Lecture Notes in Computer Science 11161

Commenced Publication in 1973
Founding and Former Series Editors:
Gerhard Goos, Juris Hartmanis, and Jan van Leeuwen

Editorial Board

More information about this series at http://www.springer.com/series/7410

Arcangelo Castiglione · Florin Pop
Massimo Ficco · Francesco Palmieri (Eds.)

Cyberspace Safety and Security

10th International Symposium, CSS 2018
Amalfi, Italy, October 29–31, 2018
Proceedings

Springer

Editors
Arcangelo Castiglione
University of Salerno
Fisciano
Italy

Florin Pop
University Politehnica of Bucharest
Bucharest
Romania

Massimo Ficco
University of Campania "L. Vanvitelli"
Caserta
Italy

Francesco Palmieri
University of Salerno
Fisciano
Italy

ISSN 0302-9743   ISSN 1611-3349 (electronic)
Lecture Notes in Computer Science
ISBN 978-3-030-01688-3   ISBN 978-3-030-01689-0   (eBook)
https://doi.org/10.1007/978-3-030-01689-0

Library of Congress Control Number: 2018956174

LNCS Sublibrary: SL4 – Security and Cryptology

This Springer imprint is published by the registered company Springer Nature Switzerland AG
The registered company address is: Gewerbestrasse 11, 6330 Cham, Switzerland

Preface

On behalf of the Organizing Committee, it is our pleasure to welcome you to the proceedings of the 10th International Symposium on Cyberspace Safety and Security (CSS 2018), held in Amalfi, Italy, during October 29–31, 2018. The papers included in the proceedings present novel ideas or state-of-the-art perspectives regarding the topics of interest of the conference.

CSS aims at bringing together international researchers and practitioners from both academia and industry who are working in the areas of cyberspace safety- and security-related topics.

CSS 2018 was the next event in a series of highly successful events focusing on cyberspace safety and security. In the past 9 years, the CSS conference has been successfully held and organized all over the world: Xian, China (2017), Granada, Spain (2016), New York, USA (2015), Paris, France (2014), Zhangjiajie, China (2013), Melbourne, Australia (2012), Milan, Italy (2011), Chengdu, China (2009), and Sydney, Australia (2008).

In this edition, the value, overall quality, and scientific and technical depth of the CSS conference continued to grow in strength and importance for both the academic and industrial communities. Such strength was evidenced this year by having a significant number of high-quality submissions resulting in a highly selective program. All submissions received at least two reviews according to a stringent peer review process involving about 50 Program Committee members and several additional reviewers. On the basis of the review results, 25 papers were selected for presentation at the conference, with an acceptance rate lower than 32%. In addition, the conference also featured an invited talk.

The support and help of many people is needed in order to organize an international event. We would like to thank all authors for submitting and presenting their papers. We also greatly appreciated the support of the Program Committee members and the reviewers who carried out the most difficult work of carefully evaluating the submitted papers.

We sincerely thank all the chairs and Technical Program Committee members. Without their hard work, the success of CSS 2018 would not have been possible.

Last but certainly not least, our thanks go to all the attendees who contributed to the success of the conference. Finally, we are sure that the beautiful location and the relaxing atmosphere of the venue were the perfect ingredients for a successful international event, providing a unique opportunity for both researchers and technologists to present, share, and discuss leading research topics, developments, and future directions in their area of interest.

October 2018

Arcangelo Castiglione
Florin Pop
Massimo Ficco
Francesco Palmieri

Organization

Steering Committee Chair

Yang Xiang   Deakin University, Australia

Honorary Chairs

Alfredo De Santis   University of Salerno, Italy
Laurence T. Yang   St. Francis Xavier University, Canada
Stefano Russo   University of Naples Federico II, Italy

General Chairs

Francesco Palmieri   University of Salerno, Italy
Albert Y. Zomaya   The University of Sydney, Australia
Willy Susilo   University of Wollongong, Australia

Program Chairs

Aniello Castiglione   University of Salerno, Italy
Guojun Wang   Central South University, China
Kim-Kwang Raymond   The University of Texas at San Antonio, USA
  Choo

Organizing Chairs

Christian Esposito   University of Naples Federico II, Italy
Raffaele Pizzolante   University of Salerno, Italy
Ugo Fiore   Parthenope University of Naples, Italy
Arcangelo Castiglione   University of Salerno, Italy

Publicity Chairs

Xinyi Huang   Fujian Normal University, China
Shang Wen   Deakin University, Australia
Chang Choi   Chosun University, South Korea

Publication Chairs

Arcangelo Castiglione   University of Salerno, Italy
Florin Pop   University Politehnica of Bucharest, Romania
Massimo Ficco   University of Campania L. Vanvitelli, Italy

Technical Program Committee

Andrea Bruno	University of Salerno, Italy
Zhe Liu	Nanjing University of Aeronautics and Astronautics, China
Umberto Ferraro Petrillo	University of Rome La Sapienza, Italy
Matteo Ferro	University of Salerno, Italy
Ciriaco D'Ambrosio	University of Salerno, Italy
Sherman S. M. Chow	The Chinese University of Hong Kong, SAR China
Christian Esposito	University of Naples Federico II, Italy
Gianni D'Angelo	University of Sannio, Italy
Gabriella Ferruzzi	University of Naples Federico II, Italy
Luigi Catuogno	University of Salerno, Italy
Ciprian Dobre	University Politehnica of Bucharest, Romania
Francesco Pascale	University of Salerno, Italy
Francesco Colace	University of Salerno, Italy
Marco Lombardi	University of Salerno, Italy
Arcangelo Castiglione	University of Salerno, Italy
Raffaele Pizzolante	University of Salerno, Italy
Mauro Iacono	Second University of Naples, Italy
Florin Pop	University Politehnica of Bucharest, Romania
Massimo Ficco	Second University of Naples, Italy
Alessio Merlo	DIBRIS- University of Genoa, Italy
Marek Ogiela	AGH University of Science and Technology, Poland
Ugo Fiore	University of Naples Parthenope, Italy
Xinyi Huang	Fujian Normal University, China
Mehrnoosh Monshizadeh	Nokia Bell Labs, Finland
Bruno Carpentieri	University of Salerno, Italy
Fang-Yie Leu	TungHai University, Taiwan
Mauro Migliardi	University of Padua, Italy
Luigi Coppolino	University of Naples Parthenope, Italy
Salvatore D'Antonio	University of Naples Parthenope, Italy
Simone Bongiovanni	Infineon Technologies, Austria
Md Zakirul Alam Bhuiyan	Fordham University, USA
Andrea Abate	University of Salerno, Italy
Silvio Barra	University of Cagliari, Italy

Contents

Cryptography, Data Security and Biometric Techniques

Social Security, Ontologies and Smart Applications

Cybersecurity

Who Is Reusing Stolen Passwords?
An Empirical Study on Stolen Passwords and Countermeasures

Chedy Missaoui[1], Safa Bachouch[2], Ibrahim Abdelkader[3], and Slim Trabelsi[3(✉)]

[1] Tessan Group, Rue des Jardins, Tunis, Tunisia
chedy.missaoui@tessan-technology.com
[2] ESPRIT, Tunis, Tunisia
safa.bachouch@esprit.tn
[3] SAP Security Research, 805, Avenue Dr. M. Donat, Mougins, France
{ibrahim.abdelkader,slim.trabelsi}@sap.com

Abstract. The combination of login passwords is still the most used identification and authentication method used on internet. Although if number of studies and articles pointed out the extreme weakness of using such authentication methods, almost every website is asking for a string password to create an account. Strong Password policies were created to reduce the risk of guessing or cracking a password string using traditional password crackers, but what is the benefit of such strong password construction if the whole credentials database is stolen and leaked? Every day hundreds of websites are breached and the content of their credential databases are exposed to the entire word. Millions of online accounts are then accessed illegally by various people with different level of damage impact. Who are these people? What is their purpose? How to prevent them from replaying stolen passwords? In this paper, we conduct an empirical study about the people who are reusing the stolen passwords found on internet or on the dark web. We deployed a fake Banking website in a honeypot mode, then we shared fake 3300 logins and passwords to the websites traditionally used for this purpose, finally we recorded their activities and made statistics. We also proposed a solution to reduce the attempts for replaying stolen passwords, and we measured the impact of this solution.

Keywords: Passwords · Hacking · Honeypot · Cyber security
Cyber criminality · Authentication

1 Introduction

According to The Breach Level Index[1] every day more than 5 million records are stolen and only 4% are encrypted. The rest is in clear text or hashed and finally easily accessible to cyber criminals. A Large portion of this data is composed of credentials and all the content is at some point of time published for free on internet. One of the

---

[1] http://breachlevelindex.com.

© Springer Nature Switzerland AG 2018
A. Castiglione et al. (Eds.): CSS 2018, LNCS 11161, pp. 3–17, 2018.
https://doi.org/10.1007/978-3-030-01689-0_1

recent biggest clear text credentials disclosure was recently released [2], with more than 1.4 Billion entries compiled from several leaks. Almost all the big internet companies suffered at some point of time from a credential leak (Apple, Amazon [3], LinkedIn [4], Twitter [5], Microsoft [6]), and according to a recent study [7] 65% of data beaches result from weak or stolen passwords. And without being paranoid we are almost all concerned by a password leak at some point of time in our digital life. In some of the cases we are not even aware about the theft.

One password leak could have much more disease that expected and this is due to the password replication custom from certain people to use the same password for many domains or a derivation a root password easy to guess. For example, if your Gmail account was leaked, a malicious user would try to replay it for Hotmail, Yahoo, LinkedIn, Facebook, Twitter or even your professional e-mail account. If the password is the same everywhere the whole digital life of a person can be ruined. This phenomenon is called domino effect [8]. The Mozilla bug tracker (Bugzilla) was severely hacked in 2014 due to a domino effect affecting one of their administrator who was using the same password Bugzilla management and his twitter account [9]. His Twitter password was leaked and the hackers replay it on Mozilla. The result of this hack was the full access to all security notes including zero-day vulnerabilities, exploit code related to all Mozilla software. All the security experts were recommending to not use Firefox until all the security breaches are fixed. The domino effect is not only concerning basic password reuse, but it concerns password reshape. Due to the human limitation of memorizing various combinations of passwords related to all their online accounts, one option is to create passwords starting from a common root word. Like example a root password is *ILikefootball* and the derivations will be {*ILikefootball1234, ILikefootball&"'$$, footballILike9871*, etc.}. Some algorithms [12] can guess those types of variations and make the domino effect much more harmful.

For many years, all the security experts agreed on the fact that passwords are weak and vulnerable authentication mechanisms. Bruce Schneider said: "As insecure as passwords generally are, they're not going away anytime soon. Every year you have more and more passwords to deal with, and every year they get easier and easier to break. You need a strategy". Despite that fact, password authentication systems are still dominating the authentication landscape especially on internet websites (less inside big companies where certificate based authentication is becoming more and more popular [10]). Many technological and cultural reasons are explaining this phenomenon [11] and this issue will stay for several years in the future. For this reason, we need to cope with this fact and try to limit the harm as much as possible by limiting the impact of a password leak. For this reason, in this paper we try to find an answer to the question of who is replaying stolen passwords? How are they behaving? And what could we disturb them before using these passwords? We also proposed a solution to try to discourage some of them to reuse those passwords and we will measure the efficiency of this dissuasive approach.

This paper is organized as follows: in Sect. 2 we describe the different reasons and factors that leads to a password leak. In Sect. 3 we list the different channels used to spread stolen credentials. In Sect. 4 we describe our honeypot case study. In Sect. 5 we introduce our solution to dissuade the stolen password reuse, and we evaluate the impact of this solution on our honeypot. In Sect. 6 we declare our ethical considerations applied to conduct this study. In Sect. 7 we describe our state of the art study, then we conclude.

2 How Credentials Are Leaked

There is a multitude of reasons at the origin of a password leak. In this section, we give a non-exhaustive list of methods and attacks used by attackers to obtain credentials from websites, systems and people.

2.1 Vulnerability Exploit

The software vulnerability is defined as a weakness of a failure existing in the source code of the system that can be exploited by an attacker to perform malicious actions. Exploiting such vulnerability can require writing a code or execute a workflow process in a different way from what it was initially designed. An SQL injection attack[2] is for example exploiting a bad input validation vulnerability and can lead to the entire database dump including the password tables.

To exploit vulnerabilities cyber criminals, had the good idea to make script kiddie's life easier by developing easy to use and automated tools called exploit kits. These tools will target a system make an analysis, identify all the potential vulnerabilities and execute the related exploit attack. This kind of tools contributed to the democratization [13] of micro-bloggings attacks and resulted of many data breaches, including credential dumps.

2.2 Social Engineering and Phishing

The social engineering attacks, is based on the exploitation of human trust to extract confidential information from a victim. It is based on a psychological manipulation that masquerades an entity of trust to the victim in order to ask for personal or confidential information. One of the most known method of this attack in information security is called Phishing attack. A phishing attack is mainly spread though e-mails, it takes the appearance of a professional or serious e-mail (management, bank, support team, etc.) but it redirects to a pitfall. For a massive Phishing attacks, Phishing kits are available to automate the fake e-mail distribution, the deployment of trap servers and the collection of credentials.

2.3 Keyloggers and Malwares

Some malwares are exploiting vulnerabilities of the systems to access their databases or file set, some others install keyloggers to capture all the keyboard entries of the victim. Credentials are then collected and sent through the network to the attacker servers. Even if most of the antiviruses can detect traditional keyloggers, some malicious

---

[2] https://www.w3schools.com/sql/sql_injection.asp.

browsers plug-ins remain undetected and continue to steal keyboard typing. Other types of malware are used to intercept system and configuration files to identify credentials.

2.4 Easy to Guess and Default Passwords

In all the best practice recommendations related to the password setup, the rule number one is to not choose an easy password. This rule is elementary event if some persons are still ignoring it. This issue becomes really dramatic when system administrators are committing the error in wide scale. We can refer to a practice that was spread among hardware vendors to set default passwords[3] for systems (usually the same one). Big industrial companies were targeted by attackers exploiting[4] the default password vulnerability. Or in some other cases system administrators chose to use personal identifiers of the users to create passwords like birthdate or social security numbers, etc. This would open the floor to easy guessing attacks like the Yale vs Princeton case.

2.5 Honeypots and Traps

Cyber criminals are permanently inventing new strategies to collect people credentials, some of them are elaborated and require a long-term effort. In some cases, they create real websites and services like discussion forums, adult websites, storage platforms or free virtual machines. These platforms are of course collecting all the credentials created by their users and rely on the domino effect [8] to compromise other accounts from their users. Even if some studies pointed out this phenomenon [14] very few statistics are available to quantify the impact of such sophisticated attacks.

3   Where Credentials Are Published

There are several sources sharing stolen credentials. Depending on the freshness and the quality of the data, these sources can be paying or free.

3.1 Commercial Sources

One of the main motivation to leak data and more specifically credential is the financial gain that could be generated from this action. We observe frequently cyber criminals selling credentials on the black markets in the dark web marketplaces. The prices and the popularity can vary with the freshness and the sensitivity of the data sold. In 2016[5] for example a hacker was selling a bunch of US government credentials in the dark web for very high prices. In this case the credentials sold are very sensitive, rare and fresh.

---

[3] https://www.scmagazine.com/russian-researchers-leak-default-passwords-packaged-to-icsscada-software/article/527829/.

[4] https://www.nytimes.com/2002/07/26/nyregion/princeton-pries-into-web-site-for-yale-applicants.html.

[5] http://www.businessinsider.fr/us/hacker-selling-credentials-government-sites-2016-7.

Then a chain of resellers will appear in order to invest in this kind of merchandize and create mini-websites to sell the credentials per entry or per package of 10. This kind of stolen credential will be cascaded through several sub-sources until becoming free at some point of time. There is a real illegal business in the password resell. Without being a talented hacker, a simple reseller can generate a lot of money just by collecting and reselling credentials. A lot of people were arrested[6] for running such kind of credential reselling business.

3.2 Free Sources

In the previous section, we exhaustively described the leaked password lifecycle in the illegal commercial circuit that ends-up in to a free sharing platform. According to most of the recent studies, text sharing websites like PasteBin are the most commonly used platforms to share free stolen credential or to advertise on sales by sharing part of the stolen databases. Hacking forums like hackforums.net, offensivecommunity.net, or bestblackhatforums.eu, are also popular places to share this kind of data, even if the access is restricted (needs account creation and works with a credit compensation system based on the contribution). Some torrent hosts are also used to share huge databases. These sources are easily accessible by most of the users on internet and offers a huge collection of stolen passwords that is maintained and enriched over the time.

Some legal websites are also offering the possibility to check whether their credentials were leaked at some point of time. Websites like have I been pwned[7] gives the possibility to provide your login or password and find how many times they were leaked. They also offer commercial services to sell the data per domain or to alert when a credential is leaked. This kind of websites are collecting the publicly available leaked databases. Some discussions are still ongoing on the morality of making legal business by offering services based on stolen passwords.

4 Experiments and Methodology

The goal of this study is to try to identify the profile of the persons that are illegally re-using leaked passwords shared on internet. We try to capture their behaviour and their anonymity degree. We also propose a counter-measure to reduce the re-usage motivation of the attacker.

4.1 Honeypot Bank Website

We decided to create a fake website of middle eastern bank. We also generated fake credentials dataset (containing Arabic names as logins). We choose Middle Est due to

---

[6] https://thehackernews.com/2018/01/leakedsource-operator-charged.html.

[7] https://haveibeenpwned.com/.

the convergence of several studies[8] identifying their banks as the most targeted ones by the various attackers.

We generated 3300 credentials distributed over 10 well known websites for credentials sharing on the surface web and the dark web. Here are the links to the sites:

- https://pastebin.com
- https://www.pastefs.com
- https://slexy.org/recent
- http://n0z.de/index.php
- https://pastie.ru
- https://justpaste.it
- https://pastelink.net/read
- https://ideone.com/recent
- http://nzxj65x32vh2fkhk.onion (Stronghold)
- http://depastedihrn3jtw.onion

We started the experience on March 2nd 2018 and we recorded for a duration of three weeks. We made 11 rounds of distribution to these sites (until March 11th), to ensure a good visibility. For every site, we publish a specific set of credentials to easily identify the site origin of the interaction.

Fig. 1. Honeypot website capture

Architecture

The Honeypot system was deployed on a cloud hosting service with a decoupled system backup to save data in case of attack (see Fig. 2).

---

[8] https://www.group-ib.com/blog/polygon.

The Web application is exposing the web interface (Fig. 1) and implementing the workflow of the user interaction including the deception system put in place (will be described further in this paper). As mentioned previously, in order to protect our system and the data collected we put in place a firewall system and an anti-DoS attack framework. This security system is intercepting all the incoming requests to the web app. All the interactions and the credentials are persisted in a local DB that is also connected to the fingerprint and the analysis engine. This component is charge of collecting the navigation information and the traces left by the users while they are accessing the website. The statistics engine is in charge of the analysis and the computing of all the events and the interactions happening in the system in order to facilitate our study.

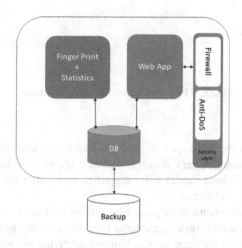

Fig. 2. Honeypot architecture

Fingerprint

A browser fingerprint is the combination of several identification parameters that will make the browser uniquely identifiable. The browser fingerprint can be quantified into a signature calculated by the combination of numerical values associated to the different parameters. In our study we choose of the following parameters to compute the signature: Browser Type, Browser version, Browser name, Operating system, Is Beta, Is Crawler, is Win16, Is Win32, Supports frames, Supports tables, Supports Cookies, Supports VB Scripts, Supports JavaScript, JavaScript version, Supports Java Applets, Supports ActiveX Controls, User IP Address, User Host name, Remote port, Country, Language, Plugins, Timezone.

All these elements combined will generate a signature used to identify distinct users running traditional browsers. In order to compute this signature, we create a matrix with all these parameters and for every new entry we increment a numerical value. The union of these values will generate a signature vector.

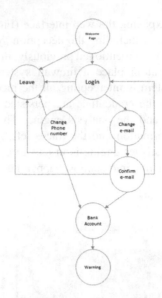

Fig. 3. Honeypot interaction state machine

State Machine

When a user accesses the honeypot website, he has the possibility to execute certain actions in the bank account. Every action is part of a global workflow that we depicted in Fig. 3. This state machine model will be used to make statistics on the behavior of every user visiting the website.

When a user visits the bank homepage page we do not record any trace (not useful). When the user logs-in with a stolen credential then the tracking starts. Once the user is logged in, an information message invites him to update the account password and the contact information. If the attacker decides to update the account information, he will have the choice to update the password, the e-mail address or the phone number. In case of e-mail address update, a conformation from the mail box is needed to check the validity of the address. There is no phone number verification. Once this information updated the attacker must login again. Now the "manage bank account" button appears in the interface, if the attacker click on this button a warning message is displayed (Fig. 7). This warning message corresponds to the countermeasure put in place to limit the stolen credential reuse. We will detail the countermeasure in the following section of the paper.

4.2   Observations

The credentials were published on March 2nd, 3rd, 5th, 6th, 8th, 9th, and 11th. We observed a slow start activity of the interactions. We started recording a reasonable activity after the third round of credential distributions (05/04/2018). The peak was reached on the 09/04/2018 (see Fig. 4).

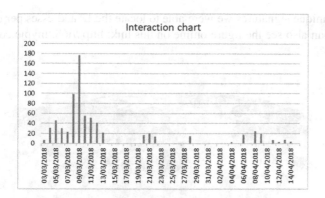

Fig. 4. Number of interactions with the honeypot

We are aware that most of the experimented hackers will first verify the authenticity of the Bank (on internet) before starting any action with the website. For this reason, this experiment target mainly curious users and intermediary and beginner's gold diggers.

We recorded in total 741 interactions (we define an interaction as an evolution in each step of the interaction workflow described in Fig. 3. These interactions are made by three categories of users: TOR protected users, Proxy protected users and non-protected users (accessing via private and public internet connections). 449 interactions are performed by non-protected users; this represents more than 60% of the total interactions. 51 interactions by TOR users 6% and the rest 244 using web proxies 33% (Fig. 5).

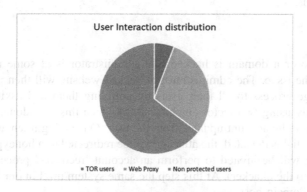

Fig. 5. User interaction distribution per browsing mode

Users using a web or a TOR proxy don't have a unique browsing finger print; those kinds of proxies are usually sharing fake browsing information in order to anonymize users and make their finger print not unique. For the non-protected users we identified 88 unique signatures (this probably corresponds to 88 unique users).

On these unique signatures we were able to locate the IP addresses per country (see Fig. 6). You can also see the figure online on this link: http://i68.tinypic.com/35buryh. png.

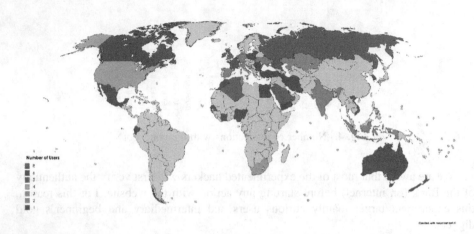

Fig. 6. IP Geo-location of the non-protected users

5 Dissuading Stolen Password Reuse

In this paper, we propose a new solution to deter and prevent malicious people from reusing stolen or hacked credentials to illegally access users accounts. We put in place a system that will threaten the authors of this illegal access tentative exploiting the stolen credentials.

5.1 Concept

When a website or a domain is hacked, the administrator is at some point of time notified about the issue. The administrator of hacked website will then put in place a password change process to all their users by notifying them and asking to change password (ideally using two factor authentication). Once this step done, the administrator will observe the account updates from the user. Once a login tentative using the old stolen credential is detected, the attacker will be redirected to a honeypot version of the website. He will be invited to perform an account 'recovery' process (that seem very legitimate to the attacker). At this step the same system used in our honeypot can be used by the domain host.

During this process (described in Fig. 8), the attacker will be asked to provide information to recover the blocked user account such as: email address, (second recovery email address), phone number and a new password. He will be then asked to confirm all this information by sending a verification email, an SMS code or a phone call. At the same time, all the attacker's navigation metadata will be collected: IP address, browser fingerprint (user agent, list of installed plugins, language, screen size,

Operating system etc. ...), VPN provider and address if used, Internet Service Provider, IP Geolocation. We also inject tracking cookies and we create a virtual profile of the attacker. We might also try to scan his IP address to detect open ports, and detect running applications.

Fig. 7. Violation warning message

When the attacker reaches the state "Warning" in Fig. 3, the honeypot will display a warning message containing all his data and explaining that he is in a law infringement that could lead him to court judgement (see the warning message displayed Fig. 7). The machine signature is then blacklisted in order to block any other tentative.

5.2 Observations and Results

Based on several parameters that we identified (date, time, selected user account, new password set) we guess that 43 unique users were using a Web or TOR. This number is not totally exact due to the difficulty to identify unique signatures. This raises the number of total unique users to 131.

On 741 interactions, the warning was reached 92 times 12%. As a reminder, according to Fig. 3, the warning is reached when the attacker decided to access the victim's account (after changing the password or not). The password was changed only 11 times. This represents only 1% of the interaction, this is an indication on the need for the attacker to leave the user account as it is and not raise any suspicion.

39 unique users changed the contact e-mail address, this represent 29% of the total users. 22 confirmed the validity of their address from their mail box, this represent 16% of the users.

The number of unique users who decided to ignore the warning and try again to access to the bank account is 19, this represents 14% of the whole users and they are all proxy/TOR protected.

Fig. 8. Dissuading password reuse process

We clearly observe the effect of the dissuading system put in place. Even if 14% of the users were not threaten by the message, 86% were. We also observe that all the non-protected users who got the waring decided to not follow-up on the illegal activity.

The table below summarizes all the numbers that we collected during the study (Table 1).

Table 1. Summary of all the measures of the study

Data	Number	Proportion
Total recorded interactions	741	100%
Non-protected interactions	449	60%
Web Proxy interactions	244	33%
TOR interactions	51	7%
Warning reached	92	12%
Password changed	11	1%
Unique users	131	100%
Non-protected users	88	60%
TOR/Proxy users	43	40%
Changed their e-mail address	39	29%
Validated their e-mail address	22	16%
Users ignored the warning	19	14%
TOR/Proxy users ignored the warning	19	100%

6 Ethical Considerations

The honeypot deployed and the honey tokens distributed are completely fake and non-exploitable by attackers. The bank is a fake one, the services are fake and the names used for the logins are generated randomly. The data collected is only used for research purpose. All the data is deleted just after the study with a retention period of one month. The users that connected to the honeypot are not identified and their data is never crossed or combined with other datasets for identification purposes. The server used in the experiments was running only with patched software to reduce the exposure risk. We used different protection tools (anti-dos, firewall, input sanitizing, etc.). During all the experiment period, we checked permanently the logs of our systems in order to detect external access. Zero abnormal access detected. All these precautions were taken in order to avoid an external attack and an eventual collection of data.

7 Related Work

Several studies were conducted to define and explain the domino effect phenomena due to the password reuse bad practice of the users [8]. Other studies explored the different password guessing techniques used from stolen credential databases [12]. These techniques are used to generate variants of a password root. These variants are frequently adopted by the users to vary their password collection set among the different domains and websites. Most of the solutions proposed in the literature suggest to bypass the multiplication of password versions by adopting complex centralized infrastructures for authentication [17] and [18].

A Google study [15] proposed the first longitudinal measurement research tracking the origin of the different credential leak sources and their impact on user account (in term of re-use rate). This study tackles the origin of the leak and not the consequences and who is behind these consequences. The proposed mitigation techniques are based on two factor authentications.

To our knowledge, very few honeypot based studies were conducted, one of them is proposed by [16]. They created 100 Gmail accounts, they shared the credentials on internet and they observed the usage. Even if the approach is interesting, the ethical risk is important. Many of the accounts were used to perform illegal actions (spamming, malware propagation, illegal purchase, etc.). Besides this legal aspect, the researchers installed a malware to track the user activity, and this approach goes far beyond a simple browser activity tracking. Finally, their study is more qualitative than quantitative; they mainly observe what a malicious user is doing with a hacked e-mail account. This study is different but complementary with ours, without proposing any countermeasure to prevent stolen credential reuse. Another study [1] also proposed to spread fake credentials for real domains redirecting to honeypots in order study the hackers targeting this domain.

8 Conclusion

In this paper we proposed a honeypot based study targeting the persons who are re-using leaked credentials published on internet. In our experiments, we created a fake banking website and spread 3300 fake credentials. We observed the behaviour of the users re-using these credentials in order to define the different profiles. We also proposed a solution to dissuade the malicious user to continue using these credentials after their first try. The results of our study gave an idea on the type of users re-using stolen credentials, their degree of security precautions taken to perform illegal actions, and the impact of our dissuading warning based message. One important observation, is that all the users who are not surfing behind an anonymous proxy are threaten by our prevention system especially when their navigation information are displayed. Concerning the other more precautious users only 19% ignored the system. This ratio is quite interesting according to our opinion, and reflects that fear of being tracked by these kind of malicious users, that we promptly describe as vultures that want to dig some gold from crumbs resulting of big hacks.

In our future work, we want to explore and measure the proportion of malicious honeypot websites deployed in the internet with the purpose to collect user's credentials. Currently this phenomenon is not fully explored, except for the cloud VM honeypots.

Acknowledgement. Special thanks to Anis Zouaoui from ESPRIT for the students advisory.

References

1. Catuogno, L., Castiglione, A., Palmieri, F.: A honeypot system with honeyword-driven fake interactive sessions. In: 2015 International Conference on High Performance Computing and Simulation (HPCS), pp. 187–194. IEEE, July 2015
2. Database of 1.4 Billion Credentials Found on Dark Web. https://www.securityweek.com/database-14-billion-credentials-found-dark-web
3. How Apple and Amazon Security Flaws Le to My Epic Hacking. https://www.wired.com/2012/08/apple-amazon-mat-honan-hacking/
4. LinkedIn Lost 167 Million Account Credentials in Data Breach. http://fortune.com/2016/05/18/linkedin-data-breach-email-password/
5. Passwords for 32M Twitter accounts may have been hacked and leaked. https://techcrunch.com/2016/06/08/twitter-hack/
6. Password Leak Lists Contain 20 Percent of Microsoft Login Credentials. https://www.forbes.com/sites/adriankingsleyhughes/2012/07/16/hackers-have-20-percent-of-microsoft-login-credentials/#54cb833c7e0d
7. 63% of Data Breaches Result From Weak or Stolen Passwords. http://info.idagent.com/blog/63-of-data-breaches-result-from-weak-or-stolen-passwords
8. Ives, B., Walsh, K.R., Schneider, H.: The domino effect of password reuse. Commun. ACM **47**(4), 75–78 (2004)
9. Mozilla: data stolen from hacked bug database was used to attack Firefox. https://arstechnica.com/information-technology/2015/09/mozilla-data-stolen-from-hacked-bug-database-was-used-to-attack-firefox/?utm_content=buffer1c53c&utm_medium=social&utm_source=twitter.com&utm_campaign=buffer

10. 2017 state of authentication report. https://fidoalliance.org/wp-content/uploads/The-State-of-Authentication-Report.pdf
11. Herley, C., Van Oorschot, P.: A research agenda acknowledging the persistence of passwords. IEEE Secur. Priv. **10**(1), 28–36 (2012)
12. Das, A., Bonneau, J., Caesar, M., Borisov, N., Wang, X.: The tangled web of password reuse. In: NDSS, vol. 14, pp. 23–26
13. Akiyama, M., Yagi, T., Aoki, K., Hariu, T., Kadobayashi, Y.: Active credential leakage for observing web-based attack cycle. In: Stolfo, S.J., Stavrou, A., Wright, C.V. (eds.) RAID 2013. LNCS, vol. 8145, pp. 223–243. Springer, Heidelberg (2013). https://doi.org/10.1007/978-3-642-41284-4_12
14. Claycomb, W.R., Nicoll, A.: Insider threats to cloud computing: directions for new research challenges. In: 2012 IEEE 36th Annual Computer Software and Applications Conference (COMPSAC), pp. 387–394. IEEE (2012)
15. Thomas, K., et al.: Data breaches, phishing, or malware?: understanding the risks of stolen credentials. In: Proceedings of the 2017 ACM SIGSAC Conference on Computer and Communications Security, pp. 1421–1434. ACM (2017)
16. Onaolapo, J., Mariconti, E., Stringhini, G.: What happens after you are pwnd: understanding the use of leaked webmail credentials in the wild. In: Proceedings of the 2016 Internet Measurement Conference, pp. 65–79. ACM (2016)
17. Sun, H.M., Chen, Y.H., Lin, Y.H.: oPass: a user authentication protocol resistant to password stealing and password reuse attacks. IEEE Trans. Inf. Forensics Secur. **7**(2), 651–663
18. Kontaxis, G., Athanasopoulos, E., Portokalidis, G., Keromytis, A.D.: SAuth: protecting user accounts from password database leaks. In: Proceedings of the 2013 ACM SIGSAC Conference on Computer and Communications Security, pp. 187–198. ACM (2013)

A Survey of Keylogger and Screenlogger Attacks in the Banking Sector and Countermeasures to Them

Hugo Sbai[1]([⊠]), Michael Goldsmith[1], Samy Meftali[2], and Jassim Happa[1]

[1] Department of Computer Science, Oxford University, 15 Parks Rd, Oxford OX1 3QD, UK
{hugo.sbai,michael.goldsmith,jassim.happa}@cs.ox.ac.uk
[2] Centre de Recherche en Informarique, Signal et Automatique (Cristal), Université de Lille 1, Batiment M3 extension Avenue Carl Gauss, 59655 Villeneuve-d'Ascq Cedex, France
samy.meftali@univ-lille1.fr

Abstract. Keyloggers and screenloggers are one of the active growing threats to user's confidentiality as they can run in user-space, easily be distributed and upload information to remote servers. They use a wide number of different techniques and may be implemented in many ways. Keyloggers and screenloggers are very largely diverted from their primary and legitimate function to be exploited for malicious purposes compromising the privacy of users, and bank customers notably. This paper presents a survey of keylogger and screenlogger attacks to increase the understanding and awareness of their threat by covering basic concepts related to bank information systems and explaining their functioning, as it presents and discusses an extensive set of plausible countermeasures.

Keywords: Keyloggers · Screenloggers · Virtual keyboards Optical character recognition · Neural networks · SVM · Noise

1 Introduction

Currently, banking data is digital, integrated into banking information systems and accessible to employees, bank supervisors and customers. Thus, all users of such an information system connect with passwords to their accounts and get some privileges. The privileges can, for instance, be a simple consultation of an account balance, closing or creation of an account or transactions of large financial amounts from an account to another.

This simplicity of access and the large amount of money that can be manipulated or diverted by any malicious person with an adequate password make these systems privileged targets of many computer attacks using various software and malware. Among these, the use of keyloggers or screenloggers is often particularly effective and dangerous for banking information systems.

A. Castiglione et al. (Eds.): CSS 2018, LNCS 11161, pp. 18–32, 2018.
https://doi.org/10.1007/978-3-030-01689-0_2

Keyloggers and screenloggers are software used to capture and save, without the user's knowledge, keystrokes or screenshots into files. Most currently available keyloggers are considered "legitimate" applications and they are used to fulfil many legitimate and legal functions such as tracking children's use of the internet, tracking cases of inappropriate use of business computers [29]. Yet, they are very largely diverted from their primary and legitimate function to be exploited for malicious purposes, and unfortunately, the theft of various online payment systems credentials has become one of the main application of keyloggers/screenloggers [4]. Many keyloggers/screenloggers try to conceal themselves, and unlike other types of malware, they do not affect its functioning. Despite that, they can be very dangerous for the user privacy and the organisation to which the information system belongs.

A keylogger can intercept passwords or other confidential information entered by the user with his keyboard, when a screenlogger is capable of capturing screenshots. This information is then passed to the source of the malicious program. This paper will only target the case of banking institutions, even if the theft of such data can have very serious consequences in other sectors, for example regarding economic and political intelligence operations, commercial or state secrets, compromising the security in public and private organisations. To the best of our knowledge, there is no document that provides a clear synthesis of the current knowledge about screenloggers. This is the aim of this paper. The existing works in the literature presenting an overview of this type of malware, concentrate generally on keyloggers especially on the detection phase as in [29] or on the processing and implementation details as in [30]. One of the originalities of this paper is that it presents the vulnerabilities of screenloggers at all stages of their operation, and focuses particularly on the most critical phase, which is data automatic recognition.

The rest of this document is organised as follows: in Sect. 2 we define the basic concepts related to keyloggers and screenloggers and their illegitimate use against bank information systems. Section 3 aims to present the general functioning of these attacks step by step and to propose countermeasures. Section 4 focuses on the data extraction process, showing the different techniques that can be used, and discussing their weaknesses and possible countermeasures. Finally, in Sect. 5 we conclude by summarising the work and discuss potential directions for future research.

2   Basic Concepts

2.1   Keyloggers Classification

Keyloggers: a keylogger might be either a piece of software or a hardware component that monitors key presses on a computer. These details will be saved into files and sent later to the person specified in the keylogger settings. We distinguish two types of keyloggers: software and hardware ones.

Hardware (HW) Keyloggers: they devices connected to the keyboard or the computer. Their detection needs a physical human verification [5]. These boxes can intercept all the data transmitted by the keyboard including the recovery of BIOS password and bank identifiers.

The oldest ones are Module type keyloggers and have a PS2 interface; they are usable on keyboards having this same interface [19], and often have a form extremely close to that of USB-PS2 adapters. There are also USB versions that look like the USB/Wifi or USB/Bluetooth peripheral. A third form is less accessible to the general public but is quite efficient. It consists of a tiny electronic card connected inside the keyboard. Lastly, probes can be used for side channel attacks. For wireless keyboards, there is no need for a specific additional box to recover the keys entered [9]. This can be done just by capturing the waves emitted by the keyboard to communicate with the receiver and then decrypt the communication, which employs weak encryption in most cases.

Software (SW) Keyloggers: they are much more common because they can be installed remotely, e.g. via a network, and generally, do not require physical access to a certain device for recovering collected data (the data can be transmitted periodically by email) [12]. Although these keyloggers are more easily detectable by other software tools, they still have more advantages than hardware keyloggers.

A hardware keylogger is only capable of recording keystrokes *out of context* i.e. that have no relation to the user environment. A software keylogger records not only keystrokes but also the state of the target machine. The most targeted applications are web browsers because they allow the recovery of usernames and passwords (bank accounts login for example) [14]. One of the main strengths of this type of keyloggers is that they can be deployed indifferently on computers, tablets or smartphones.

Screenloggers (also known as touch logger, tap logger): they are a variant of keyloggers software [8]. Their main use is to take screenshots and even make videos retracing all computers' activity. A Screenlogger records the movements of the mouse, along with screen captures during the click event.

2.2 Comparative Evaluation Between Screenloggers, HW Keyloggers and SW Keyloggers

As shown in Table 1 below, screenloggers have some important advantages comparing to HW or SW keyloggers. Indeed, they can be used to affect a device remotely and at a very large scale in the same way as SW keyloggers, providing the hacker with a complete set of data and information. In fact, screenshots give additional details, making passwords extraction much easier.

The only way to detect hardware keyloggers is to become familiar with these devices or to check the device internally and externally [10] regularly. Even the NSA catalogue published in late 2013 reflects the difficulty of finding one's own recording devices that are barely bigger than a fingernail. This constitutes the main advantage of HW keyloggers, but still, the hacker must have physical access to the device to affect it, this represents a significant drawback. For software keyloggers, the infection tracks are the same as for other malware.

Table 1. Screenloggers vs HW keyloggers vs SW keyloggers: features, infection capabilities and detection.

	HW keyloggers	SW keyloggers	Screenloggers
Keys	Yes	Yes	Yes but not their main use)
Use of multiple inputs (mouse, pad, ..etc)	No	No	Yes
Screenshots	No	No	Yes
System context	No	Yes	Yes
Ease of infection	****	*	*
Large scale infection	*	****	****
Ease of exploitation	*****	***	*
Ease of detection by SW	No	***	***
Ease of detection by user	***	*	*

2.3 Screenlogger Attack Against Banking Information Systems

The main objective of any hacker attacking a banking information system is to steal confidential information such as authentication information. He could try to remotely install a screenlogger program on a client device or directly on a computer inside the bank [15]. This last alternative should give more privileges to the hacker, but it is harder than attacking simple client account.

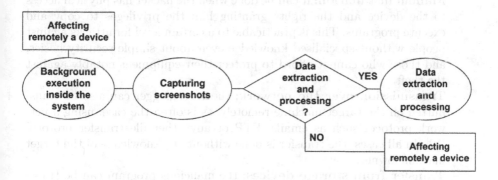

Fig. 1. Screenloggers operating process.

The most common process of a screenlogger might be separated into five steps as shown in Fig. 1. First, the hacker must affect a device, generally in a remote way, using emails or any other files transmission technique [16]. Second, after the malicious program has been installed, it will run as a background service. Then comes the main job of screenloggers, which consists in recording screenshots at regular periods or triggered by mouse clicks. The resulting captured screenshots might be treated or not on the host device depending on the nature of the screenlogger. Finally, the raw or processed data is transmitted to the hacker through the network.

Each of the above steps utilises a certain number of vulnerabilities to make the whole process as efficient as possible. The objective of the next section is to give more details about operating mode of each part, vulnerabilities used, and with countermeasures that can be taken by users to protect their devices.

3   Screenloggers Processing Steps and Countermeasures

At each stage of their operating mode, screenloggers exploit a number of flaws, using resources to optimise their performance and ability to collect and quarrying data [18]. However, there are measures allowing to minimise as far as possible the risk of an infection by a screenlogger before its installation on the target machine on the one hand, and a set of actions to detect the existence of malware after infection, on the other hand, trying to reduce its damages.

The purpose of the current section is to give an overview of the weaknesses used by screenloggers at each stage of their functioning (as seen in Fig. 1) as well as countermeasures that could be taken by the victim to ensure his safety.

- **Device infection:** the first step of a Screenlogger process is to infect the target machine, as seen in Fig. 1. The way in which such software gets on a machine is quite similar to the infection by almost all modern malware. Indeed, a Screenlogger infects a machine (a computer, a tablet, or a smartphone) through one of these main methods:
  - **Manual installation:** it can be done when the hacker has physical access to the device and the rights granting him the privileges to copy and execute programs. This is practicable to a certain level for attacks against people without specialised knowledge even about simple security basics, and those who cannot afford to protect their equipment notably against the theft.
  - **Transmission over the network:** the Screenlogger can also be transmitted on the target machine remotely, as is often the case, using a network protocol such as emails, FTP or any other file transfer protocol [12]. In all cases, the transfer is done without the knowledge of the target machine owner.
  - **Transfer from storage devices:** the malicious program can be transferred via a device such as a USB key, a memory card or an external hard disk that the user connects to the device without being aware of the malware presence.
- **Countermeasures to prevent device infection:** although zero risks can reasonably not be guaranteed on any machine connected to the internet, there are nevertheless many measures allowing to reduce the risk of a screenlogger infection substantially. As well as how a device can be infected, these measures can be divided into three parts:

- **Countermeasures to prevent manual installation:** to avoid any manual transfer of the malware, the user should take awareness in consideration as a measure, to ensure and protect the system from any possible access (especially the administrator mode).
- **Countermeasures to prevent transmission over the network:** the first recommendation is to open e-mails only coming from known senders, which can be authenticated by digital signature when possible. Second, is to not open any attachments without being sure of the non-dangerous nature of its content. It is the same for hypertext links. Indeed, the transmission of Screenloggers as attachments to emails or as files on a remote server accessible via a hypertext link is a widespread practice.
- **Countermeasures to prevent transmission via storage devices:** an effective practice, especially for professional business users, is to never use a removable storage media on their devices. Indeed, a rigorous separation of the machines for professional or personal use makes it possible to ensure their non-infection by any malware in general and Screenlogger in particular. Another measure to reduce the risk of being infected is to systematically check any external storage device using an up to date anti-virus before each use.

- **Background execution mode:** once the screenlogger is installed on the target machine, it works as an active process, continually scanning the events triggered by keyboard keys or mouse clicks. Under a windows-based system, a basic and primitive version of a keylogger/screenlogger can be based on calling the **GetAsyncKeyState** system function [11] to return the key state (pressed or released).

  This active wait is a resource consuming (CPU, storage and power). Additionally, data transmission towards the attacker may require intensive use of the network, especially if they are transmitted without prior treatment on the victim's machine. In the last few years, some keyloggers integrated dissimulation methods to prevent their files from being discovered manually or using anti-virus software. They mainly use two types of dissimulation methods: user or kernel mode [31].

- **Countermeasures for screenloggers detection:** in information systems belonging to companies, and particularly to banks, there is usually an IT department that should monitor resources used to detect any unnatural overhead. This potential overhead might be more or less important depending on the nature and performances of the screeenlogger. Thus screenloggers detection is not always guaranteed. In the case of private devices belonging to individuals, monitoring device resources still possible by the mean of some integrated tools.

- **Keys captures and screenshots:**
  - **Keys recording:** the basic function of any simple keylogger is to capture pressed keys on the keyboard. An application requiring such data is generally not considered as illegitimate by operating systems or by any common anti-virus programs since reading pressed keys is a standard operation required by several legal tools. Basic Keyloggers can capture

all keystrokes and save them in files which will be sent to the hacker's server [14].

- **Screenshots capturing and storing:** the general idea behind Screenloggers is to capture all the bits displayed in a DC (Device Context). A DC is a GDI (Graphic Device Interface) window object that defines a set of objects and properties representing a graphical output. The image format used by screenloggers for recording screenshots is Bitmap. This is the simplest graphic format; where every pixel is coded in RGB. They can use another file format (JPG, GIF ...) but the size of the generated files could cause memory congestion and CPU overload of the target device [32].

- **Countermeasures against keys captures and screenshots:**
  - **Countermeasures against key recording:** at present all banking applications use virtual keyboards on smartphones (natively present in the device or integrated in the application), and some even use them on laptops (Axa bank, Oney, Abanca ...). This is an efficient countermeasure against basic keyloggers capturing only pressed keys [7]. However, hackers have adapted themselves to this new situation and have improved their programs to capture more than just keyboard keys but also screenshots and even videos. So virtual keyboards are no longer a sufficient countermeasure. Several approaches have been proposed to try to counter these modern keyloggers.
  - **Countermeasures against screenshots recordings:** if a screenlogger is installed on a device without being detected and is capable of taking screenshots, there is no way to prevent it from working and taking pictures without the risk of altering the execution of other legitimate applications. A suggestion mentioned in [6] consists in adding artefacts on the screen when a click occurs. For example, it can be the display of an artificial mouse pointer to prevent the malware from knowing which part of the screen has been clicked. Some researchers also suggested a dynamic virtual keyboard that mixes keys layout after each click [1].

    A colour code is used to remember characters positions easily. The user can enter one character at a time. Initially, the user should note the position of the character he wants to use. They must then click on the *hide keys button* to hide all characters. Assuming the password is **xyz**, the user can then click to type **x**. After this action, the keyboard layout changes again and the process is repeated one more time. A similar approach was proposed by Parekh et al. [2].

- **Transmission to the hacker's machine:** once the screenshots (or extracted data) are stored on the victim system they can be transmitted to the hacker in two forms: raw images or data extracted after treatment using an Optical Character Recognition (OCR).

In the first alternative, transferring captured images as they were taken over the network will result in high bandwidth consumption. The data flow exchanged between the attacker and the target must be minimised. Some solutions can be considered to reduce the importance of this data flow. The first one is to use various compression methods (LZ77, RLE ...) [33]. The second one is not to send the entire screen, but only the target window.

In the second alternative, the volume of transmitted data via the network will be less. However, the OCR processing on the target machine consumes a lot of resources (e.g. CPU, memory, disk storage), which can facilitate the detection of the screenlogger.

- **Countermeasures against data transmission:** a very close examination of the network usage might reveal the presence of a keylogger. A firewall is an efficient defence against key/screenloggers because it will monitor the computer's activity, and upon detecting that a program desires to send data to the hacker, the firewall will ask for permission or display a warning.

4   Focus on the Data Exploitation Step

The data exploitation can be performed either by the human eye or automatically. In the following, we will present these two alternatives and discuss their weaknesses.

4.1   Manual Screenshots Exploitation

To avoid the use of OCRs on the victim machine, and thus reduce the use of resources to minimise the risk of being detected, some screenloggers directly transmit screenshots to the hacker's server without processing them locally. These screenshots are sometimes checked and processed manually by the hacker without using any program. This type of screenloggers is particularly effective not only because of the difficulty in detecting them but also because of the use of the human eye and brain to analyse screenshots.

4.2   Countermeasures Against Manual Exploitation

Since it is harder to prevent a human from recognising a character than automatic algorithms, the simplest countermeasure would be to hide the character completely. Several ways of doing so were found in the literature. The keyboard hiding method [1] is one example. Another method presented in [17] uses retinal persistence, and its goal is to divide each character into segments and display them one after the other in quick succession. At sufficiently high speed, a human can see the whole character while the software does not. On a screenshot, the numbers are never fully visible. On the other hand, if the malicious software could take enough screenshots, it could rebuild characters.

4.3   Automatic Extraction from Screenshots

A text is a collection of characters belonging to an alphabet, united in words of a given vocabulary. OCR locates and identifies characters in an image (scanned

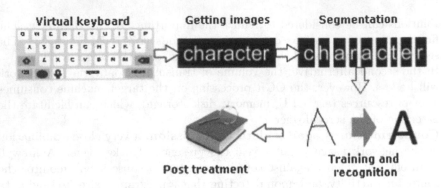

Fig. 2. Main steps of an OCR system: once the screen is captured (*Getting images*), each character is isolated (*Segmentation*) and recognized by an OCR software (*Recognition*). Then, the result can be post-processed using a dictionnary to detect possible mistakes (*Post treatment*).

or captured). Since the recognition is done character by character [24] the recognition system depends on several phases, which are presented in Fig. 2.

Acquisition: it is the aspect which consists in capturing the image of a text, and converting it into appropriate digital magnitude for the processing system using screenlogger software (screenshots).

Segmentation: the purpose of segmentation is to find in images where the text is located and to isolate each character. The segmentation can be performed by run length smearing algorithm that consists of blackening the white pixels situated between two black pixels if their number is less than n [28]. The algorithm is performed vertically and horizontally. By varying n, we can segment characters, words, lines or paragraphs. Before this, the image must be binarised *thresholding*. All the pixels having a value lower than the threshold will be encoded 0 and become black. All the pixels having a value above the threshold will be encoded 255 and will become white. The higher the threshold chosen, the cleaner the binarized image will be. Once the image binarised and the characters are isolated, the recognition itself will be performed.

Recognition: before taking any decision, we need to acquire knowledge and organise it into class models. In this context, we can find two main types of algorithms: supervised and unsupervised learning [25]. Once the learning is achieved, the decision module has to make a decision on the input character by giving an answer [25]. This answer can take three forms: success if the answer is unique; confusion in case of multiple answers; or rejection of the form if no model matches its description. In the first two cases, the decision may be accompanied by a *likelihood* measure. Recognition approaches can be grouped into five main groups: template matching, statistical, structural, stochastic and hybrid.

- *Template matching:* this approach compares pixel by pixel the image taken from the character with a library consisting of a set of different types of characters called *Template* or *library models*. The system compares the grey levels of the model with those of the library different elements, and then it assigns the image the model class in which it matches the most.

- *Statistical approaches:* in the statistical approaches [25], the recognition consists in finding the class to which the character has the highest probability to belong to, and assessing the risk involved in making such a decision. There are different types of statistical approaches:

  - *Bayesian approach:* the Bayesian method allows the introduction of probability notions in solving problems about pattern recognition [20]. From the physical representation of the forms to be recognised, characteristic vectors are extracted. These vectors to classify are considered as realisations of a random vector x characterised by a probability density $f(x)$. The Bayesian model is easy to build and particularly useful for extensive data sets.

  - *Neural networks:* a neural network is a weighted oriented graph. The nodes of this graph are simple automaton called *formal neurons*. Neurons have an internal state, by which they influence other neurons in the network. This activity propagates in the graph along weighted arcs called *synaptic links*. In OCR, the primitives extracted on a character image are the inputs of the network. The activated output of the network corresponds to the recognised character [22].

  - *Support vector machines (SVM):* these algorithms are supervised learning binary classifiers, designed to solve prediction problems. The algorithm search for a decision borderline between multiple classes. This approach was initially used to optimise the linear hyperplane of discrimination between classes [21]. Then, the use of the kernel functions made it possible to project the non linearly separable data in an increased space to make them linearly separable.

- *Structural approach:* the structural methods are based on the physical structure of the character; they represent the topological and geometrical properties of the form [25]. These characteristics are extracted from the form representation in the *skeleton* or *the outline*. In these approaches, the characters are generally represented by a set of primitives connected by a relation. The primitives are of a topological type such as an arc, a point, a ball, a corner, or a segment. Many structural classification methods have been developed from an application in character recognition.

The matching of graph representations consists in building a graph where the nodes contain the primitives and the links between these primitives [25]. Thus, the recognition consists in making a mapping between this graph and other graphs representing reference characters and constructed during the learning phase. Another method is the *metric techniques*, in which characters are represented by strings of primitives [25]. It consists in measuring the similarity between the strings of the character to be recognised and a reference model by a *distance estimation*.

The main disadvantage of structural methods is related to the extraction of primitives directly from the physical representation of the form [25]. This represents a real barrier because this description is not very resistant to geometric transformations but mostly to *noise*.

- *Stochastic approach:* in the stochastic approach, the character is modelled as a *state graph*, where each state represents an observation, we talk about a *stochastic chain*. Stochastic recognition consists of searching within a state graph the shortest path describing the observed elements. The employed technique is essentially based on the use of *Markov chains* [27].

  Markov models are commonly used for character recognition. Each character is a *hidden state* or a *Markov chain of N states*. The observations extracted from the images are called *primitives* or *characteristic vectors*. An HMM is constructed for each vocabulary word, and the corresponding likelihoods are calculated. We choose the word of the vocabulary that maximises this likelihood.

- *Hybrid approach:* to improve recognition performances, the trend is to build hybrid systems [23] that use different types of features, and that combine several layered classifiers. This combination improves the quality of the classification in terms of accuracy. We can find three types of classifiers combination. The first one is the *sequential combination*, where classifiers are used one after the other, progressively to reduces the number of possible classes. Another type of combination is the *parallel combination*, where classifiers are driven independently in parallel, and final results are then merged. Parallel methods are the most widespread due to their simplicity but also their effectiveness in terms of accuracy. The third approach is the *hybrid combination*, which is a mixture of both previous approaches.

Post-treatment: post-treatment represents the last step in OCR operation. It aims to reduce the number of errors. In fact, depending on the quality of the original screenshot, there are often some errors because characters are broken or blurred. Thus the OCR tool must now resolve these errors so that the characters can be properly interpreted. During this step, OCRs generally use dictionary support to improve the recognition quality. Some characters like ('1', 'I') and ('C', 'G') can look very similar, and a dictionary might help to make the differences and then take decisions. Moreover, some works [3] proposed an additional step to OCR operation consisting of a manual evaluation based on error probabilities evaluation. The method employs an error estimator neural network that learns to assess the error probability of every word from *ground-truth* data. The estimated error probability is used to decide which words are inspected by humans.

4.4   Countermeasures Against Automatic Extraction

Acquisition: they are the same measures as the third step of a screenlogger.

Segmentation: the bigger the image is, the longer and difficult the segmentation will be, so it is preferable not to give indications about relevant data location to the OCR software. The virtual keyboard area gives an indication, and if in addition there is the cursor of the mouse on the keys composing the password in the screenshots, the indication will be much too precise and would greatly facilitate the OCR's task, because it will merely segment the very specific areas corresponding to the virtual keyboard on which the cursor appears.

Recognition: finding countermeasures to the algorithms presented in section 4.3 requires a concrete implementation of the different methods and some testing. This will be the next focus of our work. However, a first step would be to analyse

Table 2. Strengths and weaknesses of the main OCR techniques

Approaches		Advantages	Disadvantages
Template matching		Requires only little information about the forms to recognize	−Long processing time −Sensitivity to noise
Structural		Fast and does not require many learning examples	−The determination of the characteristic attributes can be quite difficult −Difficult to extract the primitives directly from the physical representation of forms
Statistical	Neural networks	−The ability to generalize from training examples −Fast testing step −Fixed problem size	−Learning time can be very long −Over-fitting problem
	SVM	−Avoid over-fitting problem	−The high cost of memor-izing support vectors that are numerous −Recognition phases is quite slow
	HMM	−Allow segmentation and recognition at the same time −Short processing time	−Not effective for isolated characters classification −This method limited by the risks of discontinuity of contours
	K-nearest neighbor	−Effective when there are enough learning examples −Easy to implement	−Low classification speed due to the large number of distances to calculate
	Bayesian classifier	− Fast and easy to implement	−Long learning time in order to compute class probabilities

the strengths and weaknesses of each algorithm to get some insight about possible countermeasures. This is done in Table 2.

Template matching relies on a distance calculation between the captured character and the models. Therefore, a countermeasure would aim to maximise this distance. We can think of two main ways of achieving this. The first one would be to introduce noise in the image (replacing some black bits by white ones and whites by blacks). Such a method was developed in [26].

The second way would be to use different fonts such that the distance between the captured character and the model would be significant even if it is the same character. In turn, OCRs can try to encompass the largest possible number of fonts for each character, but that would imply an intensive use of memory on the victim's machine. This potentially intensive use of resources can be a major disadvantage and might be exploited by the user to detect the screenlogger.

The same problem can be found with the structural approach. Indeed, there are many ways of writing the same character and therefore many representations in terms of geometric primitives. To be accurate, the algorithm will have to memorise numerous vectors of primitives for each character, which leads to the same problem of resources consumption and ease of detection.

The large number of labelled examples to memorise and distances to calculate for KNN classification implies both a high memory cost and a long running time. Similarly, SVM requires to memorise all the support vectors and to determine the position of the points to classify with respect to the boundaries.

It is also possible to avoid the computational resource consumption problem by combining these methods with lighter ones such as Bayesian classifier or neural networks.

Post-treatment: banks must forbid the use of simple passwords that could be found in dictionaries. Indeed, an application forcing the user to use long passwords, containing special characters and not found in the dictionaries can make the step of post-processing OCRs useless.

5   Conclusion

Among all vulnerabilities to which a bank or its customers are exposed, there is certainly one more prejudicial than the others; it is the theft of confidential data and money. One of the most used attacks for this is known as key/screenloggers. It aims at stealing confidential information from users by recording the keystrokes. This paper has presented the main steps of the screenloggers process, from capturing screenshots to the extraction of relevant information by insisting on the operating mode of the different types of OCRs. Some countermeasures corresponding to each stage were given and discussed, but it turns out that there is no completely effective solution against this malware. Thus, there are still many possible improvements to be made to the techniques used by these countermeasures and the safest way to defend against screenloggers seems to be using several countermeasures covering the largest number of stages of their operating mode.

References

1. Agarwal, M., Mehara, M., Pawar, R., Shah, D.: Secure authentication using dynamic virtual keyboard layout. In: Proceedings of the International Conference and Workshop on Emerging Trends in Technology, ISSN 2349–516, vol. 2, February 2011
2. Parekh, A., Pawar, A., Munot, P., Mantri, P.: Secure authentication using anti-screenshot virtual keyboard. Int. J. Comput. Sci. Issues **8**(5), 3 (2011)
3. Abdulkader, A., Casey, M. R.: Low cost correction of OCR errors using learning in a multi-engine environment. In: 2009 10th International Conference on Document Analysis and Recognition, Barcelona, pp. 576–580 (2009)
4. Bakhtiyari, S., Tahir, U.: Phishing attacks and solutions (2010)
5. Cengage Learning: Malware and Social Engineering Attacks, Chap. 2 (2011)
6. Dadkhah, M., Jazi, M.D.: Secure payment in E-commerce : deal with keyloggers and phishings. Int. J. Electron. Commun. Comput. Eng. **5**(3), 656–660 (2014)
7. Dheeraj Bansal (2014). https://www.shoutmeloud.com/online-virtual-keyboard-secure-passwords-from-keyloggers.html
8. Echallier, N., Grimaud, G., et al.: Virtual keyboard logging counter-measures using common fate's law. In: International Conference on Security and Management (SAM 2017), Las Vegas, USA, 17–20 July 2017
9. Gerdes, R.M., Mallick, S.: Physical-layer detection of hardware keyloggers. In: Bos, H., Monrose, F., Blanc, G. (eds.) RAID 2015. LNCS, vol. 9404, pp. 26–47. Springer, Cham (2015). https://doi.org/10.1007/978-3-319-26362-5_2
10. Guerra, E.: Keyloggers: A Threat to Your Data (2011)
11. Grebennikov, N.: March 2007. https://securelist.com/keyloggers-how-they-work-and-how-to-detect-them-part-1/36138/
12. Pathak, N., Pawar, A., Patil, B.: A survey on Keyloggers: a malicious Attack. Int. J. Adv. Res. Comput. Eng. Technol. (IJARCET), **4**(4) (2015)
13. Olzak, T.: Keystroke logging (keylogging), April 2008
14. Lopez, W., Guerra, H., Pena, E., Barrera, E., Sayol, J.: Keyloggers - Ethical Hacking (2014)
15. Kaur, N.: A survey on online banking system attacks and its countermeasures. IJCSNS Int. J. Comput. Sci. Netw. Secur. **15**(3), 57 (2015)
16. Ollmann, G.: The phishing guide understanding and preventing phishing attacks (2014)
17. Lim, J.: Defeat spyware with anti-screen capture technology using visual persistence. In: Proceedings of the 3rd Symposium on Usable Privacy and Security, SOUPS 2007, 147–148. ACM, New York (2007)
18. Roche, M.: Wireless hacking tools (2007)
19. Magazine Numerique XMCO: Cybercriminalite keylogger botnet attaques (2011)
20. Echi, A.K., Belaid, A.: Impact of features and classifiers combinations on the performances of Arabic recognition systems. In: 2017 1st International Workshop on Arabic Script Analysis and Recognition (ASAR), pp. 85–89 (2017)
21. Bautista, R.M.J.S., Navata, V.J.L., Ng, A.H., Santos, M.T.S., Albao, J.D., Roxas, E.A.: Recognition of handwritten alphanumeric characters using Projection Histogram and Support Vector Machine. In: 2015 International Conference on Humanoid, Nanotechnology, Information Technology, Communication and Control, Environment and Management (HNICEM), Cebu City, pp. 1–6 (2015)
22. Das, T.K., Tripathy, A.K., Mishra, A.K.: Optical character recognition using artificial neural network. In: 2017 International Conference on Computer Communication and Informatics (ICCCI), Coimbatore, pp. 1–4 (2017)

23. Kumar, B.B., Bansal, M., Verma, P.: Designing of licensed number plate recognition system using hybrid technique from neural network template matching. In: 2015 International Conference on Computing, Communication and Security (ICCCS), Pamplemousses, pp. 1–6 (2015)
24. Lu, T., Palaiahnakote, S., Tan, C.L., Liu, W.: Character segmentation and recognition. In: Lu, T., Palaiahnakote, S., Tan, C.L., Liu, W., et al. (eds.) Video Text Detection. ACVPR, pp. 145–168. Springer, London (2014). https://doi.org/10. 1007/978-1-4471-6515-6_6
25. Chaudhuri, A., Mandaviya, K., Badelia, P., Ghosh, S.K.: Optical character recognition systems. In: Chaudhuri, A., Mandaviya, K., Badelia, P., Ghosh, S.K. (eds.) Optical Character Recognition Systems for Different Languages with Soft Computing. STUDFUZZ, vol. 352, pp. 9–41. Springer, Cham (2017). https://doi.org/ 10.1007/978-3-319-50252-6_2
26. Bacara, C., et al.: Virtual keyboard logging counter-measures using human vision properties. In: 2015 IEEE 17th International Conference on High Performance Computing and Communications, 2015 IEEE 7th International Symposium on Cyberspace Safety and Security (2015)
27. Jeng, B.S., Chang, M.W., Sun, S.W., Shih, C.H., Wu, T.M.: Optical Chinese character recognition with a hidden Markov model classifier-a novel approach. Electron. Lett. **26**(18), 1530–1531 (1990)
28. Malakar, S., Halder, S., Sarkar, R., Das, N., Basu, S., Nasipuri, M.: Text line extraction from handwritten document pages using spiral run length smearing algorithm. In: 2012 International Conference on Communications, Devices and Intelligent Systems (CODIS), Kolkata, pp. 616–619 (2012)
29. Yahye, A., Mohd, M., Fuad, H., Mohamed, M.A.: Survey of keylogger technologies. Int. J. Comput. Sci. Telecommun. **5**, 25–31 (2014)
30. Damopoulos, D., Kambourakis, G., Gritzalis, S.: From keyloggers to touchloggers: take the rough with the smooth. Comput. Secur. **32**, 102–114 (2013)
31. Tuli, P., Sahu, P.: System monitoring and security using keylogger. Int. J. Comput. Sci. Mob. Comput. IJCSMC **2**(3), 106–111 (2013)
32. Chawla, S., Beri, M., Mudgi, R.: Image compression techniques: a review. Int. J. Comput. Sci. Mob. Comput. IJCSMC **3**(8), 291–296 (2014)
33. Sharma, P., Mahajan, R.: A review on compression techniques with run length encoding. Int. J. Appl. Innov. Eng. Manage. (IJAIEM). **2**(8), (2013)

Classification of Malware Families Based on Runtime Behaviour

Munir Geden[✉] and Jassim Happa

Department of Computer Science, University of Oxford, Oxford, UK
{munir.geden,jassim.happa}@cs.ox.ac.uk

Abstract. This paper distinguishes malware families from a specific category (i.e., ransomware) via dynamic analysis. We collect samples from four ransomware families and use Cuckoo sandbox environment, to observe their runtime behaviour. This study aims to provide new insight into malware family classification by comparing possible runtime features, and application of different extraction and selection techniques on them. As we try many extraction models on *call traces* such as bag-of-words, ngram sequences and wildcard patterns, we also look for other behavioural features such as *files*, *registry* and *mutex* artefacts. While wildcard patterns on call traces are designed to overcome advanced evasion strategies such as the insertion of junk API calls (causing ngram searches to fail), for the models generating too many features, we adapt new feature selection techniques with a classwise fashion to avoid unfair representation of families in the feature set which leads to poor detection performance. To our knowledge, no research paper has applied a classwise approach to the multi-class malware family identification. With a 96.05% correct classification ratio for four families, this study outperforms most studies applying similar techniques.

Keywords: Malware · Dynamic analysis · Feature selection · Security

1 Introduction

According to McAfee's recent report [13], the number of total malware samples has already exceeded 680M, out of which 63M new instances were released in the last quarter of 2017. Despite the widespread use of Anti-Virus (AV) systems for a long time, new malware families and its variants continue to infect computers, smartphones and even small IoT devices. The recent Mirai and WannaCry cases have once again shown how the malware problem can harm our economy at large scales and can stop our critical infrastructures within hours.

There have been many studies trying to solve the malware problem by using different static [5,19,26] and dynamic analyses techniques [6,8,24]. Despite the advantage of full code coverage, static techniques mainly suffer from evasion techniques such as repackaging, obfuscation and polymorphism. To overcome these challenges, dynamic techniques can be used as they focus on actual runtime

© Springer Nature Switzerland AG 2018
A. Castiglione et al. (Eds.): CSS 2018, LNCS 11161, pp. 33–48, 2018.
https://doi.org/10.1007/978-3-030-01689-0_3

behaviour of malware. In this study, we aim to contribute to the state-of-the-art by proposing how improvements of dynamic techniques can in-turn mean protection of millions of more devices. Although the priority of end-users would be the protection of their devices via malware detection, we focus on family classification—as a more challenging task—which can provide more insight for security companies and researchers to understand the recent trends and how families evolve.

Thus, this study distinguishes malware families from the same category by analysing the runtime behaviour with different feature extraction models and selection techniques. Our study makes the following contributions:

1. **Design and implementation of a scalable dynamic analysis framework** that can identify different families from the same category (i.e., ransomware) by using *call traces* and other behavioural artefacts such as *files, registry edits, mutex names*.
2. **Comparing different feature extraction models** from API and system calls such as *bags-of-words, ngrams* or *wildcard* patterns.
3. **Applying new feature selections** and adapting them to a class-wise manner to avoid the domination of a selected feature set by specific families.

2   Related Work

A dynamic analysis technique by Salaehi et al. [17] detects malware by using API calls with their arguments. After the generation of traces via *WINAPIOverride32* tool for 826 malicious and 385 benign samples, the features are selected via document frequencies to create binary vectors for each sample. With 10-fold cross-validation, the authors observed 98.4% accuracy by using Adaboost meta-classifier of Weka. Another similar study by Uppal et al. [23] also uses API calls with ngram models without arguments. The authors use *odds ratio* to select the features. Similar to the previous study, the authors train the classifiers with a 10-fold cross validation resulting in 98.5% accuracy for SVM and 4-grams. Based on their methodology sections, both studies seem to be subject to overfitting bias since the feature selection is applied prior to the cross-validation phase.

Instead of malware detection, MEDUSA [14] classifies metamorphic engines by using the frequencies of API calls. The authors use statistical measures to distinguish metamorphic families by creating signature vectors for each. These vectors are created based on the average frequencies of selected critical API calls for the given family. Furthermore, there are studies [11,15] achieving category and family identification by using API calls in different ways and adding other feature sources such as DNS requests and accessed files to their classifications. For instance, Pirscoveanu et al. [15] distinguish malware types (i.e., trojan, worm, adware, and rootkit) via API sequences, API frequencies and their counter behaviour such as level of DNS requests. Their experiments yield 0.896 True Positive Rate (TPR) for the identification of four categories. Hansen et al. [11] detect malware and distinguishes their families by using similar feature models by including API arguments. The study achieves 0.864 TPR for five families that have different functionalities and components which issues the category bias for the results. Both studies generate the runtime features by *Cuckoo Sandbox* [2] and achieve the best results with Random Forest classifier. Another study by Tsyganok et al. [22] propose a dynamic analysis framework supposed to be resilient against evasion mechanisms such as polymorphic and metamorphic malware. The study uses WinAPI calls and files as features. To decide for the similarity of two samples, they extract *Longest Common Subsequences (LCS)* from the call traces.

Lastly, Canali et al. [7] offer a systematic approach to demonstrate how different feature extraction models—applied on API calls—can influence the accuracy of the detection. They provide a benchmark and elaborate the computational limitations of different models such as bags-of-words, ngram sequences and tuple models which care only about the order of the calls regardless of the distance in between. However, since the authors do not define a threshold distance for their tuple model, its maximum cardinality is very limited compared to other models and performs poorly in some configurations.

Although many studies have tried various feature models to detect malware, there is a lack of a comprehensive approach that assesses the value of different behavioural artefacts and feature extraction/selection models for the classification of malware families from the same category.

3   Problem Definition

Our study aims to demonstrate new and diverse experiment settings in order to answer these four key research questions.

- **RQ1: Can API and system calls be used to differentiate malware families from the same category? (i.e., ransomware).** We investigate the usability of API and system calls as features to distinguish families from the same category. All samples are picked as ransomware to minimise the behavioural bias of different categories since we expect them to show similar characteristics such as encryption of the files in the system and displaying payment instructions for the ransom.
- **RQ2: Which feature models extracted from API and system calls perform better for family classification and are more resilient against evasion mechanisms such as junk API calls?** By different extraction models on call traces such as bag-of-words, ngrams, wildcard patterns with or without arguments, we explore the drawbacks and advantages of them regarding the accuracy, scalability and resiliency to evasion techniques.
- **RQ3: To what extent other behavioural artefacts can be used to classify malware families?** In addition to API and system calls, we do classifications by using more coarse-grained artefacts such as files accessed, registry keys obtained, mutexes created or Dynamic-Link Libraries (DLL) loaded. Although the call traces can provide the same information through the function arguments, we try to understand the usability of these artefacts without the noise of call traces.

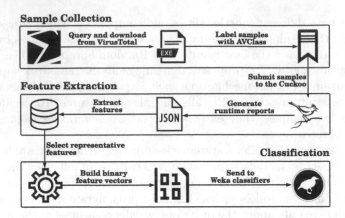

Fig. 1. Design of the experiment framework

– **RQ4: Which configuration settings regarding feature selections and classifier algorithms yield better results?** Since some models generate too many features beyond the limits of classifiers that can handle, we have used different feature selection techniques which is an important factor affecting the accuracy. Moreover, each classifier can perform differently. Thus, we aim to understand optimum settings that provide better results.

4   Methodology

Our experiment framework consists of three stages: *1-Sample Collection, 2-Feature Extraction* and *3-Classification*, as seen in Fig. 1. We first collect and label samples from different families, followed by the generation of their runtime behaviour in Cuckoo sandbox to extract the features. After applying feature selections on different models, we represent the samples as (binary) feature vectors to be sent to Weka [10] classifiers.

4.1   Dataset Collection

To collect samples, we firstly queried for recent 10–11 well-known ransomware families [1] via VirusTotal API. The queries were designed to return the samples with similar characteristics concerning file type (portable exe), first submission date/year, and file size to avoid any bias issues. However, these queries with family names do not provide reliable evidence about the family belongings since VirusTotal returns any files if at least one of the 82 AV engines labels it with the searched keyword. To address this problem, we used AVClass [20] which extracts the most common family name from AV labels and picked four ransomware families that gave the highest number of samples which were *cerber, crysis, hydracrypt* and *wannacry*.

Table 1. Number of samples for each family in training and test portions

	Cerber	Crysis	HydraCrypt	WannaCry	Total
Training	48	47	24	39	159
Test	24	23	11	19	77

Although the initial queries returned more than a thousand samples, the number of usable samples dropped to hundreds (see Table 1) after filtering with AVClass. In other words: to eliminate any concerns about the soundness of the study, we favoured more meaningful samples and preferred to experiment with the samples that AV engines have a consensus on the family.

Next, we split the samples into training and test portions randomly with a 2:1 ratio as a commonly used ratio in malware domain. We used separate portions instead of cross-validation since its proper application with a feature selection phase requires an extra effort to avoid overfitting.

4.2 Behaviour Generation

After dataset collection, we observed and collected the runtime behaviour of the samples. Due to advantages of VM-based sandbox approach such as ease of collecting many features at the same time or handling process trees, we used *Cuckoo* [2] analysis environment. It enabled us to monitor API calls, files, registry keys and mutexes accessed by the submitted samples. Setting up *Windows XP-SP3* as the experiment environment, we ran samples within for 120 s which generated JSON reports as behavioural logs.

4.3 Feature Models

We used call traces, files accessed, registry keys and mutexes as features while putting special effort on call traces with different extraction models since these calls represent the most valuable runtime features that even most of the evasion techniques including metamorphism cannot avoid.

Call Traces. Windows API and its subset system calls are used in different ways for malware detection (i.e., frequency-based approaches, bag-of-words and ngram models [14,17,23]). This study compares the accuracy and scalability aspect of both API calls and system calls.

The simplest feature model extracted from both API calls and system calls was the bag-of-words model without function arguments whereas bag-of-words with function arguments generated the highest number of features (see Table 2). Furthermore, we extracted ngrams as call sequences for a fine-grained representation of malicious behaviour. Although ngram extraction with function arguments was computationally infeasible with available resources, we successfully extracted 2-grams and 3-grams of both API calls and system calls.

Table 2. Number of unique features in different models

Feature model	# of features
API calls	210
API calls with args	1907098
API calls 2grams	2690
API calls w.card 2calls	6635/45769
API calls 3grams	10823
Sys calls	35
Sys calls with args	958474
Sys calls 2grams	321
Sys calls w.card 2calls	651/1369
Sys calls 3grams	1396
Sys calls w.card 3calls	6748/50653
Files accessed	55581
Dll loaded	166
Registry keys	4785
Mutexes	101

Wildcards models (A/B) represent the features found (A) and permutations generated (B).

To address samples bypassing ngrams by junk calls, our study proposes wildcard-based search models on call traces to catch the malicious activity hidden behind the broken call sequences. To search wildcard strings efficiently, we firstly assigned base-36 ID numbers to each API function (instead of using longer function names). Then, by using these IDs, we generated regular expressions as features that represent possible permutations of functions for the required size (2-calls, 3-calls) with an adjustable distance buffer between two functions. We set the distance buffer as 4 junk calls because larger distances could result in too many false positives while increasing the search cost unnecessarily.

We generated ngrams and wildcard patterns for 2-calls, 3-calls without arguments whereas function arguments are only used by the bag-of-words model. To illustrate all call trace-based models, a short fabricated trace and extractable features from this trace are given in Figs. 2 and 3.

Files. Malware can create new files or read/write the existing ones. We also used file names accessed by the samples during the execution as features to distinguish different families.

Registry Keys. Registry database of Windows systems provides additional artefacts for the executed programs which are frequently used for forensic

```
GetFileType(0)  //Assigned ID:A1
NtClose(0xb0) //Assigned ID:B2
RegCloseKey(0xa4) //Assigned ID:C3
NtTerminateProcess(0,0,1) //Assigned ID:D4
```

Fig. 2. A short example of call trace

```
A1:{GetFileType,NtClose..} //API calls
A2:{GetFileType(0),NtClose(0xb0)..} //API calls with args
A3:{GetFileTypeNtClose,NtCloseRegCloseKey..} //API calls ngram (2)
A4:{A1[0-9A-Z-]{0,12}B2, B2[0-9A-Z-]{0,12}C3..} //API calls w.card (2)
S1:{NtClose, NtTerminateProcess}  //Sys calls
S2:{NtClose(0xb0), NtTerminateProcess(0,0,1)}  //Sys calls with args
S3:{NtCloseNtTerminateProcess}  //Sys calls ngram (2)
S4:{B2[0-9A-Z-]{0,12}D4}  //Sys calls w.card (2)
```

Fig. 3. Feature examples extracted from the short trace (2)

analysis. While a few studies focus on the registry-based malware detection, there are malware [4] in the wild hiding themselves in the registry without causing any file artefacts. Moreover, specific registry operations can indicate hiding attempts from the analysis environments (e.g., checking the existence of VM environment) which we explore by extracting registry keys accessed as features.

Mutexes. Mutexes of operating systems represent the program objects managing the shared resources by different threads. Since these resources can be required by malware as well, we explore the use of created mutex names by the samples to identify malware families [3].

Dynamic-Link Libraries (DLL). Another feature used is the DLL files loaded during the execution of samples. Even though this feature type provides an overview of API calls without any details, it can be useful to understand the value of a more coarse-grained approach without any noise.

4.4 Feature Selection

For the models generating too many features beyond the limits that classifiers can handle such as calls with function arguments and wildcard/ngram models (see Table 2), we eliminated noisy and non-informative features via selection techniques. Despite the use of different techniques in malware domain such as *Document Frequency Threshold* [16], *Fisher Score* and *Chi-Square* scores [18,21], *Information Gain (IG)* [12,17,27] (adapted from text-categorisation) represents the most dominantly used selection technique. Thus, we performed our experiments by applying *Information Gain (IG)* [25], and our novel feature selection technique *Normalised Angular Distance (NAD)*—which is explained below— with their classwise adaptations.

Normalised Angular Distance (NAD). As a new feature selection technique based on our work [9], NAD uses the representation of features in a vector space where each dimension corresponds to the class likelihoods of the features which can be expressed as $P(f|C_i)$ and defined as the proportion of the samples containing the feature f for the given family class C_i.

This method relies on the assumption that feature vectors have equal class likelihoods for each class are not distinguishing and have no value to be selected. As the distinguishing power of a feature increases, the ratio of the difference between class likelihoods should increase as well, which our approach aims to measure via angular distance between the feature vector and the reference vector that has equal class-likelihoods.

After the representation of the features in vector space, by using the Eq. 1, the method firstly calculates α the angular distance between the feature vector f and any reference vector that has equal likelihoods for all classes such as $r = (1, 1, 1, 1)$.

$$\alpha = \cos^{-1} \frac{f \cdot r}{||f|| \cdot ||r||} \tag{1}$$

However, regardless of the vector magnitudes, the angle will be the same for the features that have the same likelihood ratios such as $f_1 = (0.1, 0.2, 0.3, 0.4)$ and $f_2 = (0.01, 0.02, 0.03, 0.04)$ which can result in the selection of noisy and sparse features. In order to manage this trade-off between being more common and more distinguishing, the method takes into account the magnitude of the feature vector as a normalisation factor with a degree parameter k to adjust the weight of the magnitude for the final score. During our experiments, we set $k = 2$ which could be experimented with a range of $[1.5, 4]$.

$$\text{NAD}(f) = \alpha \times ||f||^{1/k} \tag{2}$$

Classwise Selections. To prevent the domination of features from specific family classes and deliver a fair representation of each class in the selected feature set, we modified *Information Gain* and *Normalised Angular Distance* scores with a class-wise fashion. Although there are studies [16,28] proposing class-wise selection techniques to solve the issue, we offer a more practical solution which is adaptable to any naive solution. Firstly, we create separately ranked lists for each family class as seen in Eq. 3 for NAD which scores only the features with the highest class likelihood for the given class in the list. Then, we build our final feature set with the features ranked in each class list by ensuring that for every n number of features there will be $n/|C|$ features from each family class to create an equally distributed feature set for the classifiers.

$$\text{CWNAD}(f, C) = \begin{cases} \text{NAD}(f), & \text{if } C = argmax_{C_i} P(f|C_i) \\ 0, & \text{otherwise} \end{cases} \tag{3}$$

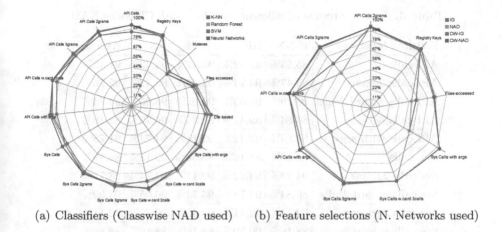

(a) Classifiers (Classwise NAD used)   (b) Feature selections (N. Networks used)

Fig. 4. Weighted TPRs of feature models for different classifiers and selections

4.5   Classifications

After extracting features from Cuckoo reports and selecting features for necessary models, we created binary-feature vectors with a size of 1000 for each
sample where the ones represent the existence of a feature for the given sample and zeros represent the absence of that feature. Created feature matrices
for each training and test portions are later sent to Weka [10] classifiers. As
classifier algorithms, we experimented with *k-Nearest Neighbour* (k=3), *Support
Vector Machines* (with SMO functions and poly-kernel), *Random Forests* (no.
of trees=100) and *Neural Networks* (default settings of Multilayer Perceptron).

5   Results and Discussion

Although we have defined the correct classification ratio as the key performance
metric, we assess the results from the scalability aspect as well. At some points
of the discussion, we will be using accuracy and weighted TPR interchangeably.
We experimented with 16 different feature models, 4 feature selection techniques
and 4 classifier algorithms on a dataset consisting of 236 samples. Due to the
excessive number of combinations caused by different settings, we discuss the
results with the setting yielding better results on average which is Classwise
NAD (selection technique) and Neural Networks (classifier) (see Fig. 4(b) and
4(a)).

5.1   Call Traces

All feature models relying on call traces are promising with the accuracy results
varying from 88.16% to 96.05%. Despite the small variations of different classifiers, any model using API and system call traces perform well enough to

Table 3. Accuracy results of different classifiers with Classwise NAD

Feature Model	K-NN	RF	SVM	NN	Average
API calls	85.53%	93.42%	93.42%	93.42%	91.45%
API calls 2grams	89.47%	94.74%	93.42%	93.42%	92.76%
API calls w.card 2calls	90.79%	96.05%	96.05%	96.05%	94.74%
API calls 3grams	86.84%	89.47%	86.84%	90.79%	88.49%
API calls with args	86.84%	93.42%	92.11%	94.74%	91.78%
Sys. calls	88.16%	88.16%	85.53%	92.11%	88.49%
Sys calls 2grams	94.74%	93.42%	92.11%	94.74%	93.75%
Sys calls w.card 2calls	86.84%	94.74%	94.74%	96.05%	93.09%
Sys calls 3grams	92.11%	92.11%	93.42%	90.79%	92.11%
Sys calls w.card 3calls	88.16%	90.79%	88.16%	88.16%	88.82%
Sys calls with args	85.53%	90.79%	90.79%	92.11%	89.81%
DLLs loaded	85.53%	92.11%	88.16%	92.11%	89.48%
Files accessed	73.68%	78.95%	77.63%	75.00%	76.32%
Mutexes	55.26%	59.21%	59.21%	55.26%	57.24%
Registry keys	88.16%	88.16%	86.84%	89.47%	88.16%
Average	87.89%	93.42%	92.37%	93.68%	

distinguish the malware families (RQ1). Regarding the comparison of API and system calls, API calls perform better on average although the system calls have scalability advantages with a less number of features.

Bag-of-Words Model. With 210 API and 35 system functions extracted, the simplest model of call traces is the bag-of-words model not using function arguments. Despite the lack of information such as function arguments and order between the calls, bag-of-words model on API calls has yielded 93.42% accuracy and followed by system calls with a 92.11%.

With Arguments. Feature models using function arguments generate the highest number of features (i.e., 1.9M unique features from API and 958 K from system call traces) which makes them infeasible for ngrams/wildcards (n-calls) due to the number of possible features ($\sim 10^{6n}$). Regarding the accuracy, API calls (94.74%) performs slightly better than system calls (92.11%) with Neural Networks and Classwise NAD settings. One benefit of function arguments is having more insight about the calls whereas standalone function names do not reveal much information about the intention of the called functions.

Another point is that due to the large feature space, these models demonstrate how the feature selection techniques can suffer from unfair representation without classwise adaptations. Since the features extracted have unbalanced distributions (e.g., feature distributions of API calls with arguments can be seen

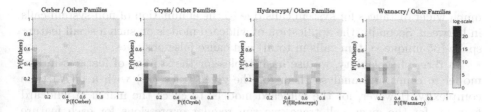

Fig. 5. Extraction distributions of features for *API Calls with args* (1.9M extracted)

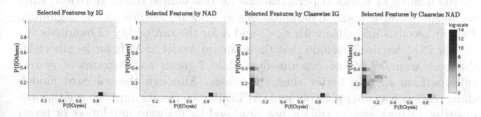

Fig. 6. *Crysis*-based selection distributions for *API Calls with args* (10K selected)

in Fig. 5), naive versions of *Information Gain* and *Normalised Angular Distance* inevitably favour one class for the selected feature sets. Figure 6 illustrates how the selection can differ for naive and classwise techniques on the basis of *Crysis* family. Figure 4(b) shows how the selection bias of naive techniques causes classifiers to perform poorly compared to the classwise selections.

Ngrams. Call sequences are expected to represent the malicious intentions better than the bag-of-words model while this is the case for most models (except API 3-grams). Based on the average results (see Table 3), both 2-grams (93.75%) and 3-grams (92.11%) of system calls have performed better than API 2-grams (92.76%) and 3-grams (88.49%) which conclude that the malicious characteristics are identified better via system calls due to possible existence of noisy and junk calls on API traces. Concerning scalability, the limited number of unique sequences found on traces makes ngrams more scalable than the feature models with arguments (see Table 2).

Wildcard Searches. These models are designed to have resiliency against the evasion mechanisms such as the insertion of junk API calls. The wildcard model running on API calls for 2-calls and with the distance buffer of 4-calls has yielded the best results of all models with an accuracy of 96.05% for three classifiers. Compared to the 2-grams of API calls, it is a legitimate assumption that there are samples in our dataset inserting junk API calls caught by the wildcard model. For system calls of which wildcard models seem to have slightly worse performance than the ngrams correspondents, the results are reasonable because of following issues. Firstly, as malware developers may not prefer to inject specifically junk system call functions, the distance buffer that we set (4-calls) corresponds to much wider distances for system calls due to the elimination of non-system calls in between. Secondly, the application of wildcard models on such a small feature space (35 unique system calls in total) can cause false positives.

In term of scalability, we use hash tables for the storage of features in any model to count and analyse them for the given trace (N) with a $\mathcal{O}(N)$ time complexity. However, for the wildcard models: to check the match of wildcard features for the given call trace, we run regular expressions for each feature which means an additional $\mathcal{O}(N)$ complexity layer that needs be to multiplied by the number of wildcard permutations for one sample trace. Moreover, since we generate all the possible permutations as wildcard features at the beginning, $P(n,r)$ becomes infeasible with $r > 3$ and n for the cardinality of hundreds.

For RQ2, we can conclude that the wildcard model of APIs for 2-calls yields the best accuracy of the experiments, while 2-grams and 3-grams of system calls perform slightly better than the others. Although the wildcard models show resilience against possible junk API calls, the results imply that either the insertion of junk system calls is not practised by malware developers or larger buffer distances (due to the elimination of non-system calls at the beginning) for a small feature space such as system calls cause false positives.

5.2   Other Artefacts

Other feature models relying on *registry keys* and *DLLs loaded* have also produced promising results whereas the *files accessed* and *mutexes* have performed poorly. DLLs and registry keys used during the analyses have yielded 89.45% and 88.16% accuracy on average respectively. The files accessed has produced 76.32% correct classification ratio, while the mutex names represent the worst performing model with a 57.24% (RQ3).

5.3   Optimum Settings and Comparison

As a response to our RQ4, regarding classifier algorithms, Neural Networks and Random Forest have performed quite well with classwise selection techniques. Experiment results manifest that unfair representation of classes by the selected feature sets is an important issue that needs to be addressed by selection techniques. While both classwise adaptations produce significantly more accurate results than the naive ones (see Fig. 4(b)), experiment results demonstrate that our selection technique NAD is able to compete with IG without any significant difference (t-tests are applied). With Neural Networks and Classwise NAD settings, the wildcard model of API calls for 2-calls is the best performing feature model of which detailed class-based performance metrics can be seen in Table 4. Despite the selection of all samples from the same malware category, this study outperforms the majority of similar studies identifying malware categories [15] or families [11] from different categories.

Table 4. Class-based performance metrics and comparison with related work

	TPR	FPR	Prec.	Recall	F-M	ROC
Cerber	0.957	0.019	0.957	0.957	0.957	0.993
Crysis	1	0.038	0.92	1	0.958	0.995
Hydracrypt	0.909	0	1	0.909	0.952	0.996
Wannacry	0.947	0	1	0.947	0.973	0.999
Our study (weighted)	0.961	0.017	0.963	0.961	0.961	0.995
Hansen et al. [11]	0.864	0.035	0.872	N/A	0.864	0.978
Pirscoveanu et al. [15]	0.896	0.049	0.907	N/A	0.898	0.980

5.4 Discussion and Future Work

As this study provides insights into which type of behavioural information can
be used for family classification, and to what extent, it also reveals the benefits
and drawbacks of different feature extraction models from the same information
(e.g., call traces) such as bag-of-words, ngrams, and adjustable and computationally optimised wildcard search models. In addition to the introduction of a new
feature selection technique, the study shows how naive selection techniques for
high-dimensional models without classwise adaptation causes poor performance.
Additionally, this study minimises the potential bias of different categories by
selecting all samples from the same category which is an issue that most studies
do not address.

   While this research focuses on the performance comparison of different feature models and selection techniques, there are other factors defining the success
on which we do not have much control. The first issue is various VirusTotal family labels of AV engines. Even though the queries made by family names return
too many file hashes, filtering them with a labelling tool [20] reduces the number
of usable samples significantly. As we apply supervised-learning techniques and
our classifiers use the most common VirusTotal family names as training labels,
the performance of the classifiers are still dependent on the way how these AV
engines analyse and label these samples.

   Our research relies on analysis reports generated by Cuckoo sandbox.
Although Cuckoo integrates some mechanisms to avoid the detection of analysis environment by samples and we have eliminated the samples that do not
execute, there may be samples hiding the malicious behaviour and acting like
legitimate software. Since the study relies on the sandbox approach as a dynamic
analysis technique, we are not fully aware of these samples possibly modifying
behaviour within the analysis environment. As a future work, we plan to integrate code coverage mechanisms that can measure the confidence of observed
behaviour or other heuristics to detect such behaviour modification attempts.

6 Conclusion

In this study, we have implemented a malware family classifier that uses the runtime behaviours collected by Cuckoo Sandbox as features. Although the focus is the exploration of feature models that can be extracted from call traces such as the application of bag-of-words, ngrams or wildcard search models to the API and system call functions, we have also investigated the value of other artefacts such as registry keys, files and mutexes as features. Our experiments have shown that any feature model relying on call traces and DLL libraries and registry keys used during the execution yield promising results which are mostly above 88%. Two other feature models, files accessed (76.32%) and mutexes (57.24%) have produced less accurate results.

In addition to the application of *Information Gain* during our experiments, we have also adapted a new feature selection technique *Normalised Angular Distance*, to family classification as an example of the multi-class classification problem. We have also demonstrated that the adaptation of these feature selection techniques with classwise fashion yields better results since they do not suffer from the unfair representation of specific families.

Acknowledgements. We want to thank VirusTotal community for providing a private API to our research that enabled us to search for and download the ransomware samples.
Cuckoo reports (1.4GB) of the samples and framework's source code: Reports: https://goo.gl/e8jbXq
Source code: https://bitbucket.org/msgeden/familyclassifier

References

1. 11 of the worst ransomware - we name the internet nastiest extortion malware - Gallery - Computerworld UK. https://goo.gl/wNDoL4
2. Cuckoo Sandbox: Automated Malware Analysis. https://cuckoosandbox.org/
3. Hunting the Mutex - Palo Alto Networks Blog. https://researchcenter.paloaltonetworks.com/2014/08/hunting-mutex/
4. TrendLabs Security Intelligence BlogPOWELIKS: Malware Hides In Windows Registry - TrendLabs Security Intelligence Blog. https://goo.gl/3nrgo7
5. Abou-Assaleh, T., Cercone, N., Keselj, V., Sweidan, R.: N-gram-based detection of new malicious code. In: Proceedings of the 28th Annual International Computer Software and Applications Conference, 2004, COMPSAC 2004. vol. 2, pp. 41–42. IEEE (2004). https://doi.org/10.1109/CMPSAC.2004.1342667
6. Bayer, U., Kruegel, C., Kirda, E.: TTAnalyze: A tool for analyzing malware. In: 15th Annual Conference on European Institute for Computer Antivirus Research, pp. 180–192 (2006)
7. Canali, D., Lanzi, A., Balzarotti, D., Kruegel, C., Christodorescu, M., Kirda, E.: A quantitative study of accuracy in system call-based malware detection. In: Proceedings of the 2012 International Symposium on Software Testing and Analysis - ISSTA 2012, p. 122 (2012). https://doi.org/10.1145/2338965.2336768

8. Fukushima, Y., Sakai, A., Hori, Y., Sakurai, K.: A behavior based malware detection scheme for avoiding false positive. 2010 6th IEEE Workshop on Secure Network Protocols (NPSec), pp. 79–84 (2010)
9. Geden, M.: Ngram and signature based malware detection in android platform. Msc dissertation, University College London (2015). https://goo.gl/uKJsHv
10. Hall, M., Frank, E., Holmes, G., Pfahringer, B., Reutemann, P., Witten, I.H.: The WEKA data mining software. ACM SIGKDD Explor. **11**(1), 10–18 (2009). https://doi.org/10.1145/1656274.1656278
11. Hansen, S.S., Larsen, T.M.T., Stevanovic, M., Pedersen, J.M.: An approach for detection and family classification of malware based on behavioral analysis. In: 2016 International Conference on Computing, Networking and Communications, ICNC 2016, pp. 1–5. IEEE (2016). https://doi.org/10.1109/ICCNC.2016.7440587
12. Kolter, J.Z., Maloof, M.A.: Learning to detect and classify malicious executables in the wild. J. Mach. Learn. Res. **7**, 2721–2744 (2006). https://doi.org/10.1002/asi.20427
13. McAfee: McAfee Labs Threats Report March (2018). https://goo.gl/ZeugSV
14. Nair, V.P., Jain, H., Golecha, Y.K., Gaur, M.S., Laxmi, V.: MEDUSA: MEtamorphic malware dynamic analysis using signature from API. In: Proceedings of the 3rd International Conference on Security of Information and Networks - SIN 2010 (January), p. 263 (2010). https://doi.org/10.1145/1854099.1854152
15. Pirscoveanu, R., Hansen, S.S., Larsen, T., Stevanovic, M. Pedersen, J., Czech, A.: Analysis of malware behavior: type classification using machine learning. In: International Conference on Cyber Situational Awareness, Data Analytics and Assessment (CyberSA), pp. 1–7 (2015). https://doi.org/10.1109/CyberSA.2015.7166128
16. Reddy, D.K.S., Pujari, A.K.: N-gram analysis for computer virus detection. J. Comput. Virol. **2**(3), 231–239 (2006)
17. Salehi, Z., Ghiasi, M., Sami, A.: A miner for malware detection based on API function calls and their arguments. In: The 16th CSI International Symposium on Artificial Intelligence and Signal Processing (AISP 2012), pp. 563–568. IEEE, May 2012. https://doi.org/10.1109/AISP.2012.6313810
18. Sami, A., Yadegari, B., Peiravian, N., Hashemi, S., Hamze, A.: Malware detection based on mining API calls. In: Proceedings of the 2010 ACM Symposium on Applied Computing - SAC 2010, p. 1020 (2010). https://doi.org/10.1145/1774088.1774303
19. Schultz, M., Eskin, E., Zadok, F., Stolfo, S.: Data mining methods for detection of new malicious executables. In: Proceedings 2001 IEEE Symposium on Security and Privacy. S&P 2001, pp. 38–49. IEEE Computer Society (2001). https://doi.org/10.1109/SECPRI.2001.924286
20. Sebastián, M., Rivera, R., Kotzias, P., Caballero, J.: AVCLASS: A tool for massive malware labeling. In: Monrose, F., Dacier, M., Blanc, G., Garcia-Alfaro, J. (eds.) RAID 2016. LNCS, vol. 9854, pp. 230–253. Springer, Cham (2016). https://doi.org/10.1007/978-3-319-45719-2_11
21. Shabtai, A., Fledel, Y., Elovici, Y.: Automated static code analysis for classifying android applications using machine learning. In: Proceedings - 2010 International Conference on Computational Intelligence and Security, CIS 2010, pp. 329–333 (2010). https://doi.org/10.1109/CIS.2010.77
22. Tsyganok, K., Tumoyan, E., Babenko, L., Anikeev, M.: Classification of polymorphic and metamorphic malware samples based on their behavior. In: Proceedings of the Fifth International Conference on Security of Information and Networks - SIN 2012, pp. 111–116 (2012). https://doi.org/10.1145/2388576.2388591

23. Uppal, D., Sinha, R., Mehra, V., Jain, V.: Malware detection and classification based on extraction of API sequences. In: 2014 International Conference on Advances in Computing, Communications and Informatics (ICACCI), pp. 2337–2342. IEEE, September 2014. https://doi.org/10.1109/ICACCI.2014.6968547
24. Willems, C., Holz, T., Freiling, F.: Toward automated dynamic malware analysis using CWSandbox. IEEE Secur. Priv. Mag. 5(2), 32–39 (2007). https://doi.org/10.1109/MSP.2007.45
25. Yang, Y., Pedersen, J.O.: A comparative study on feature selection in text categorization. In: Machine Learning-International Workshop Then Conference, pp. 412–420 (1997). https://doi.org/10.1093/bioinformatics/bth267
26. Ye, Y., Wang, D., Li, T., Ye, D., Jiang, Q.: An intelligent PE-malware detection system based on association mining. J. Comput. Virol. 4(4), 323–334 (2008). https://doi.org/10.1007/s11416-008-0082-4
27. Yerima, S.Y., Sezer, S., McWilliams, G.: Analysis of Bayesian classification-based approaches for android malware detection. IET Inf. Secur. 8(1), 25–36 (2014). https://doi.org/10.1049/iet-ifs.2013.0095
28. Zhang, P., Tan, Y.: Class-wise information gain. In: 2013 IEEE Third International Conference on Information Science and Technology (ICIST), pp. 972–978. IEEE, March 2013. https://doi.org/10.1109/ICIST.2013.6747700

Botnet Detection in Software Defined Networks by Deep Learning Techniques

Ivan Letteri, Giuseppe Della Penna[✉] ⓘ, and Giovanni De Gasperis ⓘ

Department of Information Engineering, Computer Science and Mathematics,
University of L'Aquila, L'Aquila, Italy
ivan.letteri@graduate.univaq.it,
{giuseppe.dellapenna,giovanni.degasperis}@univaq.it

Abstract. Botnets are nowadays one of the most widespread and dangerous kind of malware on the internet, so their detection is a very important task. However, many works in this field exploit general malware detection techniques and rely on old or biased traffic samples, which make their results not completely reliable. Moreover, software-defined networking (SDN), which is increasingly replacing conventional networking, drastically limits the number of features that can be extracted from the network traffic and therefore used to detect botnets. In this paper we propose a novel botnet-specific detection methodology based on deep learning techniques, which has been experimented on a new, SDN-specific dataset and reached a very high (up to 96%) traffic classification accuracy. Our algorithms have been implemented on two state-of-the-art frameworks, i.e., Keras and TensorFlow, so we are confident that our experimentation results are reliable and easily reproducible.

Keywords: Botnet detection · Machine learning
Neural networks · Deep learning
Software defined networking · Network security

1 Introduction

A *botnet* consists of a number of internet-connected devices, each of which runs one or more *bots*, i.e., systems compromised by some kind of malware controlled by an attacker (the *botmaster*). Botnets can be very difficult to detect and eradicate due to their size and distribution. Therefore, in the last twenty years, botnets have gained a lot of attention from security researchers (see, e.g., [2–4,32]).

Software-defined networking (SDN) [16] is an emerging networking approach that enables an easy and efficient (re)configuration in order to improve network performance. To this aim, SDN centralizes the network intelligence in a single component, separating the packet forwarding process (*Data Plane*) from the

This work was partially supported by the *Cyber Trainer* project (POR FESR Abruzzo 2014–2020).

© Springer Nature Switzerland AG 2018
A. Castiglione et al. (Eds.): CSS 2018, LNCS 11161, pp. 49–62, 2018.
https://doi.org/10.1007/978-3-030-01689-0_4

routing (*Control plane*). Elements on the control plane (the controllers) can communicate with elements on the data plane (e.g., switches) through the *OpenFlow* [24] protocol.

Due to this particular structure, a SDN differs form a conventional network also for traffic monitoring-related aspects: indeed, there are traffic features, such as the packet ratio, that can be easily measured on both conventional and SDN networks, whereas some other features are hard or impossible to obtain from the data plane through OpenFlow requests. Obviously, talking directly with data plane such elements is sometimes possible through ad-hoc protocols, but this would break the SDN abstraction or make the approach very specific to the software running on the elements.

Therefore, analysing network traffic in order to detect botnet attacks in a SDN requires a very different approach with respect to conventional networks. On the other hand, being very suitable for the modern high-bandwidth applications, SDN will increasingly replace conventional networking in the near future, and then it will rapidly become the main diffusion field for botnets. Thus, SDN-based botnet analysis and detection is a very interesting field.

Current state-of-the-art approaches to botnet detection often exploit the so called *behavioural analysis* (for a general discussion on this technique and its applications see, e.g., [7,8]). Indeed, botnets are continuously evolving and changing their behaviour, making quickly ineffective more established techniques as, e.g., signature analysis, which is still widely adopted in malware detection engines, whereas behavioural analysis approaches have proved more appropriate to address the constant evolution of botnets [22]. Behavioural analysis is often supported by machine learning techniques, to further improve its adaptability to the botnet evolution: indeed, by exploiting machine learning, it is possible to detect new attack schemes which have similarities with known attacks, thus preventing the so-called "zero day" exploits.

In a previous paper [20], we started working in this context by exploiting a very basic neural network classifier for such a task, and obtained encouraging results from tests carried out on a small dataset with simple features. In this paper we propose a novel botnet-specific detection methodology that exploits machine learning techniques, in particular multi layered neural networks (which fall in the field of *deep learning* techniques [19]), and has been experimented on a new SDN-specific dataset, obtaining a very high (up to 96%) accuracy. In particular, the employed dataset derives from the *HogZilla* dataset [27], which combines selected parts of the well-known CTU-13 [11] and ISCX 2012 IDS [29] datasets in order to obtain a large, complex set of more than 990,000 samples. From this dataset, we performed a further feature selection and filtering in order to make it a realistic dataset for a SDN. Therefore, our experiments have been carried out using real, recent botnet traffic samples that could be observed in a SDN.

Finally, our neural networks have been implemented and experimented relying on two state-of-the-art frameworks, i.e., Keras and TensorFlow, so we are confident that our experimentation results are reliable and easily reproducible.

To the best of our knowledge, there is no work in the literature that combines these three components, i.e., botnet-specific detection mechanisms, SDN-specific traffic features and behavioural analysis through multi-layered neural networks.

The paper is organised as follows. Section 2 lists some related works relative to our areas of interest, i.e., SDN, machine learning and botnet detection. Then, in Sect. 3 we present the dataset used in this paper and describe the SDN traffic features is contains, whereas in Sect. 4 we describe the architecture and technical details of the neural network exploited in the experiments. Finally, Sect. 5 shows our experimental results and Sect. 6 comments them, describing also our future work in this field.

2 Related Work

As discussed in the introduction, to the best of our knowledge there is no work in the literature that focuses on our exact combination of technologies and aims. However, there are works in the recent literature focusing on botnet detection or, more in general, malware analysis in SDN networks and machine learning based malware detection. Here we give an overview of the most recent and interesting ones.

A few works address the malware detection problem in SDN, possibly exploiting machine learning techniques. Among these, in [31] Tang et al. propose a deep learning based approach for general network intrusion detection in SDN using self-taught learning (STL) and the NSL-KDD dataset. In particular, they exploit a simple five-layer deep neural network with an input dimension of six and an output dimension of two, which is instructed trough six features: *duration, protocol type, source bytes, destination bytes, count,* and *service count*. Even if the approach is interesting and similar to ours, the current results are not particularly good, probably due to the insufficient number of features exploited.

In [33] the authors exploit a SDN-oriented botnet grading strategy based on the collection of OpenFlow *flow counters* and on the use of a monitored C4.5 tree grading algorithm. The experiments show that such features are suitable for distinguishing between malware and general network traffic flows.

In [14] the authors employ Self-Organizing Maps as classifiers in order to build an intrusion prevention system for DDoS attacks mitigation in SDN architectures.

With respect to the approaches above, in this paper we exploit a multilayer perceptron as classifier and use a different set of selected SDN traffic features to perform botnet detection.

Finally, in [38] Wijesinghe et al. propose a machine learning technique to detect botnets by analysing traffic flows directly from SDN switches through the IPFIX protocol [26], thus bypassing the data plane isolation and the OpenFlow protocol. This approach, however, introduces a significant delay in the botnet detection, since measurements extracted with the IPFIX protocol are available only when the corresponding connection is closed. Moreover, the authors exploit five different machine learning algorithms to classify the traffic but do not take in consideration their performance. To avoid these problems, in the present work we used only features that can be read from the SDN controller and collected through the OpenFlow protocol.

On the other hand, many works exploiting machine learning methods for malware detection (or, more in general, network traffic classification) can be cited. Kalaivani et al. [15] compare several different machine learning algorithms such as SVM, naive bayes, decision trees and neural networks in the context of network traffic classification. They exploit the CTU-13 dataset and evaluate the model performance through 10-fold cross-validation. Surprisingly, they conclude that neural networks are the worst classifiers in this context, whereas the results presented in this paper show that neural networks can be employed in botnet detection with very good results. Our feeling is that [15], being aimed to a comparison rather than to the optimization of a specific approach, lacks an accurate feature selection, which is indeed at the heart of a good neural network classifier.

In [37], the authors encode traffic data as images and then exploit a convolutional neural network for traffic classification. Their experiments, carried out in two different scenarios with three classifiers, reach an accuracy rate of roughly 99%.

In [35] the authors exploit deep learning techniques in an intrusion detection system and experiment it on the KDDCup99 dataset [9] with good accuracy results.

Finally, in [39] the authors propose a novel *flow-based* inductive intrusion detection system using a One-Class Support Vector Machines and reaching an accuracy rate of 98%.

However, for these works, the addressed problem is much more general (not botnet-specific), not SDN-specific, or exploits outdated datasets.

3   The Dataset

Ideally, a dataset should represent realistic traffic, providing a variety samples taken from both botnet attacks and legitimate traffic. Finding a publicly available dataset fulfilling these requirements is a challenging task and a true concern in the network security community with respect to reproducibility and comparability. Indeed, often datasets are *biased* due to the specific experiment they were initially aimed to, and therefore do not constitute a good source of knowledge for a machine learning process.

The *HogZilla* dataset [27] is a recently published dataset obtained by merging a fragment of the well-known CTU-13 dataset [11], which contains 13 network traces of 7 distinct botnet malwares, and a large set of normal/background traffic traces taken from the ISCX 2012 IDS dataset [29]. This traffic is further preprocessed and classified, resulting in 990,000 samples, each associated with 192 behavioural features.

To support our experiments, we refine the dataset above, that we shall call the *complete dataset*, by extracting from it a *fair dataset*, i.e., a balanced dataset containing exactly the same number (180, 000) of normal and botnet samples. This dataset is used for the neural network training phase, since the complete dataset exhibits much more normal traffic than malicious traffic, and this could bias the neural network making it *learn* only the normal traffic [18].

3.1 Feature Selection

Feature selection aims to devise the minimal subset of flow features that are enough to detect the behaviour of a botnet. This is especially useful for machine learning based behavioural analysis, where too many (useless) features to take into account may confuse the classifier. In this paper, we focused on 22 features, taking into account the ones more suitable for botnet detection that can be actually collected in a SDN.

Indeed, in a SDN, only statistics like the *number of packets*, the *number of bytes*, and the *flow duration* can be read from the controller (control plane element), which obtains it through the OpenFlow calls to the data plane. However, other useful features can be manually computed from the statistics exposed by the controller.

Table 1. SDN traffic features extracted from the controller

#	Feature	SDN feature	HogZilla feature
1	Length of the connection	Duration	Flow duration
2	Maximum expire time of a flow	Hard time out	Flow use time
3	Protocol type	Protocol	Protocol
4	Data bytes in bidirectional flow	Bytes count	Bytes
5	Packets in bidirectional flow	Packets	Packets
6	Data bytes from source to destination	Tx packets	src2dst packets
7	Data bytes from destination to source	Rx packets	dst2src packets
8	Flow permanence time	Idle time out	Flow idle time

The eight features from the HogZilla dataset shown in Table 1 can be directly obtained from the SDN controller through appropriate calls. In particular, all the features are read from the *flow and port stats* obtained by an OpenFlow call, with the exception of the *Protocol*, which is the result of a OVSDB [31] call executed by the controller. In the table, we show both the SDN feature name and the HogZilla feature corresponding to the selected feature. As an example, the *Protocol* feature (e.g., tcp, udp, icmp, etc.) is useful for botnet detection since bots usually employ different protocols in different phases of their lifecyle (setup, attack, update, etc.)

On the other hand, the other 14 HogZilla features exploited in our experimentation and described in Table 2 can be suitably derived in a SDN environment as follows:

Table 2. Derived SDN traffic features

#	Feature	HogZilla feature
9	Packet per second (PPs) from source to destination	Packet rate (src2dst)
10	Packet per second from destination to source	Packet rate (dst2src)
11, 12, 13, 14	Inter Arrival Time (IAT) (min, avg, max, std)	Inter time
15, 16, 17, 18	Inter Arrival Time from source to destination (min, avg, max, std)	Inter time (src2dst)
19, 20, 21, 22	Inter Arrival Time from destination to source (min, avg, max, std)	Inter time (dst2src)

$$- PPs = \frac{number\ of\ packets}{duration}$$
$$- IAT = \frac{Start\ time\ of\ flow(n)}{Start\ time\ of\ flow(n-1)}$$

Note that we actually exploit the PPs and IAT features relative to the packets exchanged in both directions as well as those travelling in a specific direction (source to destination and destination to source). As an example, the bidirectional variant of the *Packet per second* is indeed the *Packets* feature in Table 1. Having direction-specific features is useful to detect particular botnets since, for example, most of spam botnets generate unidirectional flows.

Moreover, we consider the minimum, maximum, average and standard deviation of such values. Indeed, bot traffic tends to be uniformly distributed over time but, as a bot progresses through its lifecyle and accomplishes different tasks, the characteristics of the generated traffic varies. The use of such statistic measures helps to capture the behavioural differences between these tasks, so that the overall bot behaviour can be detected.

4   The Neural Network

Neural networks have been widely used in classification tasks, since they have a high tolerance of noisy data and can be used when there is a little knowledge of the relationships between features and classes. This is very important in the botnet detection scenario, since bots are continuously evolving and thus their behaviour quickly changes. This makes deterministic classifiers (e.g., signature scanners) not suitable for such a task.

In our experiments, we used a multi layer perceptron with the following characteristics:

- the *input layer* consists of 22 neurons, as the number of features selected;
- there are 7 *hidden layers* with a specific distribution of neurons: 44, 88, 176, 88, 44, 22, 11. Such neurons are activated using the *rectified linear unit*

(ReLU) [12] function, whereas the more common *sigmoid* function has not been employed due to its known *vanishing gradient* issue, which proved to considerably slow down the training in our first experiments;
- the *output layer* consists of two neurons with a *softmax* activation function. Indeed, softmax is commonly used in the last layer of neural networks in order to transform the results into *classes*. In our case, the possible output values are 10 for botnet traffic and 01 for normal traffic, whereas the two other combinations value are not considered.

Note that the shape of the neural network, which initially grows by duplicating the number of neurons in each subsequent hidden layer up to the half, and then reduces by halving them, is quite usual [36], whereas the number hidden layers required by our application has been devised with a set or experiments that, for sake of brevity, we do not report here.

We used *cross entropy* as the loss function, e.g., the mean squared error between the predictions and the true values. This choice makes more evident the situations where the predictions are far from the true values. In each experiment, weights were randomly initialized according to a *Gaussian distribution* with zero mean and small (0.05) standard deviation.

Starting from such a base architecture, we tried several different configuration parameters for the neural network, e.g., different learning rates, training epochs and batch sizes. We also exploited different *optimization algorithms* for *error backpropagation*. In Sect. 5 we report the results obtained with a first guess of these parameters/algorithms combination, and then we show how other possible choices may influence the accuracy of the resulting neural network.

4.1 Network Implementation: Keras and Tensorflow

To run our neural network we used TensorFlow 1.7.0 [1], an open source software library, originally developed by the Google Brain team, which offers a state-of-the-art support for machine learning algorithms. Its main advantages are being cross-platform and able to transparently exploit both GPUs and CPUs to achieve the best computation performances. TensorFlow exposes a low-level Python frontend, upon which sits the so-called Layers API, a mid-level API providing simpler interface to define the most common neural network layers, i.e., dense and convolutional. In our setup, Tensorflow was installed in an Ubuntu Server 16.04.3 machine with 16 GB DDR4 RAM and an Intel Core I7 CPU.

To quickly prototype the neural network we did not rely directly on Tensor-Flow, but exploited the neural networks API of Keras [6], which is also written in Python and capable of running on top of TensorFlow (as well as on CNTK [28] and Theano [34]). This allowed us to abstract from the actual underlying engine and rapidly develop our network with a very compact code, which is shown in Fig. 1. In the code it is possible to read, for each layer, the number of neurons, the weight initializer function (`kernel_initializer`, except for the input layer) and the `activation` function (relu or softmax). All the layers are *Dense*, and each is concatenated with a further *Dropout* layer. This kind of layer

```
model = Sequential()
model.add(Dense(44, input_dim=22, activation='relu'))
model.add(Dropout(0.3))
model.add(Dense(88, kernel_initializer='normal', activation='relu'))
model.add(Dropout(0.3))
model.add(Dense(176, kernel_initializer='normal', activation='relu'))
model.add(Dropout(0.3))
model.add(Dense(88, kernel_initializer='normal', activation='relu'))
model.add(Dropout(0.3))
model.add(Dense(44, kernel_initializer='normal', activation='relu'))
model.add(Dropout(0.3))
model.add(Dense(22, kernel_initializer='normal', activation='relu'))
model.add(Dropout(0.3))
model.add(Dense(11, kernel_initializer='normal', activation='relu'))
model.add(Dropout(0.3))
model.add(Dense(2, kernel_initializer='random_normal',
activation='softmax'))
model.compile(loss='binary_crossentropy',
optimizer= keras.optimizers.Adam(lr=0.001),
metrics=['accuracy'])
```

Fig. 1. Perceptron definition with Keras

(offered by Keras) does not actually contribute to the network capabilities, but is used during training to randomly set a given percentage (30% in our case) of its inputs (which are then directly fed to the subsequent hidden layer) to zero. This helps to prevent overfitting [30]. The chosen loss function and optimizer are specified in the last code line.

Finally, we exploited the *scikit-learn* [25] and *numpy* [23] libraries to calculate the neural network performance metrics related to accuracy and loss. Thanks to the chosen technology setup above, we are confident that our experimentation results are reliable and easily reproducible.

5   Experimentation

To test our approach, we first extract five different training and test sets from the *fair* dataset (see Sect. 3). To this aim, we shuffle the dataset and then partition it in 50%/30%/20% parts. The first and last parts will be used for training and testing, respectively, whereas the remaining 30% is discarded.

We configure our neural network using the Adam optimizer [17], setting the *learning rate* to 0.001, the *batch size* to 100 and the number of *epochs* to 10, since, in general, these settings proved to be a good choice in our earlier experiments. The training sets are fed to the network, and the resulting training accuracy is shown in the second column of Table 3. Figure 2 shows the accuracy increase during the ten training epochs for each training set. We can see that the fifth

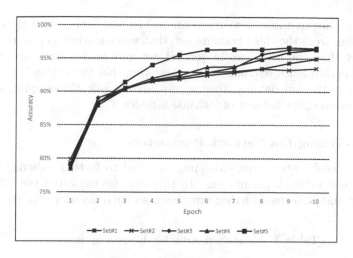

Fig. 2. Neural network training

Table 3. Neural network traning and testing on different sets extracted from the *fair* dataset

Train/Test set number	Training accuracy	Prediction accuracy	
		Test set	Complete set
1	94.94	94.95	92.24
2	93.50	93.42	82.55
3	96.44	96.42	93.18
4	96.36	96.38	92.41
5	96.52	96.59	92.63

set's accuracy quickly increases, exceeding 95% in the fifth epoch, and then remains substantially stable, whereas the third and fourth training sets reach a similar accuracy only on the last epoch. It is worth noting that, in all the five experiments, the training took less than one minute to conclude. Therefore, our classifier could be synthesized and updated almost in real time.

Then we evaluate the prediction accuracy (i.e., the percentage of exact predictions) of the trained networks on the corresponding test sets, which are completely unknown to the network since they were not used during the training. Such accuracy values are reported in column 3 of Table 3 and show that, with the last three training sets, we reach a prediction accuracy greater than 96%. In particular, training set 5 gets the best result of 96.59%.

Finally, we evaluated the prediction accuracy also on the complete HogZilla dataset, most of which is completely unknown to the network, obtaining an accuracy that ranges from 82.55% to 93.18%, as reported in column 4 of Table 3. The lowest value belongs to the second training set, that shows an anomalous behaviour also on the test set, probably because the training samples had a low variance and thus contained less information. The best accuracy on the complete dataset comes from the third training set, that was slightly less accurate on the test dataset than the fifth one. In general, we note an accuracy decrease, but the overall performance remains good considering that the network was trained on the 50% of the fair dataset, thus approximately 180, 000 samples, and then tested on the compete dataset of 990, 000 samples.

5.1 Fine-Tuning the Network Parameters

Even if the results above are satisfying, we tried to further enhance them by changing some network parameters. To this aim, we exploited the fifth training/test set and performed further experiments with different parameter choices.

Table 4. Accuracy metrics for different optimizers

Optimizer	Training accuracy	Prediction accuracy
Adamax	93.41	93.43
AdaDelta	92.22	92.38
AdaGrad	68.80	68.25
Nadam	49.94	50.14
RMSprop	49.92	50.18
SGD	50.07	49.86
Adam	**96.83**	**97.00**

First we tried to increase the accuracy by changing the network optimizer. We tried the *Stochastic Gradient Descent (SGD)* optimization algorithm as well as its variants *RMSprop* [13], *Adadelta* [40], *AdaGrad* [10] and *Adam* [17] with the corresponding further variants *Adamax* and *Nadam*. Note that the stochastic nature of such algorithms helps to converge in a lower number of epochs on datasets with redundant data, as traffic flows are, and gives better possibility of escaping from local minima [5].

The results are shown in Table 4. As we can see, Adam remains the best choice in our case. Note that the values reported here (as well as in the other tables below) may be slightly different from the ones of Table 3 even when using the same parameters (the Adam optimizer in this case) due to the random weight initialization that makes each training of the network behave differently, even if the train and test sets are the same.

Then we tried to change the *learning rate* parameter (also known as the step size), which controls the size of the updates applied to the network weights. Table 5 shows that when the learning rate is higher or lower than 0.001, the accuracy decreases considerably, especially in the prediction phase. Therefore, the value 0.001 seems to be the best choice to make the network suitably generalize the notions coming from the training set.

Table 5. Accuracy metrics for different learning rates

Learning Rate	Training accuracy	Prediction accuracy
0.0001	89.48	89.63
0.001	**96.19**	**96.34**
0.01	49.92	50.14
0.1	50.08	50.86

Table 6. Accuracy metrics for different number of epochs

Epochs	Training accuracy	Prediction accuracy
10	96.86	96.92
15	96.33	96.31
20	96.28	96.23
25	**96.87**	**96.96**
30	94.03	94.04

We further tried to change the number of epochs used for training, i.e., the number of times the network is exposed to the training set. Table 6 shows that with 25 epochs we get the higher prediction accuracy (96.96%). On the other hand, the accuracy obtained with 10 epochs (96.92%) is only slightly less than the maximum and, in this case, the training is significantly faster (less than 1/3 of the time required by 25 epochs). Thus, we may conclude that 10 epochs is an optimal value to get a good accuracy/performance compromise.

Table 7. Accuracy metrics for different batch sizes

Batch size	Training accuracy	Prediction accuracy
10	88.38	88.63
100	**96.77**	**96.79**
1000	94.42	94.64
10000	86.16	86.25

Finally, we tested the impact of changing the batch size, i.e., the number of training instances observed before the optimizer performs a weight update. Table 7 shows that the batch size impacts learning significantly. In general, larger batch sizes result in faster training, but do not always get an acceptable accuracy. Smaller batch sizes train slower, but get higher accuracies. Indeed, the right batch size will provide the optimizer with a stable estimate of the gradient to apply. In our case, a batch size of 100 gets the best results.

6   Conclusions

Botnet detection is a very important issue for modern cybersecurity applications. Many research works currently address this issue, but their results are often biased by unrealistic datasets. Indeed, public datasets are commonly published in a pre-processed format, where specific features have already been extracted, or in raw format, leaving the user with the hard task of correctly extracting a meaningful set of features. In both cases, the samples come from standard internet traffic, whereas in some network architectures raw packet data is not available and therefore some features cannot be deduced. This is the case of SDN networks, that are becoming very popular, where the traffic statistics should be obtained only from the controller, and observing in real time the raw traffic through the data plane is, in general, not allowed.

In this paper we performed botnet detection experiments on a new dataset, containing a very large amount of normal and botnet traffic samples, from which we extracted a set of botnet-specific meaningful features that can be actually derived in a SDN environment. Starting from this realistic basis, we applied behavioural analysis techniques using a multilayer perceptron as the classifier, showing that, with a good selection of parameters, this simple kind of neural network can reach very good accuracy rates, up to 96%.

For sake of transparency, both our dataset and the definition of the employed perception are publicly available [21], so our experiments can be easily reproduced by other researchers. In particular, in our implementation we exploited two state-of-the art public libraries, i.e., TensorFlow and Keras, to minimize any possible implementation problem that could invalidate the results and make our models easily executable in any environment.

Our future work on this field will include a more in-depth analysis of the SDN traffic features, to further reduce the amount of data needed to reach the current accuracy levels. To this aim, we are studying the correlations between the current set of features and also plan to employ deep leaning techniques to perform an automatic feature selection.

References

1. Abadi, M., et al.: TensorFlow: large-scale machine learning on heterogeneous systems (2015). https://www.tensorflow.org/, software available from tensorflow.org
2. Abu Rajab, M., Zarfoss, J., Monrose, F., Terzis, A.: A multifaceted approach to understanding the botnet phenomenon. In: Proceedings of the 6th ACM SIG-COMM Conference on Internet Measurement, pp. 41–52. IMC 2006. ACM, New York, NY, USA (2006). https://doi.org/10.1145/1177080.1177086
3. Antonakakis, M., et al.: Understanding the mirai botnet. In: Proceedings of the 26th USENIX Conference on Security Symposium, SEC 2017, pp. 1093–1110. USENIX Association, Berkeley, CA, USA (2017)
4. Bailey, M., Cooke, E., Jahanian, F., Xu, Y., Karir, M.: A survey of botnet technology and defenses. In: Proceedings of the 2009 Cybersecurity Applications & Technology Conference for Homeland Security, CATCH 2009, pp. 299–304. IEEE Computer Society, Washington, DC, USA (2009). https://doi.org/10.1109/CATCH.2009.40

5. Bottou, L.: Stochastic gradient learning in neural networks. In: Proceedings of Neuro-Nîmes 91. EC2, Nimes, France (1991). http://leon.bottou.org/papers/bottou-91c
6. Chollet, F., et al.: Keras: the python deep learning library (2018). https://keras.io
7. D'Angelo, G., Rampone, S., Palmieri, F.: An artificial intelligence-based trust model for pervasive computing. In: 2015 10th International Conference on P2P, Parallel, Grid, Cloud and Internet Computing (3PGCIC), pp. 701–706 (2015). https://doi.org/10.1109/3PGCIC.2015.94
8. D'Angelo, G., Rampone, S., Palmieri, F.: Developing a trust model for pervasive computing based on Apriori association rules learning and Bayesian classification. Soft Comput. **21**(21), 6297–6315 (2017). https://doi.org/10.1007/s00500-016-2183-1
9. Dheeru, D., Karra Taniskidou, E.: UCI machine learning repository: KDD cup 1999 data data set (2018). https://archive.ics.uci.edu/ml/datasets/kdd+cup+1999+data
10. Duchi, J., Hazan, E., Singer, Y.: Adaptive subgradient methods for online learning and stochastic optimization. J. Mach. Learn. Res. **12**, 2121–2159 (2011)
11. Garca, S., Grill, M., Stiborek, J., Zunino, A.: An empirical comparison of botnet detection methods. Comput. Secur. **45**, 100–123 (2014). https://doi.org/10.1016/j.cose.2014.05.011
12. Glorot, X., Bordes, A., Bengio, Y.: Deep sparse rectifier neural networks. In: Proceedings of the Fourteenth International Conference on Artificial Intelligence and Statistics, pp. 315–323 (2011)
13. Hinton, G.: RMSprop: divide the gradient by a running average of its recent magnitude (lecture 6e) (2018). http://www.cs.toronto.edu/~tdijmen/csc321/slides/lecture_slides_lec6.pdf
14. Jankowski, D., Amanowicz, M.: Intrusion detection in software defined networks with self-organized maps. J. Telecommun. Inf. Technol. **2015**(4), 3–9 (2015)
15. Kalaivani, P., Vijaya, M.: Mining based detection of botnet traffic in network flow. IRACST-Int. J. Comput. Sci. Inf. Technol. Secur. **06**, 535–541 (2016)
16. Kamal, B., Abdeslam, E.F., Abdelbaki, E.E.: Software defined networking (SDN): a survey. Secur. Commun. Netw. **9**(18), 5803–5833 (2016). https://doi.org/10.1002/sec.1737
17. Kingma, D.P., Ba, J.: Adam: a method for stochastic optimization. CoRR (2014). http://arxiv.org/abs/1412.6980
18. Kotsiantis, S., Kanellopoulos, D., Pintelas, P.: Handling imbalanced datasets: a review. GESTS Int. Trans. Comput. Sci. Eng. **30**, 25–36 (2005)
19. LeCun, Y., Bengio, Y., Hinton, G.: Deep learning. Nature **521**(7553), 436 (2015)
20. Letteri, I., Del Rosso, M., Caianiello, P., Cassioli, D.: Performance of botnet detection by neural networks in software-defined networks. In: Proceedings of the Second Italian Conference on Cyber Security, Milan, Italy, 6th–9th February 2018. (2018). http://ceur-ws.org/Vol-2058/paper-03.pdf
21. Letteri, I., Della Penna, G.: Sources for botnet detection experiments on SDN networks through machine lerarning techinques (2018). https://github.com/gdellapenna/BotNet-SDN-ML
22. Miller, S., Busby-Earle, C.: The role of machine learning in botnet detection. In: 2016 11th International Conference for Internet Technology and Secured Transactions (ICITST), December 2016. https://doi.org/10.1109/ICITST.2016.7856730
23. Oliphant, T.: Numpy (2018). http://www.numpy.org

24. Open Networking Foundation: Openflow switch specification, version 1.3.0 (2012). https://www.opennetworking.org/images/stories/downloads/sdn-resources/onf-specifications/openflow/openflow-spec-v1.3.0.pdf
25. Pedregosa, F., et al.: Scikit-learn: machine learning in Python. J. Mach. Learn. Res. **12**, 2825–2830 (2011)
26. Quittek, J., Zseby, T., Claise, B., Zander, S.: Requirements for IP flow information export (IPFIX) (2004). https://tools.ietf.org/html/rfc3917
27. Resende, P.A.A., Drummond, A.C.: The hogzilla dataset (2018). http://ids-hogzilla.org/dataset
28. Seide, F., Agarwal, A.: CNTK: microsoft's open-source deep-learning toolkit. In: Proceedings of the 22nd ACM SIGKDD International Conference on Knowledge Discovery and Data Mining, KDD 2016, pp. 2135–2135. ACM, New York, NY, USA (2016). https://doi.org/10.1145/2939672.2945397
29. Shiravi, A., Shiravi, H., Tavallaee, M., Ghorbani, A.A.: Toward developing a systematic approach to generate benchmark datasets for intrusion detection. Comput. Secur. **31**, 357–374 (2012). (report)
30. Srivastava, N., Hinton, G., Krizhevsky, A., Sutskever, I., Salakhutdinov, R.: Dropout: a simple way to prevent neural networks from overfitting. J. Mach. Learn. Res. **15**, 1929–1958 (2014). http://jmlr.org/papers/v15/srivastava14a.html
31. Tang, T.A., Mhamdi, L., McLernon, D., Zaidi, S.A.R., Ghogho, M.: Deep learning approach for network intrusion detection in software defined networking. In: 2016 International Conference on Wireless Networks and Mobile Communications (WINCOM), October 2016. https://doi.org/10.1109/WINCOM.2016.7777224
32. Tanwar, G.S., Goar, V.: Tools, techniques & analysis of botnet. In: Proceedings of the 2014 International Conference on Information and Communication Technology for Competitive Strategies, ICTCS 2014, pp. 92:1–92:5. ACM, New York, NY, USA (2014). https://doi.org/10.1145/2677855.2677947
33. Tariq, F., Baig, S.: Machine learning based botnet detection in software defined networks. Int. J. Secur. Appl. **11**, 1–12 (2017)
34. Theano Development Team: Theano: A Python framework for fast computation of mathematical expressions. arXiv e-prints abs/1605.02688, May 2016. http://arxiv.org/abs/1605.02688
35. Van, N.T., Thinh, T.N., Sach, L.T.: An anomaly-based network intrusion detection system using deep learning. In: 2017 International Conference on System Science and Engineering (ICSSE), pp. 210–214, July 2017. https://doi.org/10.1109/ICSSE.2017.8030867
36. Vincent, P., Larochelle, H., Lajoie, I., Bengio, Y., Manzagol, P.A.: Stacked denoising autoencoders: Learning useful representations in a deep network with a local denoising criterion. J. Mach. Learn. Res. **11**(Dec), 3371–3408 (2010)
37. Wang, W., Zhu, M., Zeng, X., Ye, X., Sheng, Y.: Malware traffic classification using convolutional neural network for representation learning. In: 2017 International Conference on Information Networking (ICOIN), pp. 712–717, January 2017. https://doi.org/10.1109/ICOIN.2017.7899588
38. Wijesinghe, U., Tupakula, U., Varadharajan, V.: Botnet detection using software defined networking. In: 2015 22nd International Conference on Telecommunications (ICT), pp. 219–224 (2015)
39. Winter, P., Hermann, E., Zeilinger, M.: Inductive intrusion detection in flow-based network data using one-class support vector machines. In: 2011 4th IFIP International Conference on New Technologies, Mobility and Security, February 2011
40. Zeiler, M.D.: ADADELTA: an adaptive learning rate method. CoRR abs/1212.5701 (2012). http://arxiv.org/abs/1212.5701

A Bio-inspired Approach to Attack Graphs Analysis

Vincenzo Conti[1(✉)], Simone Sante Ruffo[1], Alessio Merlo[4], Mauro Migliardi[3], and Salvatore Vitabile[2]

[1] Faculty of Engineering and Architecture, University of Enna KORE, Enna, Italy
vincenzo.conti@unikore.it, simonesante.ruffo@unikorestudent.it
[2] Department of Biopathology and Medical Biotechnologies, University of Palermo, Palermo, Italy
salvatore.vitabile@unipa.it
[3] Department of Information Engineering, University of Padua, Padua, Italy
mauro.migliardi@unipd.it
[4] Department of Informatics, Bioengineering, Robotics and Systems Engineering, Genoa, Italy
alessio@dibris.unige.it

Abstract. Computer security has recently become more and more important as the world economy dependency from data has kept growing. The complexity of the systems that need to be kept secure calls for new models capable of abstracting the interdependencies among heterogeneous components that cooperate at providing the desired service. A promising approach is attack graph analysis, however the manual analysis of attack graphs is tedious and error prone. In this paper we propose to apply the metabolic network model to attack graphs analysis, using three interacting bio-inspired algorithms: topological analysis, flux balance analysis, and extreme pathway analysis. A developed framework for graph building and simulations as well as an introductory use case are also outlined.

Keywords: Attack graphs · Network security
Bio-inspired techniques

1 Introduction

Over the years, computer security has acquired a central role in all the systems as the modern world has become more and more dependent from a seamless and timely flow of information and data. In gaining this central role, Computer Security has developed branches dealing with different aspects, from the most practical ones such as the one dedicated to the identification of vulnerabilities [9] and the development of automated protection techniques [2], to the more theoretical ones that strive to leverage mathematical methodologies to evaluate the security (or lack of) of systems [19] and of the Cloud [7]. While the importance

© Springer Nature Switzerland AG 2018
A. Castiglione et al. (Eds.): CSS 2018, LNCS 11161, pp. 63–76, 2018.
https://doi.org/10.1007/978-3-030-01689-0_5

of the practical approaches is paramount and cannot be in any way denied, we claim that the growing complexity of the systems and the compositional nature of systems developed under the umbrella of the Internet of Things requires the development of modeling tools capable of capturing the characteristics and the behavior not just of the components but of the whole system as a network of interacting entities. To achieve this goal, in this paper we propose to apply the model of metabolic networks to complex computer-based systems. This formalism allows identifying critical paths and highlight spots that present the highest level of vulnerability for the system as a whole, hence, it is our opinion that it is well suited to the task of performing a holistic security analysis to complex systems. More in details, after describing the formalism we show an introductory use-case, namely the analysis of attack graphs.

Our use case will analyze a network, assuming that the vulnerabilities are already known. Starting from this information an attack graph will be created and then it will be analyzed using a tool that allows us to obtain values that determine which is the greatest risk and the minimum number of changes needed to morph the network into a new version that could be considered at least partially safe.

In the literature there are several techniques used for attack graph analysis. In [4], the attack graph is seen as a game to which the Stacklberg equilibrium is applied to search for the best strategy that defenders must apply to defend against attackers. Other applications are based on GREEDY algorithms, transforming the problem of finding the minimum set of critical attacks into the problem of Minimum hitting set. Through this technique it is possible to find a solution in a time that is linearly related to the size of the network. The graphs used in these articles are generated by the tool MulVAl. Many approaches, however, for the analysis of networks exploit the application of PageRank of Google [3,22] on Bchi automata [11]. The approaches from which this work is inspired leverage attack graphs in which each node is associated with a probability. In [8] a methodology is proposed for the research of the minimum graph, that is the minimum path that allows the attacker to reach his goal. In [18], the attack graph is analyzed using the Monte Carlo method in order to obtain significant information on the economic value of the attack as well as on the risk of it. In [25] the network is studied using the probability theory. Similar works use exponential distributions to simulate the success of an attack and analyze network security using Markov models.

In this paper we propose a new approach that leverages the application of bio-inspired algorithms to tackle the problem of attack graphs analysis. The paper envisions some new application scenarios for these algorithms that show a high level of adaptability to different fields of applications, as already seen in [5,24]. The implemented and proposed framework is an extension of the BIAM software proposed in [5]. The framework allows the drawing and managing of complex networks and their analysis by means of bio-inspired algorithms derived from techniques of analysis originally designed for usage with metabolic networks. The framework also allows saving both the generated graph and the results obtained, hence it is possible to perform a design, analysis, implement strengthening measures loop over a candidate network. Because a network can be represented with a graph, the following article will use the two terms as synonyms.

The paper is organized as follows: in Sect. 2 we briefly introduce some of the security issues in modern networks; in Sect. 3 we describe our bio-inspired framework; in Sect. 4 we describe the case study; in Sect. 5 we present our experimental results and, finally, in Sect. 6 we provide some concluding remarks.

2 Security Assessment Through Attack Graph

As actual computing systems are far too complex to be manually analyzed by a security analyst, there is a growing demand for techniques and tools that allow automatizing the security assessment of complex systems. At the basis of a successful automatic methodology there lie proper models enabling (1) to provide an abstract, simplified but complete view of the system under validation (SUV), and (2) to define strategies for the automatic assessment of the SUV.

Current literature is plenty of proposals allowing to formalize the behavior of parallel systems, mobile applications [16], wired [2,13] and wireless [6,17] networks and so on. The primary challenge with such modeling activities is to prove the provided abstraction is general but complete enough to support a comprehensive analysis of the system. Regarding assessment strategies, these are expected to allow defining assessment/testing methodologies of the modeled SUV. The reliability of both models and assessment strategies depends on the number of vulnerabilities of the actual SUV that they allow unveiling. Among these, attack graphs provide a pure formalism to define the steps to attack an SUV to uncover vulnerabilities.

Nowadays security analysts exploit attack graphs to keep track of the attack steps, manually. Albeit several approaches have been put forward in the literature to support a semi-automatic building of attack graphs, most of the proposal fail to provide reliable solutions. With the adjective reliable, we refer to the possibility to assess the security of the SUV regarding both the time needed to carry out the analysis phase as well as the number of successful vulnerabilities that such analysis allows to discover. The current solutions for generating attack graphs provide only slight improvements of such metrics when compared to the manual building carried out by an expert security analyst.

We argue that novel models should be put forward to try improving the reliability of automatic generation of attack graph. However, the mere building of SUV-specific graph attacks is a limited contribution, as each attack graph must be tested and evaluated on the SUV. Therefore, there is the need for comprehensive frameworks able to (1) generate attack graphs automatically, (2) automatically carry out security tests on the SUV by exploiting the generated attack graph, (3) evaluate the reliability of the attack.

The previous considerations are valid for any type of SUV in a computing systems, e.g., from concurrent processes to mobile environments. We argue that each category of SUV requires specific solution for attack graph generation and validation. In this paper we put forward a solution based on bio-inspired algorithms for the definition and the building of attack graphs, and we specifically focus on LANs as SUV.

3   Framework Description: Characteristics and Functionalities

The proposed developed framework is based on three bio-inspired algorithms for networks security analysis, namely: Topological analysis, Extreme Pathway analysis (Expa) and Flux Balance analysis (FBA). These three algorithms were designed to analyze metabolic networks, particular networks that describe the reactions that, in the case of cellular metabolism, lead to the production of nutrients for the cell. The topological analysis [15] allows obtaining information on the structure and topology of the network as: the number of vertex and edge, the hub nodes, the clustering and participation coefficients, and the diameter. The extreme pathway analysis [20], working on the stoichiometric matrix, allows to obtain all the paths from a source to a destination of the graph. The FBA [12] calculates the optimal path and the related optimal fluxes. However, this path must have a minimum input flux (called nutrient uptake) in order to cellular survival.

The framework we describe in this paper, namely BIAM 2.0, is the enhanced version of the framework proposed by the same authors in [5]. The first version of BIAM framework was able only to generate scale-free networks and analyze them with bio-inspired methodologies. This new and enhanced version also allows building and handling random and small-world networks. Furthermore, BIAM 2.0 is equipped with a user-friendly GUI capable of showing in real time: the generated graph, the changes made and the results obtained from the analyses (see Fig. 1).

By clicking the "Generate" button, it is possible to modify the generated graph before performing the analysis of the same. In addition, the framework also gives the option to save the generated graphs and then reload them later. Finally, once the analyses have been carried out, the framework allows saving the results on text files and also to save images of the graphs, with the possibility to assign a name to each node and link, to be able to draw up (see Fig. 2).

Figure 1 shows the first window of BIAM 2.0, where a combo box allows selecting among three types of complex network; in this step it is possible to choose the desired graph and set the parameters for the random generation; then the graph can be generated pressing the related button. After this step has been performed, it is possible to modify the network/graph to be analyzed customizing it according to a model (see Fig. 3).

Using the "Perform analysis" button, the framework (see Fig. 4) shows the available types of analysis. It is possible to select to apply, to the generated network, each one of the three algorithms to single out the results of that specific analysis, or, using the "Save Result" button, all three algorithms can be simultaneously applied and the obtained results are saved into a text file. Figure 4

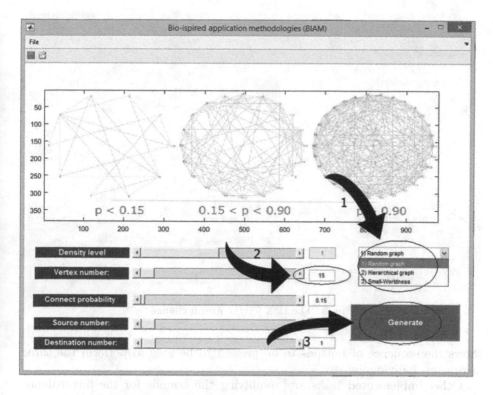

Fig. 1. The task for the graph generation

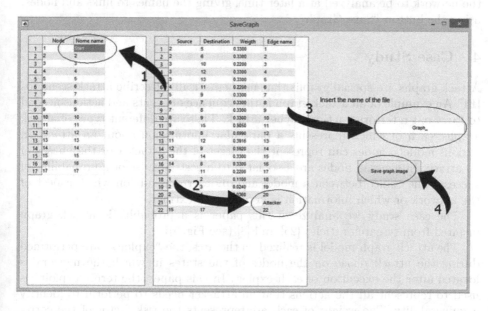

Fig. 2. The task for the graph saving

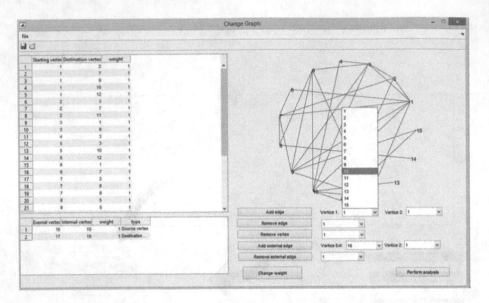

Fig. 3. The task for the graph change

shows the sequence of buttons to be pressed to be able to perform the three algorithms individually.

Other implemented tasks are: modifying the bounds for the flux balance analysis, using the buttons "Calculate Bounds" and "Set bounds", and to save the network to be analyzed at a later time, giving the names to links and nodes, using the button "Save Graph".

4   Case Study

Attack graphs are special graphs that mathematically describe attack scenarios [14]. An example of an attack graph is the sequence of events and actions needed to carry out a terrorist act or a cyber attack. There are different types of attack graphs, each of which represents a particular information about an attack. In various models, nodes can represent the target of the attacker or the phases of an attack. In general, nodes are associated to a cost, a cause or a probability of success. The choice between a model and another depends on which aspect of the network or which information is necessary to extract.

The case study we analyze in this paper is a probabilistic attack graph inspired from research articles [25] and [8] (see Fig. 5).

The attack graph model is realized on the arcs, the "exploits" are performed during the attack phase on the nodes of the states in which the network is located after the execution of each exploit. In this paper, the term "exploit" is used to represent all the actions that an attacker needs to perform to identify a vulnerability. The weight of each arc represents the risk factor of the corresponding exploit, calculated as the product between the damage suffered and the

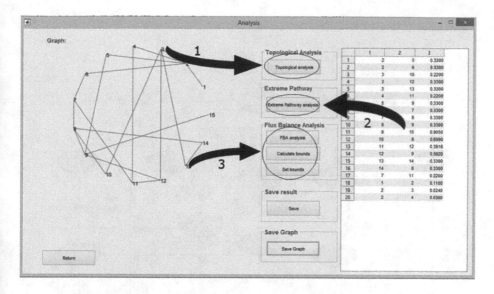

Fig. 4. The sequence of task to perform the bio-inspired analysis

likelihood of suffering that damage. The variable damage acts with a random variable. For simplicity, it can be written as:

$$R = D * P \tag{1}$$

It represents the risk for a system to receive some damages. The probability of the exploit being performed is taken from the Common Vulnerability Scoring System (CVSS) score [1] of the same. The algorithm used to calculate the CVSS takes the name of the Common Vulnerability Scoring System and can be found on the NIST (national Institute of Standard and Technology) site [23]. The current version of the algorithm is version 3.0. The values of CVSS score were obtained from the National Vulnerability Database (NVD) located on the same NIST site we have previously cited. The initial probability was calculated as the number of exploits executable in that machine over the total exploits number. For the calculation, the formulas shown in Fig. 6 were used.

Each event was considered independent from the previous and the analysis is considered independent from the attacker's knowledge. For the calculation of bounds in Flux Balance Analysis, two limit values have been considered, these two values correspond to the maximum risk (CVSS equal to its actual value) and to the minimum risk (CVSS equal to 1). The CVSS value of each exploit is calculated on the parameters shown in Fig. 7, giving each of these characteristics a score.

The algorithm used to calculate a CVSS from a metrics base and described in Fig. 7 is based on a main equation derived from two sub-equations: the Exploitability Subscore equation and the impact subscore equation. While the

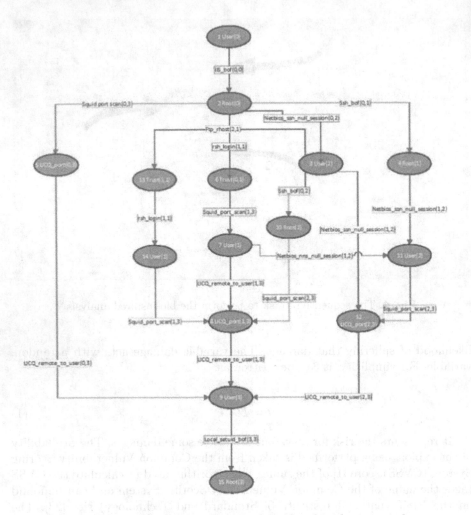

Fig. 5. The probabilistic attack graph analyzed in the case study

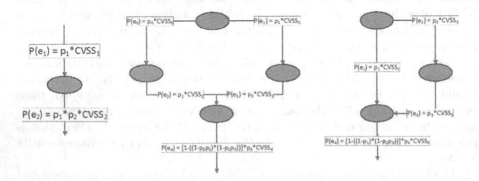

Fig. 6. Formulas used to calculate the initial probability

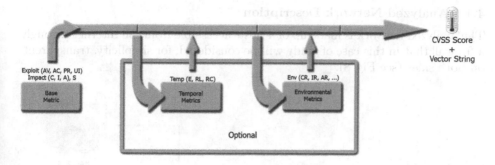

Fig. 7. Process for CVSS calculation

Exploitability Subscore equation comes from the base metric exploitable metrics, the Impact Subscore equation is derived from the impact metric base. Typically, baseline and temporal metrics are specified by vulnerability analysts or vendors of security products or applications, because they generally have more accurate information. In contrast, environment metrics are specified by the end user of organizations because they know the impact information that has that vulnerability.

The CVSS score for each vulnerability has been derived from the NIST NVD looking for the vulnerability from its CVE ID. As previously mentioned the case study is based on two fundamental hypotheses, since everything is independent from the attacker's knowledge. It was considered that the attacker knows the right exploit for each vulnerability and that he is able to use it to his advantage. The first hypothesis is that the system knowledge is very good and so on how the attack must be performed. The second hypothesis is that every exploit performed has no effect on successive events, so each event becomes independent from the previous ones (see Fig. 8).

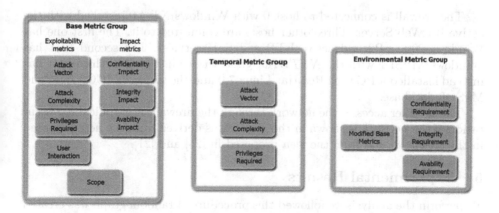

Fig. 8. Parameters for the CVSS calculation

4.1   Analyzed Network Description

The analyzed network is made up of 4 hosts accessible from the Internet through a firewall that in this case of study will be considered, for simplicity, transparent on both sides (see Fig. 8).

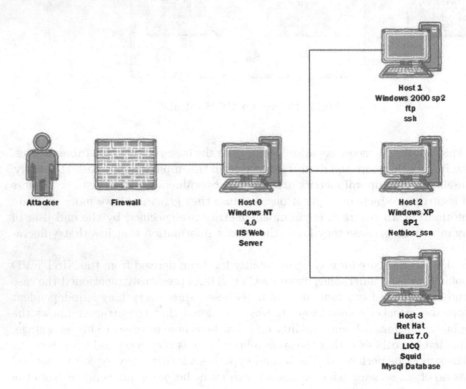

Fig. 9. The scenario analyzed in this work

The firewall is connected to host 0 with Windows NT 4.0 installed with the active IIS Web Server. Three other hosts are connected to it. The first one has Windows 2000 SP2 and active FTP and SSH services. The second host has Windows XP SP1 with the $NETBIOS_SSN$ service install. The third host has instead installed a PC with Red Hat Linux 7.0 and the services LICQ, squid and MySQL database.

The attacker accesses the network through the firewall. A graphical representation of the network is shown in the Fig. 9. It is derived from the nets proposed in the article [8] and from the idea proposed in [25] and [21].

5   Experimental Results

To perform the analysis we followed this procedure: a random graph was created starting from Fig. 7, the weight of each arc was calculated and inserted after which the network was saved (see Fig. 10).

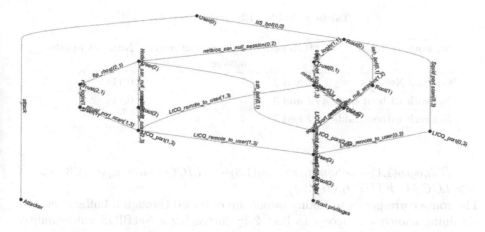

Fig. 10. The analyzed network in this work

Then, the Topological analysis, the Extreme Pathway analysis, and the Flux Balance analysis were performed. After saving the obtained results from the analysis of the original network, nodes 4 and then the 3 were deleted (attacks) in order to repeat the analysis and compare obtained results of the three different networks. From these analyses it is possible to identify the sequences of exploits that optimize the damage; furthermore, it is also possible to identify the minimum number of arcs (i.e., the minimum number of vulnerabilities of the network) which, if eliminated, would make the network partially sure.

The analysis of the original network provides the results shown in Table 1. A first result is the fact that the connectivity is high for node 2, in other words this fact makes multiple attack paths possible in the network. A second result is the identification of nodes that have the role of "connector hubs" [10]. In the analyzed network, these "connector hubs" are nodes 2 and 3. In the analyzed network there are 7 extreme pathways and a best path with a uptake nutrient of 0.11. Deleting node 4, the exploit that allows host 1 administrator privileges, does not significantly change the results of the analysis. On the contrary, by deleting node 3, which is a hub node, some differences in the results of the analysis can be observed. Nodes 2 and 7 become the new hub nodes, both with the role of "connector hub". Besides, the number of extreme pathways change from 4 to "no best path is found".

With more details, the weight of each arc of the network represents the risk that an exploit can cause a certain damage equal to the CVSS score of the exploit itself. The best path represents the path, which is the sequence of exploits, which maximizes the risk. This represents the sequence of exploits that maximizes both the damage suffered and the likelihood of suffering such damage. Examining the original network we observe that nodes 2 and 3 are hub nodes. The number of extreme pathways found is equal to 7 and the uptake nutrient of the best path is equal to 0.11. The best path consists of the following sequence of exploits: $IIS_BOF(0.0)- > Netbios_ssn_null_session(0.2)- > Ftp_rhost(2.1)- >$

Table 1. Table with analysis results.

Network analyzed	Hub nodes	Extreme pathways number	Nutrient uptake
Original Network	2 and 3	7	0.11
Network without node 4	2 and 3	6	0.11
Network without node 3	2 and 7	4	-

$- > Rsh_login(1.1) - > Squid_port_scan(1.3) - > LICQ_remote_to_user(1.3) - > $
$- > LOCAL_SETUID_BOF(3.3)$

The route corresponds to taking ownership of host 0 through a buffer overflow, obtaining anonymous access to host 2 by leveraging a NetBIOS vulnerability, gaining host 1 confidence, and logging in it through the reverse shell, using Squid to make the scanner using open ports in machine 3 obtaining remote control of the machine and performing a local buffer overflow by obtaining host 3 Administrator privileges. By deleting node 3, no best path is found, this result can be interpreted as a state in which a potential hacker cannot find a sequence of exploits that maximizes the risk. By deleting node 4, the number of extreme pathways varies slightly while best path does not vary.

For a computational point of view, the proposed approach and toolset allow obtaining results in a real time. For the network we just analyzed, the run time using a PC with an i7 CPU and 4 GB of RAM running Windows 8.1 is just 5 s. Breaking down the total amount of time we observe that 0.16 s are employed by the topological analysis, 0.67 s are employed by the ExPa algorithm, while 2 s are employed by the FBA (measured by Matlab functions). We can compare our results with some data regarding algorithm performance provided in papers present in the literature. The authors in [8] show a computational cost algorithm of $M*N^3$ where M is the number of exploits and N is the number of hosts present. The computational cost of the extreme pathway is equal to N^3 with N number of graph nodes. Because the presence of each node is not dependent on the exploits in the hosts number but on states number in which the network can be found, the algorithm computational cost is not easy to calculate. An estimate can be obtained by assuming the best case in which each exploit allows to reach only one state, in this case, at most, the result is k * m knots, with m the number of exploits and K integer. The application of this algorithm is useful if the objective is used to get all paths that an attacker can follow to get own goal.

6   Conclusions

In this paper we have proposed a bio-inspired approach, based on algorithms used to study the metabolic network behavioural, to tackle the problem of attack graphs analysis. An automated tool has been implemented and its use has been described by means of an introductory attack graph analysis use case. In the proposed use case we have assumed that the vulnerabilities are already known.

The usage of the tool allowed us to obtain values related the greatest risk and the minimum number of changes needed to morph the network into a new version that could be considered at least partially safe. With more details, the application of this bio-inspired approach allowed us to identify all paths that an attacker can follow to get own goal and to identify the most efficient way to thwart the attacker malicious will. The computational complexity of the used algorithms allowed observing the results of network modification in real-time, however, in more complex cases, additional optimization might be needed to keep this real-time behavior. Such optimization, together with the study of additional types of analysis will be the object of future work.

References

1. Common Vulnerability Scoring System Version 3.0 Calculator (2017). https://www.first.org/cvss/calculator/3.0
2. Baddar, S.A.H., Merlo, A., Migliardi, M.: Anomaly detection in computer networks: a state-of-the-art review. J. Wirel. Mob. Netw. Ubiquit. Comput. Dependable Appl. (JoWUA) 5(4), 29–64 (2014)
3. Brin, S., Page, L.: The anatomy of a large-scale hypertextual web searchengine. Comput. Netw. ISDN Syst. 30(1), 107–117 (1998). https://doi.org/10.1016/S0169-7552(98)00110-X. Proceedings of the Seventh International World Wide Web Conference
4. Chokshi, I., Das, S., Ghosh, N., Ghosh, S., Kaushik, A., Sarkar, M.: NetSecuritas: an integrated attack graph-based security assessment tool for enterprise network. In: Proceedings of the 2015 International Conference on Distributed Computing and Networking (2015)
5. Conti, V., Ruffo, S., Vitabile, S., Barolli, L.: BIAM: a new bio-inspired analysis methodology for digital ecosystems based on a scale-free architecture. Soft Comput. 1–18 (2017)
6. Feng, P.: Wireless LAN security issues and solutions. In: 2012 IEEE Symposium on Robotics and Applications, ISRA, pp. 921–924, June 2012. https://doi.org/10.1109/ISRA.2012.6219343
7. Ficco, M.: Security event correlation approach for cloud computing. Int. J. High Perform. Comput. Netw. 7(3), 173–185 (2013)
8. Ghosh, N., Ghosh, S.K.: An intelligent technique for generating minimal attack graph. In: First Workshop on Intelligent Security (Security and Artificial Intelligence), SecArt (2009)
9. Gobbo, N., Merlo, A., Migliardi, M.: A denial of service attack to GSM networks via attach procedure. In: Cuzzocrea, A., Kittl, C., Simos, D.E., Weippl, E., Xu, L. (eds.) CD-ARES 2013. LNCS, vol. 8128, pp. 361–376. Springer, Heidelberg (2013). https://doi.org/10.1007/978-3-642-40588-4_25
10. Guimer, R., Amaral, L.: Functional cartography of complex metabolic network. Nature 433, 895–900 (2005)
11. Jalan, S., Kumar, P., Das, S.: Formalization of digital forensic theory by using Buchi Automaton. In: 2015 Third International Conference on Image Information Processing, pp. 102–108 (2015)
12. Kauffman, K., Prakash, P., Edwards, J.: Advances in flux balance analysis. Curr. Opin. Biotechnol. 14(5), 491–496 (2003)

13. Khoussainov, R., Patel, A.: LAN security: problems and solutions for Ethernet networks. Comput. Stand. Interfaces **22**(3), 191–202 (2000). https://doi.org/10.1016/S0920-5489(00)00047-7
14. Kramer, D.: Attack-defence graph - on the formalisation of security-critical system. Master's thesis. Saarland University, Germania (2015)
15. Lacroix, V., Cottret, L., Thbault, P., Sagot, M.: An introduction to metabolic networks and their structural analysis. IEEE/ACM Trans. Comput. Biol. Bioinform. **5**(4), 594–617 (2008)
16. Merlo, A., Migliardi, M., Fontanelli, P.: On energy-based profiling of malware in Android, pp. 535–542 (2014). https://doi.org/10.1109/HPCSim.2014.6903732
17. Migliardi, M., Merlo, A.: Modeling the energy consumption of distributed IDS: a step towards Green security, pp. 1452–1457 (2011). https://www.scopus.com/inward/record.uri?eid=2-s2.0-80052297709partnerID=40md5=f36e30763ec3bc927c69575ba628cf18
18. Noel, S., Wang, L., Singhal, A., Jajodia, S.: Measuring security risk of networks using attack graphs. Proc. Int. J. Next-Gener. Comput. **1**(1), 135–147 (2010)
19. Pasha, M., Qaiser, G., Pasha, U.: A critical analysis of software risk management techniques in large scale systems. IEEE Access **6**, 12412–12424 (2018). https://doi.org/10.1109/ACCESS.2018.2805862
20. Schilling, C., Letscher, D., Palsson, B.: Theory for the systemic definition of metabolic pathways and their use in interpreting metabolic function from a pathway-oriented perspective. J. Theoret. Biol. **203**(3), 229–248 (2000)
21. Singhal, A., Ou, X.: Security risk analysis of enterprise networks using probabilistic attack graph. NIST Interagency Report (7788) (2011)
22. Treinen, J.J., Thurimella, R.: Application of the PageRank algorithm to alarm graphs. In: Qing, S., Imai, H., Wang, G. (eds.) ICICS 2007. LNCS, vol. 4861, pp. 480–494. Springer, Heidelberg (2007). https://doi.org/10.1007/978-3-540-77048-0_37
23. US-CERT Security Operations Center: Security Operations NVD-2017 (2017). https://nvd.nist.gov/info/contact
24. Vitello, G., Alongi, A., Conti, V., Vitabile, S.: A bio-inspired cognitive agent for autonomous urban vehicles routing optimization. IEEE Trans. Cogn. Dev. Syst. **9**(1), 5–15 (2017)
25. Wang, L., Islam, T., Long, T., Singhal, A., Jajodia, S.: An attack graph-based probabilistic security metric. In: Atluri, V. (ed.) DBSec 2008. LNCS, vol. 5094, pp. 283–296. Springer, Heidelberg (2008). https://doi.org/10.1007/978-3-540-70567-3_22

Confidence Curve for Continuous Authentication

Tony Quertier[⊠]

Systancia, Rennes, France
t.quertier@systancia.com

Abstract. In this paper, we present an algorithm that continuously measures a user's legitimacy by monitoring his behavior in real time using his mouse activity. The proposed algorithm can also be used to analyze a user's log files and determine if it is the right user and if his behavior can be described as normal. We built our own database, with employee data from a computer company. We use Support Vector Machine (SVM), a supervised machine learning algorithm, to detect abnormal behavior as quickly as possible. A graph, representing the confidence level, is also drawn in real time to visualize the confidence level given to the user. We save it in case we need to check the user's legitimacy later. Experimental results show that our system can accurately authenticate a user and quickly detect an impostor. We can either set confidence thresholds that block the computer if the confidence curve decreases below or just monitor the tendency of the curve. A significant advantage is the ease of analyzing the result and also that we have tested it on real data.

Keywords: Machine learning · Behavioral authentication
Mouse dynamics · Security

1 Introduction

Authentication has become a main topic in computer security. Indeed, the number of database containing stolen passwords has significantly increased over the last years. It is very difficult for a company to make sure that every employee has good practices to choose his password and change it. Then two critical issues can occur: password cracking and password theft. Once the attacker has recovered the password, the damage it causes can be catastrophic, for the business as for the image of the company (data ex-filtration, malware, financial identity theft ...).

In order to increase the security of identification (multi class), we use authentication (binary class). The aim is to verify the legitimacy of the user basing on his physiological or behavioral biometric data. Unlike physiological authentication, behavioral authentication makes it possible to proceed to a continuous authentication in real time, and not only punctual. The benefits of behavioral authentication are twofold. First of all, it helps protect the user from password

© Springer Nature Switzerland AG 2018
A. Castiglione et al. (Eds.): CSS 2018, LNCS 11161, pp. 77–84, 2018.
https://doi.org/10.1007/978-3-030-01689-0_6

theft or hacking but also, for a company, to report unexpected or even abnormal user behavior. This approach should not be negligible since it is applicable not only to users outside the company but also within it. In addition, by keeping track of this continuous authentication, we can a posteriori analyze logs for detect of suspicious behavior.

For continuous behavioral authentication, the two main methods are: mouse dynamics (mouse movements) and keystroke dynamics (keystroke and keyboard keys used). Authentication based on keystroke dynamic and used with machine/deep learning has recently given excellent results. For this purpose, we need to install a key logger on different computer, which may cause problems concerning privacy. Indeed, keyboard data contains more sensitive information for the user (mails, passwords, network research ...).

In this paper, we use a machine learning algorithm to make continuous authentication and log analysis on some employees of a computer company using their mouse activity data.

2   Related Work

In the state of art of behavioral authentication, articles [1,3,5] make very interesting comparison between keystroke dynamics and mouse dynamics. Shen, Cai and Guan [7] describe an algorithm based on fixed mouse-operation task from 37 subjects. Their aim is to characterize a user's unique mouse behavior. Results are very good but the fixed mouse-operation task does not match with our problem. Ahmed et al. [2] build their authentication in monitoring the mouse activity of users during their daily tasks. They achieve a very high accuracy, but their method is not effective in real time, due to the number of actions needed to verify the user's identity. In contrast to the histogram approach in [2], Feher et al. [4] work directly on individual mouse actions. They also proposed a hierarchy of mouse actions from which the features are extracted. Mondal and Bours [6] use different machine learning algorithms on the same data set than [2] to authenticate a user per mouse event performed. For each movement, they give a score to the user. Results and method are very interesting but the way they choose threshold is not effective in real system. Indeed, they select the threshold sightly below the least attained trust value, when evaluating the test data.

In our paper, we do not use the same public data as in [2,4,6], because we build a data set of real employees of a computer company. However, we use a preprocessing to have data in the same format.

3   Data

3.1   Data Description

We collect our own data set. For this, 10 users have accepted to install a mouse tracker on their work computer during one month. They are of different ages and have different jobs (research, development, consulting, direction). Mouse movement data are recorded during their routine computing activities.

The raw mouse movements are represented as:

- Date in the format dd/mm/yyyy hh:mm:ss:fff where fff are the milliseconds.
- Type of action: mouse-move, mouse-click, mouse-wheel.
- Cartesian coordinates: x, y.
- Process name in which the action is done.

3.2 Feature Extraction

As we want to extract a score from the data to make a continuous authentication, we cannot use global statistics on data. Then, we compute new features from original data:

- Type of action: 1 for mouse movement, 2 for point and click and 3 for drag and drop.
- Direction of action: we compute direction in radian from the Cartesian coordinate.
- Distance of action in pixels.
- Speed of action: this equals to the distance of action/the action time.
- Acceleration: this equals to speed of action/action time.
- Zone of action: we split the screen into 9 equal zones, we keep the zone in which the action ends.
- Regular process: 0 if the process has already been used during training phase, 1 otherwise.

3.3 Data Preparation

For each user, we split the data into three unequal sets. The training set corresponds to the two first weeks of data and the third week is for the validation set. We keep the last week for the test set and we simulate the real time by injecting the data one by one. To complete the training and validation sets, we add some samples from other users to have a 50/50 ratio in the training set and a 80/20 ratio in the validation set. To not skew the test phase, we split the users in two groups. A first group of 5 users is for the training and validation data and the others are simply used as impostors in the test phase.

To simulate continuous authentication with streaming data, we inject the data from the test set one by one and we compute the user's score for each data item. After a random number of data, we inject data of another user and we analyze how long the algorithm takes to detect the impostor. Here, for a better readability of the graphs, we set the number of data to 500 before injecting the impostor data.

4 Computation of Confidence Curve

4.1 Support Vector Machine

Support Vector Machine (SVM) is a supervised machine learning algorithm more often used in classification problems. Here, we use SVM for binary classification. For this, if n is the number of features ($n = 7$ in our data), we consider each data point x as a point in n-dimensional space. Then, we compute a hyperplane $w \cdot x + b = 0$, where w is a vector of size n and b is a scalar constant, that separates the data points in two classes. The aim is not just to **separate** the two classes but also to **maximize** the separation. In our case, we use a non-linear SVM with a Radial Basis Function (RBF).

4.2 Confidence Curve

The purpose of this system is to alert a supervisor in case of anomalies, or even to block the computer if an impostor is detected. For that, we want to draw a confidence curve in real time for each user. If this curve decreases below a given threshold, we consider that it is not the right user or that his behavior is abnormal. For this curve, we have three possibilities:

- **Data Graph:** For each data item, we draw the graph corresponding to the probability of being the right user.
- **Average Streaming Curve:** We make a simple moving average in streaming to get a smoother curve and reduce the impact of false positives. We denote by s the size of the sliding window.
- **Smooth Curve:** We make a kernel regularization of the data graph. The advantage of this method is that we have the tendency of the confidence curve, more than just the score. Then, if there are some consecutive suspicious mouse movements, the curve decreases. This method gives excellent results on log analysis.

5 Experiments

The training and test phases were performed on a computer with 8 GB of RAM and an Intel(R) Core i5 CPU 2.70 GHz. The algorithm is very fast because, for each user, we compute the weights of the SVM during training and we save them. So, when we compute the score of confidence, we just load the weights and we compute the anomaly score in real time.

5.1 Log Analysis

If we just want to detect anomalies on mouse log, we can be very accurate in drawing the **Smooth Curve**. We do not even have to set a threshold (but we can set t = 0.5) because the most important is the tendency of the curve. Indeed, as we can see in figures below, when the data of an impostor are injected, the curve decreases very fast. The rest of the time, it is very constant between 0.6 and 1. The results of the algorithm on log files are very well and easy to interpret.

5.2 Real Time Curve

On real time, it is harder because we cannot make a kernel regularization on the complete curve, we have to do it step by step. For this, we have two possibilities.

Either we can compute the regularization at regular intervals, or we can compute the simple moving average. For each of these solutions, we set a confidence threshold after the training of the SVM and we announce an anomaly when the curve decreases below this threshold. In our experiments, the simple moving average gives better results then we choose it.

5.3   Results and Analysis

To test our algorithms, we use the test data that we have prepared and we add two samples of impostor data. This allows us to test the log analysis method and the real time method. We denote by **FFR** the false reject rate and by **FAR** the false accept rate. In our case, the most important is to have a FAR very close to 0, then we can adapt our confidence threshold value after training to have it. We compute FRR and FAR because it gives a numerical value to our results, but it only has sense for continuous authentication in real time. Indeed, the most important thing in log analysis is the tendency of the curve more than the value of each point.

For each user, we have drawn the Average Streaming Curve with $s = 2$ and $s = 10$, and the Smooth Curve. We have limited the number of data in input for a better visibility of the curves (Figs. 1, 2, 3, 4, 5, 6 and 7).

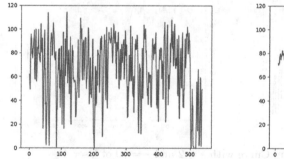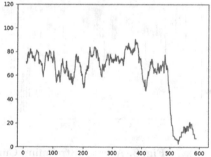

Fig. 1. Average Streaming Curve with $s = 2$ and $s = 10$ of User 1

The results depends on several features. For example, the different tasks done by a user. The second user, by his job, does more varied tasks, so it is more difficult to learn a pattern for him and we have more false negatives. The second important point is the difference between the real user's job and the impostor's job. It is easier to detect an anomaly if the two jobs are different. The most complicated case here is between two developers who work on the same subject. Moreover, learning a pattern is easier for some users, because they have specific habits, as we can see with user 4.

Below, we have a table with the results (FRR and FAR) for the simple moving average method with a size $s = 10$.

	FRR	FAR
User 1	1.4%	0%
User 2	4%	0%
User 3	1.2%	0%
User 4	0.2%	0%
User 5	2.1%	0.6%

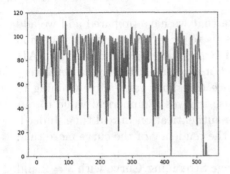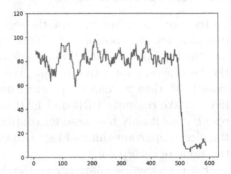

Fig. 2. Average Streaming Curve with $s = 2$ and $s = 10$ of User 3

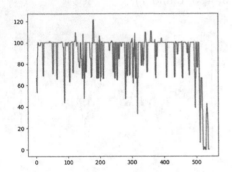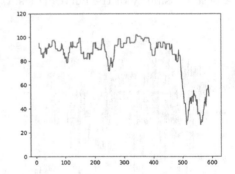

Fig. 3. Average Streaming Curve with $s = 2$ and $s = 10$ of User 4

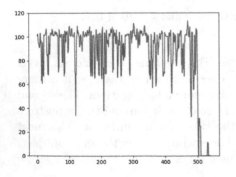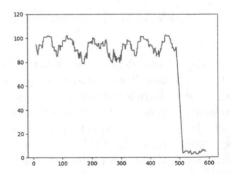

Fig. 4. Average Streaming Curve with $s = 2$ and $s = 10$ of User 5

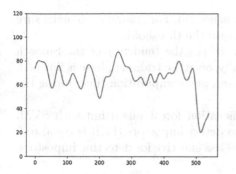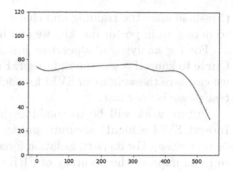

Fig. 5. Smooth Curve of User 1 and User 2

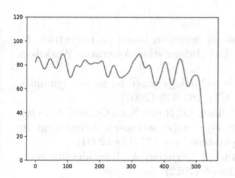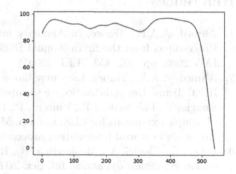

Fig. 6. Smooth Curve of User 3 and User 4

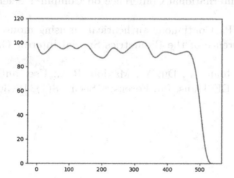

Fig. 7. Smooth Curve of User 5

6   Conclusion

In this paper, we present an effective algorithm to perform behavioral authentication in real conditions. Depending on the needs, it can be used in real time or on log files. The advantages of our method are that we have tested it under real conditions, that we can also detect abnormal user behavior and that the results are very easy to interpret. Furthermore, we can easily set the confidence threshold after the training and change it as needed. For example, to make sure to detect an impostor quickly, we can increase the threshold.

For log analysis, a supervisor just has to see the tendency of the Smooth Curve to know if it was the right user. Finally, once the training phase is finished, we can save the weights of SVM for each user, and computation time during the test phase is very fast.

Future work will be to combine the isolation forest algorithm with SVM. Indeed, SVM is highly accurate and fast to detect impostors (FAR is equal to 0 or very close). For its part, isolation forest is less effective for detecting impostors, but can improve the accuracy of FRR.

References

1. Ahmed, A.A.E., Traore, I.: Anomaly intrusion detection based on biometrics. In: Proceedings from the Sixth Annual IEEE SMC Information Assurance Workshop, IAW 2005, pp. 452–453. IEEE (2005)
2. Ahmed, A.A.E., Traore, I.: A new biometric technology based on mouse dynamics. IEEE Trans. Dependable Secure Comput. 4(3), 165–179 (2007)
3. Bengio, Y., Paiement, J.F., Vincent, P., Delalleau, O., Roux, N.L., Ouimet, M.: Out-of-sample extensions for LLE, isomap, MDS, eigenmaps, and spectral clustering. In: Advances in neural information processing systems, pp. 177–184 (2004)
4. Feher, C., Elovici, Y., Moskovitch, R., Rokach, L., Schclar, A.: User identity verification via mouse dynamics. Inf. Sci. 201, 19–36 (2012)
5. Hashia, S., Pollett, C., Stamp, M.: On using mouse movements as a biometric. In: Proceeding in the International Conference on Computer Science and its Applications, vol. 1 (2005)
6. Mondal, S., Bours, P.: Continuous authentication using mouse dynamics. In: 2013 International Conference of the Biometrics Special Interest Group (BIOSIG), pp. 1–12. IEEE (2013)
7. Shen, C., Cai, Z., Guan, X., Du, Y., Maxion, R.A.: User authentication through mouse dynamics. IEEE Trans. Inf. Forensics Secur. 8(1), 16–30 (2013)

SCADA Security: Concepts
and Recommendations

Dragos Ionica, Florin Pop(✉), Nirvana Popescu, Decebal Popescu,
and Ciprian Dobre

Faculty of Automatic Control and Computers, Computer Science Department,
University Politehnica of Bucharest, Bucharest, Romania
ionicadrgs@gmail.com,
{florin.pop,nirvana.popescu,decebal.popescu,ciprian.dobre}@cs.pub.ro

Abstract. SCADA systems are the computers that control essential, complicated, and often dangerous physical processes, many of which constitute the physical infrastructure critical to modern societies. These physical processes are powerful tools, and their misuse generally has unacceptable consequences. Preventing such abuse is the goal of SCADA security. To understand misuse and how to avoid it, we need some understanding of what a SCADA system is, and how it works under different forms of attacks. These are the primary objectives of this paper.

Keywords: SCADA system · Security update · SCADA security
Cyber attacks over SCADA systems · Hacktivists · Cyber insiders

1   Introduction

To understand SCADA security, we must understand something about both SCADA systems and cybersecurity. The concepts presented in this paper represents a collections of already well-known terms and definitions. The novelty of our approach is represented by the classification and the analysis of several cyber attacks.

A SCADA (Supervisory Control and Data Acquisition) system is an industrial control system that spans a wide-area network (WAN) over long distances. Electric grids, pipelines and water distribution systems use SCADA systems. A DCS (Distributed Control System) is an industrial control system where no WAN is involved, and the entire physical process is contained in one comparatively small site. Power plants, refineries and chemical Plants use DCSs. Historically, SCADA systems and DCSs were different - one kind of software could not control the other kind of process. Nowadays, general-purpose control system software has all of the features of both SCADA Systems and DCSs, so the difference between the two terms is more useful than technology. The modern term encompassing DCSs, SCADA systems and all other kinds of control systems is ICS (Industrial Control System) [1,2].

A. Castiglione et al. (Eds.): CSS 2018, LNCS 11161, pp. 85–98, 2018.
https://doi.org/10.1007/978-3-030-01689-0_7

Industrial processes can be subdivided as well. Most critical infrastructures are examples of "process industries". In process industries, the material being manipulated is more or less "goo" at some point in the physical process: water purification systems manipulate water, refineries manipulate oil, and pipelines move fluids. Electric grids are considered process industries as well because electricity is produced in a continuous stream that can be modelled as more or less a fluid'. Even railway and traffic control systems are considered process systems, though this pushes the concept just a bit. Within process industries, there are batch industries and continuous industries. Batch industries, such as refining and pharmaceuticals, are industries where the production line does not run continuously. Instead, it produces identifiable batches of outputs. Continuous sectors, such as water treatment plants, power plants and offshore oil production platforms, consume inputs and provide outputs more or less continuously.

Discrete manufacturing is the opposite of process industries. While process industries work with continuous inputs, discrete manufacturing assembles small, separate components into larger outputs, such as automobiles, ah-craft, and home appliances. There are many similarities between process and discrete manufacturing, but there are significant differences as well. For example, when a controls system in a process plant is sabotaged, and the physical process is misoperated, there is often a real risk to human life at the plant and the safety of the public in the immediate vicinity. When a control system in a discrete manufacturing plant is sabotaged, there can be a risk to any human operator working close to the affected machines or robots, but there is generally no immediate public safety risk. In both cases though, there is a real risk that the physical industrial process will be shut down as a protective measure. Such shutdowns are always costly to the business operating the industrial process and can have societal consequences when the physical process constitutes critical infrastructure [4].

An important aspect common to all SCADA systems is the human operator. Control systems at critical industrial facilities almost always have one or more human operators charged with ensuring the safe and reliable operation of the physical process. These operators use tools known as "Human-Machine Interface" (HMI) software. This software almost always includes a graphical visualisation of the state of the physical process and often includes other elements such as alarm managers and historical trending tools. By policy and sometimes by law, these operators are required to permit the physical process to operate only if they have a high degree of confidence that the process is operating safely. If the operator ever loses such confidence, for example, because their displays freeze or a message pops up saying "you have been hacked," they must take action. An affected operator may transfer control of the process to a secondary or redundant HMI or control system. If however, after some seconds or minutes, the operator is still not sufficiently confident of the correct and safe operation of the physical process, that operator, most often, must trigger a shutdown of the physical process. This means that most often, the simplest way for an attacker to cause physical consequences is to impair the operation of some part of an operator's HMI or the systems supporting the HMI. The most straightforward physical implications of such attacks are shutdowns of the physical process. Many industrial processes can be shut down much faster than they start up, and can take days to recover full production again after an emergency shutdown. In some cases, regulatory approvals must be obtained before restarting physical processes, delaying plant restarts by as much as months. Worse, emergency shutdowns can often put physical stress on industrial equipment, leading to immediate equipment failures or premature equipment ageing [3,5–7].

The paper presents the cyber security aspects, focusing on the three laws of SCADA Security in Sect. 2. Then Sect. 3 presents Cyber Attacks in SCADA systems. The paper ends with conclusions.

2   Cybersecurity

Cybersecurity is focused on preventing different attacks, as we mentioned in Introduction. SCADA security is focused on avoiding any unauthorised operation of SCADA system computes. SCADA security is a more recent discipline than SCADA systems or automation systems but is no less confusing. Newcomers to the security field see a bewildering variety of types of vulnerabilities, attacks, and defensive schemes. Combine this with the perennial warning that "a chain is only as strong as its weakest link" and the task of defending controls systems can seem insurmountable. This bewildering variety is an illusion. All vulnerabilities in software and indeed in systems of hardware, software and networks, are bugs or defects. The bewildering variety is simply the result of people trying to classify somehow, all possible defects – all the possible ways people can produce software and systems incorrectly. All such classification systems are doomed to fail – people can make mistakes in an uncountable number of ways. This perspective simplifies much "security research" as well. When the only results of such "research" are new vulnerabilities in existing software products, this research is no more than post-product-release quality assurance (QA). To be fair, not all security research produces QA-like results. For example, the most useful research into vulnerabilities identifies entirely new kinds of vulnerabilities that nobody had before considered, and that all product developers must now start to recognise and avoid [21–24].

Research into defensive techniques, their application and their effectiveness is of course also much more than QA. However, the vast majority of previously-undiscovered "zero-day" vulnerabilities and exploits revealed at events such as the annual Black Hat conference are no more than new security defects discovered by unpaid post-release QA "security researchers" [8].

In hopes of simplifying the field of cybersecurity to the point where SCADA practitioners can make sense of and routinely apply sound security practices, the three laws of SCADA security were proposed. Yes, in modern times, scientists prefer the terms "principle" and "theory" to "law," but we are trying to simplify things here. These laws address fundamental cyber-security concepts that are poorly understood, and poorly communicated.

1. **Nothing is secure** - Security is a continuum, not a binary value. Given enough time, money and talent, any security posture can be breached. Anyone using terms such as "secure communications," "secure boot" or "secure operating system" is either selling something or has just been sold a bill of goods. This is important. It changes the conversation from "never you mind, I have security covered" to "just how secure are we?" and ultimately "how secure should we be?"

2. **All software can be hacked** - All software has bugs. Software development teams eliminate what bugs they can, but in spite of their best efforts, essentially all software has flaws, even security software. Some bugs result from exploitable security vulnerabilities. For evidence of this, look at the support section of any software vendor's website and see how many security updates have been issued recently. In practice then, all software can be hacked. Too many of us believe that patching known bugs and vulnerabilities makes us invulnerable. Others think that the way to build software systems "secure" is to deploy more security software. This is all nonsense – there are vulnerabilities to be found in any software system, even security software.

3. **Every piece of information can be an attack** - Even a single bit of information – a one or a zero – can be an attack. If a plant operator is trying to turn off a piece of equipment with a zero, but an attacker changes that zero to a one, that is an attack. Passwords and malicious intent carried in the brains of people entering a plant can be an attack. Malware installed on brand new computers, or in the tiniest of computers embedded in USB keyboards, can be an attack.

3   Cyber Attacks

If IT-class protections are inadequate, then how should we be protecting SCADA systems? To address this question, we must first understand cyber-attacks. Too many SCADA security practitioners do not study modern attack techniques, and so they produce singularly vulnerable "secure" SCADA systems.

Instead of attacks, too many of today's SCADA security and IT security practitioners spend far too much time thinking about vulnerabilities. Classic risk assessment calculations maintain that risk is a function of threats, vulnerabilities, exploits and consequences. Many practitioners, therefore, conclude that their job is to eliminate weaknesses. They reason that if we could only, somehow, eliminate all failings, then our systems would be invulnerable. This chain of reasoning quickly devolves into a preoccupation with known vulnerabilities and security update programs.

The first law of cybersecurity states that nothing is ever secure. For example, security updates repair only known product vulnerabilities, leaving countless unknowns waiting to be discovered and exploited. More generally, SCADA systems as a whole may have vulnerabilities that stem from how the systems are organised and configured, independent of any security defects in the product code.

These systems vulnerabilities are at the heart of many kinds of recent attacks. Frankly, our attackers are lazy they prefer to use permissions we have configured into our SCADA networks rather than software vulnerabilities because exploiting agreements is less work. It takes considerable time and talent to analyse software applications to find undiscovered software vulnerabilities. It makes even more work to write the code needed to exploit those newly-discovered vulnerabilities. The standard permissions-based attack described in the section on intelligence agencies below easily defeats security updates, antivirus systems, intrusion detection systems, remote access jump hosts, firewalls and other IT-class protections routinely installed on SCADA systems. To anyone focused on vulnerabilities rather than attack techniques, this targeted, remote-control, permissions-based type of attack comes as a horrible surprise.

3.1 Corporate Insiders

Corporate insiders are people who have access to IT networks, and who are to some degree trusted by the organisation. These may be employees, contractors, business partners or even third-party vendors. Insiders generally have some accounts, passwords and other credentials that let them legitimately use equipment and applications on the IT network. These trusted insiders tend to be well-positioned to gain access to additional accounts, passwords and other credentials through social engineering. Social engineering can encompass many activities, for instance, learning other people's passwords by turning their keyboards over and reading the sticky notes on the bottom, impersonating authorised users to distant administrators and asking for password changes, or watching people type as they enter their "strong" passwords. Corporate insiders though, tend to know little about security and less about industrial control systems [16].

The most common targets of insider attacks are IT systems, yielding either leaked information or financial fraud. Insiders in many organisations have logged into accounting systems, created fictitious vendors, faked invoices and issued payments to themselves either directly or indirectly. Insiders may have the means to steal control-system passwords and log into SCADA systems, but generally, lack the skills to do much damage there. An exception to this rule is corporate IT personnel. For example, well-meaning IT personnel have been known to use administrative privileges on SCADA systems to log in and tell all of the equipment on the SCADA network to reboot. Before coming back online, these administrators apply all outstanding security updates for all software on the machines, carry out full backups of all hard drives to the corporate backup system, and carry out a full antivirus scan. This, of course, cripples the control system for hours. The plant operator, seeing that she no longer has any way to determine if the physical process is running correctly or safely, has no choice but to lift the cage on the "big red mushroom button," press the button, and trigger a safety shutdown. This might be funny if it did not cost so very much.

3.2 Organized Crime

Organized crime is responsible for the vast majority of email Spam and common malware, such as viruses, worms, Trojans, botnets and ransomware. Criminal organisations pay professional malware developers to create these attack tools and evolve these tools regularly to stay ahead of the professional anti-malware developers producing antivirus, intrusion detection and other anti-malware tools. Organized crime has the money and talent to apply to the task of creating malware that spreads indiscriminately and infects or compromises as many machines as possible. This malware generally compromises as many spreads by deceiving victims into deliberately installing it, or by exploiting known vulnerabilities on devices that have not yet applied security updates. These criminal groups typically extract an average of a few dollars value from each compromised device. This value may take the form of stolen credit card numbers, bank account credentials, or the use of compromised computers to issue countless millions of spam messages. The most common impact of such infection is nothing at all – the SCADA system continues unimpeded [17].

Common malware has been known to cause enough symptoms on SCADA systems to trigger shutdowns, but such cases are rare. For example, anecdotal reports from security assessment consultants suggest that a significant minority of SCADA systems are still infected with the decade-old Conflicker worm, with no apparent ill-effects. There is a cost to all infections by common malware though: when such diseases are discovered, SCADA administrators generally feel obliged to do the work to "clean out" the system. Removing all traces of malware addresses the risk that the malware may someday impair important processing. This cleaning can be costly. Removing the most persistent malware often requires the assistance of external, third-party experts. An exception to this "low impact" rule of thumb is ransomware. Ransomware is malware that encrypts files and demands payment to restore the data. It is easy to imagine how encrypting data on SCADA computers could render essential files unusable. This could impair the system enough to affect the operator's confidence levels, thus bringing about a safety shutdown. As ransomware becomes more pervasive, this class of common malware on SCADA networks will become a more significant threat to the physical reliability of industrial systems than was the case in the past.

3.3 SCADA Insiders

Like IT insiders, SCADA insiders are people with access to SCADA networks and systems which are to some degree trusted by the organisation. Again, they may be employees, contractors or third-party vendors. SCADA insiders generally have some access to accounts, passwords and other credentials that let them use equipment and applications on the SCADA network. As with IT insiders, SCADA insiders tend to be well-positioned to use social engineering attacks to gain additional privileges. While these insiders often know little about cybersecurity, they are familiar with industrial systems to a greater or lesser extent. This means that malicious insiders are generally able to manipulate the SCADA systems they log into and affect physical/industrial operations. The most common motivation for such insider attacks is revenge for some real or imagined slight [18].

3.4 Hacktivists

Hacktivists are individuals or groups with "an axe to grind" who carry out cyber-attacks. Hacktivists often have some degree of security knowledge, and can occasionally be highly skilled they do after all spend much of their spare time hacking into other people's computers and networks. Hacktivists are amateurs though, in the sense that they generally do not profit personally from breaking into things. This means hacktivists generally cannot afford to purchase the most sophisticated attack tools, and cannot afford to spend the enormous amounts of time and effort needed to write their world-class hacking tools. This means that hacktivists generally rely on wrong permissions for their attacks, and use open source or other freely-available attack tools [19].

For example, the December 2015 attack that turned off power to over 200,000 people in Ukraine used common hacktivist-class attack techniques. Note that this attack was not necessarily carried out by hacktivists experts argue that the degree of coordination among many attackers in a far-flung attack pattern suggests that professionals were involved.

Published reports, however, indicate that no matter who the attackers were it was only hacktivist-class attack techniques and tools that were used:

- A spear-phishing campaign against employees of electric distribution systems in Ukraine yielded remote access credentials for at least three distribution companies.
- The attackers used these stolen credentials to log in to their tar, networks, look around, and take additional credentials.
- The attackers used their access to compromise their targets, Windows domain controllers and create new accounts arid passwords for themselves, with all the privileges they needed to continue their attacks.
- They then logged into SCADA computers over a period of months, studying how these systems worked They Presumably also used Internet-based and other learning resources to understand how these SCADA systems were designed and configured.
- On the day of the attack, they logged in to at least three distribution companies published reports include only lower bounds on how many companies were targeted and how many people were affected. On two systems, they activated features of the SCADA software that disabled the operators' mice and keyboards and gave the attackers control of the SCADA HMI. On the third distribution system, the attackers had acquired a copy of the SCADA HMI software on their computers. To attack this third system, the attackers used a VPN to connect their copy of the SCADA HMI to the distribution system's SCADA infrastructure.

- Over a period of about 30 min, the attackers used the fall software to navigate to screens for at least 30 substations and turn off power flows through those substations. They also logged into the substation control computers and erased the hard drives on those computers so that the machines could not be used to turn on power flows again remotely.

At least 200,000 people were affected for up to several hours. Concurrent with this attack, the attackers flooded the distribution companies' custom: support lines with faked phone calls. This way the targets' customers we not able to report that they had no power, which served to increase the duration of the power outage.

This class of attack is known as an "Advanced Persistent Threat" (APT). APTs differ from more-widely-known, organised-crime attack in two ways:

1. The Ukrainian/Russian conflict most likely motivated the attack, and so had a specific target: distribution companies serving Ukrainian consumers. Even if the attackers had found a dozen less-well-defended targets in neighbouring countries, it seems unlikely that they would have been distracted by those targets. The common wisdom of needing only to be protected better than our neighbours do not apply to targeted attacks.
2. This attack used interactive remote control attackers were sitting at keyboards and giving commands to compromised systems for months before the 30-min attack on substations, and for the entire duration of the 30-min substation attack. Common malware spreads indiscriminately, and automatically. Remote-control attacks rely on people "sipping coffee on the other side of the planet" while manually driving the attack, minute by minute.

Note that organised crime has been known to use targeted techniques as well. Ransomware groups have started to seed modified ransomware into networks, to extort more significant sums of money for decrypting an entire targeted system that could have been extracted for individual machines [9,10].

3.5   Intelligence Agencies

State-sponsored national and regional intelligence agencies are disciplined groups of attackers using both targeted remote control techniques and when necessary, sophisticated low-volume malware. Different levels of government in China are accused of having pioneered this method of cyber espionage, and many other nations today are accused of using these same techniques. At present, these attacks are used routinely to steal information about dissidents, governments, competing corporations, product designs, source code, and even designs for weapons and industrial sites [11,12].

Many governments and authorities have expressed concern that these same attack techniques could be used to carry out sabotage rather than espionage. Some governments have declared that the destruction of critical national infrastructures will be regarded as an act of war [13]. This sounds impressive, but the reliable attribution of this class of attack to a specific state or private actors can be difficult or impossible. For example, the "Shamoon" malware erased the hard drives of 30,000 IT computers at Saudi Aramco, crippling business functions [14]. In spite of claims by what appears to be an Iranian hacktivist group, and widespread speculation that the group acted with the support of Iran's government [15], no reliable attribution was ever published, nor were military, or other retaliatory steps were taken against any nation.

Worse, these intelligence-agency-grade attack techniques are not limited to use by nation-states. Any organisation with a budget to develop custom malware can improve the ability to use these techniques. Many experts are concerned that organised crime will start using this class of attack to sabotage industrial sites to extort money from those sites, manipulate stock markets or otherwise derivate significant profits from cyber-sabotage attacks [20].

A typical attack of this type has many steps:

1. The attackers scour social networking sites for Personal information and use spear-phishing techniques to deceive an individual in a targeted organisation into clicking on an attachment or downloading a file to activate a malware payload.
2. Antivirus (AV) sensors in the focused organisation are blind to the attack because the payload has been used sparingly. AV sensors are designed to defeat high-volume, organised-crime malware. New AV signatures are created when an AV vendor detects many thousands of copies of a new variant of malware on the vendor's Internet honeypot machines. Intelligence-agency class malware is typically deployed to a few hundred victims' sites at most. The malware does not spread automatically, and so never no AV reaches AV-vendor honeypots on the Internet. This means the vendor produces AV signatures for the malware.
3. The malware payload "phones home." connecting to and reporting to an Internet command and control (C&C) centre. Professional operators use the C&C to connect to the malware and operate it remotely. This class of malware often has features built into it that are similar to the popular "secure shell" and "remote desktop" remote access tools. The malware allows remote operators to issue commands to compromised machines, see the results of those commands, and even take over the screen, keyboard and mouse.
4. The malware's operators use compromised computers to look around the compromised network very quietly, spread the malware to other machines where the compromised account might have permissions to create and run executable files, and most importantly, steal account names and passwords.
5. When the attackers take Windows domain administrator credentials, they often create new administrator and VPN accounts for themselves, so that they no longer need to use their particular malware to continue the attack. They also use these credentials to pivot deeper, through intervening firewalls and other layers of protection, into more-protected networks such as SCADA networks.
6. When they reach their goals, they are in a position to start stealing large volumes of information, modifying information or misoperating industrial systems.

For high-value targets, the attackers may seed several kinds of malware in the target organisations, each reporting to a different control centre. The least-valuable, least-sophisticated malware is used first. This may be a standard attack tool circulating free on the Internet. If that tool is detected and erased, the attackers can fall back to more-sophisticated tools, such as those available on black markets. If these tools are identified and cleaned out of the target system, they may revert to their own, custom-written, highly-stalled tools to re-establish their presence on the compromised network at some later time, when the site's investigation and clean-up of the less-valuable tools are complete.

This class of attack has been beneficial and is very hard to detect. Authorities and researchers are investigating some C&C centres often find evidence that large numbers of organisations have been compromised. When these authorities reach out to these targeted organisations, the vast majority report that they had no idea they had been compromised. For example, in the Ukrainian attack, post-incident investigators found BlackEnergy malware on SCADA computers. BlackEnergy is a sophisticated malware tool with many features, including full remote control of compromised machines.

The investigators reported that while they believed the BlackEnergy malware had enough features to attack the power system, there was no evidence the malware was, in fact, part of the attack, or that the same attack group even deployed the malware. In conclusion, the intelligence-agency-class attacks often use the most straightforward attack methods available. Such an adversary might use a hacktivist-class remote access attack, with more sophisticated tools such as BlackEnergy malware kept in reserve until they might become necessary.

3.6 Military-Grade

As we mentioned early in this paper, nothing is secure. Military-grade attacks prove this point. Military-grade attacks not only have access to all of the attack techniques used by all of the other classes of attackers, but they also have enormous financial and technical resources, as well as physical attack techniques to all back on. Military-grade attacks can physically break into targets to steal their private encryption keys and other credentials. They can intercept equipment and software on the way to customers, and insert custom hardware and malware into those shipments. Military-grade attackers can pay large sums of money for newly-discovered "zero-day" vulnerabilities in applications and cyber-security products and defences, and can spend more money to produce custom malware to exploit and weaponise those vulnerabilities.

These attackers can deceive, buy, blackmail, or otherwise coerce cooperation from trusted insiders at a target site. If an attacker has the means to bribe or coerce insiders into revealing all of the details of how an industrial system is designed, and how that industrial system is protected, and that attacker has the means to find vulnerabilities in and defeat any cybersecurity protections, then such an attacker's target does not have an exact cyber-security problem. There is no cyber-security technology the site can deploy that will defeat this grade of attacker reliably.' Instead, the industrial site has a classic cold-war-style cyber-espionage problem and needs to escalate that problem to its national intelligence agencies.

Stuxnet is widely regarded as the best-documented example of a military-grade attack. In this example, the attackers appear to have deceived insiders, and may not have needed to coerce or bribe them. The attackers though, indeed seem to have had the means to produce an expensive, compelling, very complicated piece of free attack malware.

3.7 Transmitting Attacks

Cyber-attacks are information and are embedded in data. Every piece of information can be an attack, even a single one/zero bit, and also information transmitted using analogue signalling. What does this mean? Pretty much everyone knows that sophisticated attack code can be embedded in complex files, such as PDF files. Any communications mechanism that transmits data, including people carrying such data on removable media or cell phones in so-called "sneakernet" communications, can transmit attack code. Most people know that any continuous stream of complex messages can encode attacks as well, such as message streams arriving across the Internet. Most of us also understand that a compromised machine can be used to pivot attacks to heavily-protected targets through one or several more-easily-accessible targets.

Many people though, even security experts who should know better, regard the simplest and most primitive analogue signalling systems as "secure" in the sense that they believe that attacks cannot be communicated through such mechanisms. For example, an electric signal on a network cable can indicate whether a connected device is turned on or turned off, even if no messages are exchanged on the wire. Experts sometimes recommend that this sort of primitive signalling be used when a minimal number of simple values must be communicated from external systems into a SCADA system.

These experts may regard such signalling mechanisms as too primitive to communicate an attack, even though they do deliver minimal amounts of information. In practice, such signals to transmit data, and so even these most primitive signals can constitute an attack, in two different ways:

- When the signal is used as a control signal, indicating that, for example, a motor should be turned on or off, or a valve should be opened or closed, the signal may be deliberately incorrect. In this way, a compromised source for the signal may misoperate an industrial process or device.
- More subtly, if malware has somehow been planted in the SCADA system, any signal entering the system can be used to trigger the operation of the malware. The on/off signal may itself serve to activate and de-activate the malware, or the timing of the signal may serve that function or some other characteristic of the signal.

3.8   Failure of Defense in Depth

In response to the attacks described previously and many other kinds of attacks, the IT approach to cybersecurity has been held up as the "gold standard" for SCADA security, pretty much ever since SCADA security started. SCADA security emerged as a discipline only after the World Trade Center attack in 2001 and naturally took inspiration from what was then the more mature IT security field. This tendency to take inspiration from IT security was reinforced by the IT software and hardware products that had become nearly ubiquitous in control systems by the early 2000s.

What most people recognised almost immediately was that some IT techniques were a poor fit for the needs of SCADA systems, which led to a doctrine of "compensating measures" and "defence in depth." IT reasoning here postulates that if we cannot solve some of the security problems directly, we need to put compensating measures in place. A comprehensive system of such measures was seen as a "defence in depth" posture, where "layers of security" would save us from the inherent limitations of any single defensive measure.

Defence in depth has failed. Modern attacks routinely compromise both IT and SCADA networks protected by IT-style defence-in-depth systems. SCADA security standards, regulations and advice are evolving beyond IT defence-in-depth, but only slowly. In spite of its evident deficiencies, many experts, and especially IT experts, still, maintain that IT-style defence-in-depth is the right approach for SCADA security. It is, after all, the "hammer" they know.

To understand why defence in depth has failed, we examine the IT-style approach to SCADA security in this chapter. The method is summarised in Table (2). In the table, the line demarking the boundary between threats we are reasonably confident of defeating reliably, and threats we are not satisfied with defeating reliably, is labelled as the design-basis threat. Design-basis threat is a concept from physical security. A design-basis threat document describes the most capable adversary a site is required to defeat with a high degree of confidence. At many sites, the document is confidential or classified.

4   Conclusions

In this paper we highlighted the main security issues and cyber attacks in SCADA systems. We considered several types of attacks and gave some recommendation for each case: corporate insiders, organized crime, SCADA insiders, intelligence agencies, military-grade, transmitting attacks, and failure of defense In depth. This paper represents an overview on what exists in the presents (2018) in SCADA security domain, based on well-known aspects and concepts.

References

1. Igure, V.M., Laughter, S.A., Williams, R.D.: Security issues in SCADA networks. Comput. Secur. **25**(7), 498–506 (2006)
2. Pollet, J.: Developing a solid SCADA security strategy. In: 2nd ISA/IEEE Sensors for Industry Conference, pp. 148–156. IEEE (2002)
3. Chandia, R., Gonzalez, J., Kilpatrick, T., Papa, M., Shenoi, S.: Security strategies for SCADA networks. In: Goetz, E., Shenoi, S. (eds.) ICCIP 2007. IIFIP, vol. 253, pp. 117–131. Springer, Boston, MA (2008). https://doi.org/10.1007/978-0-387-75462-8_9
4. Nicholson, A., Webber, S., Dyer, S., Patel, T., Janicke, H.: SCADA security in the light of Cyber-Warfare. Comput. Secur. **31**(4), 418–436 (2012)
5. Adamo, F., Attivissimo, F., Cavone, G., Giaquinto, N.: SCADA/HMI systems in advanced educational courses. IEEE Trans. Instrum. Meas. **56**(1), 4–10 (2007)
6. Salihbegovic, A., Marinkovi, V., Cico, Z., Karavdi, E., Delic, N.: Web based multi-layered distributed SCADA/HMI system in refinery application. Comput. Stand. Interfaces **31**(3), 599–612 (2009)
7. Endi, M., Elhalwagy, Y.Z.: Three-layer PLC/SCADA system architecture in process automation and data monitoring. In: 2010 The 2nd International Conference on Computer and Automation Engineering (ICCAE), vol. 2, pp. 774–779. IEEE (2010)
8. Radvanovsky, R., Brodsky, J.: Handbook of SCADA/Control Systems Security. CRC Press, Boca Raton (2016)
9. Gallagher, S.: Two more healthcare networks caught up in outbreak of hospital ransomware. Ars Technica **29**(03) (2016)
10. CBC News: University of Calgary paid $20K in ransomware attack (2016). http://www.cbc.ca/news/canada/calgary/university-calgary-ransomware-cyberattack-1.3620979
11. Mandiant: Mandiant APT1 Exposing One of China's Cyber Espionage Units (2013). https://www.fireeye.com/content/dam/fireeye-www/services/pdfs/mandiant-apt1-report.pdf
12. Alperovitch, D.: Revealed: Operation Shady RAT, vol. 3. McAfee (2011)
13. United States. White House Office, and Barack Obama. International Strategy for Cyberspace: Prosperity, Security, and Openness in a Networked Worldr. White House (2011)
14. Leyden, J.: Hack on Saudi Aramco Hit 30,000 Workstations, Oil Firm Admits-First Hacktivist-Style Assault to Use Malware? (The Register) (2012)
15. Zetter, K.: The NSA acknowledges what we all feared: Iran learns from US cyber-attacks. Wired (2015)
16. Daryabar, F., Dehghantanha, A., Udzir, N.I., bin Shamsuddin, S.: Towards secure model for scada systems. In: 2012 International Conference on Cyber Security, Cyber Warfare and Digital Forensic (CyberSec), pp. 60–64. IEEE (2012)
17. Rege-Patwardhan, A.: Cybercrimes against critical infrastructures: a study of online criminal organization and techniques. Crim. Justice Stud. **22**(3), 261–271 (2009)
18. Bigham, J., Gamez, D., Lu, N.: Safeguarding SCADA systems with anomaly detection. In: Gorodetsky, V., Popyack, L., Skormin, V. (eds.) MMM-ACNS 2003. LNCS, vol. 2776, pp. 171–182. Springer, Heidelberg (2003). https://doi.org/10.1007/978-3-540-45215-7_14

19. Fiaidhi, J., Gelogo, Y.E.: SCADA cyber attacks and security vulnerabilities. In: SERSC, Research Trend of Computer Science and Related Areas, ASTL, vol. 14, pp. 202–208 (2012)
20. Kerr, P.K., Rollins, J., Theohary, C.A.: The Stuxnet Computer Worm: Harbinger of an Emerging Warfare Capability. Congressional Research Service, Washington, DC (2010)
21. Colombini, C.M., Colella, A., Mattiucci, M., Castiglione, A.: Cyber threats monitoring: experimental analysis of malware behavior in cyberspace. In: Cuzzocrea, A., Kittl, C., Simos, D.E., Weippl, E., Xu, L. (eds.) CD-ARES 2013. LNCS, vol. 8128, pp. 236–252. Springer, Heidelberg (2013). https://doi.org/10.1007/978-3-642-40588-4_17
22. Palmieri, F., Ficco, M., Castiglione, A.: Adaptive stealth energy-related dos attacks against cloud data centers. In: 2014 Eighth International Conference on Innovative Mobile and Internet Services in Ubiquitous Computing (IMIS), pp. 265–272. IEEE (2014)
23. De Santis, A., Castiglione, A., Fiore, U., Palmieri, F.: An intelligent security architecture for distributed firewalling environments. J. Ambient Intell. Hum. Comput. 4(2), 223–234 (2013)
24. Bertino, E., Casola, V., Castiglione, A., Susilo, W.: Security and privacy protection vs sustainable development, pp. 250–251 (2018)

Towards the Evaluation of End-to-End Resilience Through External Consistency

Thomas Clédel[1(✉)], Simon N. Foley[1], Nora Cuppens[1], Frédéric Cuppens[1],
Yvon Kermarrec[1], Frédéric Dubois[2], Youssef Laarouchi[3],
and Gérard Le Comte[4]

[1] IMT Atlantique, Lab-STICC, Université Bretagne Loire, Rennes, France
{thomas.cledel,simon.foley,nora.cuppens,
frederic.cuppens,yvon.kermarrec}@imt-atlantique.fr
[2] Airbus Defence and Space CyberSecurity, Rennes, France
frederic.dubois@airbus.com
[3] EDF Labs, Palaiseau, France
youssef.laarouchi@edf.fr
[4] Société Générale, Paris, France
Gerard.Le-Comte@socgen.com

Abstract. Contemporary systems are built from complex arrangements of interoperating components implementing functional and other non-functional concerns that are necessary to ensure continuing service delivery. One of these concerns—resilience—relies on components that implement a variety of mechanisms, such as access controls, adaptability and redundancy. How these mechanisms interoperate with each other and the systems' functional components to provide resilience is considered in this paper. External consistency, defined as the extent to which data in the system corresponds to its real-world value, provides a natural interpretation for the definition of resilience. A model of resilience is developed that can be used to trace how the functional and non-functional components in a system contribute to the determination of our confidence in the external consistency of the data that they process.

1 Introduction

Contemporary systems are complex arrangements of frameworks, software stacks, services and third party components. It is in this complexity, that vulnerabilities are often introduced and that threats emerge. Added to this is a variety of controls, protocols and design patterns that are, in turn, intended to provide resilience in the system to these threats, be they through malicious attack or system failure. For example, access control mechanisms are used to prevent the threat of unauthorized access to resources; replication and redundancy help provide fault tolerance; software diversity helps to avoid threats arising from software mono-cultures, along with a range of other resilience mechanisms that provide robustness to failure/threat [1,13,20]. A challenge is determining whether

© Springer Nature Switzerland AG 2018
A. Castiglione et al. (Eds.): CSS 2018, LNCS 11161, pp. 99–114, 2018.
https://doi.org/10.1007/978-3-030-01689-0_8

the chosen mechanisms and their deployment provide adequate resilience for a given arrangement of the system.

Resilience is typically defined as encompassing a number of characteristics, including redundancy, diversity, adaptability and restore ability [3,21]. It is succinctly described by Laprie [13] as *"the persistence of service delivery that can be justifiably be trusted, when facing changes"*. In principle, this definition can be formalised using techniques such as [8,18] where the design of the system, protected by its resilience mechanisms, is formally proven to uphold the requirements of the service in the presence of threats. However, in practice this does not scale to contemporary systems, as it requires formal specification of the requirements and behaviour of system components, mechanisms and the attacker [8]. While feasible for relatively small critical components, this is not feasible when one considers contemporary systems that are constructed from a large number of components and often originating from many different developers. A case in point, for instance, is the REST_API in the JavaScript NPM repository, implemented using 293 packages from 226 different developers, at the time of writing.

We are interested in more lightweight approaches to determining resilience in such contemporary complex systems. Rather than taking a behaviour-based approach, we trace, at an abstract level, how the individual components and mechanisms in a system can influence our degree of confidence in the resilience of a service. For instance, we may have a low-degree of confidence in the resilience provided by a browser that retrieves pages only via the http protocol. However, if the browser is configured to support https and uses an up-to-date certificate store, then we can have a higher degree of confidence in the overall resilience of the browser service and, in particular, in the authentication, secrecy and integrity of loaded pages. This confidence increases further if the browser also uses a certificate revocation component implementing the Online Certificate Status Protocol. In practice, many components are involved in the loading of a web-page [5] and each can impact resilience, positively or negatively. This gives us an end-to-end view of resilience: how does the resilience of the individual components that retrieve the page, check the certificates, etc. contribute to the overall resilience for the rendered page?

In this paper we propose a model that supports this view of resilience. The contribution in the paper is the proposed approach, which uses the notion of external consistency [6] to define end-to-end resilience. A data item has external consistency if its value corresponds to its real-world value [6]. In the web-browser example, resilience is defined in terms of the confidence that we have in the external consistency of the page rendered in the browser, that is, it matches the page on the server. The effectiveness of the model is evaluated by considering the resilience provided by a browser, containing a variety of security components.

This paper is organized as follows. Section 2 defines the model of a system as a set of components communicating information over channels. Section 3 presents the model of end-to-end resilience for a system, defined in terms of external consistency. A simple running example of the resilience provided in loading a web-page is used throughout and Sect. 4 provides a more detailed exposition of this use-case. Related work is considered in Sect. 5 and Sect. 6 provides the conclusion.

2   System Model

Definition 1. *Representation of a system.* A system is defined as:

$$sys = \langle V, E, L, \mathcal{R} \rangle$$

where the set V of system components corresponds to vertices of a directed oriented graph and the set of edges E corresponds to relationships between components (described in Sect. 2.1). Lattice L characterizes the kind of data communicated between components and $\mathcal{R}$ defines the resilience of the system components. L and $\mathcal{R}$ are described in Sects. 2.2 and 3, respectively.

2.1   System Components and Sources

The set of vertices $V = S \cup C$ is partitioned into system components C and data sources S. Components are system elements that sink and source data and can be software, hardware, servers or end-users. For example, Fig. 1 depicts the retrieval of a web-page, and includes software components pl and pr and fs_1 and fs_2; the latter can be considered as a mix of software and hardware: a data storage device and an operating system. Sources are part of the system that are considered to produce data from nothing, as opposed to components which source data from received data. For example, in Fig. 1, the vertex f corresponds to the content of a file that is stored in fs_1 and CA is the source of data for certificates or trusted CA. Other components of this system are the window that displays data such that users can read the file, the Internet that can alter data passing by it if it is not protected and the *tls* protocol.

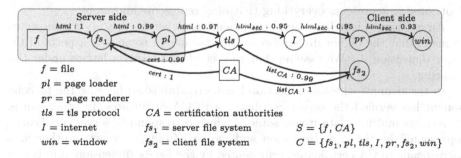

$f = $ file
$pl = $ page loader
$pr = $ page renderer
$tls = $ tls protocol $CA = $ certification authorities
$I = $ internet $fs_1 = $ server file system $S = \{f, CA\}$
$win = $ window $fs_2 = $ client file system $C = \{fs_1, pl, tls, I, pr, fs_2, win\}$

Fig. 1. Retrieval and rendering of a remote webpage

The set of edges of *sys* is $E \subset (V \times C)$. Sources do not have input edges. Edges represent connection relationships between components. Continuing the example in Fig. 1, if component *tls* sends data, such as the content of a file, to the Internet I, it means that there is a channel from *tls* to I, and this channel is represented by an edge $(tls, I) \in E$, as shown in Fig. 1. Edges do not represent data. They are channels through which data flows.

2.2   Lattice of Data Dimensions

Components communicate with each other by sending data. *Data dimensions* are used to characterize the different kinds of, or interpretations for, communicated data. For example, in Fig. 1, the data communicated over a secure connection between a webserver and a browser can be considered to have a data dimension *html*, representing the webpage content; equally, since it is over a secure connection, the connection also has a secure html dimension *tls* representing the TLS relationship, along with a dimension for the certificate, and so forth. This is illustrated by the page loader *pl* sending data to *tls*. On the client side, the web client receives a X509 certificate to trust the web server, then it receives the web page. The server certificate is sent from the server file system fs_1 to the component *tls*. Then *tls* can verify that this server certificate has been signed by a trusted CA, can perform a secured connection and can send data to the client page renderer *pr* through the Internet. The list of CA trusted by the client is represented by the data dimension $list_{CA}$ and is stored in the client file system. Thus, different types of data are sent and different data dimensions can be attributed: *html* for the web page, *cert* for the server certificate, $html_{sec}$ for a web page sent through a secured channel and $list_{CA}$ which corresponds to a list of trusted CA.

Let $D = \{d_1, d_2, \ldots, d_n\}$ represent the set of all data dimensions.

Data dimensions do not just represent what data contain. For example, a web page sent using a *tls* connection can be represented by a data dimension *html*, reflecting wed data. However, as it is known that the data representing the web page has been protected by *tls* over the Internet, another data dimension $html_{sec}$, is attributed to this data. These two data dimensions are not independent: $html_{sec}$ represents everything that *html* represents and more.

An ordering $\leq$ is defined between dimensions, whereby $d_1 \leq d_2$ is interpreted to mean that the higher dimension d_2 incorporates in some way aspects of the lower dimension d_1. We assume that the set $(D, \leq)$ forms a lattice under this ordering.

In the example, the *tls* connection has been established because the *tls* component has verified the server certificate with CA-certificates. In other words, *tls* receives multiple data items, some of which correspond to server certificates, represented by the *cert* dimension and received from fs_1, whereas other data corresponds to CA certificates, represented by the $list_{CA}$ dimension, and is sent by fs_2. Thus, *tls* can verify whether the server certificate has been signed by a trusted CA. A result of this verification is that *tls* can confirm that the server certificate has been delivered by a trusted CA and can ensure the establishment of a secured connection. Thus, other data dimensions and their relationships can be inferred. For the above example, a corresponding lattice is given in Fig. 2.

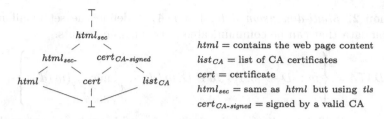

Fig. 2. Lattice of data dimensions

3   Resilience

The external consistency of data is used as a measure of the resilience of a system. In [13], resilience is defined as *"the persistence of service delivery than can be justifiably be trusted, when facing changes"*. Consequently, representing system's services and their delivery is necessary. In the proposed model, services are represented by data produced in the system and a service is considered delivered if the corresponding data is sufficiently likely to be externally consistent.

3.1   External Consistency

In [6], external consistency is defined as *"the correspondence between the data object and the real world object it represents"*. This definition has been generalized in [23] whereby *external consistency is the ability of a computing system to give correct information about its external environment*. For instance in Fig. 1, data arriving to the component *win* is externally consistent if it exactly represents the desired file represented by the component f. In the same way, data sent by fs_1 to *tls* is externally consistent if it represents a certificate of this server.

In the proposed model, data dimensions are used to characterize the different kinds of data that exist in the system. And thus, data is considered externally consistent relative to these data dimensions. For example, data sent by fs_1 to *pl* is intended to be externally consistent regarding the *html* dimension because it represents the desired web page, but it is not supposed to be externally consistent regarding the *cert* dimension because it does not represent a server certificate.

3.2   Representation of Data

Data relationships between components are represented by a mapping of data dimensions to the degree of confidence that one has in the external consistency of the data at the corresponding dimension on the communications channel. These degrees of confidence are in the metric space $[0, 1]$.

Definition 2. *Multi-dimension data.* Let $DATA$ define the set of all multi-dimension data that can be communicated between components.

$$DATA = \left\{ m : D \to [0,1] \mid \forall d \in D, m\left(d\right) \leq \max_{\substack{d' \in D, \, d' \leq d \\ d' \neq d, \, d' \neq \perp}} \left(m\left(d'\right)\right) \right\}$$

where for $m : DATA$, $m(d)$ gives the degree of confidence in the external consistency of data at dimension d.

For ease of exposition and when there is no ambiguity, these degrees of confidence of external consistency will be denoted as external consistency values of data or simply as external consistency of data. Note this definition reflects our assumption that the external consistency of data at higher dimensions is dependent on the external consistency of data at lower dimensions, and therefore, our degree of confidence in the external consistency at one dimension must be less than our degree of confidence in the external consistency on which it is based. For example if data is externally consistent at the $html_{sec}$ dimension, it is also externally consistent at the $html$ dimension since $html \leq html_{sec}$. In the same way, if some data is more or less trusted to be externally consistent regarding the $cert_{CA-signed}$ dimension, the same data is at least as much trusted regarding lower data dimensions such as $cert$ and $list_{CA}$.

3.3 Aggregation of External Consistency

Components are parts of the system that receive or produce data. Received data can be used by a component to produce output data. However the produced data is restricted by the input data of these components. Indeed, in Fig. 1, if the *tls* component tries to verify the signature of a server certificate with an untrusted list of CA, the result of this verification is also untrusted and the same goes for the external consistency. Besides, if the web server had two file systems and if the page loader *pl* loaded the web page from this two different file systems, the input data of *pl* would be more likely to be externally consistent to the web page than if the web page was loaded from only one of these file systems.

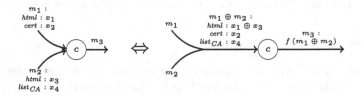

Fig. 3. Input data aggregation

Because external consistency is defined in the metric space $[0,1]$, triangular norms [7,19] can be used as aggregation operators. Triangular norms are operations that generalize the fuzzy logic operators such as the use of probabilistic sum and product or the use of min/max operators and have already been used to describe aggregation of trust [10] or aggregation of risk attributes [9]. Triangular norm operators, such as the min operator or the probabilistic product, are noted $\otimes$ whereas triangular conorm operators such as the max operator or the probabilistic sum, are noted $\oplus$.

As represented in Fig. 3, when a component $c \in C$ has several incoming edges, the input data of c corresponds to the aggregation of data of all input edges. In Fig. 3, it is represented by the aggregation of data m_1 and m_2 and is noted $m_1 \oplus m_2$.

3.4   Resilience of Sources and Components

The resilience of a component $v \in V$ is the measure of its ability to preserve the external consistency of its input data into its output data. But it is not possible to produce any output data from any set of input data. The produced data is restricted to what contains or represents the input data, as shown in Fig. 3. For the rest of this article, sets of input data and sets of output data are represented as mappings, from the vertices that produced the data, to data $m \in DATA$.

Example 1. Input data of *tls* is a mapping $M_{tls} \in (V \nrightarrow DATA)$ from $\{pl, fs_1, fs_2\}$ to $DATA$:

$$M_{tls} = \{(pl, m_1), (fs_1, m_2), (fs_2, m_3)\} \in (V \nrightarrow DATA)$$

Preservation of external consistency means the external consistency of data generated by the component is limited by the external consistency of its input. This is reflected in the definition of Θ which is the set of all valid data combinations, that is, solutions to aggregate input data to produce valid output data.

Definition 3. *Set of valid transformations*

$$\Theta = \left\{ \begin{array}{l} \tau : (V \nrightarrow DATA) \nrightarrow (V \nrightarrow DATA) \mid \\ \exists! v_d \in V \mid dom(\tau) = \{M \mid \text{cond}_1 \wedge \text{cond}_2 \wedge \text{cond}_3\} \end{array} \right\}$$

with $\text{cond}_1 : dom(M) = \{v_s \mid (v_s, v_d) \in E\}$

$\text{cond}_2 : dom(\tau(M)) = \{v_d\}$

$\text{cond}_3 : \forall d \in D, \tau(M)(v_d)(d) \leq \max_{\substack{d' \in D \\ d' \leq d, d' \neq \perp}} \left(\bigoplus_{v_s \in dom(M)} M(v_s)(d') \right)$

These transformation functions $\tau \in \Theta$, that produce data from input data, are partially defined such as the definition domain of their input data is consistent with the graph and matches the input edges. For example, input data of a transformation τ associated to *tls*, which receives data from fs_1, fs_2 and pl, would be defined on the domain $\{fs_1, fs_2, pl\} \subset V$, as depicted by cond_1. Produced data is also represented by a partial mapping even if the definition domain of this mapping is restricted to a single element: the vertex that combines the input data to output data, therefore the vertex to which the transformation is associated. This is expressed by $cond_2$.

The third constraint, $cond_3$, means that the external consistency of produced data is limited by the aggregation of the external consistency of input data. A component cannot improve the external consistency from nothing. However, a component can aggregate external consistency of different dimensions to produce data externally consistent to higher dimensions than those present in the input data. For example, the *tls* component can aggregate data corresponding to a certificate (data dimension *cert*) and data corresponding to a list of valid CA (dimension $list_{CA}$) to produce data corresponding to a certificate that is known to have been signed by a CA (data dimension $cert_{CA-signed}$) and can use this data with *html* data to produce $html_{sec}$ data.

The produced data also depends on the component to which the data is destined. In Fig. 1, the source CA sends a certificate to fs_1 and sends a list of valid CA to fs_2. Components and sources are restricted to produce data only for components they are connected to. For this reason, a partial mapping $\mathcal{R}^v$ is attributed to every component or source $v \in V$ and assigns a transformation function to every component to which v can send data.

Definition 4. *Resilience function of an element $v \in V$*

$$\mathcal{R}^v : C \nrightarrow \Theta \mid dom\left(\mathcal{R}^v\right) = \{c_d \in C \mid (v, c_d) \in E\} \text{ and}$$
$$\forall c_d \in dom\left(\mathcal{R}^v\right), dom\left(dom\left(\mathcal{R}^v\left(c_d\right)\right)\right) = \{v_s \mid (v_s, v) \in E\}$$

These are partial functions and their domains are restricted by components to which they can send data. For example, $dom\left(\mathcal{R}^{fs_1}\right) = \{pl, tls\}$. But another constraint concerns transformation functions that can be assigned. Indeed, the only transformations allowed are those whom the definition domain is input data sent by vertices that are directly connected to v.

Example 2. Input data definition domain of the transformation function of fs_1 for the production of data meant for *pl*. As shown in Fig. 1, only f and CA can provide data to fs_1.

$$dom\left(dom\left(\mathcal{R}^{fs_1}\left(pl\right)\right)\right) = \{f, CA\}$$

Note that sources of the system are specific cases as they produce data from nothing. For that reason, transformations associated to sources do not depend on input data and are not restricted by it. Thus data produced by sources can have any external consistency values. Given $f_\emptyset = \emptyset$, then

$$\forall s \in S, \forall c_d \in dom\left(\mathcal{R}^s\right), dom\left(\mathcal{R}^s\left(c_d\right)\right) = \{f_\emptyset\}, \mathcal{R}^s\left(c_d\right)\left(f_\emptyset\right)$$

Definition 5. *Resilience function of a system.* The element $\mathcal{R}$ given in $sys = \langle V, E, L, \mathcal{R} \rangle$ is the collection of the resilience of all components and sources of the system:

$$\mathcal{R} : V \to (C \nrightarrow \Theta)$$

where, $\mathcal{R}^v$ defines the external consistency (dimensions) of the output of element v based on its inputs.

3.5   Computing Resilience Across the System

Now that components of the system and data have been defined, it is possible to evaluate the external consistency of data in the system. For that purpose, a metric, named global resilience and denoted $\mathcal{R}_{glo}$, is presented.

Definition 6. *Global resilience.* Global resilience allows the evaluation of the external consistency of data arriving to a specific component. This is a recursive computation of the external consistency of data from input edges of a node to involved sources of the system.

$$\mathcal{R}_{glo} : V \rightarrow (V \nrightarrow DATA)$$
$$v_d \mapsto \mathcal{R}_{glo}\left(v_d\right) : V \ \nrightarrow DATA \mid dom\left(\mathcal{R}_{glo}\left(v_d\right)\right) = \{v_s \in V \mid$$
$$\left(v_s, v_d\right) \in E\}$$
$$v_s \mapsto \begin{cases} \mathcal{R}^{v_s}\left(v_d\right)\left(\mathcal{R}_{glo}\left(v_s\right)\right)\left(v_s\right) \text{ if } v_s \in C \\ \mathcal{R}^{v_s}\left(v_d\right)\left(f_\emptyset\right)\left(v_s\right) \text{ if } v_s \in S \end{cases}$$

Note that since sources do not have input data, it can be noticed that $\forall s \in S, \mathcal{R}_{glo}\left(s\right) = f_\emptyset \in (V \nrightarrow DATA)$, the empty function.

Example 3. Global resilience of tls and fs_1 Considering Fig. 1, it is possible to compute the global resilience of different components.

$$\mathcal{R}_{glo}\left(tls\right) = \left\{\left(fs_1, \mathcal{R}^{fs_1}\left(tls\right)\left(\mathcal{R}_{glo}\left(fs_1\right)\right)\left(fs_1\right)\right), \left(fs_2, \mathcal{R}^{fs_2}\left(tls\right)\left(\mathcal{R}_{glo}\left(fs_2\right)\right)\left(fs_2\right)\right),\right.$$
$$\left.\left(pl, \mathcal{R}^{pl}\left(tls\right)\left(\mathcal{R}_{glo}\left(pl\right)\right)\left(pl\right)\right)\right\} \in (V \nrightarrow DATA)$$

This computation results in the external consistency values of input data of tls: data arriving from fs_1, from fs_2 and from pl. And it should be noticed that this data itself results in the computation of external consistency of data arriving to these previous components. For example:

$$\mathcal{R}_{glo}\left(fs_1\right) = \left\{\left(f, \mathcal{R}^f\left(fs_1\right)\left(f_\emptyset\right)\right), \left(CA, \mathcal{R}^{CA}\left(fs_1\right)\left(f_\emptyset\right)\right)\right\} \in (V \nrightarrow DATA)$$

The main purpose of this metric is to compute external consistency of data arriving to components that correspond to end users, such as the component *win* in Fig. 1 which represents the final user of the system. By considering the external consistency of data arriving to these nodes, it is possible to evaluate if one is enough confident in the system to produce externally consistent data. For example, in Fig. 1, it can be considered that the main service of the system is that the client receives data corresponding to a desired file stored in the server file system. It is interpreted as the input data of *win* having to be externally consistent regarding the data dimension *html*.

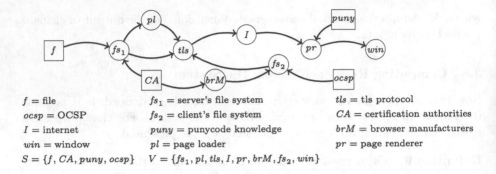

f = file fs_1 = server's file system tls = tls protocol
$ocsp$ = OCSP fs_2 = client's file system CA = certification authorities
I = internet $puny$ = punycode knowledge brM = browser manufacturers
win = window pl = page loader pr = page renderer
$S = \{f, CA, puny, ocsp\}$ $V = \{fs_1, pl, tls, I, pr, brM, fs_2, win\}$

Fig. 4. A more extensive secured connection

4   The HTTPS Browser Use-Case Extended

To illustrate the use and the interest of this metric and this model, the same system than presented before will be considered as a use-case, but with additional components and sources. If a client wants to access a file from a distant server, the establishment of a secured connection requires the involvement of more actors and more types of data. In this case, the tls component needs to receive a certificate from the server and to have CA certificates to validate its authenticity but it also needs data to confirm that it has not been prematurely revoked. The client uses a browser plugin that highlights punycode to make sure that there is no hidden data in data received from the Internet. This more extensive example is described by Fig. 4. The lattice shown in Fig. 5 describes all data dimensions that will be considered and how they are organised.

As a system is defined by $sys = \langle V, E, L, \mathcal{R} \rangle$, the given graph and lattice define most of the system's elements: S, V, and E are retrieved from Fig. 4 and L from Fig. 5. Only $\mathcal{R}$ remains to be defined. The resilience function of each source and component is defined separately. Their resilience regarding each of their output data recipient components are also defined separately. Let $\mathcal{R}^{v_1}(v_2)$: $dim_1 \mapsto x$ be data produced by v_1 to v_2 equal to x regarding the dim_1 data dimension, and equal to 0 regarding all others.

Sources Description:

$$\mathcal{R}^f(fs_1) : html \mapsto 1 \qquad\qquad \mathcal{R}^{puny}(pr) : puny \mapsto 1$$
$$\mathcal{R}^{CA}(fs_1) : cert \mapsto 1 \qquad\qquad \mathcal{R}^{CA}(brM) : list_{CA} \mapsto 1$$
$$\mathcal{R}^{ocsp}(fs_2) : list_{revoked} \mapsto 0.99$$

Concerning components of the system, the following notations are used: $\mathcal{R}^{v_2}(v_3)$: $dim_1 \mapsto v_1 : dim_2 * y$ means that the data produced by v_2 for v_3 is, regarding dim_1 data dimension, equal to the external consistency value for dim_2 of the data received from v_1, multiplied by y. The y factor characterizes a loss of external consistency. This loss can be due to an imperfect work of the

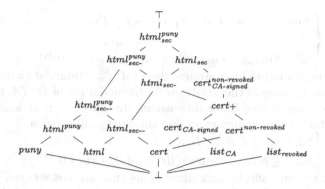

$html$ = contains the web page content $list_{revoked}$ = list of revoked certificates

$list_{CA}$ = list of CA certificates $html_{sec}$ = same as $html$ but using tls

$cert$ = certificate $puny$ = knowledge about puny-code

$cert_{CA\text{-}signed}$ = certificate signed by a valid CA $cert^{non\text{-}revoked}$ = non revoked certificate

Fig. 5. A complete lattice of data dimensions

component on the input data (failure, fault) or because the component is vulnerable to attacks. Following these notations, resilience functions of the system components are given:

Components Description:

- $\mathcal{R}^{win}$: $\emptyset$, because the resilience of this component is meaningless, only its input data is of interest.
- $\mathcal{R}^{fs_1}(pl)$: $\forall d \in D, d \mapsto f : d * 0.99$, the component fs_2 represents a storage device and just sends data received from f to pl. It is considered that this component has some chances of failing to preserve the external consistency of stored data because of faults, attacks, failures, etc. (and the same goes for fs_2). This is the meaning of the factor 0.99.
- $\mathcal{R}^{fs_1}(tls)$: $\forall d \in D, d \mapsto CA : d * 0.99$
- $\mathcal{R}^{fs_2}(tls)$: $\begin{cases} list_{CA} \mapsto brM : list_{CA} * 0.99 \\ list_{revoked} \mapsto ocsp : list_{revoked} * 0.99 \end{cases}$
- $\mathcal{R}^{pl}(tls)$: $\forall d, html \leq d \mapsto fs_1 : d * 0.98$, with pl a software that loads data stored in fs_1 and sends it through the Internet. This component has a little rate of failing or of corrupting the loaded data, represented by 0.98.
- $\mathcal{R}^{brM}(fs_2)$: $list_{CA} \mapsto CA : list_{CA} * 0.95$. Even if the CA component is idealized in this use case (it does not produce imperfect data), it is not the same considering browser manufacturers that can be considered not entirely trustworthy or not perfectly competent and they can introduced illegitimate or untrustworthy CA into the list of valid CA stored in the client web browser.

$$- \mathcal{R}^{tls}(I) : \begin{cases} html_{sec} \mapsto pl : html * fs_1 : cert * fs_2 : list_{CA} \\ * fs_2 : list_{revoked} \\ \forall d \le html_{sec} \mapsto \max(tls : html_{sec}, \max(\forall v, v : d)) \end{cases}$$

The tls component produces secured data ($html_{sec}$) from data with lower data dimensions. Because of the constraint in the definition of $DATA$, the external consistency considering lower dimensions than $html_{sec}$ is at least preserved by the external consistency regarding the $html_{sec}$ dimension.

$$- \mathcal{R}^I(pr) : \begin{cases} \forall d, html_{sec} \le d \mapsto tls : d \\ \forall d, d \le html_{sec} \mapsto \max(tls : html_{sec}, tls : d * 0.75) \end{cases}$$

The Internet only affects data dimensions that are not secured. The external consistency of data dimensions $html_{sec}$ and higher is untouched whereas considering lower dimensions, external consistency can be lost.

$$- \mathcal{R}^{pr}(win) : \begin{cases} puny \mapsto puny : puny \\ \forall d, \mathrm{LUB}(puny, html) \le d \mapsto I : \mathrm{GLB}(html, d) \\ * puny : puny * 0.98 \\ \forall d, \mathrm{GLB}(d, puny) = \bot \mapsto I : d * 0.98 \end{cases}$$

This last component receives data from the Internet and prepares it for the client to see it, with a possible loss of external consistency. Moreover, this component checks and highlights the presence of punycode.

Results: Now that the system has been entirely defined, it is possible to compute end-to-end external consistency of data. Data of interest id data received by the client, in other words, input data of the win component:

$$\mathcal{R}_{glo}(win) = \{(pr, \{(puny, 1), (d, x \approx 0.87) \text{ if } d \ne puny\})\} \in V \nrightarrow DATA$$

This result means that whatever data dimension is considered - except $puny$ - the degree of confidence for the input data of the win component to be externally consistent is 0.86. In particular, the external consistency for the $html$ and $html^{puny}$ is 0.86. It does not mean anything by itself but it can be used to compare with another system configuration.

Indeed, if another system configuration is considered, their global resilience values for the component win can be compared. For example, if the tls component is replaced by a fake component that do not produce secured data, the external consistency of the input data of win would be different. The description of the resilience the fake tls component is :

$$\mathcal{R}^{tls^{fake}}(I) : \forall d \in D, d \mapsto \max(\forall v, v : d)$$

This component just produces data with the highest external consistency of its input data for every data dimension. As the produced data is not protected by a secured connection, ($html_{sec} \mapsto 0$), the Internet component will affect the external consistency of lower dimensions than $html_{sec}$. At the end, the external consistency of input data of win is different :

$$\mathcal{R}_{glo}(win) = \{(pr, \{(puny, 1), (html, x \approx 0.71), (html^{puny}, x \approx 0.71),$$
$$(d, 0) \text{ if } d \nleq html^{puny}\})\} \in V \nrightarrow DATA$$

It can be noticed that the external consistency values for $html$ and $html^{puny}$ are lower than previously with a secured connection. On top of that, the external consistency value for all other dimensions - except $puny$ - is equal to 0, because the component pl does not produce data from dimensions corresponding to certificates (dimensions lower than $cert_{CA-signed}^{non-revoked}$).

5   Related Work

Originally, resilience was studied in psychology [22] to refer to the ability to recover from trauma and crisis, and in ecology [12] as a measure of persistence of systems to changes and disturbances. In engineering, existing work has looked at how to define and evaluate resilience. The work in [3,11] focuses on resilience analysis, that is an evaluation of capacities of a system, from risk assessment, that is an analysis of possible harms and losses. In [21], resilience is defined as a combination of three system capacities: absorptive, adaptability and restorative capacities. However both metrics suggested in [11,21] for evaluating resilience of a system are based on costs and time to recover from a disturbance so that the resilience evaluation is specific to a determined set of changes or attacks.

In [2], resilience of a network is improved by evaluating paths between nodes and by selecting the most efficient path in order to overcome edge removal. This approach improves the adaptability of a system but do not consider the need to recover from a disturbance. On the other hand, in [14], a system is designed to detect corrupted components and to restore them once the corruption is detected. This detection mechanism is based on a voting-system such that the system is tolerant to failures and attacks unless a majority of voting components are compromised. In this case, the system can not recover anymore and fails. In [20] and in [15], the system is defined in term of states and state transitions and a game-theoretic approach is proposed in [15] to avoid failure states while [20] evaluate resilience as the capacity of the system to avoid unacceptable states. In both cases, failure and unacceptable states are needed to be known and defined.

On the opposite of an overall evaluation of the resilience of a system, some studies suggest to evaluate a system by describing it as a set of components that interact with each others to achieve some property. For example, in [10] the calculation of trust between two principals is treated as a quantity that flows through a delegation graph. In this case, the trust a principal has into another is the result of the aggregation of trust all across the delegation graph, from the former principal to the latter one.

6   Conclusion

A model of resilience was proposed that can be used to compute the degree of confidence in the external consistency of data as it is operated upon, stored and transformed across a system. This provides a measure of the external consistency of data at any point in the system relative to the data's origin. It is used to determine whether the various non-functional mechanisms in the system are sufficient to ensure that data values are as expected, that is, they ensure a *persistence of service delivery that can be justifiably be trusted, when facing changes* [13].

Rather than using a behavior-based model of external consistency [8], we model how individual components and resilience mechanisms influence our degree of confidence in the external consistency of the data that they process. Intuitively, this is not unlike a max-flow style problem, measuring the 'flow' of external consistency across a graph of constraining nodes (although it is quite different in formulation). The advantage of the proposed approach is that node resilience definition (resilience function $\mathcal{R}$) is relatively straightforward, in terms of the degree of confidence in the external consistency of its outputs relative to its inputs. Node resilience could be subjective, for example based on component developer reputation or a threat assessment; it could be based on past vulnerability reports for the components, or a symbolic data-flow analysis could be used to identify reliable data-paths in the component software indicating a preservation of external consistency.

The proposed model provides a static snapshot of resilience in terms of the confidence in the external consistency of data. Investigating the temporal aspects of resilience is a topic for future research, for example, how one's confidence in the proper operation of a software component may change over time [16]. Such changes can be managed conventionally in terms of threats, whereby the current degree of confidence is calculated according to the outcome of ongoing audit tests on the efficacy of the existing components [9]. Alternatively, techniques, such as [4,17], that consider how the probability of failure of individual components impact the overall probability of failure of the system could be used in modelling how the degree of confidence in external consistency can change over time.

A preliminary evaluation of the potential of the model has been conducted by the encoding of the https use-case (Sect. 4). With this encoding it is possible to effectively compute how the various security components contribute to the overall end-to-end resilience of the browser. In particular, it allows one to determine how confident we can be in the external consistency of the rendered page relative to the original server page, on the basis of the security configuration of the browser. How this might be incorporated into the browser run-time in practice is a topic for future research.

Acknowledgements. This work was supported the Cyber CNI Chair of Institute Mines-Télécom which is held by IMT Atlantique and supported by Airbus Defence and Space, Amossys, BNP Parisbas, EDF, Orange, La Poste, Nokia, Société Générale and the Regional Council of Brittany; it has been acknowledged by the French Centre of Excellence in Cybersecurity.

References

1. Alsberg, P.A., Day, J.D.: A principle for resilient sharing of distributed resources. In: Proceedings of the 2nd International Conference on Software Engineering, ICSE 1976, pp. 562–570. IEEE Computer Society Press, Los Alamitos (1976). http://dl. acm.org/citation.cfm?id=800253.807732
2. Andersen, D., Balakrishnan, H., Kaashoek, F., Morris, R.: Resilient overlay networks, vol. 35. ACM (2001)
3. Arghandeh, R., von Meier, A., Mehrmanesh, L., Mili, L.: On the definition of cyber-physical resilience in power systems. Renew. Sustain. Energy Rev. **58**, 1060–1069 (2016)
4. Bourget, E., Cuppens, F., Cuppens-Boulahia, N., Dubus, S., Foley, S.N., Laarouchi, Y.: Probabilistic event graph to model safety and security for diagnosis purposes. In: Kerschbaum, F., Paraboschi, S. (eds.) DBSec 2018. LNCS, vol. 10980, pp. 38–47. Springer, Heidelberg (2018). https://doi.org/10.1007/978-3-319-95729-6_3
5. Clark, D.D.: Control point analysis. TRPC (2012). https://doi.org/10.2139/ssrn. 2032124
6. Clark, D.D., Wilson, D.R.: A comparison of commercial and military computer security policies. In: 1987 IEEE Symposium on Security and Privacy, p. 184. IEEE (1987). http://ieeexplore.ieee.org/abstract/document/6234890/
7. Dubois, D., Prade, H.: A review of fuzzy set aggregation connectives. Inf. Sci. **36**(1–2), 85–121 (1985). https://doi.org/10.1016/0020-0255(85)90027-1
8. Foley, S.N.: A non-functional approach to system integrity. IEEE J. Sel. Areas Commun. **21**(1) (2003)
9. Foley, S.N.: Security risk management using internal controls. In: Proceedings of the First ACM Workshop on Information Security Governance, pp. 59–64. ACM (2009)
10. Foley, S.N., Mac Adams, W., O'Sullivan, B.: Aggregating trust using triangular norms in the keynote trust management system. In: Cuellar, J., Lopez, J., Barthe, G., Pretschner, A. (eds.) STM 2010. LNCS, vol. 6710, pp. 100–115. Springer, Heidelberg (2011). https://doi.org/10.1007/978-3-642-22444-7_7
11. Francis, R., Bekera, B.: A metric and frameworks for resilience analysis of engineered and infrastructure systems. Reliab. Eng. Sys. Saf. **121**, 90–103 (2014)
12. Holling, C.S.: Resilience and stability of ecological systems. Ann. Rev. Ecol. Syst. **4**(1), 1–23 (1973)
13. Laprie, J.C.: From dependability to resilience. In: 38th IEEE/IFIP International Conference on Dependable Systems and Networks, pp. G8–G9. Citeseer (2008)
14. Liu, D.: Resilient cluster formation for sensor networks. In: 27th International Conference on Distributed Computing Systems (ICDCS 2007), p. 40. IEEE (2007)
15. Lucia, W., Sinopoli, B., Franze, G.: A set-theoretic approach for secure and resilient control of cyber-physical systems subject to false data injection attacks. In: Science of Security for Cyber-Physical Systems Workshop (SOSCYPS), pp. 1–5. IEEE (2016)
16. Morrison, P., Herzig, K., Murphy, B., Williams, L.: Challenges with applying vulnerability prediction models. In: Proceedings of the 2015 Symposium and Bootcamp on the Science of Security, HotSoS 2015, pp. 4:1–4:9. ACM, New York (2015). http://doi.acm.org/10.1145/2746194.2746198
17. Piètre-Cambacédès, L., Bouissou, M.: Attack and defense modeling with BDMP. In: Kotenko, I., Skormin, V. (eds.) MMM-ACNS 2010. LNCS, vol. 6258, pp. 86–101. Springer, Heidelberg (2010). https://doi.org/10.1007/978-3-642-14706-7_7

18. Ryan, P.Y.A.: Mathematical models of computer security. In: Focardi, R., Gorrieri, R. (eds.) FOSAD 2000. LNCS, vol. 2171, pp. 1–62. Springer, Heidelberg (2001). https://doi.org/10.1007/3-540-45608-2_1
19. Schweizer, B., Sklar, A.: Probabilistic metric spaces (1983)
20. Sterbenz, J.P., et al.: Resilience and survivability in communication networks: strategies, principles, and survey of disciplines. Comput. Netw. **54**(8), 1245–1265 (2010).   http://www.sciencedirect.com/science/article/pii/S1389128610000824, Resilient and Survivable Networks
21. Vugrin, E.D., Warren, D.E., Ehlen, M.A.: A resilience assessment framework for infrastructure and economic systems: quantitative and qualitative resilience analysis of petrochemical supply chains to a hurricane. Process Saf. Prog. **30**(3), 280–290 (2011)
22. Werner, E.E., Bierman, J.M., French, F.E.: The Children of Kauai: A Longitudinal Study from the Prenatal Period to Age Ten. University of Hawaii Press, Honolulu (1971)
23. Williams, J.G., La Padula, L.J.: Automated support for external consistency. In: Proceedings of Computer Security Foundations Workshop VI, pp. 71–81. IEEE (1993). http://ieeexplore.ieee.org/abstract/document/246637/

Optimal Partitioning of LLC in CAT-enabled CPUs to Prevent Side-Channel Attacks

Ugo Fiore[1] , Adrian Florea[2]() , Arpad Gellert[2] , Lucian Vintan[2] , and Paolo Zanetti[1]

[1] Parthenope University, Napoli, Italy
[2] Lucian Blaga University, Sibiu, Romania
adrian.florea@ulbsibiu.ro

Abstract. Over the last years, timing channels that exploit resources shared at the microarchitectural level have attracted a lot of attention. The majority of such side-channel attacks target CPU caches. Cache-based side-channel attacks are based on monitoring cache accesses performed by a victim process through measurements of access times by a spy process that shares the cache with the victim. Among the counter-measures proposed to frustrate cache-based side-channel attacks, cache partitioning seems most effective. The recently introduced Cache Allocation Technology (CAT) enables fine control over the LLC and how cores allocate into it. In this work, we introduce the problem of optimizing cache partitioning under dynamically configurable schemes such as Intel CAT, in the perspective of thwarting access-based side-channel attacks.

Keywords: LLC partitioning · Side-channel attack
Cache allocation technology

1 Introduction

The recent discovered Meltdown and Spectre present-day hardware commercial CPU security vulnerabilities shocked the IT world [13,14]. Billions of devices, from smart phones to servers, were affected. The authors present and analyze the profound intrinsic causes of these hardware vulnerabilities. One main cause consists in the fact that transient instructions—out of order and speculatively executed dynamic instructions—processed by the superscalar/SMT processors, unfortunately can allocate privileged data in the CPU's cache even if they are processed by user-level threads. Particularly, speculative instructions bypass privilege violation exceptions, additionally facilitating the vulnerability in this way. After having been allocated in the cache through transient instructions,

Authors acknowledge the financial support provided by the Research grant of Università Parthenope, DR no. 793, november 28th, 2017.

A. Castiglione et al. (Eds.): CSS 2018, LNCS 11161, pp. 115–123, 2018.
https://doi.org/10.1007/978-3-030-01689-0_9

the secret accessed data can be learned by another attacker's thread in an ingenious manner. An open problem, at least for us, is the following: in the case of a L1 direct mapped cache instruction access (for example, the Pentium 4 case), the corresponding subsequent speculative instructions could facilitate another CPU insecurity niche, too? Anyway, the Spectre bug suggests that revisiting the design of microarchitectures with instruction values prediction and speculation from the hardware security point of view should be a must in the nearest future. More generally, these bugs show us that we haven't understood in sufficient depth some fundamental computer architecture concepts like temporal/spatial/value locality, prediction and speculation, concurrency and parallelism, virtualization, and so on. Such vulnerabilities are working at the interfaces between these fundamental concepts in a subtle manner [20].

With a flattening in the growth curve for single-thread speed, CPU performance enhancement is frequently achieved by virtue of microarchitectural improvements. Additional modules with specialized functions are being added to cores and the trend indicates an increasing recourse to this strategy. Complexity is thus being shifted towards lower levels in the hierarchy. Unsurprisingly, attacks also are seen to follow this path. Over the last years, microarchitectural timing channels have received much attention. Some of these side-channels also exploit resources shared between cores and across packages [6], making them a substantial threat to sensitive information in environments where co-residency and multi-tenancy occur (e.g., tenants in a cloud). It should be added, nevertheless, that cache timing can also be used to discover whether any other tenant was co-located in the same hardware [26].

When using many-core processors in High-Performance Computing (HPC), the number of memory channels creates a performance bottleneck on simultaneous accesses to RAM. A simple solution is to avoid allocating multiple cores on the same package to a specific computational task. This exacerbates the issues caused by resource sharing, since other activities should be allocated on the other cores and the degree of conflict cannot be established *a priori*. In this context, an optimized allocation of the last-level cache (LLC) can play a vital role in improving predictability of the performance, which is an essential aspect.

In this work, as a first step of a wider research endeavor, we focus on the optimization of shared resources—in particular, LLCs–to mitigate access-driven side-channel attacks. This paper is structured as follows. Section 2 presents caches as main target of side-channel attacks, revealing some countermeasures and elaborating on cache partitioning, advantages and disadvantages of inclusive and exclusive cache hierarchies. Section 3 analyses the opportunity of using as optimization solution for cache partitioning with CAT from Intel. Finally, Sect. 4 highlights the main contributions and proposes some possible further work.

2   Timing Side-Channels

In an access-driven side-channel attack, an attacker learns secret information about a victim running on the same computer by observing (and sometimes provoking) the effects the execution of the victim onto microarchitectural components shared between attacker and victim. No attempt is therefore made to bypass access control and isolation provided by operating systems (OS), virtual machine hypervisors, or orchestrators. Leaking channels at the microarchitectural level bypass sandboxing techniques.

One of the microarchitectural components popular among researchers investigating side-channel attacks is the branch predictor unit (BPU). The BPU, which is unique within a physical core, attempts to guess the direction of conditional branches in the code to ensure an uninterrupted delivery of instructions to the execution pipeline of a superscalar processor. The targets recently taken conditional branches are stored in the branch target buffer (BTB). Since the BPU is shared between virtual cores, if the spy program is running on the same physical core as the victim, information in the BTB can be extracted to infer the direction of conditional branches in the victim. The attacker mistrains the branch predictor [5] and measures the performance of some branches. Although co-residency is not trivial to accomplish in practice, techniques for forcing it have been proposed [4]. More advanced hardware structure supporting prediction can also be targeted. The Selective Load Value Prediction (SLVP) unit exploits locality in load values by anticipating the next output of a load instruction based on its previous outputs. Prediction process is applied only on long-latency loads, leveraging upon the correlation between the load instruction addresses and their actual values. Prediction will selectively apply to load instructions with a miss in the data cache [7].

The majority of side-channel attacks target CPU caches. Cache-based side-channel attacks monitor cache accesses performed by a victim process through a spy process that shares the cache with the victim. Cache attacks are based on variations of access times when retrieving data from the cache and from the RAM. The difference can be used to decide whether a specific portion of the memory resides in the cache–and therefore it has been accessed recently. Access times below a threshold indicate a cache hit and times above that threshold indicate a cache miss. Early attacks exploited the core caches, the L1 and L2 caches that are not shared by cores. To achieve sharing, the attacker needs co-residency with the victim on the same core. In addition, effective mitigation techniques have been proposed for this case [3,21,22]. The focus of recent attacks has therefore shifted from core caches to the L3 cache, also termed the Last Level Cache (LLC), which is shared by all the cores in most modern processors Cross-core and cross-VM attacks have been demonstrated [11] that exploit the LLC. LLC-based side-channel attacks capable of disclosing information from a victim computation fall boradly into two categories. The FLUSH-RELOAD variety [23], can access fine-grained data but it relies on the attacker sharing a physical page of memory with the victim. This may happen because of memory deduplication mechanisms, which are not uncommon with OSes and hypervisors. PRIME-PROBE attacks, instead, do not have that requirement. Rather, the condition for PRIME-PROBE attacks to be viable is that attacker and victim share the same sets in the LLCs [11,16]. The attacker primes the LLC by reading a purposely crafted set of memory addresses which exactly fills a cache set. Later, it probes the cache by accessing the same data and measuring the time to load them, inferring information about the memory accessed by the victim. Secret data can be also recovered because code is often structured in such a way that the execution path is different for different values of security-critical data.

2.1 Caches

During the last three decades, the latency of memory has been unable to keep the pace with the clock rate of processors: Compare a typical RAM bandwidth of 34 GiB/s with the peak 409.6 GiB/s of instruction and data references that an Intel Core i7 running at 3.2 GHz is able to generate [9]. Memory hierarchies provide an architectural solution to this mismatch. Caches are memory areas organized in levels, each level being bigger but slower that the preceding one. When the processor references a memory address, the corresponding word, if not found in the cache must be fetched from a lower level in the hierarchy (another cache or the main memory) and placed in the cache before continuing. Because of spatial locality, addresses close to the requested one are likely to be referenced soon, and so multiple words, called a *line*, are moved in a single fetch operation. The minimum storage unit of a cache is a line and the cache is divided into sets consisting of the same number of lines. A cache line holds one aligned, power-of-two-sized block of adjacent bytes loaded from memory and it contains a tag to indicate which memory address it corresponds to. A line is first mapped onto a set, usually through a string of consecutive bits. The line can then be placed anywhere within the set. Looking a line up involves mapping the line address to the set and then searching (usually in parallel–the number of lines a set can contain is called the number of *ways*) the set to find the line.

In a Chip multiprocessor (CMP), the L3 cache is often shared by cores. For example, the Core i7 has a 32 KiB L1 cache (split into data and instruction caches), with 64 sets with 8 ways each. Cache lines are 64 bits of data. The L2 unified cache is an 8-way 256 KiB cache. The L3 cache, the largest and slowest cache, can be up to 8 MiB (8192 sets and 16 ways). Fourth generation Xeon processors host from 6 to 12 cores with an L3 cache of 2.5 MiB per core.

2.2 Countermeasures

Defenses against cache attacks can be grouped into several broad areas.

Modifying Critical Code. Making critical code sections constant-execution time would be greatly reduce the potential of side-channel attacks. Crypthographic libraries in particular should avoid key-dependent code path patterns, so that branch instructions conditioned on the state of secret data are avoided. Compiler optimizations that remove conditional branches from target code have been proposed [2], but the automated Conversion of real-world applications into branch-free code is challenging.

Preventing Attackers from Accessing High-Resolution Timers. This approach is very restrictive, possibly impacts other functions, and may be thus difficult to implement. Further, attackers could resort to external events to achieve such measurements.

Attempt to Detect Attacks. Cache attacks tend to generate a lot of cache misses, which can be monitored. The victim itself, the OS or the VMM can measure times to detect misbehavior.

Obfuscate/Shuffle Addresses. A condition precedent for an attack is that the attacker needs to be able to create colliding lines with the victim. To create obstacles for this, randomizing the mapping of caches has been proposed by Wang and Lee [21].

Pin Sensitive Data into the Cache. In this way, such data cannot be evicted. As an example, Wang and Lee [21] suggested a partition-locked cache (PLcache) where locking attributes are associated to every cache line. This would require the definition of additional specific instructions and, in addition, the effects on cache management are not trivial and should be carefully analyzed.

Other techniques such as hardware transactional memory TSX (Intel Transactional Extensions) can be considered to have pinning as a side effect. With TSX, if a cache line is evicted, the entire transaction aborts. It is worth noting that TSX has been adopted both as a protection against attacks and as a timing side-channel [8].

Using Specialized Protection Structures. Hardware-based isolated execution environments such as Intels Software Guard Extensions (SGX) designed to protect application secrets from compromised system software could offer protection. SGX consists in a set of instructions an application can use to create a secure enclave embedded in its address space, inaccessible to even system software. While memory is protected, CPU hardware resources still remain shared between enclave and non-enclave code. SGX in its present form can, thus, be vulnerable to side-channel attacks.

Resource Partitioning. Eliminating the sharing of resources neutralizes side-channel attacks. The BPU may be partitioned so that victims and attackers do not share the same structures. For example, a separate branch predictor could be reserved for SGX code. Alternatively, mechanisms to request a private partition of the BPU may be introduced [15]. With partitioning, the attacker can no longer create collisions with the victim. Percival [18] was the first to note that a thread-aware cache eviction logic could restrict a thread to only evict cache lines "owned" by itself. He recommended that CMP designers *either avoid sharing caches between the processor cores or use thread-aware cache eviction strategies.* Page [17] proposed a partitioned architecture for caches as a countermeasure against side-channel attacks, where the cache is dynamically split into protected regions. As a result, the level of cache interference is drastically reduced and the cache can be configured specifically for an application rather than optimizing for the average case. Cache partitioning will be analyzed in more depth in the next section.

2.3   Cache Partitioning

Because of cache sharing in multicore systems, the cache usage—hence the performance—of a program depends on the cache occupancy of concurrent programs. A good defence is reducing the degree of sharing resources or to eliminate sharing altogether. Moreover, security is not the sole motivation for isolation: Sharing also reduces predictability of performance, an aspect that is sometimes essential to customers. Avoiding sharing of cores between different tenants could be viable in clouds [6]. However, cloud operators are strongly incentivized to use resources as efficiently as possible, so exclusive use of all cores in a package is difficult to achieve in practice.

Cross-core cache attacks rely on *inclusivity*, the property that the contents of every cache level are a subset of the contents at the level below. Countermeasures have therefore targeted inclusivity. In an exclusive cache hierarchy, lines evicted from a level are stored in the level below, so that the intersection of contents of different levels is empty. The exclusive cache management policy has long been adopted by AMD multicore processors. Exclusive caches have two drawbacks: storing evicted values in cascade down the hierarchy raises timing issues due to latencies, and losing the semantics of the LLC as a directory of all cache contents complicates the management of data being written to. On the other hand, since no data duplication is possible in exclusive caches, cache space is utilized in a better way than it is with inclusive caches [24]. Jaleel *et al.* have shown, however, that the performance penalty suffered from inclusive cache management policies is mainly due to *back-invalidations*. When a line gets evicted from the LLC, its presence in core caches would violate inclusion. For this reason, that line needs to be invalidated in all core caches, but if it has survived there, then it has necessarily been accessed more recently than the lines at the same level which were, instead, evicted. Hence, there is something fundamentally wrong with back-invalidations. A interesting solution is Temporal Locality Aware (TLA) inclusive cache management policies [12], in particular Query Based Selection (QBS), where the LLC, instead of asking core caches to invalidate lines on the verge of eviction, queries them to check whether the line is resident with them. In case the line is resident in any of the core caches a new victim is chosen. The overhead of QBS victim selection process is typically masked by memory latency.

Intel recently introduced CAT [10] to enable fine control over the LLC and how cores allocate into it. CAT associates portions of the LLC with a Class of Service (CoS) identifier termed CLOS. A resource capacity bitmask indicates, for each CLOS, whether a part of the cache can be used by the given CLOS, governing the degree of overlap and isolation between classes. A mask bit set to '1' specifies that the corresponding CLOS can allocate into the cache subset represented by that bit. One capacity mask bit generally corresponds to some number of ways, but CAT maintains flexibility by leaving the specific mapping to implementation. Further adding to flexibility, the CLOS can be assigned to various types of entities: threads, applications, VMs, or containers. Binding of CLOS to such entities is the responsibility of the system administrator, who interacts with the processor through an architecturally exposed mechanism. A system administrator thus can, for example, reserve portions of the LLC for individual cores so that other cores may not evict cache lines from these reserved portions.

3   Optimizing Cache Partitioning with CAT

While resource sharing improves performance scalability and throughput in cloud environments, prioritizing important or interactive applications in multitenant VMs with heterogeneous types of applications can represent a serious challenge. In addition, for workloads where substantial amounts of computing resources are involved, the reliability of an estimate of how long a job will run or the stability of running times over repeated executions are fundamental matters that can bear serious financial consequences. The increasing number of cores in CMPs exacerbates the contention for shared resources, making cache partitioning even more a pre-eminent problem. A recent empirical study by Qin [19] explores the impact of cache configuration, memory usage of programs, and partitioning type on the performance of cache partitioning.

Optimization of cache partitioning is a difficult problem in no uncertain terms. Bui *et al.* showed that just partitioning the LLC is a NP-complete problem [1], while finding the partition which minimizes the overall cache bandwidth has been shown to be NP-hard [25]. Although cache partitioning through CAT opens countless opportunities, its effective use is requires careful study. Thus, the optimization of LLC partitioning in a CAT-enabled CMP is a problem worth studying. Aspects that characterize this specific optimization problem include:

- CAT partitions can be either non-overlapped, enforcing complete separation, or overlapped, which would allow some (or all) of the space allocated to a CLOS to be shared with another CLOS.
- A constraint present in CAT that must be satisfied in the optimization is that cache portions reserved in the capacity bitmasks must be contiguous[1].

4   Conclusions and Future Work

We have introduced a new problem, the optimization of cache partitioning under dynamically configurable schemes such as Intel CAT, in the perspective of thwarting access-based side-channel attacks. The newly formulated problem involves several conflicting objectives, including isolation, performance, energy absorption and thermal behavior. It also has unique constraints, derived from

---

[1] Vol 3B, Section 17.19.2 of the Intel 64 and IA-32 Architectures Software Developer's Manual.

the structure of CAT. Finally, the flexibility of CAT allows the control variables to vary, since the malleable definition of CLOS permits to consider entities at different levels, such as threads, applications, and application groups.

In further research, we will compare the performance of optimization techniques on specific instances of the CAT-enabled cache optimization problem, study the effectiveness of operating at each of the various granularity levels supported by CLOS, evaluate the overlapping and non-overlapping partition schemes, and extend the optimization logic applied to CPU design which has been presented in [7] to address the wider problem of an integrated approach to resource allocation in CAT-enabled CMPs, with a special emphasis on accomplishing simultaneously an improved performance, a decrease in energy consumption, and an increased security.

References

1. Bui, B.D., Caccamo, M., Sha, L., Martinez, J.: Impact of cache partitioning on multi-tasking real time embedded systems. In: 14th IEEE International Conference on Embedded and Real-Time Computing Systems and Applications, RTCSA 2008, pp. 101–110. IEEE (2008)
2. Coppens, B., Verbauwhede, I., De Bosschere, K., De Sutter, B.: Practical mitigations for timing-based side-channel attacks on modern x86 processors. In: 2009 30th IEEE Symposium on Security and Privacy, pp. 45–60. IEEE (2009)
3. Domnitser, L., Jaleel, A., Loew, J., Abu-Ghazaleh, N., Ponomarev, D.: Non-monopolizable caches: low-complexity mitigation of cache side channel attacks. ACM Trans. Archit. Code Optim. (TACO) 8(4), 35 (2012)
4. Evtyushkin, D., Ponomarev, D., Abu-Ghazaleh, N.: Jump over ASLR: attacking branch predictors to bypass ASLR. In: The 49th Annual IEEE/ACM International Symposium on Microarchitecture, p. 40. IEEE Press (2016)
5. Evtyushkin, D., Riley, R., Abu-Ghazaleh, N.C., Ponomarev, D., et al.: Branch-Scope: a new side-channel attack on directional branch predictor. In: Proceedings of the Twenty-Third International Conference on Architectural Support for Programming Languages and Operating Systems, pp. 693–707. ACM (2018)
6. Ge, Q., Yarom, Y., Cock, D., Heiser, G.: A survey of microarchitectural timing attacks and countermeasures on contemporary hardware. J. Cryptogr. Eng. 8(1), 1–27 (2018)
7. Gellert, A., Florea, A., Fiore, U., Zanetti, P., Vintan, L.: Performance and energy optimisation in cpus through fuzzy knowledge representation. Inf. Sci. (2018, in press)
8. Gruss, D., Lettner, J., Schuster, F., Ohrimenko, O., Haller, I., Costa, M.: Strong and efficient cache side-channel protection using hardware transactional memory. In: 26th USENIX Security Symposium (USENIX Security 17), pp. 217–233. USENIX Association, Vancouver (2017)
9. Hennessy, J.L., Patterson, D.A.: Computer Architecture: A Quantitative Approach, 6th edn. Morgan Kaufmann, Burlington (2017)
10. Intel Corporation: Improving real-time performance by utilizing cache allocation technology. White paper (2015)
11. Irazoqui, G., Eisenbarth, T., Sunar, B.: S$A: a shared cache attack that works across cores and defies VM sandboxing-and its application to AES. In: 2015 IEEE Symposium on Security and Privacy (SP), pp. 591–604. IEEE (2015)

12. Jaleel, A., Borch, E., Bhandaru, M., Steely, S.C.J., Emer, J.: Achieving non-inclusive cache performance with inclusive caches: temporal locality aware (TLA) cache management policies. In: Proceedings of the 2010 43rd Annual IEEE/ACM International Symposium on Microarchitecture, pp. 151–162. IEEE Computer Society (2010)
13. Kocher, P., et al.: Spectre attacks: exploiting speculative execution. arXiv preprint arXiv:1801.01203 (2018)
14. Lipp, M., et al.: Meltdown. arXiv preprint arXiv:1801.01207 (2018)
15. Liu, F., et al.: CATalyst: defeating last-level cache side channel attacks in cloud computing. In: 2016 IEEE International Symposium on High Performance Computer Architecture (HPCA), pp. 406–418. IEEE (2016)
16. Liu, F., Yarom, Y., Ge, Q., Heiser, G., Lee, R.B.: Last-level cache side-channel attacks are practical. In: 2015 IEEE Symposium on Security and Privacy (SP), pp. 605–622. IEEE (2015)
17. Page, D.: Partitioned cache architecture as a side-channel defence mechanism. IACR Cryptology ePrint archive 2005(280) (2005)
18. Percival, C.: Cache missing for fun and profit. In: BSDCan2005, Ottawa, Canada (2005)
19. Qin, H.: When partitioning works and when it doesn't: an empirical study on cache way partitioning. In: Zu, Q., Hu, B. (eds.) HCC 2017. LNCS, vol. 10745, pp. 595–607. Springer, Cham (2018). https://doi.org/10.1007/978-3-319-74521-3_62
20. Vintan, L.: About some security niches in present-day microprocessors (in Romanian, asupra unor brese de securitate in microprocesoarele actuale). Buletinul AGIR XXIII(2), 55–65 (2018)
21. Wang, Z., Lee, R.B.: New cache designs for thwarting software cache-based side channel attacks. In: ACM SIGARCH Computer Architecture News, vol. 35, no. 2, pp. 494–505. ACM (2007)
22. Wang, Z., Lee, R.B.: A novel cache architecture with enhanced performance and security. In: Proceedings of the 41st Annual IEEE/ACM International Symposium on Microarchitecture, pp. 83–93. IEEE Computer Society (2008)
23. Yarom, Y., Falkner, K.: Flush+Reload: a high resolution, low noise, L3 cache side-channel attack. In: 23rd USENIX Security Symposium (USENIX Security 14), pp. 719–732. USENIX Association, San Diego (2014)
24. Ye, C., Ding, C., Luo, H., Brock, J., Chen, D., Jin, H.: Cache exclusivity and sharing: theory and optimization. ACM Trans. Archit. Code Optim. (TACO) 14(4), 34 (2017)
25. Yu, C., Petrov, P.: Off-chip memory bandwidth minimization through cache partitioning for multi-core platforms. In: 2010 47th ACM/IEEE Design Automation Conference (DAC), pp. 132–137. IEEE (2010)
26. Zhang, Y., Juels, A., Oprea, A., Reiter, M.K.: HomeAlone: co-residency detection in the cloud via side-channel analysis. In: 2011 IEEE symposium on security and privacy, pp. 313–328. IEEE (2011)

GER-EN – GNSS Error Reduction Using an Elastic Network Based on V2V and LiDAR

Walter Balzano[✉] and Fabio Vitale

Università degli Studi di Napoli Federico II, Naples, Italy
walter.balzano@unina.it, fvitale86@gmail.com

Abstract. Vehicle2Vehicle is an emerging and promising research area, with several applications in IoT and in self-driving vehicles. It allows vehicle to establish ad-hoc connections for information sharing and improve users security while driving. V2V systems are strongly dependent on localization accuracy. In a common outdoor scenario, it is possible to use satellite-based navigation systems in order to determine user position in space, but the accuracy may vary due to interferences and when the sky visibility is sub-optimal.

In this paper we present *GER-EN – GNSS Error Reduction using an Elastic Network based on V2V and LiDAR*, a novel methodology for reducing satellite-based systems error using a combination of V2V, LiDAR-based distances and an elastic graph generated by the vehicles in the area.

Keywords: Vehicle-2-Vehicle · LiDAR
Global Navigation Satellite System

1 Introduction

Latest developments in computation-enabled devices has contributed to the diffusion of dynamic and powerful networks of physical devices able to communicate and exchange information. These kind of devices are well known under the name of Internet of Things (IoT), and are getting increasing interest from the literature for their potential. One of the most interesting application of IoT is in vehicular embedded devices, allowing vehicles to sense and communicate security warnings about traffic [13,16] and road conditions (like accidents, closed roads, works in progress etc.). These technologies have even higher importance considering self-driving vehicles.

Several application of V2V [3,4,6,8,12,14,15] technologies also depend on localization accuracy, which is still not satisfactory in several common situation, for instance inside urban canyons and in indoor scenarios. Several methodologies have been proposed in this regard, like using wireless positioning [9–11] (WPS) or inertial positioning using several kind of sensors (gyroscopes, accelerometers and digital compass) known as Inertial Navigation Systems (INS)[5].

© Springer Nature Switzerland AG 2018
A. Castiglione et al. (Eds.): CSS 2018, LNCS 11161, pp. 124–131, 2018.
https://doi.org/10.1007/978-3-030-01689-0_10

Global Navigation Satellite Systems (GNSS), which are nowadays quite common in modern personal devices like smartphones and tablets, allow good positioning accuracy for several application like navigation, location-based services and photo geo-tagging, but may have precision issues (up to 30 m) in narrow urban canyons and situations in which the sky visibility is limited.

Elastic graphs are graphs in which the edges are able to alter their length with regards to forces applied to the nodes. We can have *pulling* and *pushing* forces, which alter the direction in which the connected nodes tend to move. Pulling forces try to reduce the distance between the nodes, while pushing forces try to increase the distance. All the forces are applied iteratively until the system reaches a balance, which in turn is the most accurate solution.

In this paper we present GER-EN, a novel methodology which aims to improve GNSS-based localization precision. We use a smart combination of GNSS error estimation, LiDAR sensors and an elastic graph in order to reduce satellite-based error over time. In our model, we use LiDAR-detected distances and GPS error as forces in an elastic graph in order to find the best possible solution is a short time frame.

Related Works

LiDAR-based systems are having a lot of attention in current literature. In *A lidar and vision-based approach for pedestrian and vehicle detection and tracking*[22], authors present an architecture able to detect, track and classify entities in outdoor scenarios using LiDAR sensors. In *Sensorfusion using spatio-temporal aligned video and lidar for improved vehicle detection*[18], authors provide a novel approach to cross-calibrate automotive vision and ranging sensors in real time. In *Model based vehicle detection and tracking for autonomous urban driving*[21] authors provide a method which allows detection and tracking of moving vehicle in the road, which is extremely important for self-driving vehicles.

Vehicle-2-Vehicle and other IoT applications are also getting high interest from the research. In *Scudware*[23], authors present a complex system which allows communication between entities in a smart vehicle space, while in *Making cars a main ICT resource in smart cities*[1] authors consider using cars and other roadside infrastructures for processing power and storage. In *A cloud-based architecture for emergency management and first responders localization in smart city environments*[20] authors present a hybrid cloud infrastructure which allows management of resources in emergency scenarios, with an additional localization methodology which uses sensors (properly placed by first responders) and motion sensors.

With regards to user movement, in *Hybrid indoor and outdoor location services for new generation mobile terminals*[17], authors provide a novel hybrid location approach which chooses and switches between available localization methodologies in the surrounding area, while also being dynamic and transparent to the user.

Finally, in *Hypaco – a new model for hybrid paths compression of geodetic tracks*[7] authors provide a high-quality method for compression of geodetic tracks which may be used in our project to store traffic analysis for statistical purposes.

Outline

The rest of the paper is organized as follows: in Sect. 2 we present the well known V2V and LiDAR technologies used by our framework, then in Sect. 3 we present our project and detail the procedure used, finally in Sect. 4 we have some conclusions and some suggestions for future work opportunities.

2 V2V and LiDAR

In this preliminary section we introduce the well-known concepts of **V**ehicle-**2**-**V**ehicle (V2V) and **L**ight **D**etection **A**nd **R**anging (LiDAR) as the main ingredients of our framework, which will be described in the next section.

Vehicle-2-Vehicle (V2V) systems are wireless networks, in which all vehicles are able to communicate and provide safety warnings and traffic information. Normally, they use GNSS and a wireless LAN module for communication up to 1000 m range. Each node is also able to relay information to other vehicles, extending the effective communication range.

Light detection and ranging (LiDAR) is a method that measures distances illuminating the target using a pulsed laser and reading the reflected pulses with a sensor. Commonly used nowadays for obstacle detection in self-driving vehicles, has rapidly increased in popularity in latest years due to the cost reduction for laser emitters and sensors. With regards to RADAR systems, LiDAR offers a much wider field of view, provides cleaner measurements but also has higher cost and is more sensible to rain, snow and dust.

3 GER-EN Proposal

In this paper we describe GER-EN, a framework which uses vehicle-2-vehicle and LiDAR in order to improve current GNSS-based localization.

Each second, all the vehicles detect and measure their distance with regards to nearby visible cars using LiDAR. These distances are then shared via V2V and are compared, in order to determine elastic network edges.

The framework performs several operations:

1. LiDAR scans nearby area looking for vehicles;
2. for each vehicle, minimum distance is evaluated;
3. distances are shared among nearby vehicles in order to find matches, i.e. $md(A, B) = md(B, A)$ where md is the minimum-distance function;
4. minimum distance is applied to the GNSS-generated elastic graph;
5. the elastic graph iteratively tries to balance the distances in order to find the most accurate solution.

Correction c is calculated as the difference between GNSS distance d_G and LiDAR distance d_L:

$$\forall A, B \in V \quad c = d_G(A, B) - d_L(A, B) \tag{1}$$

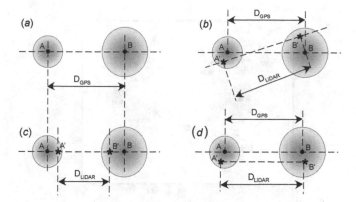

Fig. 1. When LiDAR is added to GPS-only distance (a), we may have rotations (b), difference in measured distances (c), translations (d) or any combination of (b, c, d).

and is applied proportionally to relative GNSS deviation GD:

$$GD_A = k \cdot GD_B \quad c_A = k \cdot c_B \quad c = c_A + c_B \tag{2}$$

We decided to use the concept of elastic network in order to further improve positioning correction. In fact, with only two vehicles, any correction may be inaccurate: rotation and translation of the line between the vehicle centers cannot be determined. In Fig. 1 we can see several possible errors using only two points: in (a) we only have GNSS positions and distance, but when we add LiDAR measurement we may have 8 situations:

- in (b) vehicles centers line is rotated;
- in (c) vehicles centers line is correct but LiDAR shows a different distance;
- in (d) vehicles centers line is translated;
- any combination of (b), (c) and (d).

When only two vehicles are present, for simplicity we will consider only (b) as an option.

However, having more than two vehicles allows us to address this issue using a polymorphism with an elastic network, granting better positioning and error correction. In this elastic network there are two forces: one caused by the GNSS localization and one from LiDAR distance estimations.

3.1 GNSS Forces

In the proposed model, we exploit the GNSS ability to find its own estimated error range. Inside the elastic network, this acts as a force which pulls the vehicle toward the center of the error area, i.e. the estimated GNSS localization, as this is the most probable location for the user. Since we assume the error evaluation

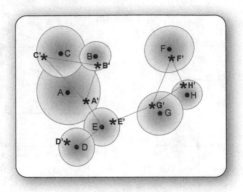

Fig. 2. With several vehicles in the area, we can use an elastic network in order to better estimate car positions. All the LiDAR-measured distances are used as forces on graph edges, incrementally moving vehicles to their correct position.

is correct, this force rapidly grows toward the edge of the error radius:

$$F_G = \begin{cases} \frac{d}{e-d+1} & \text{for } d \le e \\ \infty & \text{for } d > e \end{cases} \tag{3}$$

The second rule is set in order to avoid a limit condition on forces which may take the user positioning outside the maximum GNSS range, which we assume is fully accurate.

3.2   LiDAR Forces

LiDAR forces are calculated based on detected vehicular distances. They strongly depend on the difference between GNSS-evaluated distance and the true distance as measured by the LiDAR system. There are three distinct situations:

- LiDAR distance matches GNSS-evaluated distance: no LiDAR force is applied;
- LiDAR distance is shorter than GNSS-evaluated one: in this case we have a *pulling force*, which tries to draw the two element closer;
- LiDAR distance is higher than the GNSS-evaluated one: in this case we have a *pushing force*, which tries to repel the two elements.

LiDAR force module (F_L) is proportional to the difference between the LiDAR-evaluated distance and the GNSS-evaluated distance, multiplied by k, an elastic coefficient:

$$F_L = \frac{(d_L - d_I) \cdot k}{2} \tag{4}$$

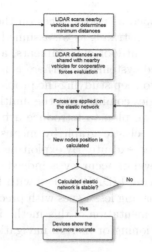

Fig. 3. Procedure flowchart, as detailed in Subsect. 3.3. The procedure is repeated as long as the GPS receiver is active.

3.3   System Behavior

We are now going to detail each step of the aforementioned procedure.

The first network building is made by V2V in cooperation with each GNSS receiver.

Each vehicle then scans the nearby area using LiDAR and detect nearby nodes minimum distances, which are broadcasted via V2V to nearby cars.

This step determines LiDAR forces, while GNSS forces are currently null (since all elements are still in their GNSS-detected position).

This allows us to build the first iteration of the elastic graph, which only uses LiDAR forces. Forces are then balanced in order to find a better positioning for each node. With this new position, we are also able to calculate GNSS forces which can be applied in the next iteration. This balancing-evaluating iteration is repeated in order to find the best possible condition.

Each node is able to calculate its own forces, and therefore the network computation is distributed among the V2V nodes.

When a valid condition is found, the process restarts from the first step. From the user perspective, it only stops when the GPS tracking is disabled, but the on-board unit may still help nearby vehicles positioning using the last known position and the LiDAR sensor.

4   Conclusions and Future Work

In this paper we presented GER-EN, which aims to reduce GNSS-based localization error using a smart combination of LiDAR sensors and an elastic network. LiDAR sensors are very precise in evaluating distances between objects and are therefore valuable when applied as nodes forces on the generated elastic graph, while GNSS error acts as a constraint, as we assumed it is totally reliable. This methodology only applies in outdoor environments, as indoor it is not possible to make use of satellite-based systems since there is no sky visibility.

As future work, we plan to keep studying the problem addressed in this paper by also applying methodologies coming form the multi-agent strategic reasoning area [2, 19]. More precisely, we plan to introduce a fresh multi-agent structure that is able to simulate the elastic graph by means of constraints along the possible actions the agents can execute. By exploiting such an approach, we aim at checking that a certain level of accuracy is indeed satisfied.

Moreover, we plan replacing LiDAR sensors with RADAR, since they share similar accuracy while also having less issues with precipitations. It is also worth considering a different implementation of this method for indoor situations, for instance using wireless positioning or inertial navigation systems.

References

1. Altintas, O., Dressler, F., Hagenauer, F., Matsumoto, M., Sepulcre, M., Sommery, C.: Making cars a main ICT resource in smart cities. In: 2015 IEEE Conference on Computer Communications Workshops (INFOCOM WKSHPS), pp. 582–587. IEEE (2015)
2. Aminof, B., Murano, A., Rubin, S., Zuleger, F.: Verification of asynchronous mobile-robots in partially-known environments. In: Chen, Q., Torroni, P., Villata, S., Hsu, J., Omicini, A. (eds.) PRIMA 2015. LNCS (LNAI), vol. 9387, pp. 185–200. Springer, Cham (2015). https://doi.org/10.1007/978-3-319-25524-8_12
3. Balzano, W., Barbieri, V., Riccardi, G.: Car2Car framework based on DDGP3. In: The 23rd International DMS Conference on Visual Languages and Sentient Systems (2017)
4. Balzano, W., Del Sorbo, M.R., Murano, A., Stranieri, S.: A logic-based clustering approach for cooperative traffic control systems. Advances on P2P, Parallel, Grid, Cloud and Internet Computing. LNDECT, vol. 1, pp. 737–746. Springer, Cham (2017). https://doi.org/10.1007/978-3-319-49109-7_71
5. Balzano, W., Formisano, M., Gaudino, L.: WiFiNS: a smart method to improve positioning systems combining WiFi and INS techniques. In: De Pietro, G., Gallo, L., Howlett, R.J., Jain, L.C. (eds.) KES-IIMSS 2017. SIST, vol. 76, pp. 220–231. Springer, Cham (2018). https://doi.org/10.1007/978-3-319-59480-4_23
6. Balzano, W., Murano, A., Stranieri, S.: Logic-based clustering approach for management and improvement of VANETs. J. High Speed Netw. **23**(3), 225–236 (2017)
7. Balzano, W., Murano, A., Vitale, F.: Hypaco-a new model for hybrid paths compression of geodetic tracks. In: CCPS-2016: The International Conference on Data Compression, Communication, Processing and Security (2016)
8. Balzano, W., Murano, A., Vitale, F.: V2V-EN-Vehicle-2-Vehicle elastic network. Proc. Comput. Sci. **98**, 497–502 (2016)
9. Balzano, W., Murano, A., Vitale, F.: WiFACT-wireless fingerprinting automated continuous training. In: 2016 30th International Conference on Advanced Information Networking and Applications Workshops (WAINA), pp. 75–80. IEEE (2016)

10. Balzano, W., Murano, A., Vitale, F.: EENET: energy efficient detection of NET-work changes using a wireless sensor network. In: Barolli, L., Terzo, O. (eds.) CISIS 2017. AISC, vol. 611, pp. 1009–1018. Springer, Cham (2018). https://doi.org/10.1007/978-3-319-61566-0_95

11. Balzano, W., Murano, A., Vitale, F.: Snot-WiFi: Sensor network-optimized training for wireless fingerprinting. J. High Speed Netw. **24**(1), 79–87 (2018)

12. Balzano, W., Stranieri, S.: LoDGP: a framework for support traffic information systems based on logic paradigm. In: Xhafa, F., Caballé, S., Barolli, L. (eds.) 3PGCIC 2017. LNDECT, vol. 13, pp. 700–708. Springer, Cham (2018). https://doi.org/10.1007/978-3-319-69835-9_66

13. Balzano, W., Vitale, F.: DGP application for support traffic information systems in indoor and outdoor environments. In: Xhafa, F., Caballé, S., Barolli, L. (eds.) 3PGCIC 2017. LNDECT, vol. 13, pp. 692–699. Springer, Cham (2018). https://doi.org/10.1007/978-3-319-69835-9_65

14. Balzano, W., Vitale, F.: DiG-park: a smart parking availability searching method using V2V/V2I and DGP-class problem. In: 2017 31st International Conference on Advanced Information Networking and Applications Workshops (WAINA), pp. 698–703. IEEE (2017)

15. Balzano, W., Vitale, F.: PAM-SAD: ubiquitous car parking availability model based on V2V and smartphone activity detection. In: De Pietro, G., Gallo, L., Howlett, R.J., Jain, L.C. (eds.) KES-IIMSS 2017. SIST, vol. 76, pp. 232–240. Springer, Cham (2018). https://doi.org/10.1007/978-3-319-59480-4_24

16. Dhondge, K., Song, S., Choi, B.Y., Park, H.: WiFiHonk: smartphone-based beacon stuffed WiFi Car2X-communication system for vulnerable road user safety. In: 2014 IEEE 79th Vehicular Technology Conference (VTC Spring), pp. 1–5. IEEE (2014)

17. Ficco, M., Palmieri, F., Castiglione, A.: Hybrid indoor and outdoor location services for new generation mobile terminals. Pers. Ubiquit. Comput. **18**(2), 271–285 (2014)

18. Mahlisch, M., Schweiger, R., Ritter, W., Dietmayer, K.: Sensorfusion using spatio-temporal aligned video and lidar for improved vehicle detection. In: 2006 IEEE Intelligent Vehicles Symposium, pp. 424–429. IEEE (2006)

19. Murano, A., Perelli, G., Rubin, S.: Multi-agent path planning in known dynamic environments. In: Chen, Q., Torroni, P., Villata, S., Hsu, J., Omicini, A. (eds.) PRIMA 2015. LNCS (LNAI), vol. 9387, pp. 218–231. Springer, Cham (2015). https://doi.org/10.1007/978-3-319-25524-8_14

20. Palmieri, F., Ficco, M., Pardi, S., Castiglione, A.: A cloud-based architecture for emergency management and first responders localization in smart city environments. Comput. Electr. Eng. **56**, 810–830 (2016)

21. Petrovskaya, A., Thrun, S.: Model based vehicle detection and tracking for autonomous urban driving. Auton. Robots **26**(2–3), 123–139 (2009)

22. Premebida, C., Monteiro, G., Nunes, U., Peixoto, P.: A lidar and vision-based approach for pedestrian and vehicle detection and tracking. In: IEEE Intelligent Transportation Systems Conference, ITSC 2007, pp. 1044–1049. IEEE (2007)

23. Wu, Z., Wu, Q., Cheng, H., Pan, G., Zhao, M., Sun, J.: ScudWare: a semantic and adaptive middleware platform for smart vehicle space. IEEE Trans. Intell. Transp. Syst. **8**(1), 121–132 (2007)

A Dynamic Security Policies Generation Model for Access Control in Smart Card Based Applications

B. B. Gupta$^{(\boxtimes)}$ and Megha Quamara

National Institute of Technology Kurukshetra, Kurukshetra, India
gupta.brij@gmail.com

Abstract. Significant increase in the use of smart cards in diverse set of real-time applications has lead to the proliferation of number of attack scenarios including physical and logical attacks. Since the security of smart card based systems and applications depends upon the security of smart cards being a key element of communication, it provokes researchers from enterprises and academia to come forward and to exchange their ideas to ensure security of these systems. To authenticate different users in different application scenarios requires the development of security policies that can effectively satisfy the heterogeneous security requirements. In this paper, we propose a contextual security policy generation model for applications involving authentication using smart cards. The paper illuminates the factors that are crucial in determining a dynamic set of security policies. We also implement our model on Access Control Policy Testing (ACPT) tool in order to test and verify its correctness.

Keywords: Security policies · Smart cards · Access control · Authentication
ACPT

1 Introduction

Smart cards have entered the global market seamlessly regardless of the geographical and industry specific barriers. There is a noticeable increase in the use of smart cards as an alternate to conventional mechanisms of security, such as passwords, barcodes, magnetic cards etc., due to the advancements in the underlying technological paradigms, such as Internet of Things (IoT), Near Field Communication (NFC), Machine-to-Machine (M2M) communication etc. They are being used in multiple application domains for storage, processing and exchange of information. They provide a convenient way of doing online transactions in a secure manner.

Remote user authentication mechanisms provide a mean to verify the identity of the users in insecure communication scenarios to ensure that only legitimate users are able to access the resources and therefore, have become an essential part of smart card based applications to restrict illegal access. Protection of remote user authentication mechanisms from standard ways of compromise including physical and logical attacks must be ensured in order to satisfy the security and privacy of the applications, services and

A. Castiglione et al. (Eds.): CSS 2018, LNCS 11161, pp. 132–143, 2018.
https://doi.org/10.1007/978-3-030-01689-0_11

the authentication data being transmitted. In other words, to preserve the integrity of the authentication process, each and every component of the authentication system needs protection.

With increasing user dependency, imposition of security policies during user authentication has become crucial in order to ensure the security of smart card based systems and applications. Security policies associated with access control determines which entity of the system has access to what resources. However, with diverse set of applications having varying levels of security requirements, which in turn depend on a number of factors, implementing a security policy model is a complicated task. Misconfigurations in policies may lead to unexpected consequences that include allowing a malicious user to access critical resources of the system or denying access to the legitimate users. In such scenarios, it is required to develop an integrated model which can work in compliance with these security levels, thereby encapsulating the security requirements of the system. In this paper, we propose a security policy generation model for smart card based applications having different levels of security requirements. We also implement and verify the correctness of the model over Access Control Policy Testing (ACPT) tool.

Rest of the paper is organized as follows. Section 2 discusses the different application areas of smart cards. Section 3 discusses the related work. Section 4 covers the proposed security policy generation model in detail. Section 5 contains the implementation results of our proposed model. Finally, Sect. 6 concludes the paper.

2   Application Areas of Smart Cards

Industries across the world are leveraging the benefits of smart cards in diverse applications and products, thereby promoting an integration of smart cards in our everyday lives. Improving convenience of transactions, enhanced security against wide range of security attacks, tamper-proof storage, reliability, durability, lower cost of system maintenance, adaptability, portability, on-the-chip processing and intuitive user interface are some of the salient advantages of using smart cards in these applications over traditional mechanisms of security and authentication.

Some of the key applications of smart cards are discussed as follows:

1. Healthcare – Smart cards are being extensively used in healthcare applications and are termed as eHealth cards [1]. They provide a secure platform to authenticate a patient by storing patient specific information over the card itself. They enable portable storage and online distribution of patient's health records in compliance with Government initiatives and standards.
2. Transportation and Public Transits – Public transit agencies are utilizing smart cards for automated fare collection and parking fee payment as they offer fraud resistance, flexibility and speed of transactions. A corporate information system validates the use of smart cards through a network and stores the data of each transaction for financial processing. Integrated Transport Smartcard Organization (ITSO) and Calypso Network of Associations are two well known standard making organizations for use of smart cards in transportation industry [2].

3. Banking – With Europay-Mastercard-Visa (EMV) cards and standards for PIN based security gaining momentum across the world, smart cards have acquired a prime place in fund transfer applications over the Internet [3]. Debit cards and credit cards not only offer high level of security, but also support offline transactions, PIN management, user authentication and risk management.
4. Telecommunications – Use of Subscriber Identity Modules (SIM) cards under Global System for Mobile Communication (GSM) standard is one of the most prominent application of smart cards [4]. A unique identification value is stored over the SIM which is associated with a particular user subscribed to a particular network.
5. User Identification (Physical and Logical Access Control) – Government, Private and Defense organizations across the world are making use of smart cards as identity cards for the identification of individuals to ensure legitimate access to systems, data, specific locations and other resources. These days, national ID cards and passports contain smart chips embedded in them that are accessible during the normal travelling [5]. Identity details of the person are stored on the card which are then scanned and checked to prove the legitimacy of the user.
6. Multi-media – Satellite TV is an example multi-media application where smart cards are used to access audio or video programs that are broadcasted by remote service providers [6]. Direct-To-Home (DTH) cards provide accessibility to the services and information coming from the satellites.

Other application areas include e-commerce, retail, e-ticketing etc. Figure 1 shows the forecasts of smart card deployment in various applications across the world for the year 2018 [7].

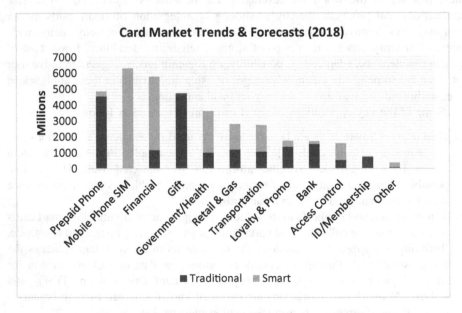

Fig. 1. Global card market trends and forecasts (2018).

3   Related Work

Sharp et al. [8] described a policy-based framework to define the privileges for the logical entities of a system to perform system-wide operations associated with elements over which access control has been imposed by considering different security levels and protocols for performing these operations. Belanche-Gracia et al. [9] proposed a theoretical model considering security and privacy as the key determinants reflecting the use of smart cards in smart cities. Among all the factors described in the model, the level of personal interaction with the services was also considered as an expansion force for this technology.

Peltier et al. [10] defined the key attributes of organizational information security policies including understandability, applicability, compliance with organizational objectives, enforceable and proactivity. Celdrán et al. [11] proposed a contextual framework called Semantic Web-based Context Management (SeCoMan) for the development of smart applications policies including operational, location and authorization policies for the users.

Guccione et al. [12] proposed a smart card product having independent functionalities for security domain and domain manager. The security domain is responsible for defining the privileges based on the level of trust with the external stakeholder, while the domain manager is responsible for the enforcement of security policies based on the received privileges. Narasinghanallur et al. [13] proposed a model which implements role based access control policies based on the parameters and conditions of the application environment.

4   Proposed Security Policy Generation Model

In this section, we discuss our proposed dynamic security policy generation model in detail. We outline the key factors that are responsible for defining the security policies for diverse set of applications, and lastly, we describe the phases involved in our model.

4.1   Determining Factors

A policy is a security governance tool which defines a course of actions that are adopted by the organizations to manage their resource usage. Security policy formulation is a multi-faceted task and a single policy cannot fit with all the applications. While generating security policies for different applications, following factors play a major role:

1. Organizational or Enterprise Decisions – An organization hosting an application over its private or public server can determine the level of security required to access that particular application based on which it can define, enforce and automate the access control policy statements.
2. Previous Login Sessions – The frequency with which the user has logged into a particular application and user habits also determine the security policies.

3. Subject Attributes – Security policies also depend on the role of user trying to log into a particular application which includes age of the user, clearance, associated department, job title, and so on.
4. Action Attributes – Security policies can also be determined based on the type of action being attempted by the user. A user may try to simply access the data, or manipulate the same which adds on to extra security.
5. Resource Attributes – Security policies are also determined based on the application being accessed. The application may be highly security intensive, such as online banking and may deal with critical data which demands for extra security and hence, strict policies are defined for them.
6. Contextual or Environmental Factors – These factors include the date of login, time of login, location from which that application has been logged in and other dynamic aspects, such as IP address, MAC address, and so on.

4.2 Phases Involved in Policy Development

The methodologies and the practices for the development of security policies differ from organization to organization which in turn depends on the determining factors as described in the previous sub-section. In this sub-section, we present a general model for the development of security policies for smart-card based applications [14]. The model comprises of following phases as shown in Fig. 2:

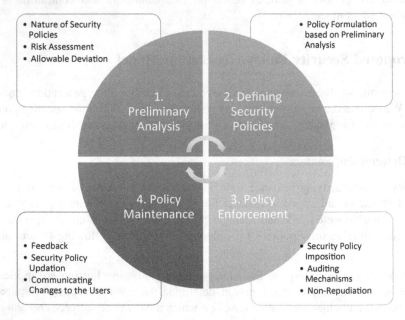

Fig. 2. Phases involved in security policy development.

Phase 1: Preliminary Analysis – This phase involves determining the nature of security policies that are needed to be developed by analyzing the nature of application, security level required for that application, nature of resources, organizational model, nature of users, organization activities, and other factors as defined in the previous subsection. In addition, the implications of not carrying out activities according to the security policies, risk assessment and allowable range of deviations are also considered.

Phase 2: Defining Security Policies – In this phase, security policies are defined based on the preliminary analysis.

Phase 3: Policy Enforcement – It involves imposition of security policies over the network for a particular application and the associated events or actions that are taken in case of non-compliance with the policy. The received user's credentials are checked to allow or deny access for a particular application or service. Auditing mechanisms and services to ensure non-repudiation can be employed for managing enforcement of policies. Figure 3 shows the steps that are involved during the policy enforcement phase that are described as follows:

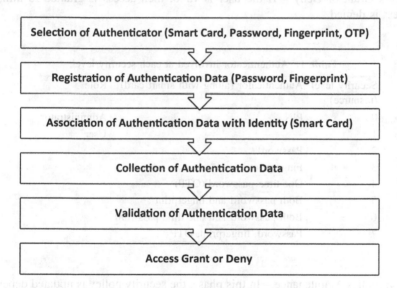

Fig. 3. Steps in policy enforcement phase.

1. Selection of Authenticator – In remote user authentication mechanism for smart card based applications, the data used for the authentication of user is called as authenticator or factor, and can be one or more out of the following:

   - Something the user knows i.e. password, One Time Password (OTP), Personal Identification Number (PIN).
   - Something the user has i.e. smart card.
   - Something the user is i.e. fingerprints.

   In our proposed model, with increasing level of security, requirement of user authenticator for a particular application becomes more rigid as shown in Table 1.

However, for the role of administrator, a PIN value along with smart card is required to access and manage the applications and services which may be computed using different identifying parameters including user's biometrics, passwords etc.

2. Registration of Authentication Data – In this step, the data associated with the respective authenticator is collected from the users based on which registration of the user is done. In our model, we consider user's password and fingerprints for the registration.

3. Association of Authentication Data with Identity – A smart card is issued to the user which contains unique information that can be used to identify that user.

4. Collection of Authentication Data – Once the smart card is issued to the user, it can be utilized to access the application. The user enters the required credentials through the application which is collected at the server side.

5. Validation of Authentication Data – The collected data is then matched with already stored one to verify its correctness and to validate the identity of the user.

6. Access Grant or Deny – If the user is valid, then access is granted to him, else access is denied.

Table 1. Authenticator involved at each security level.

Security level (resource)	Authenticator (along with smart card)	Role
0	PIN	Administrator
1	–	User
2	Password	
3	Fingerprint	
4	One time password (OTP)	
5	Both password and fingerprint	
6	Both password and one time password	
7	Password, fingerprint, OTP	

Phase 4: Policy Maintenance – In this phase, the security policy is updated depending upon the arrival of new applications and user feedback. It involves reviewing and evaluating the changes (technical, organizational and legal) periodically, and the ways to communicate these changes to the users. In group based communication, change in policies can be distributed to the users using group communication schemes [15].

5   Result and Discussion

In this section, we discuss the results obtained from the execution of our proposed model along with a comparison of the same with other related schemes on the basis of different parameters.

5.1   Access Control Policy Testing (ACPT) Tool

ACPT tool was developed by National Institute of Standards and Technology – Computer Science Division (NIST-CSD) as a prototype system for policy specification, implementation and verification [16]. It is a Java based tool which provides Graphical User Interface (GUI) templates for defining access control policies, and a Symbolic Model Verification (SMV) model checker for checking access control policy models [17]. It also provides NIST's Automated Combinatorial Testing for Software (ACTS) tool for generating test suite. Once the model is verified, the output is generated in eXtensible Access Control Markup Language (XACML) format.

5.2   Implementation Results

Access Control Policy Modelling. In our model, we use Attribute Based Access Control to define the security policies. We utilize the Graphical User Interface (GUI) provided by the ACPT tool to specify the properties associated with the access control policies. Table 2 shows the initial parameter values for this model.

Two subjects have been considered for smart card based applications – user and administrator. The user credentials that are used for controlling the access to the system services are smart card (SC), password (PW), fingerprint (FP) and one-time password (OTP) which is received on the registered mobile number or email address of the user. Similarly, the administrator who is responsible for managing the access control tasks provides the smart card SC and a security PIN to enter the system or the application. Different security levels S_L are defined ranging from integral values 0 to 7 with different credential requirements. The application with S_L = 1 is least security sensitive, while the one with S_L = 7 deals with highly secured information. S_L = 0 is kept for identifying the administrator.

Table 2. Initial parameters setting.

Parameters	Attributes	Attribute type	Attribute values
Subject	Role	String	User, Administrator
Resource	S_L	Integer	0, 1, 2, 3, 4, 5, 6, 7
Action	SC, PW, OTP, FP, PIN	String	PROVIDED, NOT_PROVIDED
Environment	VALUES	String	VALID, INVALID

Policy Implementation. After defining the policies, XACML representation is created by mapping the attributes considered in the policies to the corresponding XACML attributes. Figure 4 shows a sample rule for the security policy of the proposed model in XACML format.

```
<Rule RuleId="rule_16" Effect="Deny">
    <Target>
        <Subjects>
            <Subject>
                <SubjectMatch MatchId="urn:oasis:names:tc:xacml:1.0:function:string-equal">
                    <AttributeValue DataType="http://www.w3.org/2001/XMLSchema#string">Administrator</AttributeValue>
                    <SubjectAttributeDesignator SubjectCategory="urn:oasis:names:tc:xacml:1.0:subject-category:access-subject" AttributeId="Role" DataType="http://
www.w3.org/2001/XMLSchema#string"/>
                </SubjectMatch>
            </Subject>
        </Subjects>
        <Resources>
            <Resource>
                <ResourceMatch MatchId="urn:oasis:names:tc:xacml:1.0:function:integer-equal">
                    <AttributeValue DataType="http://www.w3.org/2001/XMLSchema#integer">0</AttributeValue>
                    <ResourceAttributeDesignator AttributeId="S_L" DataType="http://www.w3.org/2001/XMLSchema#integer"/>
                </ResourceMatch>
            </Resource>
        </Resources>
        <Actions>
            <Action>
                <ActionMatch MatchId="urn:oasis:names:tc:xacml:1.0:function:string-equal">
                    <AttributeValue DataType="http://www.w3.org/2001/XMLSchema#string">NOT_PROVIDED</AttributeValue>
                    <ActionAttributeDesignator AttributeId="SC" DataType="http://www.w3.org/2001/XMLSchema#string"/>
                </ActionMatch>
            </Action>
            <Action>
                <ActionMatch MatchId="urn:oasis:names:tc:xacml:1.0:function:string-equal">
                    <AttributeValue DataType="http://www.w3.org/2001/XMLSchema#string">NOT_PROVIDED</AttributeValue>
                    <ActionAttributeDesignator AttributeId="PIN" DataType="http://www.w3.org/2001/XMLSchema#string"/>
                </ActionMatch>
            </Action>
        </Actions>
    </Target>
</Rule>
```

Fig. 4. XACML representation of defined policies.

Policy Verification. Verification of the policies is done once they have been implemented which involves static and dynamic verification.

Static Verification or Property Verification. Static verification involves checking whether the properties of a policy are satisfied or not, in order to ensure correct behavior of the policy. NuSMV is used for this purpose which verifies a policy P against its properties p_i, where p_i is a logical formula to determine whether a particular state is reachable or not for a given set of constraints. NuSMV checks for any state violating the properties of a policy by reporting with counterexamples.

Dynamic Verification or Test-Input Generation. In dynamic verification, correctness of policies in a system is verified based on the output of the test inputs which is compared with the expected output. Thus, dynamic verification adds additional level of confidence to the correctness of the policy by executing test inputs and act as complimentary for static verification. These test inputs are based on both structural and combinatorial coverage which reduces the size of the test suite and at the same time provides sufficient level of confidence for policy correctness. While the structural test input generation is called as white-box testing, combinatorial test input generation is called as black-box testing.

Figure 5 shows the results of the verification of proposed security policy model in ACPT tool. The results that are shown here cover 3 test cases out of a total of 16 test cases. Based on the access decisions of these results, i.e. Permit and Deny, we can compare them with the intended results, i.e. whether access should be granted or denied. Table 3 shows the execution time of static and dynamic verification for the proposed model. For static verification, running time is 203 ms, while for dynamic verification, it is 0.109 s.

Fig. 5. Policy verification results in ACPT.

Table 3. Results.

Verification	Running/execution time
Static verification	203 ms
Dynamic verification	0.109 s

5.3 Comparison with Existing Work

Table 4 shows the comparison of the proposed work with some of the existing works discussed in Sect. 3.

Table 4. Comparison of the proposed work with existing work.

Schemes	Operational environment	Access control model used	Access control determinants	Verification through implementation
Sharp et al. [8]	Wireless environment	General	Security element	✗
Belanche-Gracia et al. [9]	Smart card in smart city applications	General	Privacy and security of users, and level of interaction with services	✗
Celdrán et al. [11]	Context-aware smart applications	Role-based	Operational, authorization and location	✓
Guccione et al. [12]	Smart card for wireless communications	General	Trust level among external stakeholders	✗
Narasinghanallur et al. [13]	Applications in data processing systems	Role-based	Application environment	✓
Proposed work	Smart card applications	Attribute-based	Password, fingerprints, OTP, PIN	✓

6 Conclusion and Future Scope

With the advancements in computing and networking facilities, along with the advent of different technological paradigms, such as NFC, IoT etc., smart card based applications are gaining more importance in user domain due to the convenience of transactions they provide. User authentication mechanisms are adopted to ensure legitimate access to the resources associated with these applications, and organizations define security policies as safeguard for their successful execution. However, with varying levels of security requirements, implementation of security policies becomes complex.

In this paper, a dynamic security policy generation model is proposed in order to develop security policies for user authentication mechanisms in smart card based applications. Key factors that are used to determine the security policies for the users are discussed along with the phases involved in the model. The proposed model is implemented on ACPT tool in order to prove its accuracy. In future, this work can be extended by assimilating machine learning concepts for generating policies for new users entering into the system and to dynamically update the credential requirements for a particular user with respect to a particular application [18, 19].

References

1. Favier, F.: Smart cards and healthcare. Card Technol. Today **19**(11–12), 10 (2007)
2. Pelletier, M.P., Trépanier, M., Morency, C.: Smart card data use in public transit: a literature review. Transp. Res. Part C: Emerg. Technol. **19**(4), 557–568 (2011)
3. Markantonakis, K., Main, D.: Smart cards for banking and finance. In: Mayes, K., Markantonakis, K. (eds.) Smart Cards, Tokens, Security and Applications, pp. 129–153. Springer, Cham (2017). https://doi.org/10.1007/978-3-319-50500-8_5
4. Rankl, W., Effing, W.: Smart Card Handbook, 3rd edn. Wiley, Hoboken (2004)
5. Arora, S.: National e-ID card schemes: a European overview. Inf. Secur. Tech. Rep. **13**(2), 46–53 (2008)
6. Mayes, K.: An introduction to smart cards. In: Mayes, K., Markantonakis, K. (eds.) Smart Cards, Tokens, Security and Applications, pp. 1–29. Springer, Cham (2017). https://doi.org/10.1007/978-3-319-50500-8_1
7. 2014–2018 Global Card Market Trends & Forecasts The Next 5 Years. https://icma.com/wp-content/uploads/2015/04/Al_V6-2014-2018-Trends-Forecasts.pdf. Accessed 11 Feb 2018
8. Sharp, C.B., et al.: U.S. Patent No. 9,098,714. U.S. Patent and Trademark Office, Washington, DC (2015)
9. Belanche-Gracia, D., Casaló-Ariño, L.V., Pérez-Rueda, A.: Determinants of multi-service smartcard success for smart cities development: a study based on citizens' privacy and security perceptions. Gov. Inf. Q. **32**(2), 154–163 (2015)
10. Peltier, T.R.: Information Security Policies, Procedures, and Standards: Guidelines for Effective Information Security Management. CRC Press, Boca Raton (2016)
11. Celdrán, A.H., Clemente, F.J.G., Pérez, M.G., Pérez, G.M.: SeCoMan: a semantic-aware policy framework for developing privacy-preserving and context-aware smart applications. IEEE Syst. J. **10**(3), 1111–1124 (2016)
12. Guccione, L.J., Meyerstein, M.V., Cha, I., Schmidt, A., Leicher, A., Shah, Y.C.: U.S. Patent No. 9,363,676. U.S. Patent and Trademark Office, Washington, DC (2016)

13. Narasinghanallur, J., Ho, M.H., Keefe, T., Sedlar, E., Chui, C.C., Pesati, V.: U.S. Patent No. 9,886,590. U.S. Patent and Trademark Office, Washington, DC (2018)
14. Wahe, S., Petersen, G.: Open Enterprise Security Architecture (O-ESA): A Framework and Template for Policy-Driven Security. Van Haren Publishing, Zaltbommel (2011)
15. Castiglione, A., D'Arco, P., De Santis, A., Russo, R.: Secure group communication schemes for dynamic heterogeneous distributed computing. Future Gener. Comput. Syst. **74**, 313–324 (2017)
16. NIST-Compter Security Resource Center. https://csrc.nist.gov/Projects/Access-Control-Policy-Tool. Accessed 25 Jan 2018
17. Hwang, J., Xie, T., Hu, V., Altunay, M.: ACPT: a tool for modeling and verifying access control policies. In: 2010 IEEE International Symposium on Policies for Distributed Systems and Networks (POLICY), pp. 40–43. IEEE (2010)
18. Castiglione, A., De Santis, A., Masucci, B., Palmieri, F., Huang, X., Castiglione, A.: Supporting dynamic updates in storage clouds with the Akl-Taylor scheme. Inf. Sci. **387**, 56–74 (2017)
19. Castiglione, A., De Santis, A., Masucci, B., Palmieri, F., Castiglione, A., Huang, X.: Cryptographic hierarchical access control for dynamic structures. IEEE Trans. Inf. Forensics Secur. **11**(10), 2349–2364 (2016)

An Advanced Methodology to Analyse Data Stored on Mobile Devices

Flora Amato[1], Giovanni Cozzolino[1(✉)], Antonino Mazzeo[1],
and Francesco Moscato[2]

[1] DIETI - Dipartimento di Ingegneria Elettrica e Tecnologie dell'Informazione,
Università degli studi di Napoli "Federico II", via Claudio 21, 80125 Naples, Italy
{flora.amato,giovanni.cozzolino,mazzeo}@unina.it
[2] Political Science Department "Jean Monnet",
University of Campania "Luigi Vanvitelli", Caserta, Italy
francesco.moscato@unicampania.it

Abstract. Nowadays computer and mobile devices, such as mobile phones, smartphones, smartwatches, tablets, etc., represent the multimedia diary of each of us. Thanks to technological evolution and the advent of an infinite number of applications, mainly aimed at socialization and entertainment, they have become the containers of an infinite number of personal and professional information. For this reason, optimizing the performance of systems able to detect intrusions (IDS - Intrusion Detection System) is a goal of common interest. This paper presents a methodology to classify hacking attacks taking advantage of the generalization property of neural networks. In particular, in this work we adopt the multilayer perceptron (MLP) model with the back-propagation algorithm and the sigmoidal activation function. We analyse the results obtained using different configurations for the neural network, varying the number of hidden layers and the number of training epochs in order to obtain a low number of false positives. The obtained results will be presented in terms of type of attacks and training epochs and we will show that the best classification is carried out for DOS and Probe attacks.

Keywords: Network security · Intrusion detection
Multilayer perceptron · Machine learning · Neural networks

1 Introduction

Today computer networks have a widespread distribution and daily people make use of a growing number of network services [13, 14] that are becoming even more pervasive. This has led, dually, to a security problem for devices connected to a network [22–24]. In order to find out attacks against information systems, there are many tools (hardware and/or software), called IDS (*Intrusion Detection System*) [7], designed to protect the accessibility of systems, the integrity and confidentiality of data.

A. Castiglione et al. (Eds.): CSS 2018, LNCS 11161, pp. 144–154, 2018.
https://doi.org/10.1007/978-3-030-01689-0_12

Based on the location in a network, IDS can be categorized into two groups:

- **NIDS:** Network IDS. They analyse the packets transmitted through the network looking for their *"signatures"* (set of conditions) and comparing them with those stored in a database [8]
- **HIDS:** Host-Based IDS. They operate directly on a machine detecting intrusions by monitoring the operating system through its log, the file system and hard drives, etc.

There are two main techniques of analysis adopted by a NIDS [8]:

- **Pattern Matching Based:** It determines intrusions by comparing an activity with known signatures. It has a *low* false positive rate but it does not allow to recognize new kinds of attack.
- **Anomaly Detection Based:** It determines intrusions by looking for anomalies in network traffic. It has a relatively *high* rate of false positives, but allows to detect new kinds of attack, not yet stored in the database.

Existing IDS, like *Snort*, a very popular and open-source network intrusion detection system, present a limitation related to the detection of new attacks, because the detection mechanism is based on *"signatures"*. In fact, they are not able to acquire new knowledge unless the system administrator does not update the definitions, just like anti-viruses. So, if an unknown attack occurs, although it may slightly differ from another one stored in definitions database, the IDS will not be able to identify it.

Therefore, we exploit the advantages of the generalization property, typical of neural networks. We apply the perceptron algorithm in order to classify a generic attack through a predictor function, combining a set of weights with a feature vector. A such type of network is able to identify both known and unknown intrusion and, if properly trained with a series of examples, to reduce false alarms.

In literature many projects have exploited artificial intelligence approaches [20,21] (decision trees, Bayesian classifiers, multilayer perceptron, etc.) to mitigate generics intrusion detection risks or single class of anomalies. We can read them in [1–5].

2 The Multilayer Networks

Multilayer networks have been introduced to cope with the limitations of single-layer perceptrons. Minsky and Papert demonstrated in [6] how a simple exclusive OR (XOR), which is a classification problem but not linearly separable, could not be solved by a single-layer perceptron network. Therefore, it is possible to consider more levels (also called *layers*) of neurons connected in cascade [19].

The multi-layer networks are composed of:

- **Input layer:** composed of n nodes, without any processing capacity, which send the inputs to subsequent layers;

- **Hidden layer** (one or more): composed of neural elements whose calculations are input to subsequent neural units;
- **Output layer:** composed of m nodes, whose calculations are the actual outputs of the neural network.

In case of a competitive learning, the output is selected through the *Winner-Takes-All* computational principle, according to which only the neuron with the greatest "activity" will remain active, while the other neurons will be inactive. Graphically, input data can be represented on a plane and each layer draws a straight line inside. The intersections of these lines generate decision regions. This is a limit to be considered, because the inclusion of too many layers can create too many regions, which means that the perceptron loses the ability to generalize, but it specializes on the set of training data samples. This phenomenon is called **overfitting**. Dually the **underfitting** problem exists, where the network has a number of neurons unable to learn. The use of a preventive mechanisms, such as cross-validation and the early stopping, can avoid falling into similar excesses (Fig. 1).

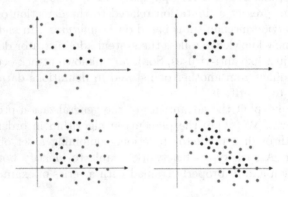

Fig. 1. Examples of not linearly separable data

Unlike to the single perceptron, supposing some hypotheses about activation functions of the individual element, it is possible to approximate any continuous function on a compact set and then to solve the problems of classification [11,12] of not linearly separable sets. This reasoning agrees to Kolmogorov theorem (1957). It state that with three layers it is possible to implement any continuous function in $[0,1]^n$, where in the first layer we place the n input elements, in the intermediate layer $(2n + 1)$ elements, and in last layer we place the m elements (equal to the number of elements of the co-domain space $\mathbb{R}^m$).

2.1   Training a Neural Network

The modeling of a multilayer neural network leads to two main problems [9]. We have to:

- **Select the architecture**, in other words, the number of layers and neurons that each layer should possess;
- **Train the network**, namely to determine the appropriate weights of each neuron and its threshold;

Typically, if we fix architecture, the training problem can be seen as the ability of the system to produce the outputs according to our needs. This is equivalent to minimizing the error between the desired error and the obtained output. The most used is the squared error:

$$E_i(w) = \frac{1}{2}\|D_i - O_i\|^2$$

where, for simplicity, D_i indicates the desired output of the generic i-th neuron (in place of y_i), and O_i indicates the obtained output (in place of $y(x_i, w)$, depending on the weight and input).

Usually, to compute and find this error, we follow two heuristic methods [9], because often the statistical theories are not adequate. The first method is **structural stabilization**: it consists in gradually growing, during the training, the number of neural elements (whose set is called *training set*). It is estimated, initially, the error of this network on the training set and on a different set, said *validation set*. Then we can select the network that produces the minimum error on the latter. Once trained, the network will be evaluated using a third set said *test set*. The second method, known as **regularization**, consists of adding penalty to the error, with the effect of restricting the choice set of weights w.

3   The Dataset KDD '99 and Features Description

We aim training a neural network to make it able to predict and distinguish malicious connections from not malicious ones (normal connections). To train our network we choose a (publicly available) labelled dataset for IDS, KDD '99, subset of DARPA (agency of U.S. Department of Defense) dataset [10]. It was created by acquiring nine weeks of raw TCP dump data from a LAN, simulating attacks on a typical military environment, like U.S. Air Force LAN. The connections are a sequence of TCP packets and each record consists of about 100 bytes.
The attacks fall into four main categories:

- **DOS:** denial-of-service, e.g. syn flood;
- **R2L:** unauthorized access from a remote machine, e.g. guessing password;
- **U2R:** unauthorized access to local superuser (root) privileges, e.g., various "buffer overflow" attacks;
- **Probe:** surveillance and other probing, e.g., port scanning.

For our data analysis, we use an open-source platform, widely used in the field of "data mining" and "machine learning": KNIME (Konstanz Information

Miner). It means the aggregation of nodes makes it possible to "pre-process data, in other words "do extractions", transformation and loading, modeling, analyzing, and displaying data".

For simplicity, during our experimental session, due to the complexity of KDD dataset (about 500.000 records), we use only a tenth part for training activities discussion. We manipulate the dataset features, originally not organized in a tabular representation, in order to change the format in ARFF type, useful to process it in KNIME environment with the components of Weka (automatic learning software developed by the University of Waikato in New Zealand). In Table 1 we show a classification of attacks according to their type.

Table 1. Classification of attacks

Type of attack	Attack
DOS	Back, Land, Neptune, Pod, Smurf, Teardrop
U2R	Ipsweep, Nmap, Portsweep, Satan
R2L	Bueroverow, Perl, Loadmodule, Rootkit
Probe	Ftpwrite, Imap, GuessPasswd, Phf, Multihop, Warezmaster, Warezclient

3.1   Preprocessing and Features Selection

Given the huge number of features of KDD dataset, we make a selection of the essential attributes. Moreover, the attributes have different types: continuous, discrete and symbolic, each with its own resolution and range of variation. We can convert symbolic attributes into numerical (attributes like *protocol_type*, *service*, *flag*) and normalize the other attributes between 0 and 1. In Fig. 2 we show the features selection meta-node.

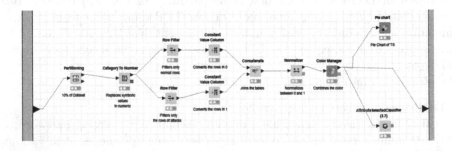

Fig. 2. Block diagram of the meta-node for the selection of the essential attributes

We can observe the following blocks:

- **ARFF Reader:** it reads the file containing the samples;
- **Partitioning:** it partitions the table considering only 10% of the dataset;
- **Category to Number:** it takes symbolic attributes and converts them to numeric;
- **Row Filter:** it filters rows of non-malicious connections by marking them with a 0 and rows of malicious connections by marking them with 1;
- **Concatenate:** it combines the changed tables;
- **Normalizer:** it normalizes between 0 and 1 the attribute values, dividing the value of each attribute to its maximum;
- **Color Manager:** it assigns a colour to the Normal class (0) and one at Attack class (1);
- **AttributeSelectedClassifier (v3.7):** it carries out the selection of the most discriminating attributes, based on various algorithms that we will show;
- **Pie Chart:** it displays a pie chart of the attributes of the training set. We can observe that, in agreement to what was said, there are more attacks that normal connections (Fig. 3);

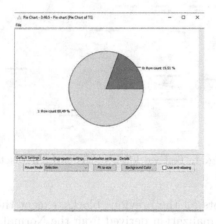

Fig. 3. Pie chart of the training set

To select the discriminating attributes, we tested different configurations for the AttributeSelectedClassifier block, also making use of an external tool, Weka Explorer, to better display the outcomes. No substantial differences were noted: both search algorithms on 41 attributes will select 11: *protocol_type, service, flag, src_bytes, dst_bytes, land, wrong_fragment, root_shell, count, diff_srv_rate, dst_host_same_src_port_rate.*

We considered the two following search algorithms:

- **GreadyStepwise:** it basically uses a Hill-Climbing algorithm. It returns a number of essential features equal to 11 and it is preferred because it employs a lower computational time (equal to 28 s).

– **BestFirst:** it is similar to GreadyStepwise but with the use of backtracking. It returns the same number of features (11) but with a higher computational time (32 s) and that's why it was decided to discard it.

In addition, we apply the ranker in order to obtain a consistency on features choices. From a list of attributes classified by an evaluator, it sorts them in descending vote and still get a consistent choice. All these blocks, for practical reasons, are encapsulated in a single meta-node: *Preprocessing.*

4   Evaluation of the Network with the Entire Dataset and Analysis

In this phase, we test the chosen configuration on the entire data set using the block diagram shown in Fig. 4. We test it also on the individual types of attacks (and not) to provide some statistical utility.

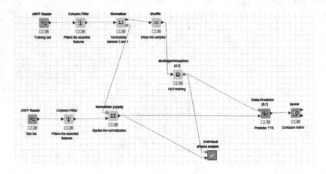

Fig. 4. Test workflow of the entire dataset

The scheme presents all the previous blocks, except the Normalizer Apply, to apply the same normalization derived from the Normalizer block applied to the test set. The out-coming classification system is characterized by an error of about 1.3% with a 98.7% accuracy (Fig. 5).

Correct classified: 487.804	Wrong classified: 6.217
Accuracy: 98,742 %	Error: 1,258 %
Cohen's kappa (κ) 0,979	

Fig. 5. Output of the final scorer

We also test the system on a dataset consisting of individual types of attacks (and same training set), through the scheme shown in Fig. 6:

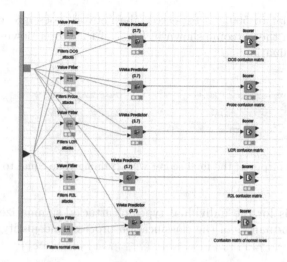

Fig. 6. Meta-node for the analysis of individual attacks

We observe that, for each category of attack, there is a "Value Filter" block that filters the rows based on the type of attack. Then we use the blocks that perform the prediction on the basis of the training of the previous block. It is possible to see the error rate, in other words the number of correctly classified (or not) of our studies in the following Table 2:

Table 2. Error rate for individual types

Type of attack	Error rate	Correctly classified	Not correctly classified
DOS	0.639%	388.958	2500
Probe	41.953%	2.384	1.723
U2R	100%	0	52
R2L	99.911%	1	1.123
Normal	0.84%	96.461	817
All	1.258%	487.804	6.217

So, with given data set and training configuration, our neural network is able to correctly distinguish between malicious and non-malicious connections. However, through malicious connections, the system classify with more precision DOS and Probe attacks. This behaviour is justified by the insufficiency of instances of the other two categories of attacks, so the network is not able to learn properly (U2R has only 52 instances, while R2L slightly exceeds thousands). This result are consistent with other studies (e.g. [5]). On the basis of these observations, we have tried to train the network with the largest training time, choosing a training time equal to 500. As expected, the network goes into over-training, as is evident from the outcome shown in Fig. 7 of the scorer downstream of the entire dataset evaluation:

Correct classified: 208.442	Wrong classified: 285.579
Accuracy: 42,193 %	Error: 57,807 %
Cohen's kappa (κ) 0,367	

Fig. 7. Output of the final scorer with training time equal to 500

while the analysis for the individual types of attacks, summarized in Table 3, shows lower performances of the classification process, and justify our previous choice.

Table 3. Error rate for individual types (Training time = 500)

Type of attack	Error rate	Correctly classified	Not correctly classified
DOS	72.367%	108.170	283.288
Probe	10.251%	3.686	421
U2R	100%	0	52
R2L	100%	0	1.124
Normal	0.711%	96.586	692
All	57.807%	208.442	285.579

5   Conclusion

In this work we have seen that MLP neural networks are well suited to classification problems. We adopted a MLP network to develop a methodology to classify hacking attacks adopting the multilayer perceptron (MLP) model with the back-propagation algorithm and the sigmoidal activation function. We analyse the results obtained using different configurations for the neural network, varying the number of hidden layers and the number of training epochs in order to obtain a low number of false positives. Through this methodology, after the analysis of various configurations and the evaluation of their pros and cons, we achieved a high classification rate and a low error rate.

Although they require time and a good knowledge to be trained, they are able to quickly detect old attacks as well as new ones. Another advantage of this model is its scalability: it isn't needed to retrain the entire network after adding a new type of attack, but only the set of layers that have the new attack as input.

Future work are focused on removing the classification errors, trying new types of attacks and changing other parameters such as learning rate and momentum, comparing the results with other machine learning models, and the application of proposed methodology to different domains [15–18].

References

1. Przemysław, K., Zbigniew, K.: Adaptation of the neural network-based IDS to new attacks detection, Warsaw University of Technology
2. Laheeb, M.I., Dujan, T.B.: A comparison study for intrusion database. J. Eng. Sci. Technol. **8**(1), 107–119 (2013)
3. Heba, E.I., Sherif, M.B., Mohamed, A.S.: Adaptive layered approach using machine. Int. J. Comput. Appl. **56**(7), 0975–8887 (2012)
4. Alfantookh, A.A.: DoS Attacks Intelligent Detection using Neural Networks. King Saud University, Arabia Saudita (2005)
5. Barapatre, P., Tarapore, N.: Training MLP Neural Network to Reduce False Alerts in IDS, Pune, India
6. Minsky, M.L., Papert, S.A.: Perceptrons: An Introduction to Computational Geometry. The MIT Press, Cambridge (1969)
7. Intrusion detection system. Wikipedia.it. https://it.wikipedia.org/wiki/Intrusion_detection_system
8. Network intrusion detection system. Wikipedia.it. https://it.wikipedia.org/wiki/Network_intrusion_detection_system
9. Grippo, L., Sciandrone, M.: Metodi di ottimizzazione per le reti neurali, Roma, Italia
10. University Of California, 28 October 1999. http://kdd.ics.uci.edu/databases/kddcup99/kddcup99.html
11. Amato, F., Moscato, F.: A model driven approach to data privacy verification in E-health systems. Trans. Data Priv. **8**(3), 273–296 (2015)
12. Amato, F., Moscato, F.: Pattern-based orchestration and automatic verification of composite cloud services. Comput. Electr. Eng. **56**, 842–853 (2016)
13. Moscato, F.: Model driven engineering and verification of composite cloud services in MetaMORP(h)OSY. In: Proceedings - 2014 International Conference on Intelligent Networking and Collaborative Systems, INCoS 2014, pp. 635–640. IEEE (2014). Article no. 7057162
14. Aversa, R., Di Martino, B., Moscato, F.: Critical systems verification in MetaMORP(h)OSY. In: Bondavalli, A., Ceccarelli, A., Ortmeier, F. (eds.) SAFECOMP 2014. LNCS, vol. 8696, pp. 119–129. Springer, Cham (2014). https://doi.org/10.1007/978-3-319-10557-4_15
15. Minutolo, A., Esposito, M., De Pietro, G.: Development and customization of individualized mobile healthcare applications. In: 2012 IEEE 3rd International Conference on Cognitive Infocommunications (CogInfoCom), pp. 321–326. IEEE (2012)
16. Sannino, G., De Pietro, G.: An evolved ehealth monitoring system for a nuclear medicine department. In: Developments in E-systems Engineering (DeSE 2011). IEEE (2011)
17. Cuomo, S., De Pietro, G., Farina, R., Galletti, A., Sannino, G.: A revised scheme for real time ECG signal denoising based on recursive filtering. Biomed. Signal Process. Control. **27**, 134–144 (2016)

18. Coronato A., De Pietro G., Sannino, G.: Middleware services for pervasive monitoring elderly and ill people in smart environments. In: 2010 Seventh International Conference on Information Technology: New Generations (ITNG). IEEE (2010)
19. Vivenzio, E.: Reti neurali: Il percettrone multilivello. Thesis. University of Naples "Federico II" (2017)
20. Colace, F., De Santo, M., Greco, L.: A probabilistic approach to tweets' sentiment classification. In: Proceedings - 2013 Humaine Association Conference on Affective Computing and Intelligent Interaction, ACII 2013, pp. 37–42 (2013). Article no. 6681404
21. Colace, F., De Santo, M., Greco, L., Amato, F., Moscato, V., Picariello, A.: Terminological ontology learning and population using latent Dirichlet allocation. J. Vis. Lang. Comput. **25**(6), 818–826 (2014)
22. Palmieri, F., Fiore, U., Castiglione, A.: Automatic security assessment for next generation wireless mobile networks. Mob. Inf. Syst. **7**(3), 217–239 (2011)
23. Ficco, M., Palmieri, F., Castiglione, A.: Hybrid indoor and outdoor location services for new generation mobile terminals. Pers. Ubiquitous Comput. **18**(2), 271–285 (2014)
24. Palmieri, F., Ficco, M., Castiglione, A. Adaptive stealth energy-related DoS attacks against cloud data centers. In: Proceedings - 2014 8th International Conference on Innovative Mobile and Internet Services in Ubiquitous Computing, IMIS 2014, pp. 265–272 (2014). Article no. 6975474

Cryptography, Data Security
and Biometric Techniques

On the Equivalence of 2-Threshold Secret Sharing Schemes and Prefix Codes

Paolo D'Arco, Roberto De Prisco$^{(\boxtimes)}$, and Alfredo De Santis

Dipartimento di Informatica, Università di Salerno, 84084 Fisciano, SA, Italy
{pdarco,robdep,ads}@unisa.it

Abstract. Kmargodski et al. have shown an equivalence between $(2,\infty)$-threshold secret sharing schemes (*evolving schemes*) and prefix codes for the integers. Their approach exploits the codewords of the prefix code to share the secret. In this paper we propose an alternative approach that exploits only the tree structure underlying the prefix code. The approach works equally well both for the finite case, that is for $(2,n)$-threshold schemes, and for the infinite case, that is for evolving 2-threshold schemes.

1 Introduction

Secret Sharing. Secret sharing has been introduced, independently, in 1979, by Shamir [12] and Blakley [1]. A secret sharing scheme is a method through which a *dealer* shares a secret among a set of participants. More in details, each participant, during the sharing phase, receives and securely stores a piece of information, called *share*. Then, in a reconstruction phase, some subsets of participants, called *qualified*, by pooling together their shares or by sending them to a trusted combiner, through the scheme reconstruction function, recover the secret. Meanwhile, the other subsets of participants, called *forbidden*, analyzing the shares they have and applying any computation on them, do not get any information about the secret. The collection of qualified subsets is referred to as an *access structure* to the secret.

2-Threshold Schemes. In the general case the access structure can contain any subsets of the n participants, with the obvious restriction that no qualified set is a subset of a forbidden one. A particular type of access structure is the one for which all subsets of at least k participants are qualified while all subsets with less than k participants are forbidden. Such an access structure is called a *threshold* access structures and a scheme implementing such an access structure is called a k-threshold, or (k,n)-threshold, scheme. The seminal papers by Shamir [12] and Blakley [1] provide (k,n)-threshold schemes. General access structures were later considered, for example, in [3,7,10,13]. Secret sharing schemes have been widely used in cryptographic protocols design and have been extended in many ways in order to exhibit additional properties. For a detailed overview of the field we refer the reader to [2]. In this paper we consider 2-threshold access structures.

A. Castiglione et al. (Eds.): CSS 2018, LNCS 11161, pp. 157–167, 2018.
https://doi.org/10.1007/978-3-030-01689-0_13

Evolving Access Structures. An interesting new variant for secret sharing schemes has been introduced recently in [8]. The authors have considered a setting in which the set of participants is *infinite* and the access structure is defined through a *collection* of access structures, not known at the beginning: precisely, at time t, a new participant arrives and new qualified subsets—if any—are added to the existing access structure. Constructions for such a new setting are given for threshold access structures. To specify that the number of participants is not fixed apriori, the scheme is called (k, ∞)-threshold. For example a $(2, \infty)$-threshold scheme is a scheme capable of accomodating new participants and each time a new participant arrives new qualified subsets are added—all the sets of 2 participants where one of the two is the new participant. Other papers that consider evolving access structures are [6,9,11].

Prefix Codes. A prefix (or more precisely, prefix-free) code is a code where no codeword is prefix of any other codeword. Let $c^1, c^2, \dots$ be a prefix code for the integers (thus there are infinite codewords, one per each integer). Let ℓ_i be the length of c^i, for $i = 1, 2, \dots$. In [8] it has been proved that $(2, \infty)$-threshold schemes for sharing a 1-bit secret are equivalent to prefix codes for the integers. More precisely, denoting with s_i the size of the share of participant i, a $(2, \infty)$-threshold scheme for sharing a 1-bit secret exists if and only if a prefix code for the integers, with $\ell_i = s_i$, exists.

This Paper. In this paper we elaborate on the connection between $(2, \infty)$-threshold schemes and prefix codes and we provide an alternative technique to show the equivalence. This alternative connection allows to build a new class of $(2, \infty)$-threshold schemes based on the binary tree underlying the prefix code.

Organization of the Paper. We proceed as follows: in Sect. 2 we provide definitions and notions needed in the rest of the paper. In Sect. 3 we show how a binary tree can be used to define a 2-threshold secret sharing scheme. Section 4 contains concluding remarks.

2   Preliminaries

2.1   2-Threshold Secret Sharing Schemes

Let $\mathcal{P}$ be a (finite or infinite) set of participants. A 2-threshold secret sharing scheme is a method to share a secret s, which in this paper is simply one bit, among members of $\mathcal{P}$ in such a way that every single participant $p_1 \in \mathcal{P}$ does not have any information about the secret s while any 2 participants $p_1, p_2 \in \mathcal{P}$ are able to reconstruct the secret s. In a secret sharing scheme there is a trusted party, called the dealer, who knows the secret and is able to generate a share for each participant. Share sh_i is given to the ith participant. When $\mathcal{P}$ is finite and $n = |\mathcal{P}|$ we talk about $(2, n)$-threshold schemes; when $\mathcal{P}$ is infinite we talk about evolving threshold schemes and use the notation $(2, \infty)$-threshold schemes. Apart from the fact the in an evolving scheme we cannot precompute all the shares, there is no difference between the two cases in terms of the properties that need to be satisfied. More specifically there must be a sharing phase in which the dealer computes and distributes the shares (this can be offline for the finite case or upon participants arrival for the evolving case) and a reconstruction phase in which the shares of participants are used as input to a reconstruction function that allows qualified sets to reconstruct the secret.

The shares produced in the sharing phase have to be such that two properties are satisfied:

- **Privacy:** for every single participant i, share sh_i does not reveal any information about the secret.
- **Correctness:** Every set of two participants i, j, have to be able to figure out the secret bit s, through the use of a reconstruction function that takes as input sh_i and sh_j and gives as output the secret.

2.2 Prefix Codes and Previous Results

A prefix (or more precisely, prefix-free) code is a code in which no codeword is prefix of any other codeword. A prefix code for the integers is an infinite prefix code $C = c^1, c^2, \ldots$, where codeword C^i encodes integer i, $i \in \mathbb{N}$.

Theorem 1 ([8]). *Let $\sigma : \mathbb{N} \to \mathbb{N}$. A prefix code for the integers $C = c^1, c^2, \ldots$ such that $|c^i| = \sigma(i)$ exists if and only if it is possible to construct an evolving 2-threshold scheme for a 1-bit scret in which the size of the share for the ith participant is $|sh_i| = \sigma(i)$.*

To show the equivalence in [8] it is proved (i) that given a prefix code for the integers $C = c^1, c^2, \ldots$ such $|c^i| = \sigma(i)$ it is possible to construct an evolving 2-threshold scheme for a 1-bit secret in which the size of the share for the ith participant is $\sigma(i)$ and (ii) that the existence of an evolving 2-threshold scheme for a 1-bit scret in which the size of the share for the ith participant is $\sigma(i)$ implies the existence of prefix code for the integers $C = c^1, c^2, \ldots$ such $|c^i| = \sigma(i)$. We briefly recall the above two implications proved (or observed, as the authors say) in [8].

Let $C = c^1, c^2, \ldots$ be a prefix code for the integers and let $\ell^i = |c^i|$ be the length of the codewords. An evolving 2-threshold scheme for a 1-bit secret can be constructed as follows. The construction makes use of an infinite random bitstring r which can be built incrementally as needed, when a new participant arrives. Let us denote $r = r_1 r_2 \ldots$ such a random string. When participant number t arrives, the random string r needs to contain at least ℓ^t bits; that is at least as many bit as the length of codeword c^t. If necessary r is extended to be at least $r_1 r_2 \ldots, r_{\ell^t}$. The share sh_t of participant number t is defined as follows

$$sh_t = \begin{cases} r_1, r_2, \ldots, r_t & \text{if } s = 0 \\ c_1^t \oplus r_1, c_2^t \oplus r_2, \ldots, c_t^t \oplus r_t & \text{if } s = 1 \end{cases}$$

The scheme satisfies the privacy property because any single participant just holds a random string. It also satisfies the correctness property because any 2 participants can recover the secret: indeed, if the secret is 0 the 2 participants hold 2 random strings such that one is the prefix of the other while if the secret is 1, since the prefixes of r are xored with the codewords and the codewords are prefix free, we have that the two string are not one the prefix of the other. Finally, notice that the size of the share of participant t is equal to $\ell(c^t)$.

The proof that given an evolving 2-threshold scheme for a 1-bit secret, where the size of the share of participant i is $|sh_i|$, a prefix code for the integers with codewords length equal to $\ell_i(c^i) = |sh_i|$ exists, is based on the following result.

Theorem 2 ([4]). *Let $\ell_i = |sh_i|$ be the length of the shares of a $(2, n)$-threshold secret sharing scheme, where sh_i is the share of participant i, $i = 1, 2, \ldots, n$. Then we have that $\sum_{i=1}^{n} \frac{1}{2^{\ell_i}} \leq 1$.*

The above result basically states that the length of the shares satisfy the well-know Kraft's inequality. It is well-known that Kraft's inequality is a necessary and sufficient condition for the existence of a prefix code whose i^{th} codeword has length ℓ_i (see [5], Theorem 5.2.2, for further details).

3   Constructing Schemes from Binary Trees

In this section we provide an alternative, constructive proof of the equivalence between $(2, \infty)$-threshold schemes for sharing a 1-bit secret and prefix codes for the integers. More specifically we provide an alternative technique to construct a $(2, \infty)$-threshold scheme for sharing a 1-bit secret starting from a prefix code. The code doesn't need to be infinite (but this is true also for the construction given in [8]).

3.1   Tree Extension

Consider a binary tree T and let a be a leaf of T. A *tree extension*, or simply an extension, makes node a internal and creates two new leaves, u and v, as, respectively, left and right child of a. Moreover node u is labeled with a freshly generated random bit r while node v is labeled with $s \oplus v$, where s is the secret bit.

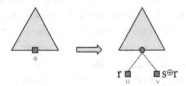

Fig. 1. Tree extension operation

We will write $(u, v) = extension(a)$ when we want to specify the nodes involved in the extension, where a is the leaf being extended and u and v are the two new leaves. See Fig. 1.

3.2   Binary Trees and $(2, n)$-Threshold Secret Sharing Schemes

A binary tree can represent a 2-threshold access structures by associating leaves to participants. We don't need to associate a participant to every leaf, that is, some leaves might remain unassociated. A participant associated to a leaf a will get a share that depends on the position of a in the tree.

The $(u, v) = extension(a)$ operation can be seen as a distribution of the secret to all participants in the left subtree of a, rooted in u and to all participants in the right subtree of a, rooted in v. The share given to each participant of the subtree rooted in u will contain the label given to u, while the share given to each participant of the subtree rooted in v will contain the label given to v. Notice that although right after the extension operation u and v are leaves, so their subtrees, do not contain other nodes, subsequent extension operations can enlarge both subtrees (Fig. 2).

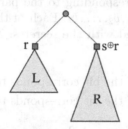

Fig. 2. Secret split between left and right participants

Notice that if two participants, one belonging to the left subtree L and another one belonging to the right subtree R get together, since the first one knows r and second knows $s \oplus r$, they can reconstruct the secret bit.

To construct a $(2, n)$-threshold scheme it is enough to build a binary tree using repeatedly the extension operation in order to have at least n leaves in the tree. Then, we associate each participant to a leaf of the tree and we give as a share of the participant the sequence of labels in the path from the root to the leaf.

Figure 3 shows an example of a tree and the corresponding splitting of the secret bit. Enumerating the nodes top-down and left-to-right, starting with 1 for the root, we have that node 1 (the root) does not have any label, node 2 gets a random value r_1 while node 2 gets $s \oplus r_1$. The nodes in the second level, namely, nodes 4, 5, 6, and 7, get, respectively, $r_2, s \oplus r_2, r_3, s \oplus r_3$, where r_2 and r_3 are random values. Similarly, in the third level of the tree, nodes 8, 9, 10, and 11, get, respectively, $r_4, s \oplus r_4, r_5, s \oplus r_5$, where r_4 and r_5 are random values. Finally, nodes 12 and 13, in the last level of the tree, get, respectively, a random value r_6 and $s \oplus r_6$.

Theorem 3. *The shares corresponding to the leaves of the tree are a $(2, n)$-threshold secret sharing scheme.*

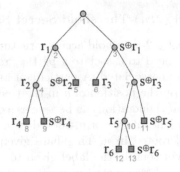

Fig. 3. An example of tree

Proof. **Privacy:** Consider a single participant p. Let ℓ be the length of the path from the root to the leaf corresponding to the participant p. The share given to p is a sequence of ℓ bits $b_1, b_2, \ldots, b_\ell$. Each of these bits is either a random value or a random value xored with the secret s. More precisely, we have, for $i = 1, 2, \ldots, \ell$,

$$b_i = \begin{cases} r_{j_i} & \text{if the bit corresponds to a left child} \\ s \oplus r_{j_i} & \text{if the bit corresponds to a right child.} \end{cases}$$

Since the random values r_{j_i}, for $i = 1, 2, \ldots, \ell$ are all independent we have that a single participant has no information about the secret s.

Correctness: Consider now two participants p_1 and p_2. Their shares are of the form $b_1^1, \ldots, b_{\ell_1}^1$ and $b_1^2, \ldots, b_{\ell_2}^2$, where

$$b_i^k = \begin{cases} r_{j_i}^k & \text{if the bit corresponds to a left child} \\ s \oplus r_{j_i^k} & \text{if the bit corresponds to a right child.} \end{cases}$$

Since the two paths of the leaves corresponding to p_1 and p_2 have a common ancestor we have that the first part of the two shares are equal. More precisely, let ℓ_0 be the level of the common ancestor (levels start from 0), we have that the sequence of bits $b_1^1, \ldots, b_{\ell_0}^1$ is the same as the sequence of bits $b_1^2, \ldots, b_{\ell_0}^2$. Moreover $b_{\ell_0+1}^1 = r_{j_{\ell_0+1}}^k$ and $b_{\ell_0+1}^2 = s \oplus r_{j_{\ell_0+1}}^k$ (or viceversa, that is $b_{\ell_0+1}^1 = s \oplus r_{j_{\ell_0+1}}^k$ and $b_{\ell_0+1}^2 = r_{j_{\ell_0+1}}^k$). The xor of these two bits reveals the secret. $\square$

Theorem 3 allows to build a $(2, n)$-threshold secret sharing scheme starting from any binary tree, that is from any prefix code. As a concrete example let us consider a specific type of tree, which contains exactly on leaf for each level, with the exception of level 0, the root, and of the last level, which has two leaves; this is a chain, as depicted in Fig. 4 for $n = 6$.

The $(2, 6)$-threshold scheme corresponding to this tree distributes the following shares to the participants:

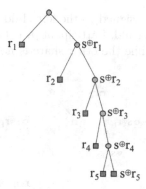

Fig. 4. A chain-tree

Participant	Share
p_1	r_1
p_2	$s \oplus r_1, r_2$
p_3	$s \oplus r_1, s \oplus r_2, r_3$
p_4	$s \oplus r_1, s \oplus r_2, s \oplus r_3, r_4$
p_5	$s \oplus r_1, s \oplus r_2, s \oplus r_3, s \oplus r_4, r_5$
p_6	$s \oplus r_1, s \oplus r_2, s \oplus r_3, s \oplus r_4, s \oplus r_5$

Any single participant has no information about the secret because each participants knows only a random bit and/or various version of the secret each masked with an unknown random bit. Two participants can recover the secret by appropriately selecting a masked version of the secret and the corresponding random bit; for example, p_2 and p_5, will use r_2, known by p_2 and $s \oplus r_2$, known by p_5. More in general p_i and p_j, with $i < j$ will use r_i, known by p_i and $s \oplus r_i$, known by p_j.

3.3 Binary Trees and $(2, \infty)$-Threshold Secret Sharing Schemes

The approach used in the previous section for the finite case can be easily extended to the infinite one. To do so it is enough to preserve (that is, not to assign) at least one share. Indeed each share can be further split into two pieces, effectively producing two new shares that can be assigned to new participants. In terms of the tree structure, this corresponds to selecting a leaf u, not yet assigned to a participant, and making it an internal node by creating two new nodes that will be inserted into the tree as children of u.

As a concrete example let us consider the construction of an evolving $(2, \infty)$-threshold secret sharing scheme based on a chain-tree. Initially the tree consists of only the root that represents the secret bit s. No shares exist. Upon the arrival of the first participant the first random bit r_1 is created and a node insertion operation is used on the root to create two new leaves making the root an internal node. The random bit r_1 is assigned to the left child and the corresponding bit $s \oplus r_1$ is assigned to the right child. Participant p_1 gets the share of the left child, that is the random bit r_1, while the other share is not assigned. See Fig. 5.

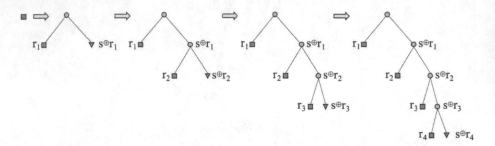

Fig. 5. Extensions in a chain-tree. Squares denote leaves assigned to participants and triangles denote unassigned leaves.

When the second participant arrives, the unassigned leaf u becomes an internal node with two new children, v and w, respectively left and right child of u. A new random bit, r_2 is generated and it is assigned to v while $s \oplus r_2$ is assigned to w. Participant p_2 gets as share all the bits on the path from to root to u, excluding the bit of the root (the secret). The share of w remains unassigned in order to accomodate future participants. Figure 5 show two more extension of the chain-tree used to accomodate two new participants. The process can obviously be repeated infinitely many times, as long as we keep at least one leaf unassigned.

We also remark that, although for simplicity we have use the chain-tree as example, the "expansion" can happen in any leaf of any tree. So in order to accomodate new participants it is enough not to assign a share.

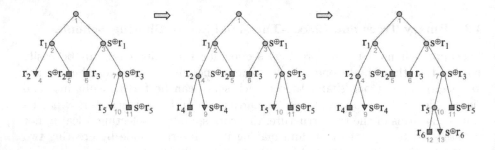

Fig. 6. Extensions in a generic tree

For example, in Fig. 6 the leftmost tree shows a situation in which leaves 5, 6 and 9 have been used to assign shares to three participants, while nodes 4 and 8

Participant	Share
p_1	$r_1, s \oplus r_2$
p_2	$s \oplus r_1, r_3$
p_3	$s \oplus r_1, s \oplus r_3, s \oplus r_5$

have not been assigned to participants so so they can be extended. At this point the shares distributed to the first three participants are

The figure then shows two extensions for two new participants, which get the following shares where the share for p_4 has been obtained by extending

Participant	Share
p_4	r_1, r_2, r_4
p_5	$s \oplus r_1, s \oplus r_3, r_5, r_6$

node 4 and assigning node 10 to p_4 and the share for p_5 has been obtained by extending node 8 and assigning node 13 to p_5. In the rightmost tree nodes 11 and 12 remain available for extensions.

3.4   Saving Randomness

In the examples used so far we generated a fresh new random bit for every internal node. We can save randomness by using only one random bit for each level of the tree. That is, instead of generating a random bit per each internal node, we generate a random bit for each level of the tree and use that random bit for the extension of all the nodes in the level.

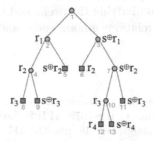

Fig. 7. One random bit per level

Figure 7 shows an example. Random bit r_1 is used for the first level, that is to expand the root. Random bit r_2 is used to expand all the nodes in the second level. Random bit r_3 is used to expand all the nodes in the third level. And so on.

Theorem 4. *The secret sharing scheme obtained by using only one random bit per level is correct.*

Proof. **Privacy:** This is as in Theorem 3, since each participant gets one bit per each level. **Correctness:** Consider two participants p_1 and p_2. Their shares are of the form $b_1^1, \ldots, b_{\ell_1}^1$ and $b_1^2, \ldots, b_{\ell_2}^2$, where

$$b_i^k = \begin{cases} r^{\ell(i)} & \text{if the bit corresponds to a left child} \\ s \oplus r_{\ell(i)} & \text{if the bit corresponds to a right child.} \end{cases}$$

Looking at the paths starting from the root the two paths must diverge at same level z. For $s > z$, we have that Moreover $b_s^1 = r_s$ and $b_s^2 = s \oplus r_s$ (or viceversa, that is $b_s^1 = s \oplus r_s$ and $b_s^2 = r_s$). The xor of these two bits reveals the secret.

$\square$

3.5   Prefix Codes and Size of the Shares

A binary tree corresponds to a prefix-code and viceversa. Hence the approach we have shown in the previous section can be applied by starting from a prefix code and consider the underlying binary tree. Notice that starting from an already constructed code (either finite or infinite) is equivalent to have executed the extension operations needed to accomodate all the participants. The size of the shares are equal to the depth of the leaves in the tree, or equivalently to the length of the codewords.

4   Conclusions

In this paper we have proposed an alternative approach to show the equivalence of prefix codes and 2-threshold secret sharing schemes. Our approach exploits the structure of the binary tree underlying the prefix code. It would be interesting to investigate possible further relations among codes and secret sharing schemes.

References

1. Blakley, G.R.: Safeguarding cryptographic keys. In: Merwin, R.E., Zanca, J.T., Smith, M. (eds.) Proceedings of the 1979 AFIPS National Computer Conference. AFIPS Conference Proceedings, vol. 48, pp. 313–317. AFIPS Press (1979)
2. Beimel, A.: Secret-sharing schemes: a survey. In: Chee, Y.M., Guo, Z., Ling, S., Shao, F., Tang, Y., Wang, H., Xing, C. (eds.) IWCC 2011. LNCS, vol. 6639, pp. 11–46. Springer, Heidelberg (2011). https://doi.org/10.1007/978-3-642-20901-7_2
3. Benaloh, J., Leichter, J.: Generalized secret sharing and monotone functions. In: Goldwasser, S. (ed.) CRYPTO 1988. LNCS, vol. 403, pp. 27–35. Springer, New York (1990). https://doi.org/10.1007/0-387-34799-2_3
4. Cascudo, I.P., Cramer, R., Xing, C.: Bounds on the threshold gap in secret sharing and its applications. IEEE Trans. Inf. Theory **59**(9), 5600–5612 (2013)

5. Cover, T.M., Thomas, J.A.: Elements of Information Theory, 2nd edn. Wiley, Hoboken (2006)
6. D'Arco, P., De Prisco, R., De Santis, A., Perez Del Pozo, A., Vaccaro, U.: Probabilistic Secret Sharing. Manuscript
7. Karchmer, M., Wigderson, A.: On span programs. In: Proceedings of the 8th IEEE Structure in Complexity Theory, pp. 102–111 (1993)
8. Komargodski, I., Naor, M., Yogev, E.: How to share a secret, infinitely. In: Hirt, M., Smith, A. (eds.) TCC 2016. LNCS, vol. 9986, pp. 485–514. Springer, Heidelberg (2016). https://doi.org/10.1007/978-3-662-53644-5_19
9. Komargodski, I., Paskin-Cherniavsky, A.: Evolving secret sharing: dynamic thresholds and robustness. In: Kalai, Y., Reyzin, L. (eds.) TCC 2017. LNCS, vol. 10678, pp. 379–393. Springer, Cham (2017). https://doi.org/10.1007/978-3-319-70503-3_12
10. Ito, M., Saito, A., Nishizeki, T.: Secret sharing schemes realizing general access structure. In: Proceedings of the IEEE Global Telecommunication Conference, Globecom 1987, pp. 99–102 (1987). Journal version: Multiple assignment scheme for sharing secret. J. Cryptol. 6(1), 15–20 (1993)
11. Paskin-Cherniavsky, A.: How to infinitely share a secret more efficiently. IACR Cryptology ePrint Archive (2016). https://eprint.iacr.org/2016/194.pdf
12. Shamir, A.: How to share a secret. Commun. ACM 22, 612–613 (1979)
13. Simmons, G.J., Jackson, W., Martin, K.M.: The geometry of shared secret schemes. Bull. ICA 1, 71–88 (1991)

An Efficient and Reliable Two-Level Lightweight Authentication Protocol

Paolo D'Arco[1], Roberto De Prisco[1], and Angel Perez del Pozo[2(✉)]

[1] Dipartimento di Informatica, Università di Salerno, Fisciano, SA, Italy
paodar@dia.unisa.it, robdep@unisa.it
[2] Departamento de Matemática Aplicada, Ciencia e Ingeniería de los Materiales y
Tecnología Electrónica, Universidad Rey Juan Carlos, Madrid, Spain
angel.perez@urjc.es

Abstract. In this paper we propose a new lightweight authentication protocol. It is a two-level protocol which supports *unbounded message transmission*. It is suitable for several settings, from the standard sender-receiver setting to unreliable broadcast and multicast communication in networks with resource-constrained devices. The key ideas underlying our design are the use of the Guy Fawkes signatures, the hash-chaining method, and some techniques used in MAC-based authentication protocols for multicast communication. To our knowledge, our protocol is the first one that solves the unbounded number of message transmission issue in unreliable settings. It does not lose efficiency and introduces only a constant-size overhead in message transmission compared to solutions for a bounded number of message transmissions.

1 Introduction

Lightweight cryptography. The Internet-of-things has extended the traditional communication network infrastructure to a pervasive system, where a huge number of computational devices with very different capabilities collect, process and transmit information to the other devices present in the system. Wired and wireless communications are used together, in order to allow fixed and moving objects to exchange data. Such a system opens plenty of new possibilities: environmental monitoring, risk control and dangerous situations management, building and sensitive areas surveillance, domotic, smart applications and projects for smart cities in general, just to name a few. However, the presence in the system of heavily-constrained devices and unreliable transmission media poses new challenges. Good and efficient solutions to the security and privacy problems are of fundamental importance. Standard cryptographic tools like symmetric and asymmetric encryption, hash functions, message authentication codes and digital signatures, play a key role in the design of secure protocols. But not all of them are suitable *for all* the devices connected to the system. In particular, low-cost devices need tailored tools and strategies, less demanding in terms of computational power and storage requirements.

© Springer Nature Switzerland AG 2018
A. Castiglione et al. (Eds.): CSS 2018, LNCS 11161, pp. 168–180, 2018.
https://doi.org/10.1007/978-3-030-01689-0_14

Guy Fawkes Signature. In [1], Anderson et al. introduced a new family of authentication protocols, based on a nice use of hash functions. The goal of the authors was to provide a tool which reduces the computational cost of digital signatures but, at the same time, retains the main properties of such schemes, e.g., authentication and non-repudiation of the origin of a message or of the reception. Assuming in the system the presence of a timestamping service, they proposed an hash-based protocol which achieves a quite similar functionality to a digital signature. They also proposed its use to setup an authenticated bidirectional channel between two parties who do not share a-priori a secret key, and outlined some other possible applications: tamper-evident audit trails, secure access to network services, authentication and non-repudiation protocols for low-power processors, design of protocols for settings in which the use of standard cryptographic tools is forbidden and secret keys cannot be stored. Besides its technical contribution, the paper also rised up an interesting meditation on what in essence a digital signature is.

MAC-Based Multicast Authentication Protocols. Cheung, in [2], proposed an authentication protocol for secure link state routing, enabling each router to authenticate the packets from other routers in the network. The key idea in Cheung's protocol is to construct MACs for packets with keys which are released only afterwards. In the protocol, every receiver optimistically accepts the packets if they are received in a certain time interval and, when the key for those MACs is released, he verifies the authenticity of the packets. Moreover, the sender uses a hash chain to generate the keys. Such a strategy enables resistance to packet loss. In [6], five authentication schemes for multicast stream over lossy channels are proposed. The first one is essentially Cheung's protocol. The others, until the final version which is the well-known TESLA protocol, refine several aspects of the basic protocol. Later on SPINS [8], a suite of security protocols for sensor networks, optimizes TESLA in the μ-TESLA version, in order to fit the hardware constraints of low-cost devices. Another work based on similar ideas is [3], which proposes an adaptive lightweight protocol for hop-by-hop authentication.

Guy Fawkes Signatures and MAC-Based Authentication Protocols. In both cases, *time is crucial.* Guy Fawkes signatures first commit to the keys that are used later on to authenticate messages. Then, keys are released, the commitments are verified and the messages are authenticated. It is important that the commitments *preceed* the use of the keys. Such a temporal relation is enforced either through a timestamping service or through interaction and message serialization, i.e., for example, in a sender-receiver communication, each message is followed by an acknowledgement. MAC-based multicast authentication protocols require a *loose synchronization* among all the parties, which is achieved for example in TESLA [6,7] with direct or indirect methods. Then, a time upper bound is used by the receivers to check that the MAC associated to a packet was computed with a key which had not been released yet by the sender. Moreover, Guy Fawkes signatures design is based on *hash functions* and are introduced as a general tool for substituting digital signatures when computational, bandwith and storage constraints of the devices do not allow their use, and for the target application a weaker primitive is sufficient; while, MAC-based multicast protocols usually use *pseudo-random functions*, and the time-gap is used to achieve efficient multicast authentication by reducing the use of digital signatures.

Our Contribution. Cheung's protocol, TESLA and its optimized versions assume that an *upper bound* on the number of messages which are transmitted during the multicast session, is available a-priori. The upper bound is needed in order to generate an hashchain of suitable length. We address, in this paper, the issue of how to modify the protocol to deal with an *unbounded* number of message transmissions. We start observing that the Guy Fawkes signatures and the applications described in [1] *do allow* an unbounded number of messages. Hence, we have looked for a strategy that maintains such a property and, at the same time, as done in Cheung's protocol and TESLA, deals with lossy channels through the use of the hash-chaining method. We ended up in the design of a two-level protocol which keeps both properties.

Organization of the Paper. In Sect. 2 we describe the cryptographic tools we are going to use: hash chains, Guy Fawkes signatures, and MAC-based multicast authentication protocols. Then, in Sect. 3 we introduce the threat model and the security guarantee we want to get. Section 4 is instead devoted to the description and the analysis of our protocol. Section 5 closes the paper.

2   Hash Chains, Guy Fawkes Signatures, and MAC-Based Multicast Protocols

In this section we briefly survey concepts and tools which are used in the subsequent sections.

Hash Chains. Hash chains were introduced by Lamport in [5], in order to provide an efficient scheme for password authentication. His protocol uses a one-way function. Informally, a function F is one-way if:

- given a word x, it is easy to compute $F(x)$
- given a word y, it is not feasible to compute a word x such that $y = F(x)$

Denoting with $F^i(x)$ the iterated application of F to x exactly i times, i.e., $F^i(x) = F(F(F \ldots F(x) \ldots))$, the authentication scheme proposed by Lamport works as follows:

- choose word x
- compute $F^1(x), F^2(x), \ldots, F^n(x)$ through iterative applications of F
- send $F^n(x)$ to the server
- at the ith authentication, send to the server $F^{n-i}(x)$
- the server checks that $F^{n-i}(x)$ is a pre-image of the value $F^{n-i+1}(x)$ received before

The protocol is secure if F is one-way and it is also robust in the sense that, if some values are lost, and the parties are not synchronized anymore, the server can still authenticate the sender by applying F a few times, until he gets the last stored value $F^j(x)$, for some j.

The sequence of values $F^1(x), F^2(x), \ldots, F^n(x)$, used in *reverse order*, have been referred since [5] to as a *hash chain*, because often the function F used is a one-way hash function. Hash chains have been widely used in cryptographic protocol design.

Guy Fawkes Signatures. Guy Fawkes signatures were introduced in [1] to achieve authentication and non-repudiation, as a lightweight alternative to digital signatures. They extend Lamport's work, who generates signatures by opening commitments that have been made by using a one-way hash function [4].

The basic idea is that, at each round of the protocol, first a commitment to a string str = (message, codeword, hash-of-the-next codeword) is released, by publishing $h(str)$, where h denotes a one-way hash function. The commitment binds the message to the codeword and its successor. Then, revealing the values of this string, the sender proves the knowledge of the codeword and, thus, authenticates himself.

Using the notation of [1], the Guy Fawkes protocol can be described as follows: in order to authenticate message M_{i+1}, the sender

- selects a random codeword X_{i+1}
- computes its hash $h(X_{i+1})$
- computes $Z_{i+1} = h(M_{i+1}, X_i, h(X_{i+1}))$ and publishes it
- reveals (later on) the values $M_{i+1}, X_i, h(X_{i+1})$

The sender, at this time, has already published Z_i, followed by the values M_i, X_{i-1}, and $h(X_i)$. Hence, when the sender reveals the content of Z_{i+1}, the receiver can authenticate the former Z_i (and, hence, message M_i).

The first message Z_0 in the protocol needs to be bootstrapped by some other authentication method. For example a digital signature. But that is the only point in which an external method/entity is needed.

MAC-Based Multicast Authentication Protocols. Cheung [2] proposed a method for reducing the cost of secure link routing.

Routers exchange routing control packets to disseminate their current states. Based on these control packets, they construct their routing tables to cooperatively forward packets from source to destination. Therefore, it is critical that these routing control packets are authenticated.

The protocol proposed by Cheung, which corresponds to the basic version of TESLA [6], authenticates packets by using a message authentication code (MAC, for short). The employed idea is similar to the two-step process in the Guy Fawkes protocol: a key used to generate a MAC for a packet at time t, will be released only at time $t + \delta$. At that time, the router checks that the previous received packet is authentic. The approach is indeed an optimistic one: when a routing control packet arrives, it is supposed to be authentic and used by the receiver router. Later on it is verified. Only in case of failed authentication, the recovery process is activated by the receiving router.

More precisely, the protocol is sub-divided into three parts: sender, receiver, and recovery. Every router runs a sender process, a receiver process, and a recovery process.

Briefly, it works essentially as follows [2]:

- The sender generates a random value r and constructs a hash chain of length ℓ, using r and a one-way hash function H. Then, he composes a *key-chain anchor* message that contains the router id, the current time T, and $H^\ell(r)$. He signs it with the private key of the router. Finally, the signed message $(id, T, H^\ell(r), Sid(id, T, H^\ell(r)))$ is distributed to other routers via flooding.
- The quantities $H^{\ell-i}(r)$, where $1 \leq i < \ell$, are used as keys to generate MAC for the packets. A *hash-chained key* message $(id, i, H^{\ell-i}(r))$ is released to other routers at time $T + i\delta$, where δ is the duration of the time intervals between consecutive key releases.
- When the receiver process gets a key-chain anchor message, he authenticates it by using the digital signature verification procedure. When he receives a hash-chained key message, he verifies the message by applying the hash function H one or more times and checking that it had not already been released by the time it was used to compute a MAC. Then, he verifies the authenticity of the packet received before, by checking the validity of the MAC computed by using a key derived from the currently received hash value. In case of error, the recovery process is activated.

The reader is referred to [2] for details. We are just interested in the authentication procedure in this abstract and the above description is enough to understand what follows. Indeed, the two key ingredients are the use of the hash chain, to deal with packet loss due to error transmission, and the two-step first-MAC then-release process. Notice that, Cheung's protocol assumes that the clocks of the routers are loosely synchronized, in order to check with sufficient confidence that the MAC of a certain packet has not been produced after the MAC key has already been released.

3   Threat Model and Security Guarantees

We describe and analyze our protocol using the model introduced in [6] for secure stream authentication. Actually, in [6–8] the model is never formally specified. Here, we provide a formal treatment.

We assume in the network the presence of a powerful adversary who can eavesdrop, capture, drop, resend, delay and modify the packets. Moreover, the adversary's resources may be very large, compared to the ones held by honest parties, but not unbounded.

A *secure stream authentication protocol* guarantees that a receiver does not accept as authentic any message M_i unless the message M_i was sent by the sender.

Using the asymptotic approach, the protocol depends on a security parameter ℓ, the *parties and the adversary* can be modeled as probabilistic polynomial time algorithms (*ppt*, for short), and events which happen with small probability, for properly chosen values of the security parameter ℓ, can be modeled through negligible functions. Specifically, we state the following definitions:

Definition 1 (stream authentication protocol). *Let ℓ be a security parameter. Let S be a sender, $\mathcal{R}_1, \ldots, \mathcal{R}_m$ be receivers, and let $\mathcal{M}$ be a set of messages. A* stream authentication protocol *is a tuple of ppt algorithms $\Pi = <\mathsf{Setup}, \mathsf{Send}, \mathsf{Upd}, \mathsf{Auth}>$ where*

- $\mathsf{Setup}(1^\ell) \to pp$, *establishes common parameters pp among the parties.*
- $\mathsf{Send}(1^\ell, pp, M, st_S) \to (O, st'_S)$, *enables S to send any $M \in \mathcal{M}$ to the receivers by outputting an authentication packet O and an updated sender's state st'_S.*
- $\mathsf{Upd}(1^\ell, pp, M, O, st_{\mathcal{R}_i}) \to st'_{\mathcal{R}_i}$, *enables any $\mathcal{R}_i$ in state $st_{\mathcal{R}_i}$ to update its state by using M and O.*
- $\mathsf{Auth}(1^\ell, pp, M, O, st_{\mathcal{R}_i}) \to b$, *with $b \in \{0, 1\}$, enables any $\mathcal{R}_i$, in state $st_{\mathcal{R}_i}$ to authenticate $M \in \mathcal{M}$, through O sent by S; it outputs a bit b, indicating if the message is successfully authenticated.*

The $\mathsf{Setup}, \mathsf{Send}$ and Auth algorithms are needed to perform the corresponding operations: setup the communication, send the messages and verify the authenticity. The algorithm Upd is introduced in order to extend the class of authentication protocols to the cases in which the receivers have states and do not verify immediately the authenticity of the received packets, but post-pone it to a subsequent moment of the execution. The protocols we deal with follow in these cases.

In the subsequent definitions, and for the sake of clarity, we will not make explicit the full list of the algorithms inputs and outputs, but only the relevant ones.

Definition 2 (correctness). *A stream authentication protocol Π is* correct *if, for any security parameter ℓ, for any probability distribution $\mathcal{P}$ on the set $\mathcal{M}$, for any potentially unbounded sequence of messages $Seq = <M_1, M_2, \ldots>$ chosen from $\mathcal{M}$ according to $\mathcal{P}$, for any receiver $\mathcal{R}_i$ and for any $j \geq 1$, there exists $k > j$ such that, if the sender S sequentially run Send for $\{M_l\}_{l=1}^k$ and updated his state at every step, then*

$$Prob[\mathsf{Auth}(M_j, O_j, st'_{\mathcal{R}_i}) \to 1 \,|\, \mathsf{Send}(M_j) \to O_j,$$
$$\mathsf{Send}(M_k) \to O_k,$$
$$\mathsf{Upd}(M_j, O_j) \to st_{\mathcal{R}_i},$$
$$\mathsf{Upd}(M_k, O_k, st_{\mathcal{R}_i}) \to st'_{\mathcal{R}_i}]$$

equals 1.

The definition essentially states that any receiver $\mathcal{R}_i$ is able to authenticate message M_j, which triggers him to move to state $st_{\mathcal{R}_i}$, later on, when he receives message M_k, which triggers him to move to state $st'_{\mathcal{R}_i}$.

Definition 3 (negligible function). *A function $f(\cdot)$ from the natural numbers to the non-negative real numbers is* negligible *if, for every positive polynomial $p(\cdot)$, there is an integer ℓ_0 such that, for an $\ell > \ell_0$, it holds that $f(\ell) < \frac{1}{p(\ell)}$.*

The threat model and the security goal we want to achieve can be stated as follows. We start by considering a security experiment.

Definition 4 (ExpForge). *Let $\mathcal{A}$ be an adversary, and let $\mathcal{P}$ be a probability distribution on the set $\mathcal{M}$, chosen by $\mathcal{A}$. Let $Seq = <M_1, M_2, \ldots>$ be a potentially unbounded sequence of messages chosen in $\mathcal{M}$ according to $\mathcal{P}$. First the* Setup *algorithm is executed on input the security parameter ℓ. Then, for every $i = 1, 2, \ldots$, the adversary $\mathcal{A}$ gets (M_i, O_i), where O_i is the output of* Send(M_i) *with appropriate state update, and immediately outputs (M_i', O_i'), before getting (M_{i+1}, O_{i+1}). At a certain point, $\mathcal{A}$ outputs an index j and stops. The adversary $\mathcal{A}$ wins the* ExpForge *experiment if, for all $i \leq j$, it holds that*

$$\mathsf{Auth}(1^\ell, pp, M_i', O_i', st) = 1 \text{ and } \exists\, k \leq j \text{ such that } M_k' \neq M_k,$$

where the state st has been updated consistently with $\{(M_i, O_i)\}_{i=1}^j$

The ExpForge experiment models a network setting in which $\mathcal{A}$ has full control. The winning condition corresponds to $\mathcal{A}$'s ability to break the authentication scheme: modify the original message stream with a message M_k' which gets accepted, even if it is not part of the original authenticated message stream.

By using the above experiment, we can state the following:

Definition 5 (security). *Let Π be a stream authentication protocol and let $\mathcal{A}$ be any ppt adversary. We say that Π is* secure *if for any probability distribution $\mathcal{P}$ on the set $\mathcal{M}$, there exists a negligible function $negl(\cdot)$ such that*

$$Prob[\mathcal{A} \text{ wins } \mathsf{ExpForge}] \leq negl(\ell).$$

4   Our Protocol: Description and Analysis

Let F and H be one-way key-derivation functions. Let $\mathtt{MAC}(\cdot, \cdot)$ denote the tag-producing algorithm of a message authentication code scheme, where the first argument is the secret key and the second argument is the message to be authenticated. Moreover, let us denote the concatenation of strings s_1 and s_2 by $s_1 \| s_2$.

We use an unbounded number of independent key chains, all of them with a fixed length $n \in \mathbb{N}$. Each chain is used during period I_i, where $i \in \mathbb{N}$, in order to authenticate n consecutive messages. At the beginning of period I_i, a value K_i is chosen uniformly at random by the sender from the set $\{0, 1\}^\ell$, where $\ell \in \mathbb{N}$ denotes the key-length. Such a value is the *seed* of the key chain. We set $K_i^n := K_i$ and, for every $j \in \{1, \ldots, n\}$, we define $K_i^{n-j} := F(K_i^{n-j+1})$. The set $\{K_i^j\}_{j \in \{0, \ldots, n\}}$ constitutes the key chain for period I_i. The key chain derivation is illustrated in Fig. 1. In the sequel we refer to the seed of the chain directly as K_i^n.

$$\begin{aligned}
&K_1 = K_1^n \xrightarrow{F} K_1^{n-1} \xrightarrow{F} K_1^{n-2} \xrightarrow{F} \ldots \xrightarrow{F} K_1^1 \xrightarrow{F} K_1^0 \\
&K_2 = K_2^n \xrightarrow{F} K_2^{n-1} \xrightarrow{F} K_2^{n-2} \xrightarrow{F} \ldots \xrightarrow{F} K_2^1 \xrightarrow{F} K_2^0 \\
&\quad\vdots \qquad\quad \vdots \qquad\quad \vdots \qquad\qquad\quad \vdots \qquad\quad \vdots \\
&K_i = K_i^n \xrightarrow{F} K_i^{n-1} \xrightarrow{F} K_i^{n-2} \xrightarrow{F} \ldots \xrightarrow{F} K_i^1 \xrightarrow{F} K_i^0 \\
&\quad\vdots \qquad\quad \vdots \qquad\quad \vdots \qquad\qquad\quad \vdots \qquad\quad \vdots
\end{aligned}$$

Fig. 1. Key chain derivation

Assume that $\{M_t\}_{t \geq 1}$ is the (potentially unbounded) sequence of messages that are going to be transmitted and authenticated. A special message M_0 will include any setup information which is needed in order to start the transmission. Message M_t is included in the packet denoted by P_t, for $t \geq 0$. We also denote by D_t the body of packet P_t, which is followed by an authentication tag.

Description of the Scheme. The initial packet is constructed as

$$P_0 := (D_0 || \texttt{AUTH}(D_0)) \text{ where } D_0 := (M_0 || K_1^0 || K_2^0)$$

where $\texttt{AUTH}$ denotes the method, for instance a digital signature, chosen for authenticating the initial packet in order to bootstrap the transmission. Notice that, the value M_0 represents the first message, the value K_1^0 is the last element of the key-chain precomputed for period I_1, which is never used for authenticating packets but is needed to check the authenticity of the other keys of the key-chain, which are instead used for authenticating packets, and K_2^0 represents the last element of the key-chain precomputed for subsequent period, i.e., period I_2.

During the first period I_1, n different packets are going to be constructed and sequentially sent. Specifically, for $j \in \{1, \ldots, n\}$, the packet

$$P_j := (D_j || \texttt{MAC}(H(K_1^j), D_j)) \text{ where } D_j := (M_j || K_1^{j-1})$$

is constructed and sent. Notice that, each packet contains the current message M_j and the key K_1^{j-1}, used for authenticating the previous packet. Moreover, each packet is authenticated by the tag $\texttt{MAC}(H(K_1^j), D_j)$.

When these n packets have been sent, period I_1 is over and a new packet, P_{n+1}, needs to be constructed for the period I_2. We construct P_{n+1} as follows:

$$P_{n+1} := (D_{n+1} || \texttt{MAC}(H(K_2^1), D_{n+1})) \text{ where } D_{n+1} := (M_{n+1} || K_2^0 || K_1^n || K_3^0).$$

Notice that, D_{n+1}, apart M_{n+1} and K_2^0 and K_3^0, contains also K_1^n. The key K_1^n, the seed used to generate the key-chain of the previous period I_1, is sent to enable the authentication of the last packet of the previous period that the receiver has received.

Moreover, notice that, during the rest of period I_2, the values K_1^n and K_3^0 are included in every packet, in order to create redundancy that allows receivers to authenticate packets from I_3, even if they miss some packets from I_2. As we explain later on, our protocol keeps working as long as *at least* one packet from each period is received. For instance, P_{n+2} is computed as

$$P_{n+2} := (D_{n+2}||\mathtt{MAC}(H(K_2^2), D_{n+2})) \text{ where } D_{n+2} := (M_{n+2}||K_2^1||K_1^n||K_3^0).$$

In general, every time a key-chain is depleted at the end of period I_i, a new one is used in a similar way at the beginning of period I_{i+1}. Figure 2 contains a complete description of the scheme, while Fig. 3 depicts the first few rounds of communication.

$$
\begin{array}{|l|}
\hline
K_1^n \leftarrow_{\$} \{0,1\}^\ell \\
K_2^n \leftarrow_{\$} \{0,1\}^\ell \\
\text{FOR } t = n-1 \text{ DOWN TO } 0 \text{ DO} \\
\quad K_1^t := F(K_1^{t+1}) \\
\quad K_2^t := F(K_2^{t+1}) \\
D_0 := (M_0||K_1^0||K_2^0) \\
P_0 := (D_0||\mathtt{AUTH}(D_0)) \\
\text{FOR } j = 1 \text{ TO } n \text{ DO} \\
\quad D_j := (M_j||K_1^{j-1}) \\
\quad P_j := (D_j||\mathtt{MAC}(H(K_1^j), D_j)) \\
\text{FOR } i \geq 2 \text{ DO} \\
\quad K_{i+1}^n \leftarrow_{\$} \{0,1\}^\ell \\
\quad \text{FOR } t = n-1 \text{ DOWN TO } 0 \text{ DO} \\
\quad\quad K_{i+1}^t := F(K_{i+1}^{t+1}) \\
\quad \text{FOR } j = 1 \text{ TO } n \text{ DO} \\
\quad\quad ind := (i-1)n + j \\
\quad\quad D_{ind} := (M_{ind}||K_i^{j-1}||K_{i-1}^n||K_{i+1}^0) \\
\quad\quad P_{ind} := (D_{ind}||\mathtt{MAC}(H(K_i^j), D_{ind})) \\
\hline
\end{array}
$$

Fig. 2. Full description of the scheme

Receiver's Computation. A receiver can check the authenticity of *any* packet from period I_{i+1} as long as he has previously received and authenticated the *initial* packet P_0 and *at least one packet* from every previous period.

Let us inductively show how the verification is done. The initial packet P_0 is verified by using the checking procedure of $\mathtt{AUTH}$, for instance, the verification procedure of the employed digital signature scheme. After that, whenever the receiver gets a packet from period I_1, say

$$P_j := (D_j||\mathtt{MAC}(H(K_1^j), D_j)) \text{ where } D_j := (M_j||K_1^{j-1})$$

he checks the validity of K_1^{j-1}, by repeated applications of F until a previously received element of the key-chain is reached[1]. In order to check the MAC, the

---

[1] Notice that this element in the worst case is K_1^0, from the initial packet P_0, in case P_j is the first packet received in I_1.

Initial packet

$P_0 := (D_0 || \text{AUTH}(D_0))$ $\qquad\qquad\qquad$ $D_0 := (M_0 || K_1^0 || K_2^0)$

Period I_1

$P_1 := (D_1 || \text{MAC}(H(K_1^1), D_1))$ $\qquad$ $D_1 := (M_1 || K_1^0)$

$P_2 := (D_2 || \text{MAC}(H(K_1^2), D_2))$ $\qquad$ $D_2 := (M_2 || K_1^1)$

$\vdots$ $\qquad\qquad\qquad\qquad\qquad\qquad\qquad$ $\vdots$

$P_n := (D_n || \text{MAC}(H(K_1^n), D_n))$ $\qquad$ $D_n := (M_n || K_1^{n-1})$

Period I_2

$P_{n+1} := (D_{n+1} || \text{MAC}(H(K_2^1), D_{n+1}))$ $\quad$ $D_{n+1} := (M_{n+1} || K_2^0 || K_1^n || K_3^0)$

$P_{n+2} := (D_{n+2} || \text{MAC}(H(K_2^2), D_{n+2}))$ $\quad$ $D_{n+2} := (M_{n+2} || K_2^1 || K_1^n || K_3^0)$

$\vdots$ $\qquad\qquad\qquad\qquad\qquad\qquad\qquad$ $\vdots$

$P_{2n} := (D_{2n} || \text{MAC}(H(K_2^n), D_{2n}))$ $\qquad$ $D_{2n} := (M_{2n} || K_2^{n-1} || K_1^n || K_3^0)$

Period I_3

$P_{2n+1} := (D_{2n+1} || \text{MAC}(H(K_3^1), D_{2n+1}))$ $\quad$ $D_{2n+1} := (M_{2n+1} || K_3^0 || K_2^n || K_4^0)$

$P_{2n+2} := (D_{2n+2} || \text{MAC}(H(K_3^2), D_{2n+2}))$ $\quad$ $D_{2n+2} := (M_{2n+2} || K_3^1 || K_2^n || K_4^0)$

$\vdots$ $\qquad\qquad\qquad\qquad\qquad\qquad\qquad$ $\vdots$

Fig. 3. First rounds of communication

receiver must wait until he receives the next packet P_t, with $t > j$. At that point, the receiver will be able to recover K_1^j, use it to compute $H(K_1^j)$, and verify the MAC. To prove this, note that if the packet P_t belongs to period I_1, it contains an element of the key-chain K_1^{t-1}; while, if P_t belongs to period I_2, it contains K_1^n. Both values allow to recover K_1^j, with the appropriate number of F evaluations.

Concerning with the general case, assume that P_t is the packet from period I_i (where $i \geq 2$) with the following structure:

$$P_t := (D_t || \text{MAC}(H(K_i^j), D_t)) \text{ where } D_t := (M_t || K_i^{j-1} || K_{i-1}^n || K_{i+1}^0).$$

In order to validate the value K_i^{j-1}, the receiver has to take into account if this is the first packet he gets from period I_i. If this is the case, then he computes K_i^0 with repeated F evaluations and checks for consistency with the value K_i^0 that he must hold from a packet received in period I_{i-1}. Otherwise, if another packet $P_{t'}$ from I_i has been received, it checks the consistency by using the key $K_i^{j''}$, contained in $P_{t'}$.

Finally, the MAC can be verified as soon as the receiver gets the next packet, either from period I_i or I_{i+1}. This is done by recovering K_i^j in a similar way as described above for I_1.

Formal Description of the Protocol. Next we provide a formal specification of our protocol in the framework of Definition 1, describing how the four algorithms in the definition work:

- Setup(1^ℓ) → pp. The parameters for the one-way functions F and H and for the AUTH and MAC protocols are chosen accordingly to the security parameter. All of them are included in pp.
- Send($1^\ell, pp, M, st_\mathcal{S}$) → ($O, st'_\mathcal{S}$). Let us first describe how the sender's state is updated. The initial state of the sender is empty. When the initial message M_0 is sent, the sender chooses uniformly at random K_1^n and K_2^n, computes the complete key chain $\{K_1^j\}_{j=0}^n$ and stores everything in his state variable. After that, the state is only updated at the beginning of each period I_i. At that point the sender chooses uniformly at random K_{i+1}^n, computes the key chain $\{K_{i+1}^j\}_{j=0}^n$, and stores both the new seed and new key chain in his state. At this point, he can erase the previous chain $\{K_{i-1}^j\}_{j=0}^n$, and the seed K_{i-2}^n from the state. On the other hand, every time a message M_t is the input of Send, the corresponding packet P_t is computed as in the description of the protocol, and the authentication tag output O_t is set as P_t.
- Upd($1^\ell, pp, M, O, st_{\mathcal{R}_i}$) → $st'_{\mathcal{R}_i}$. At the beginning of the protocol the state of receiver $\mathcal{R}_i$ is empty. When he gets the first packet, which is assumed to be P_0, it is stored in $st_{\mathcal{R}_i}$. The second packet he gets is also stored in the state. From that point, whenever the receiver gets a new packet, it is added to the state while the older one can be discarded. The index t of each packet P_t is also assumed to be stored in the state variable.
- Auth($1^\ell, pp, M, O, st_{\mathcal{R}_i}$) → b. As pointed out when describing the receiver's computation, in order to authenticate a message M_t contained in packet P_t, the receiver needs to make two different checks when a new packet $P_{t'}$ arrives. First he checks that the key chain value contained in $P_{t'}$ is consistent with the one contained in the last packet P_t, which has been received until that point. Then, he uses the new element of the key chain contained in $P_{t'}$, to obtain the correct key to verify the MAC contained in P_t. If both checks are successful, then the message M_t, contained in P_t, is considered to be authenticated, and b is set to 1; otherwise, it is set to 0.

Storage at the Receiver. It is worth pointing out that, as shown in the receiver's computation, the receiver needs to store only one packet at any given time. Whenever he receives a new packet, he is able to complete the authentication procedure for the one he is holding and discard it.

Informal Security Analysis. Our scheme is secure in the sense of Definition 5. Due to length constraints we do not provide in this work the security statement and corresponding proof, which we would like to include in an extended version. However, in order to give some intuition, let us briefly provide an informal justification of why an adversary cannot tamper with the message flow. Note that, for security, it is essential that the receiver has the guarantee that he got packet P_t before packet P_{t+1} is released, otherwise an adversary could use the key present in the latter packet in order to modify the message in the former one, and compute a valid MAC. We have not explicitly fixed a method for achieving such a guarantee: actually, both the methods employed in [2,6] and in [1] work and can be used in our protocol.

In order to argue security, first note that the adversary cannot modify the key-chain value K_i^j in any packet. This is because the sender committed to the values $K_i^{j-j'} = F^{j'}(K_i^j)$ for $j' \in \{1, \ldots, j\}$ in previous packet and also to $K_i^0 = F^j(K_i^j)$ (we remind the reader that we denote by F^x the result of applying x times F).

Once it is guaranteed that the key-chain values cannot be modified, the MAC protects the integrity of the rest of the content of the packet, namely the message M_t and the K_i^0. Finally, note that the adversary cannot compute the key used for the MAC, as he would need to be able to compute a pre-image for the function F.

An Alternative Protocol Using Guy Fawkes Signatures. The idea underlying Guy Fawkes signatures described in Sect. 2 may also be used to obtain an alternative implementation of our protocol, in case the use of a cryptographic one-way hash function h is preferred to the MAC scheme. For this, the packet $P_t := (D_t || \text{MAC}(H(K_i^j), D_t))$ from our original description is replaced with $(D_t || h(K_i^j || D_t))$. Whenever a new element of the key chain is disclosed, the receiver is able to recover K_i^j, compute $h(K_i^j || D_t)$ by himself and check consistency, instead of verifying the MAC.

A theoretical Solution for Dealing with Arbitrary Packet Loss. The scheme we have presented requires getting at least one packet from every period, consisting in n consecutive packets, in order to make the receiver able to authenticate. The parameter n can be chosen by the sender in the setup to maximize the probability of this event happening, taking into account the characteristics of the network. However, if we are interested in solving the theoretical problem of being able to send a potentially unbounded number of messages while allowing arbitrary packet loss, this can be achieved with a simple modification of our scheme. Namely, the values K_{i-1}^n and K_{i+1}^0, included in every packet from period P_i, are also included in every subsequent packet, from every period $I_{i'}$, with $i' > i$. Of course, this scheme incurs in the length of packets growing linearly with i, but it solves the posed problem.

5   Conclusions

We have proposed a two-level lightweight authentication protocol that solves the unbounded number of message transmission issue in unreliable settings. To our knowledge, the issue has not been addressed before. Moreover, it does not lose efficiency and introduces only a constant-size overhead in message transmission, compared to solutions for a bounded number of message transmissions. We have also formally defined the threat model and the security guarantees we aimed to achieve, modeling which is not present in the previous papers, and proved our protocol secure according to the model.

References

1. Anderson, R., Bergadano, F., Crispo, B., Lee, J.-H., Manifavas, C., Needham, R.: A new family of authentication protocols. SIGOPS Oper. Syst. Rev. **32**(4), 9–20 (1998)
2. Cheung, S.: An efficient message authentication scheme for link state routing. In: Proceedings of the Computer Security Applications Conference (1997)
3. Heer, T., Götz, S., Morchon, O.G., Wehrle, K.: ALPHA: an adaptive and lightweight protocol for hop-by-hop authentication. In: Proceedings of ACM CoNEXT 2008, Madrid, Spain, 10–12 December 2008
4. Lamport, L.: Constructing digital signatures from a one-way function, SRI TR CSL - 98 (1979)
5. Lamport, L.: Password authentication with insecure communication. Commun. ACM **24**(11), 770–772 (1981)
6. Perrig, A., Canetti, R., Tygar, J.D., Song, D.: Efficient authentication and signing of multicast streams over lossy channels. In: Proceedings of the 2000 IEEE Symposium on Security and Privacy, Berkeley, CA, pp. 56–73 (2000)
7. Perrig, A., Canetti, R., Song, D., Tygar, J.D.: Efficient and secure source authentication for multicast. In: Proceedings of Network and Distributed System Security Symposium (NDSS 2001), pp. 35–46 (2001)
8. Perrig, A., Szewczyk, R., Tygar, J.D., Wen, V., Culler, D.E.: SPINS: security protocols for sensor networks. Wirel. Netw. **8**(5), 521–534 (2002)

Selective All-Or-Nothing Transform: Protecting Outsourced Data Against Key Exposure

Katarzyna Kapusta[✉] and Gerard Memmi

LTCI, Telecom ParisTech, Paris, France
{katarzyna.kapusta,gerard.memmi}@telecom-paristech.fr

Abstract. This paper presents the selective all-or-nothing transform (SAONT). It addresses the needs of users who would like to use inexpensive cloud storage services, but do not trust their providers. Encrypted data are transformed and separated into a small *private* fragment kept on the user's device and a large *public* fragment which can be securely uploaded to a public cloud since decryption of the public fragment is infeasible without the private fragment. Therefore, outsourced data are protected even in a situation of key exposure. SAONT reduces performance overhead by combining block-wise fragmentation of a ciphertext with an application of an all-or-nothing transform only on a subset of the ciphertext.

Keywords: Data protection · Key exposure · Fragmentation Cloud storage · All-or-nothing transform

1 Introduction

During the last decade, inexpensive cloud storage services became widely utilized by both mere end-users and enterprises that cannot or do not want to afford the costs of a private cloud. One barrier against an even more successful deployment is the users lack of trust in the capacity of the cloud provider to sufficiently protect their data. Indeed, during recent years the world have witnessed data breaches leading to massive disclosure of sensitive data[1] and cases of misusing personal data[2].

A reasonable solution is to encrypt data before uploading them to the cloud. However, this solution is not ideal for several reasons. First and foremost, it does not protect against an adversary being able to acquire the encryption key, i.e. by exploiting flaws or backdoors in the key generation software [11]. Additional protection can be reached by combining encryption with data fragmentation and dispersal over multiple independent storage providers. Such processing will limit

---

[1] https://www.bloomberg.com/news/features/2017-09-29/the-equifax-hack-has-all-the-hallmarks-of-state-sponsored-pros.

[2] https://en.wikipedia.org/wiki/Facebook-Cambridge_Analytica_data_scandal.

© Springer Nature Switzerland AG 2018
A. Castiglione et al. (Eds.): CSS 2018, LNCS 11161, pp. 181–193, 2018.
https://doi.org/10.1007/978-3-030-01689-0_15

the adversary's access to the ciphertext, but the most common fragmentation algorithms, like [12] or [15], will not prevent her from a partial decryption. Second, even algorithms protecting fragmented data against key exposure are only efficient when data are dispersed over at least two independent storage sites. Such solution may not be acceptable for some of the users, as the use of multiple clouds may slightly increase storage costs [2]. At last, when we consider data with long life cycle (that are supposed to be kept for decades or even more), the length of encryption key which may be recommended when data are first stored, may not be sufficient anymore a decade later due to the progress in the hardware development on the one hand and in the cryptanalysis on the other hand.

In this paper, we introduce a selective all-or-nothing transform (SAONT): an algorithm protecting outsourced data against key exposure, while storing data at just one single provider. The AONT processing is applied only to a crucial part of the ciphertext making the decryption of an incomplete ciphertext quite impossible. SAONT results in a transformation of the ciphertext into two fragments: a small *private* fragment that will be kept at the user's private device and a large *public* fragment that will be uploaded to an inexpensive storage site. This separation into two fragment is remotely inspired by selective encryption (it is the reason why we gave to the algorithm the name of selective all-or-nothing-transform). Decryption of the public fragment is infeasible without the private fragment even for an attacker in possession of the encryption key. In consequence, outsourced data are protected against key exposure. Thanks to exploiting the known properties of block ciphers and combining them with a fast linear all-or-nothing transform, SAONT achieves excellent performance.

Outline. This paper is organized as follows. After describing relevant works in Sect. 2, we detail our data model in Sect. 3 and then, our three-step algorithm in Sect. 4. In Sect. 5, we evaluate the complexity of the presented algorithm as well as show performance results. An insight into future works ends up the paper in Sect. 6.

2   Relevant Works

In this section we briefly present solutions for data protection by means of fragmentation inside cloud storage systems. We also give an overview of existing all-or-nothing transforms: algorithms transforming input data into output data in a way that the reconstruction of the input data is only possible when the whole output data are being gathered.

2.1   Fragmentation Inside Cloud Storage

Several authors proposed to apply fragmentation inside distributed storage systems in order to improve data confidentiality, availability or integrity [7]. Development of the cloud storage technology reinforced the interest in fragmentation, as the possibility of data dispersal between multiple servers over several independent storage sites raises new opportunities [2,3,5]. The usual way of data fragmentation consists in dispersing encrypted data fragments over up to dozens of different locations using the Secret Sharing Made Short [12] or the AONT-RS methodology [15]. This way of processing is efficient against an adversary that is not able to compromise the totality of the storage sites and to gather all the data fragments. However, it does not protect against powerful attackers able to obtain encryption keys.

2.2 All-Or-Nothing Transforms (AONTs)

The family of the all-or-nothing transforms is composed of various algorithms aiming at transforming a sequence of input messages into a sequence of output messages, in a way that recovery of the input messages is impossible unless all (or almost all) output messages are present. During descriptions, we denote input messages as $X = x_1, \ldots, x_n$ and outputs messages as $Y = y_1, \ldots, y_m$. Usually, an all-or-nothing transform is applied on the ciphertext in order to make its partial decryption impossible (in some cases even when the encryption key is known).

Rivest's AONT. Rivest [16] was the first one to introduce an all-or-nothing transform. In his proposal, the transform should be applied as a preprocessing step on input data before their encryption. During this preprocessing step the sequence of n input messages is transformed into a sequence of $m = n + 1$ output messages. First, each input message x_i is encrypted using a random key K: $y_i = x_i \oplus E(K, i)$, where $1 \leq i \leq n$ (E is a symmetric encryption function). Second, a hash of each output message is computed: $h_i = H(K_0, y_i \oplus i)$, where $1 \leq i \leq n$, using a publicly known key K_0 (H is a keyed hash function). Third, the last output message is computed as an exclusive-or of K and of all hashes: $y_m = K \bigoplus_{i=1}^{n} h_i$. The obtained sequence of output messages Y is then ready to be encrypted. Rivest's preprocessing protects against the exposure of the key used to encrypt output messages after the transform. However, it does not protect against a situation when an attacker managed to acquire the random key K used during the preprocessing in addition to the encryption key used after the preprocessing. Moreover, Rivest's proposal requires two rounds of encryption(one during preprocessing and one after) that could be a burden for performance.

Desai's AONT. Desai [6] proposed a modification to the Rivest's proposal that skips the round computing hashes. Instead, the last output message y_n is obtained as an exclusive-or of the random key and of all previously obtained n output blocks: $y_m = K \bigoplus_{i=1}^{n} y_i$. Such processing improves the performance. However, the knowledge of the encryption key K allows the recovery of an output message.

AONT-RS. AONT-RS [4,15] limited the Rivest's proposal to a single encryption round, but in a different way than the Desai's transform. In AONT-RS, input messages X are encrypted using a random key K into output messages. Just one hash of X is then computed and exclusive-ored with the key K. Moreover, AONT-RS treats the problem of data integrity and availability by adding a canary to the input messages and by generating additional output messages using systematic Reed-Solomon codes [14]. Similarly to Desai's proposal, AONT-RS allows a partial reconstruction of the input messages in a situation when the key K has been exposed.

Bastion's AONT. Inspired by Stinson's work [17], Bastion's AONT [11] ensures that input messages cannot be recovered as long as the adversary has access to all but two output messages. Input messages are already composed of encrypted data (a message corresponds to a block of a ciphertext). During the transform, the sequence of input messages is multiplied by a square matrix A, such that: (i) all diagonal elements are set to 0, and (ii) the remaining off-diagonal elements are set to 1 (such matrix is invertible and $A = A^{-1}$, so the inverse transform $X = A^{-1} \cdot Y = A \cdot Y$). The multiplication $Y = A \cdot X$ ensures that each output message y_i will depend on all output messages y_j except from y_i. Bastion achieves excellent performance thanks to an implementation computing the transform using only $2m$ exclusive-or operations.

Mix&Slice. Mix&Slice [1] is an approach to enforce access revocation on resources stored at external cloud providers. Interdependencies are created inside an outsourced resource composed of encrypted data, so re-encrypting even a small portion of the resource with a fresh key revokes the access to a user who does not possess the new key. The algorithm used for resource transformation could be seen as a case of an all-or-nothing transform, as it is characterized by the same property: data decryption is not possible without the possession of the whole ciphertext. In Mix&Slice, input messages are composed of already encrypted data. The transformation into final output messages is performed using multiple encryption rounds - each encryption round re-encrypts (and thus creates dependencies between) different sets of the output messages obtained during the previous encryption round.

3   Data Concepts, Notations, and Prerequisite

We introduce the following key data components with their size in number of bits and their dimensions in terms of number of elements of which they are directly composed (i.e., a structure s is $|s|$ bits long and composed of $\#s$ elements):

- **(Input or Output) Block (b):** a sequence of bits of size $|b|$ corresponding to the classical concept of block. When referring to a plaintext block, the block is denoted as P, and when referring to a ciphertext the block is denoted as C.

- **Sub-block** (sb): a sequence of size $|sb|$ bits contained in a block.
- **Plaintext** (p): initial data composed of $\#p$ plaintext blocks.
- **Ciphertext** (c): encrypted plaintext composed of $\#p + 1$ ciphertext blocks.
- **Share** ($share$): result of the fragmentation of the ciphertext. An intermediary fragment.
- **Private Fragment** (f_{priv}): a small data fragment that will be stored at user chosen device.
- **Public Fragment** (f_{pub}): a large data fragment that will be uploaded to a public cloud.

3.1   Notations

Plaintext p is composed of $\#p$ input blocks $P_1, ..., P_{\#p}$. It is encrypted into ciphertext c composed of $\#p + 1$ blocks $C_0, C_1, ..., C_{\#p}$, where C_0 corresponds to the initialization vector of the cipher. A ciphertext block C_i comes from encryption of the plaintext block P_i (except for the initialization vector that is appended as the first block C_0). In a first step, blocks of the ciphertext c are separated into two shares $share_0^{pub}$ and $share_1$ of size $\frac{\#p+1}{2}$ each. A ciphertext block C_i that was attributed to the share $share_j$ is also denoted as C_i^j. In a second step, $share_1$ is fragmented into $share_{10}^{priv}$ and $share_{11}$. $share_{11}$ is then transformed using an all-or-nothing transform and fragmented into $share_{110}^{priv}$ and $share_{111}^{pub}$. The upper index of a share denotes if a share will be stored at a private or public storage location. Final data stored at a private location are denoted as f_{priv} and data stored at a public storage site are denoted as f_{pub}.

3.2   Prerequisite

Mode of Operation. To be able to apply the secure fragmentation method presented in [8], the ciphertext should be obtained as a result of symmetric encryption using a block cipher with a mode of operation creating dependencies between consecutive ciphertext blocks (like the widely used Cipher Block Chaining mode of operation).

4   Description of the Algorithm

In contrast to known techniques fragmenting encrypted data into a set of fragments of equivalent sizes, SAONT transforms a ciphertext into two fragments: a small private fragment f_{priv} and a larger public fragment f_{pub}. The private fragment will be stored at user's device, while the public fragment will be uploaded to the cloud. Decryption of even one block of the ciphertext is not possible unless both fragments are gathered. In consequence, the public fragment is protected against key exposure.

In this Section we describe in details the transformation of the ciphertext. The algorithm is composed of three steps. First step includes the encryption of the plaintext and its transformation into two interdependent shares. Second step operates only on one of these shares. In a last step private and public fragments are formed (Fig. 1).

1: **function** FRAGMENTATION(p)
2: **Step 1: Encryption and blocks dispersal**
3:     Encrypt plaintext p into ciphertext c
4:     **for** each pair of consecutive blocks (C_{i-1}, C_i) inside c, such that i is odd **do**
5:         Ciphertext block C_{i-1} goes to $share_0^{pub}$ and C_i goes to $share_1$
6: **Step 2: All-or-nothing transform on a subset of $share_1$**
7:     Fragment $share_1$ into $share_{10}^{priv}$ and $share_{11}$
8:     Apply a linear *all-or-nothing* transform over $aont(share_{11})$
9:     Fragment the transformed $share_{11}$ into $share_{110}^{priv}$ and $share_{111}^{pub}$
10: **Step 3: Forming the final public and private fragments**
11:     Form the private fragment $f_{priv} = share_{10}^{priv} + share_{110}^{priv}$
12:     Form the public fragment $f_{pub} = share_0^{pub} + share_{111}^{pub}$

Fig. 1. Pseudo-code of the fragmentation algorithm that transforms plaintext into a public and a private fragment.

4.1 Step 1: Encryption and Blocks Separation

Step 1 of the algorithm is inspired by the block-wise fragmentation and dispersal of the ciphertext technique presented in [8]. First, plaintext p is encrypted into ciphertext c using a symmetric block cipher with a mode of operation that reuses the output of the encryption of a previous block during the encryption of the current block, for instance the Cipher Block Chaining or the Cipher Feedback mode. Second, consecutive blocks of the ciphertext are separated over two shares, $share_0^{pub}$ and $share_1$. Both shares are necessary in order to decrypt ciphertext c. Therefore, an attacker in possession of the encryption key and only one of these two shares will not be able to decrypt even one ciphertext block.

Indeed, for modes of operation applying chaining between blocks, decryption of a block C_i is *infeasible* without the previous block C_{i-1}. During Step 1 consecutive blocks of the ciphertext are separated over two different shares, so the decryption of each block C_i^j from the share $share_j$ is *infeasible* without the block $C_i^{j+1 \ (mod \ 2)}$ from the share $share_{j+1 \ (mod \ 2)}$. By *infeasible* we understand that for a block C_i of size $|b|$ bits an attacker would have to perform a brute-force search over $2^{|b|}$ values to find the missing value of C_{i-1} and decrypt C_i.

Remark 1. After Step 1, a user could already save $share_1$ as the private fragment and upload $share_0^{pub}$ to the cloud as the public fragment. However, it would oblige her to keep on her private storage device 50% of the total ciphertext. The second step is going further by transforming $share_1$ into a private and a public fragment and thus, increasing the size of data that can be safely stored in the cloud.

4.2 Step 2: All-Or-Nothing Transformation over a subset of $share_1$

Step 2 operates only on data of $share_1$ (equally well, $share_0$ could be chosen for further processing instead of $share_1$). It transforms $share_1$ into two small

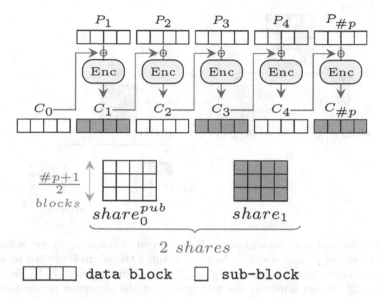

Fig. 2. Example for the cipher block chaining mode of operation: plaintext is encrypted and the resulting ciphertext is separated over two shares. It is not possible to decrypt a single share without the possession of the other share, even for an attacker in possession of the encryption key.

private shares ($share_{10}^{priv}$ and $share_{110}^{priv}$) and one public share $share_{111}^{pub}$. The transformation process is illustrated in Fig. 3.

Fragmenting $share_1$ into $share_{10}^{priv}$ and $share_{11}$. $share_1$ is fragmented into $share_{10}^{priv}$ and $share_{11}$. $share_{10}^{priv}$ will not be processed but directly stored at a private storage device. $share_{11}$ will be transformed using an all-or-nothing transform and then fragmented into a private and a public part. The choice of the size of both shares is left to the user. The only requirement is that the number of sub-blocks inside the $share_{11}$ has to be even (it is necessary for the correctness of the *all-or-nothing* linear transform). A larger size of $share_{10}^{priv}$ will lead to an increase in the occupation of the private device's memory. On the other hand, a larger size of $share_{11}$ will increase the computation overhead as the complexity of the all-or-nothing transform depends on the size of the data on which it is applied.

Transforming. $share_{11}$ Using an All-Or-Nothing Transform. Further, an all-or-nothing linear transform (we chose the Bastion's AONT presented in [11] and described previously in Sect. 2.2) is applied over $share_{11}$. The goal of this processing is to create dependencies between every sub-block of data contained in that share, in a way that a correct reconstruction of the share is not possible even if all but two sub-blocks are missing. The pseudo-code of the AONT processing is presented in Fig. 4.

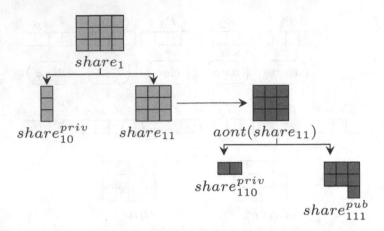

Fig. 3. Transformation of $share_1$ into public and private fragments. $Share_1$ is first fragmented into $share_{10}^{priv}$ and $share_{11}$. An all-or-nothing transform is applied to $share_{11}$ before fragmenting it into a private $share_{110}^{priv}$ and a public $share_{111}^{pub}$. By choosing a larger $share_{10}^{priv}$ a user improves the performance of the algorithm at the cost of an increase of storage on the private device.

```
1: function AONT(share11)
2:     t = 0                           ▷ t is the result of exclusive-or of all blocks
3:     for each sub-block sbi inside the share share11 do
4:         t = t ⊕ sbi
5:     for each sub-block sbi inside the share share11 do
6:         sb'i = t ⊕ sbi
```

Fig. 4. Pseudo-code of the linear all-or-nothing transform [11] applied to the share $share_{11}$. Each sub-block sb_i of the ciphertext is transformed into $sb_i' = \bigoplus_0^{m-1} sb_l, l \neq i$, where m is the number of sub-blocks contained in the $share_{11}$. In order to achieve a linear complexity, the processing is performed in two passes. In the first pass, all ciphertext blocks are exclusive-ored together in order to obtain the value t. In the second pass, each block is exclusive-ored with the value t.

Fragmenting $share_{11}$ into $share_{110}^{priv}$ and $share_{111}^{pub}$. After the all-or-nothing transformation, the absence of any two sub-blocks inside $share_{11}$ makes the correct reconstruction of this share impossible. In a next step, $share_{11}$ is fragmented into a private share $share_{110}^{priv}$ and a public share $share_{111}^{pub}$. $share_{110}^{priv}$ will be stored at the user's private device as a part of the private fragment and $share_{111}^{pub}$ will be uploaded to a public storage service. Without $share_{110}^{priv}$ data contained inside $share_{111}^{pub}$ are useless from the point of view of an attacker. Indeed, without $share_{110}^{priv}$ the $share_1$ cannot be reconstructed. Consequently, as even a block of ciphertext data cannot be decrypted without the $share_1$, it is not possible to decrypt the ciphertext without the $share_{110}^{priv}$. Obviously, one could imagine a brute-force search over the possible values of $share_{110}^{priv}$. Therefore we formulate the following recommendation:

Recommendation 1. *Recommendation about the size of $share_{110}^{priv}$ SAONT applies the Bastion's all-or-nothing transform on data inside the $share_{11}$ at the level of sub-blocks. Therefore, it efficiently protects $share_{11}$ against a situation of key exposure unless an attacker acquires all but two sub-blocks of aont($share_{11}$). Therefore, the size of $share_{110}^{priv}$ should be of at twice as large as a sub-block. However, the size of $share_{110}^{priv}$ should be also large enough to prevent a brute-force search over all possible values. Therefore, we recommend to choose $share_{110}^{priv}$ of at least 16 bytes, as then the space of the brute-force search is the same as for a 128-bits encryption key (2^{128} possible values).*

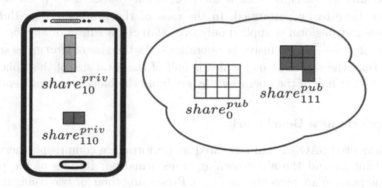

Fig. 5. Dispersing private and public fragments (here, on a smartphone with limited capacity and a public cloud) coming from different separations and the AONT transform described in Figs. 2 and 4.

4.3   Step 3: Forming Private and Public Fragments

In a final step, private and public fragments are formed. As shown in Fig. 5, the public fragment is composed of $share_0^{pub}$ (coming from the separation of consecutive blocks) and of $share_{111}^{pub}$ (coming from the all-or-nothing transformation). The private fragment is composed of $share_{10}^{priv}$ (coming from the fragmentation of $share_1$) and of $share_{110}^{priv}$ (coming from the all-or-nothing transformation). Public fragment is resistant to a key exposure attack. Indeed, a block inside $share_0^{pub}$ cannot be decrypted without its predecessor that is either stored as a part of $share_{10}^{priv}$ or transformed inside $share_{111}^{pub}$ which in turn is unrecoverable without $share_{110}^{priv}$.

5   Complexity and Performance Benchmark

In this Section, we evaluate the theoretical performance of SAONT, as well as provide results of an empirical evaluation. We compare the algorithm with simple data encryption, as well as the Bastion's scheme as it is the most relevant work. We do not make a comparison with Rivest's and Desai's transforms, as they do not achieve same properties (they allow a partial decryption of the ciphertext in a situation of key exposure). We also skip the comparison with the Mix&Slice scheme that protects against key exposure, but applies multiple encryption rounds slowing down the performance.

5.1   Complexity

Combining block-wise fragmentation of the ciphertext with application of an all-or-nothing transform only on a part of the ciphertext aims at minimizing the amount of computations. In a case when the all-or-nothing transform is applied on the totality of the ciphertext at the level of sub-blocks, $2 \times \frac{|c|}{|sb|}$ exclusive-or operations have to be performed. In the case of the proposed algorithm, the all-or-nothing transform is applied only over $share_{11}$, a subset of $share_1$. Thus, it requires $2 \times \frac{|share_{11}|}{|sb|}$ exclusive-or operations. As the size of $share_{11}$ is smaller or equal than the size of $share_1$ which is half of the total size of the ciphertext, we save at least half of the operations by applying the block-wise fragmentation.

5.2   Performance Benchmark

We implemented SAONT and measured its performance comprising encryption of the plaintext and the all-or-nothing transformation. Results of the performance comparison are presented in Fig. 6. Processing time for two configurations of SAONT is shown:

1. where the size of the private fragment is minimized and only 16 bytes are stored at the user's device.
2. where the private fragment is of the size of 25% of the ciphertext and 75% of the data are outsourced to the cloud.

Performance overhead of the SAONT is of 13% (for configuration 1) and of 6% (for configuration 2) in comparison to a simple encryption of a plaintext. In contrast, Bastion's scheme (where the whole ciphertext is transformed using an all-or-nothing transform) leads to an overhead of approximately 20%. Increasing the size of the private fragment improves the performance of SAONT, as it decreases the size of data on which the AONT is applied. However, the performance gain starts to be less interesting when the private fragment is larger than 25% of the ciphertext. Indeed, a private fragment containing 25% of the ciphertext already results in a negligible performance overhead of 6%.

Presented performance results were obtained using AES in Cipher Block Chaining (AES-CBC) mode of operation. We also compared the performance of Bastion's scheme using AES in Counter Mode (AES-CTR) with SAONT using AES-CBC. Results were similar to the comparison with Bastion's scheme using AES-CBC.

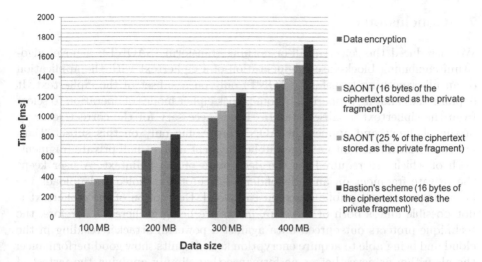

Fig. 6. Performance results for various sizes of the data sample and for two sizes of the private fragment. AES-CBC with 128 bit key was used for data encryption. We compare SAONT with simple encryption and with the Bastion's scheme (where the all-or-nothing transform (AONT) is applied over the whole ciphertext). For the smallest amount of data stored as a private fragment (16 bytes) we achieve a performance overhead twice better than the Bastion's scheme. The gain becomes larger with the increase of the private fragment (as the larger is the private fragment the smaller will be the data on which we apply the AONT).

Implementation Details. All algorithms were implemented in JAVA using the following resources: JDK 1.8 on DELL Latitude E6540, X64-based PC running on Intel® Core™ i7-4800MQ CPU @ 2.70 GHz with 8 GB RAM, under Windows 7. The standard *javax.crypto* library was used. AES-NI was enabled. A random data sample was used for each measurement.

6 Future Works

The algorithm presented in this paper divides data into a private and a public fragment by taking advantage of the chaining structure of some modes of operation of block ciphers. In the future, we would like to propose a similar technique that would be adapted for stream-ciphers. Moreover, we plan to realize a parallelized fine-grained integration of the method within the encryption process in order to make the fragmentation and all-or-nothing transformation costs negligible.

Our research focuses on systems combining data fragmentation, encryption, and dispersal (FED) [9,10,13]. Here, we present a specific method aiming at reinforcing the protection of encrypted data. In the future, we would like to propose a complete FED architecture for distributed secure storage.

7 Conclusions

We introduced the selective all-or-nothing transform (SAONT): a novel algorithm combining block-wise fragmentation of a ciphertext with the application of an all-or-nothing transform (AONT) only on a subset of the ciphertext. It exploits the chaining properties of some block cipher modes of operation to select from the ciphertext a subset of data that is necessary for the correct recovery of the plaintext and applies the AONT processing only on this subset. Data are then transformed into a large public fragment and a small private fragment, both of which are required for the decryption of the plaintext. A user keeps the private fragment on an independent device of her choice and uploads the larger fragment to a public (inexpensive) cloud. Decryption of the ciphertext is not possible unless both of these fragments are being gathered. Therefore, the technique protects outsourced data against a powerful attacker residing in the cloud and being able to acquire encryption keys. Results show good performance: the algorithm achieves better performance than simply applying the fastest of the known all-or-nothing transforms over the whole ciphertext. Moreover, a user may vary the size of the private fragment in order to balance between memory occupation and performance overhead.

References

1. Bacis, E., De Capitani di Vimercati, S., Foresti, S., Paraboschi, S., Rosa, M., Samarati, P.: Mix&Slice: efficient access revocation in the cloud. In: Proceedings of the 2016 ACM SIGSAC Conference on Computer and Communications Security, CCS 2016, pp. 217–228. ACM, New York (2016). https://doi.org/10.1145/2976749.2978377
2. Bessani, A., Correia, M., Quaresma, B., André, F., Sousa, P.: DEPSKY: dependable and secure storage in a cloud-of-clouds. Trans. Storage 9(4), 12:1–12:33 (2013). https://doi.org/10.1145/2535929
3. Bowers, K.D., Juels, A., Oprea, A.: HAIL: a high-availability and integrity layer for cloud storage. In: Proceedings of the 16th ACM Conference on Computer and Communications Security, CCS 2009, pp. 187–198. ACM, New York (2009). https://doi.org/10.1145/1653662.1653686
4. Chen, L., Laing, T.M., Martin, K.M.: Revisiting and extending the AONT-RS scheme: a robust computationally secure secret sharing scheme. In: Joye, M., Nitaj, A. (eds.) AFRICACRYPT 2017. LNCS, vol. 10239, pp. 40–57. Springer, Cham (2017). https://doi.org/10.1007/978-3-319-57339-7_3
5. Cincilla, P., Boudguiga, A., Hadji, M., Kaiser, A.: Light blind: Why encrypt if you can share? In: 2015 12th International Joint Conference on e-Business and Telecommunications (ICETE). vol. 04, pp. 361–368 (July 2015)
6. Desai, A.: The security of all-or-nothing encryption: protecting against exhaustive key search. In: Bellare, M. (ed.) CRYPTO 2000. LNCS, vol. 1880, pp. 359–375. Springer, Heidelberg (2000). https://doi.org/10.1007/3-540-44598-6_23
7. Kapusta, K., Memmi, G.: Data protection by means of fragmentation in distributed storage systems. In: International Conference on Protocol Engineering (ICPE) and International Conference on New Technologies of Distributed Systems (NTDS), pp. 1–8, July 2015. https://doi.org/10.1109/NOTERE.2015.7293486

8. Kapusta, K., Memmi, G.: Enhancing data protection with a structure-wise fragmentation and dispersal of encrypted data. In: The 17th International Joint Conference on Trust, Security and Privacy in Computing and Communications (IEEE TrustCom), August 2018

9. Kapusta, K., Memmi, G., Noura, H.: Secure and resilient scheme for data protection in unattended wireless sensor networks. In: 2017 1st Cyber Security in Networking Conference (CSNet), pp. 1–8, October 2017. https://doi.org/10.1109/CSNET.2017.8241998

10. Kapusta, K., Memmi, G., Noura, H.: POSTER: a keyless efficient algorithm for data protection by means of fragmentation. In: Proceedings of the 2016 ACM SIGSAC Conference on Computer and Communications Security, CCS 2016, pp. 1745–1747. ACM, New York (2016). https://doi.org/10.1145/2976749.2989043

11. Karame, G.O., Soriente, C., Lichota, K., Capkun, S.: Securing cloud data under key exposure. IEEE Trans. Cloud Comput., p. 1 (2017). https://doi.org/10.1109/TCC.2017.2670559

12. Krawczyk, H.: Secret sharing made short. In: Stinson, D.R. (ed.) CRYPTO 1993. LNCS, vol. 773, pp. 136–146. Springer, Heidelberg (1994). https://doi.org/10.1007/3-540-48329-2_12

13. Memmi, G., Kapusta, K., Qiu, H.: Data protection: combining fragmentation, encryption, and dispersion. In: 2015 International Conference on Cyber Security of Smart Cities, Industrial Control System and Communications (SSIC), pp. 1–9, August 2015. https://doi.org/10.1109/SSIC.2015.7245680

14. Reed, I.S., Solomon, G.: Polynomial codes over certain finite fields. J. Soc. Ind. Appl. Math. 8(2), 300–304 (1960). https://doi.org/10.1137/0108018

15. Resch, J.K., Plank, J.S.: AONT-RS: blending security and performance in dispersed storage systems. In: Proceedings of the 9th USENIX Conference on File and Storage Technologies, FAST 2011, p. 14, Berkeley, CA, USA (2011). http://dl.acm.org/citation.cfm?id=1960475.1960489

16. Rivest, R.L.: All-or-nothing encryption and the package transform. In: Biham, E. (ed.) FSE 1997. LNCS, vol. 1267, pp. 210–218. Springer, Heidelberg (1997). https://doi.org/10.1007/BFb0052348

17. Stinson, D.R.: Something about all or nothing (transforms). Des. Codes Cryptogr. 22(2), 133–138 (2001). https://doi.org/10.1023/A:1008304703074

Light Blockchain Communication Protocol for Secure Data Transfer Integrity

Jakub Guziur, Michał Pawlak, Aneta Poniszewska-Marańda(✉) ⓘ,
and Bartosz Wieczorek

Institute of Information Technology, Lodz University of Technology, Lodz, Poland
{jakub.guziur,michal.pawlak,bartosz.wieczorek}@edu.p.lodz.pl,
aneta.poniszewska-maranda@p.lodz.pl

Abstract. The integrity of data transmission is an important issue of data security. There are many methods to secure the stored and exchanged data and some of them use the cryptographic techniques. However, such techniques require an additional time for encryption and decryption of data and for trusted subject (CA).

The paper presents the alternative to existing approaches that ensure the data integrity without the need to use the public key infrastructure and time-consuming process of encrypting and decrypting data. The proposed solution uses the blockchain concept and it was named Light Blockchain Communication Protocol (LBCP). The paper also compares the performance of classic encryption and proposed protocol.

Keywords: Data security · Data transfer integrity
Blockchain technology · Cryptography

1 Introduction

The development of the global market and a significant acceleration of information exchange through network increased the importance of data quality. As a result, development of secure network communication systems became priority for many organizations. Such systems are designed to protect data from threats from within and without the systems' environment.

The main purpose of network data protection systems is to reduce potential risks to acceptable levels from the point of view of a given organization. Often, there is a need to reach a "financial compromise" between a price of an adequate level of protection and expenses due to potentially decreased quality of data resulting from unsecured exchange through a network channel. Transferring data through an open internet network is often a big security risk for users [1,3,4,9, 10]. The data may be intercepted, distorted or modified by malicious users. The most common threats include: loss of confidentiality, violation of data integrity, user impersonation.

© Springer Nature Switzerland AG 2018
A. Castiglione et al. (Eds.): CSS 2018, LNCS 11161, pp. 194–208, 2018.
https://doi.org/10.1007/978-3-030-01689-0_16

Confidentiality is a property which ensures that the transferred data is not accessible to unauthorized entities [8]. Measures undertaken to enforce this property are designed to prevent sensitive information from reaching unauthorized people, while ensuring that the data is delivered to the actual addressee. In other words, the data must be available only to the authorized entities.

Data integrity is another data property, which is often in danger. It is defined by ISO 27001 as a characteristic that secures accuracy and completeness of data assets [8]. Violation of this property can result in significant financial loses or even loss of human life in case of health-related data [21]. Data integrity can be compromised in a number of ways during transfer, replication or update. For these reasons, maintaining data integrity is a core focus of many enterprise security solutions.

As mentioned previously, securing data integrity is a major concern of many companies. There exist many solutions that are designed to enforce this property. One of the methods of keeping the data integrity intact is utilization of secure communication protocols. Their main objective is to ensure that the data exchanged over a network is kept confidential but also to keep data completeness and accuracy. Most of such methods are based on Public Key Infrastructure, which adds a significant overhead. It is a result of encryption-decryption process, which must be conducted on the exchanged data. Furthermore, third parties are often necessary for identification and authorization of both involved parties [24].

It is important to note that not all data exchanges require such levels of protection. Often, the transferred data does not need to be kept strictly confidential but its integrity is a priority. As a result, there is constant research for methods of creating more lightweight solutions of ensuring this data property [19,22,24].

Rise of new technologies creates an opportunity for new potentially more efficient ways of ensuring data integrity. One of such technologies is recently introduced blockchain technology. It consists of a chain-like data structure of blocks connected by hash references and an algorithm that ensures validity and integrity of the blockchain in a peer-to-peer network. Blockchain data structure is very expensive to modify as a result of two design properties: (i) each block stores a hash reference to the previous block, which is calculated from the content of the block; (ii) blockchain data structure is append-only, which means data can be only added to it but not changed, modified or removed [5]. These characteristics make it ideal for application requiring data integrity assurance.

The presented paper proposes a lightweight blockchain based protocol for secure communication and data transfer. The main goal of this solution is to ensure the integrity of transferred data with a minimal cryptographic overhead. The paper also describes the results of performance testing of Light Blockchain Communication Protocol and compares them with approach of symmetric cryptography.

The paper is organized as follows: Sect. 2 provides the overview of secure communication and data transfer protocols. Section 3 describes the blockchain technology with related works concerning it. Section 4 presents the lightweight blockchain communication protocol, its generals concept, while Sect. 5 deals with the results of performance testing performed for LBCP and for symmetric encryption.

2   Securing Data Integrity During Transfer

Integrity of data is the system's or network's ability to allow the modifications of data only to authorized persons or processes and to provide protection against their destruction, which is accomplished through access procedures, error control and system consistency control [13]. So far, many solutions of data transmission protection have been created, the aim of which was to ensure the confidentiality and integrity of data during their transmission through the Internet. A selection of them is presented in the following paragraphs.

Transport Layer Security (TLS) and its precursor Secure Sockets Layer (SSL) are the most widely deployed protocols for establishing secure communication over insecure Internet Protocol (IP) networks. TLS is used to secure such protocols as HTTP, POP3 or telnet. It is based on asymmetric and symmetric encryption and X.509 certificates, which allows it to ensure the integrity and confidentiality of data transmission, as well as authentication of both the server and the client. Data during transmission is encrypted with a symmetric key, which is agreed on at the beginning of the transmission through use of asymmetric algorithm. Data integrity is ensured by means of electronic signatures called Public Key Infrastructure. Providing a secure session layer on top of TCP, TLS is frequently the first defense layer encountered by adversaries who try to cause loss of confidentiality by sniffing live traffic or loss of integrity using man-in-the-middle attacks [2, 16].

SSH (Secure shell) is a cryptographic network protocol which is primarily used for securely login to a remote computer. It can be used in both client-server and server-client architectures. From the second version, it is possible to use any data encryption methods and four different authentication methods (password, RSA or DSA key and using the Kerberos protocol) [14]. SSH Protocol communication has three sub-protocols [23]:

- Transport Layer Protocol (SSH-TRANS) provides server authentication, confidentiality, and integrity. It may optionally also provide compression. The transport layer will typically be run over a TCP/IP connection, but might also be used on top of any other reliable data stream.
- The User Authentication Protocol (SSH-USERAUTH) authenticates the client-side user to the server. It runs over the transport layer protocol.
- The Connection Protocol (SSH-CONNECT) multiplexes the encrypted tunnel into several logical channels. It runs over the user authentication protocol.

Hyper Text Transfer Protocol Secure (HTTPS) is the secure version of HTTP, the protocol over which data is sent between browsers and websites. The 'S' at the end of HTTPS stands for 'Secure'. It means all communications between the browsers and the websites are encrypted. HTTPS is often used to protect highly confidential online transactions like online banking and online shopping order forms.

HTTPS pages typically use one of two secure protocols to encrypt communications – SSL (Secure Sockets Layer) or TLS (Transport Layer Security). Both the TLS and SSL protocols use what is known as an 'asymmetric' Public Key Infrastructure (PKI) system. An asymmetric system uses two 'keys' to encrypt communications, a 'public' key and a 'private' key. Anything encrypted with the public key can only be decrypted by the private key and vice-versa [15].

Standard *X.509* was published in 1988 and defined a flow diagram for issuing and revoking public key certificates. In addition, the standard defines the rules for creating certificates of an attribute used to build a hierarchical structure of the public key infrastructure. The most important element of the standard is the certification authority, which is recognized by all entities and users of certificates for the so-called trusted third party. The X.509 standard plays an important role in the process of confirming the identity of message senders [7].

An X.509 certificate contains information about the identity to which a certificate is issued and the identity that issued it.

IPSec is an IP security protocol that provides a solution for Secured Tunneling for ensuring Authenticated and Encrypted data flow. It provides security at Layer 3 (IP Network Layer) by enabling a system to select required security protocols, and determine the algorithm(s) for encryption. IPSec has two security protocols, IP Authentication Header (IPSec AH) and IP Encapsulating Security Payload (IPSec ESP). IPSec provides two types of security algorithms, symmetric encryption algorithms (e.g. Data Encryption Standard, DES) and Oneway hash functions (e.g. Message Digest, MD5 and Secured Hash Algorithm, SHA-1). IPSec is used to secure tunnels against false data origins, and encrypt traffic against unwanted network passive or active intruders from listening or modifying actions [6].

All described solutions to ensure confidentiality and data integrity use public key infrastructure and cryptographic methods. This involves additional time overhead needed to encrypt and decrypt data, as well as the need to use a trusted third party to confirm the identity of the sender.

3   Blockchain Technology

Blockchain technology was introduced in 2008 by an entity under a pseudonym Satoshi Nakamoto [20]. The technology gained a lot of attention in recent years due to its potential to revolutionize many fields and new applications are constantly researched [17].

In simple terms the blockchain technology refers to a fully distributed system of ordered, immutable and append-only ledgers connected in a chain-like structure. In general, blockchain technology is made of two main components [5]:

- *blockchain data-structure*, which is made of blocks containing transaction data connected via hash references made by hashing block contents,
- *blockchain algorithm*, which negotiates information contents of the blockchain in a peer-to-peer network of nodes.

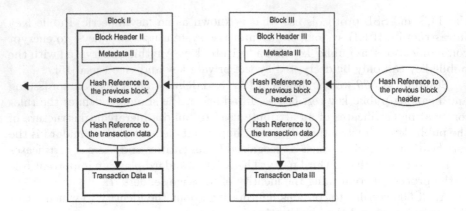

Fig. 1. Schema of blockchain data structure

Figure 1 illustrates an exemplary blockchain data-structure. Hash references, represented by ovals, point to the data from which they were generated, which is indicated by arrows. The references are result of hashing of data with one-direction hash function, for example, SHA or RIPEMD algorithms [11]. Utilization of hash functions ensure that any modification of data inside a block will be detected due to the necessity of changing the hash reference in each subsequent block. This process is computationally expensive which is discouraging for attackers. Furthermore, utilization of hash functions allows verifying integrity of the data within. This last property is crucial for the solution described in this paper.

3.1   Related Works

One of the most important attributes of blockchain technology is ensuring immutability of blockchain data structure. As a result, its application in controlling data integrity is very promising. Zikartov et al. in [24] investigate blockchain technology from the point of view of assuring data integrity in a decentralized network. The authors create a two-part model consisting of: (i) user side, made of a web application providing users with access to their data; (ii) server side, which manages transactions and verifies integrity of data with hash values.

The accuracy and the internal quality of data are crucial in case of *Electronic Health Records (EHR)*. In [21] this aspect of EHR systems is discussed and analysed. The process of ensuring data integrity in such systems is described in three successive phases. Finally, the authors present a method for reducing pseudonymisation to protect patients' health information.

In [22] a method of repeating verification of data integrity in cloud storage environment is discussed. The presented approach is based on *Message Authentication Code (MAC)* and assumes there is no third party involved. The proposed method involves generation of check metadata unique for blocks of data.

The check metadata is randomly inserted into the datablocks and used for later verification based on one-direction hash functions and values.

On the other hand, the authors of [19] analyse the existing solutions called *Remote Data Integrity Checking (RDIC)*, which are methods of data integrity checking that allow users to verify their data without downloading it. The paper presents a study of protocols for cloud storage and divides them into two major groups: (i) RDIC protocols based on Public Key Infrastructure; (ii) RDIC protocols based on identity. What is more, the article presents a comparison of the selected protocols and discuses challenges in designing RDIC protocols.

In [12] methods of ensuring data integrity and availability in electronic documents management systems are analysed. For the purpose of the research, the authors analysed architecture and elements of this type of systems such as: (i) technology of WebSockets; (ii) RFC6455 standard; (iii) JSON in JavaScript format.

4   Light Blockchain Communication Protocol

Light Blockchain Communication Protocol (LBCP) is a data transfer protocol utilizing SHA-3 based seeds and blockchain technology for ensuring the integrity of a data transfer.

Light Blockchain Communication Protocol is a request-response protocol for data transfer between a client application and a server. A communication process with LBCP is composed of the following subsequent steps:

1. seed generation,
2. client's seed transmission,
3. data partition,
4. blockchain creation,
5. data transfer,
6. blockchain verification,
7. data fragments merging.

Seed generation is the first step of the LBCP communication process. When the data transfer is initiated, the client application generates a unique seed value which is one of the components responsible for data integrity assurance. The seeds are generated using SHA-3 cryptographic hash function based on BLAKE algorithm [18]. It is one of the SHA-3 candidates that made it to the final round of the NIST competition. The algorithm uses 64 bit words, so it's works best on 64-bit platforms. The digest size using in LBCP is 256 bits.

Client's seed transmission is the second step of the data transfer process. Before the actual data can be exchanged the client application sends the generated in the previous step seed value to the server. The transmission is conducted using a standard communication procedure based on asymmetric cryptography. The process of seed transmission in conducted only once, which further reduces the overhead of the whole data transfer process. Figure 2 presents a schema of this phase of the communication process.

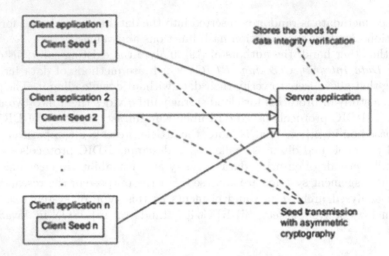

Fig. 2. Schema of the client's seed transmission stage in Light Blockchain Communication Protocol

Data partition is the third step of LBCP communication process. When the client application is provided with data for transfer (e.g. text, image, sound, etc.) the received data is partitioned by the application into equal-sized fragments of a fixed size equal to 64 kB (Fig. 3). The only exception may be the last fragment which may be smaller than the defined size. After this process is completed the next step can be started.

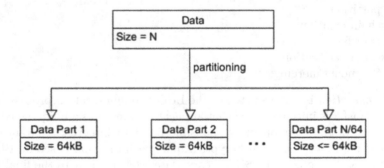

Fig. 3. Schema of the data partitioning in Light Blockchain Communication Protocol

Blockchain creation is the fourth step of LBCP communication process and the last before the actual transfer of the data. Data fragments obtained in the previous step are transformed into connected data blocks. Each of the LBCP blocks is made of one of the data fragments and a block header containing a block index, a creation *timestamp*, a hash reference to the data fragment and a hash reference to the previous block header, which is calculated from the content of the whole header (Fig. 4).

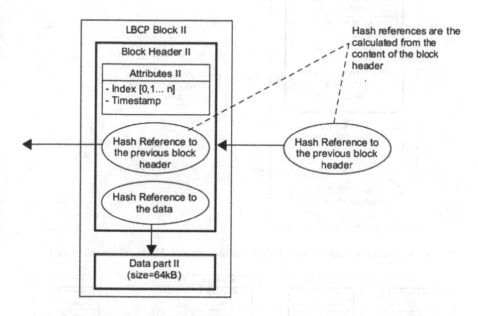

Fig. 4. Model of Light Blockchain Communication Protocol block

The creation of a blockchain starts with formation of a "genesis block" which is a block without hash reference to the previous block (as it is the first in the chain) and indexed with "0". Moreover, its data consist of the client's name. However, the hash reference to the previous block is not removed. Instead, it is replaced with a hash value of the whole blockchain calculated from hash values of all blocks of the blockchain and unique seed of the client application (Fig. 5). The reference is calculated after the whole blockchain is created.

The next blocks follow the standard format of blocks described previously. All blocks subsequent to the genesis block are created in the same way:

1. a block header is created containing the described attributes,
2. the index attribute is incremented by "1",
3. the timestamp attribute is assigned a value of the block creation time,
4. the data hash reference is calculated and assigned to the corresponding attribute,
5. the hash reference to the previous block is assigned an appropriate value,
6. a hash reference of the whole current block is calculated and stored for eventual next block.

Finally, the whole blockchain data structure is obtained (Fig. 6). The length of it is equal to the number of data fragments plus genesis block.

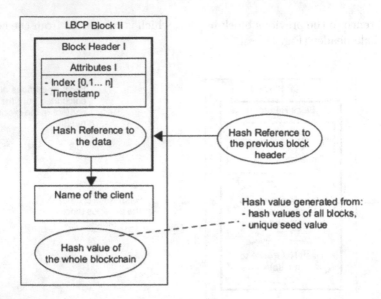

Fig. 5. Model of Light Blockchain Communication Protocol genesis block

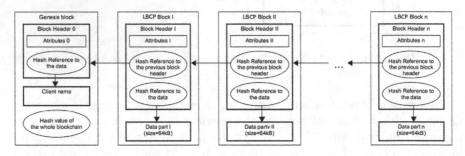

Fig. 6. Model of Light Blockchain Communication Protocol blockchain

Data transfer is the fifth step of the LBCP communication process. It consists of transmitting of the prepared blockchain to the destined recipient application on the server.

Blockchain verification is the sixth step of the LBCP communication and consists of the server verifying the correctness and integrity of the received blockchain. Firstly, the server checks the format and attributes of the blockchain to ensure it is structurally correct. Secondly, all hash references are recalculated and compared to the originals. Finally, the hash of the whole blockchain is calculated using the seed transmitted in the first step. The obtained value is compared to the one stored in the genesis block.

Data fragments merging is the last step of the LBCP data transfer process. Assuming the received blockchain is correct the data contained within is extracted and merged to recreate the initial file (Fig. 7).

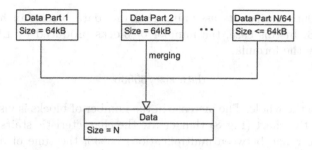

Fig. 7. Schema of the LBCP data merging stage

The most important advantage of this solution is high resistance to unauthorized modification. Due to the utilization of cryptographic hash functions for hashing block contents and blockchain data structure the proposed solution is difficult to change. Any potential attacker who would want to change even a single block would be instantly discovered due to the properties of the hash values. The only way to change the blockchain would be to replace the whole data structure. However, because the genesis block contains a hash value calculated from the whole block and unique for each client seed value it is improbable that the potential attacker would be able to change the whole blockchain without being discovered during the blockchain verification stage.

Another important advantage of LBCP is that the solution is relatively lightweight. LBCP uses cryptographic methods of encryption and decryption only for the initial transfer of seeds, while the remaining transfer is completed without any additional cryptographic security measures. Instead, it only uses cryptographic hash functions which ensure data integrity and a detection of attacks. Therefore, it has a potential to be faster than more traditional approaches to data transfer. On the other hand, the security of this solution heavily depends on the actual security of the unique seeds. If the seeds are compromised in some way there is no way to stop attackers and to ensure data integrity during the transfer. Furthermore, the cryptographic hash functions are in theory one-way functions but it is possible that after a prolonged eavesdropping the seeds will be discovered by a brute force attack.

Finally, because LBCP does not use any form of message encryption-decryption mechanism but is actually possible to eavesdrop the data transfer and discover the contents of the blockchain along with the contained within data. For this reason, LBCP should not be used for transferring sensitive data.

5   Performance Testing of Light Blockchain Communication Protocol

This section presents the results of the LBCP performance using the Blake algorithm, which returns a shortcut of 256 bits in length to the classical symmetric encryption using the AES algorithm with a key length of 256 bits.

Figure 8 presents the results assuming that one data block can have a maximum of 64 kB. In this case, the number of blocks produced by LBCP will be determined by the formula:

$$\text{data size}/65536$$

rounded up to the whole. The increase in the number of blocks is visible through the jumps on the chart (Fig. 8) that create the characteristic stairs. In the case of data in the range between multiplications 65536, the time of data creation and validation does not change (the hash function calculated for the previous blocks has no significant effect on the time of creating the entire block chain).

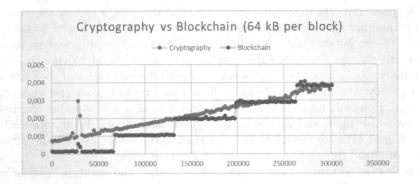

Fig. 8. Performance results of Cryptography vs Blockchain for 64 kB per block

For the AES algorithm, a linear increase in time as the file size increases is performed. For such defined per-block limit, the LBCP shows a better data transfer time for data up to 190 kB. The most time-consuming element of LBCP is the creation of a new block. For this reason, the same simulation was performed, but increasing the maximum block size from 64 kB to 512 kB (the largest file on which the LBCP was tested). Such approach guaranteed obtaining the length of block chain equals to "2" (one starting block and one block for data from a file). Figure 9 presents the results of the simulation.

Increasing the maximum block size allowed to obtain the better times for all sizes of the set of test files. The time of creation and validation of the block chain is practically independent of the size of the data.

Figures 10 and 11 present how individual parts of the entire transmission (encryption/decryption and creation/validation of blockchain) affect the total time of the process. In the case of LBCP, it can be seen that the chain formation is more time-consuming than its validation. These data make sense, because in the case of validation, we only deal with hashes verification, while the creation of the chain also requires a time to create the blocks (the difference of these times will allow to calculate how much time the calculation of the hash function takes, and how much time the physical block creation takes). It should be noted

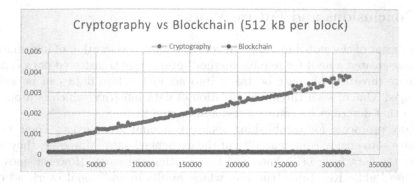

Fig. 9. Performance results of Cryptography vs Blockchain for 512 kB per block

that the use of multithreading or graphics processors will give the possibility to shorten the block creation time even further.

In the case of the AES algorithm, the time of encryption and decryption is almost the same. It results directly from the characteristics of symmetric algorithms, which is why these data are not a surprise.

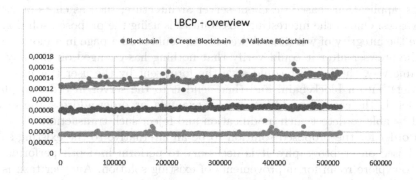

Fig. 10. Performance results of LBCP – overview – create and validate blockchain

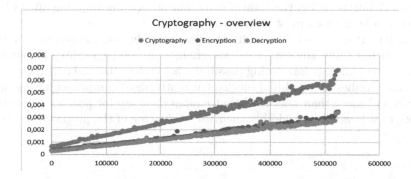

Fig. 11. Performance results of Cryptography – overview – encryption and description

6   Conclusions and Future Works

Development of the global market and corresponding acceleration of information exchange created a need for reliable methods of securing transferred data. There are many threats that must be taken into account before data can be safely exchanged. One of such threats is violation of data integrity, which is property of data that describes its compactness and accuracy.

Many protocols for establishing secure communication exist. Their main objective is to ensure confidentiality of the exchanged data. Moreover, they also protect the data form being modified by unauthorized party. However, most of them use Public Key Infrastructure, which results in additional overhead due to the process of encryption and decryption. Often, the process also includes a third party for identity confirmation of both sides. Such security measures are not always necessary, some data exchanges require only to ensure the integrity of the data remains intact.

In this paper, Light Blockchain Communication Protocol is presented. As the name suggests, it is a protocol utilizing blockchain technology for conducting relatively lightweight exchanges of data which does not need to be strictly confidential.

LBCP can be applied in industrial networks, devices using the Internet of Things, applications based on client-server architecture, such as chats or video conferences. One of the interesting possibilities is using the proposed solution to ensure the integrity of websites. A web server could send a page in a blockchain, and the browser after it could verify that nothing has changed on the way. In the same way, the browser could save the form sent by the user (for example an order), into a blockchain, and then send it to the server in order to place an order. In the case of modifications, for example, an order address, the server would be able to detect such modification and reject such transaction.

In order for the proposed solution to be an alternative to the existing solutions based on cryptography, it is necessary to perform in-depth performance tests to explore room for improvements of existing solution. Another task is to empirically verify the safety of the proposed solution. In particular, the maximum possible time of seed use before a change becomes necessary must be determined. Furthermore, the time of communication eavesdropping after which the seed can be guessed must be measured.

Next important aspect is to verify solution in production environment to verify how much it fulfils the real scenarios: changes in web pages, http requests or Internet chats. Another interesting possibility is to use GPUs and multithreading to calculate hashes of individual blocks. Currently, most computers have graphics cards and more than one CPU that enable their use for parallel processing of tasks, so it is worth considering their use in the case of the proposed solution.

References

1. Apostolaki, M., Zohar, A., Vanbever, L.: Hijacking bitcoin: routing attacks on cryptocurrencies. In: IEEE Symposium on Security and Privacy (SP), pp. 375–392. IEEE (2017)
2. Atighetchi, M., Soule, N., Pal, P., Loyall, J., Sinclair, A., Grant, R.: Safe configuration of TLS connections. In: International Conference on Communications and Network Security (CNS), pp. 415–422. IEEE (2013)
3. Barrows, R., Paul, D.: Privacy, confidentiality, and electronic medical records. J. Am. Med. Inform. Assoc. 3(2), 139–148 (1996)
4. Chen, D., Zhao, H.: Data security and privacy protection issues in cloud computing. In: International Conference on Computer Science and Electronics Engineering (ICCSEE), vol. 1, pp. 647–651. IEEE (2012)
5. Drescher, D.: Blockchain Basics: A Non-Technical Introduction in 25 Steps. Apress, Frankfurt am Main (2017)
6. Elkeelany, O., et al.: Performance analysis of IPSec protocol: encryption and authentication. In: IEEE International Conference on Communications, vol. 2, pp. 1164–1168. IEEE (2002)
7. Gerck, E.: Overview of certification systems: X.509 (2000). http://www.mcg.org.br/cert.htm
8. ISO/IEC. Information technology - security techniques - information security management systems - requirements (2005)
9. Kaufman, C., Perlman, R., Speciner, M.: Network Security: Private Communication in a Public World. Prentice Hall Press, Upper Saddle River (2002)
10. Li, M., Lou, W., Ren, K.: Data security and privacy in wireless body area networks. IEEE Wirel. Commun. 17(1), 51–58 (2010)
11. Morabito, V.: The security of blockchain systems. In: Business Innovation Through Blockchain, pp. 61–78 (2017)
12. Nyrkov, A., Sokolov, S., Chernyi, S., Chernyakov, A., Karpina, A.: Providing the integrity and availability in the process of data transfer in the electronic documents management systems of transport-logistical clusters. In: 2nd International Conference on Industrial Engineering, Applications and Manufacturing (ICIEAM), Chelyabinsk, Russia (2016)
13. Poniszewska-Maranda, A., Pawelska, J., Majchrzycka, A.: Selected aspects of security mechanisms for transactions in bitcoin virtual commerce. In: Software Engineering Research for the Practice, pp. 91–104 (2017)
14. Poornachandran, P., Soman, K.P., Vinayakumar, R.: Evaluating shallow and deep networks for secure shell (SSH) traffic analysis. In: International Conference on Advances in Computing, Communications and Informatics (ICACCI), Udupi, India (2017)
15. Rescorla, E.: HTTP Over TLS (2000). https://tools.ietf.org/html/rfc2818
16. Rescorla, E.: The transport layer security (TLS) protocol version 1.3 (2018). https://tools.ietf.org/html/draft-ietf-tls-tls13-26
17. Risius, M., Spohrer, K.: A blockchain research framework - what we (don't) know, where we go from here, and how we will get there. Bus. Inf. Syst. Eng. 59(6), 385–409 (2017)
18. Saarinen, O., Aumasson, J.P.: The BLAKE2 Cryptographic Hash and Message Authentication Code (MAC) (2012)
19. Sasikala, C., Bindu, C.S.: A study on remote data integrity checking techniques in cloud. In: International Conference on Public Key Infrastructure and its Applications (PKIA), Bangalore, India (2017)

20. Satoshi, N.: Bitcoin: a peer-to-peer electronic cash system (2008). https://bitcoin.org/bitcoin.pdf
21. Vimalachandran, P., Wang, H., Zhang, Y., Heyward, B., Whittaker, F.: Ensuring data integrity in electronic health records: a quality health care implication. In: International Conference on Orange Technologies (ICOT), Melbourne, Australia, pp. 557–564. IEEE (2018)
22. Li, L., Chen, Y., Chen, Z.: An approach to verifying data integrity for cloud storage. In: 13th International Conference on Computational Intelligence and Security, Hong Kong, China (2017)
23. Ylonen, T., Lonvick, C.: The secure shell (SSH) protocol architecture (2006). https://www.ietf.org/rfc/rfc4251.txt
24. Zikratov, I., Kuzmin, A., Akimenko, V., Niculichev, V., Yalansky, L.: Ensuring data integrity using blockchain technology. In: 20th Conference of Open Innovations Association (FRUCT), St. Petersburg, Russia (2017)

Towards the Blockchain Technology for System Voting Process

Michał Pawlak, Jakub Guziur, and Aneta Poniszewska-Marańda$^{(\boxtimes)}$ (ID)

Institute of Information Technology, Lodz University of Technology,
Lodz, Poland
{michal.pawlak,jakub.guziur}@edu.p.lodz.pl,
aneta.poniszewska-maranda@p.lodz.pl

Abstract. There are many existing voting solutions which have different benefits and issues. The most significant ones are lack of transparency and auditability. Recently developed blockchain technology may be a solution to these issues. This paper describes Auditable Blockchain Voting System (ABVS), which integrates e-voting process with blockchain technology into one supervised non-remote internet voting system which is end-to-end verifiable. In addition to the description of components and overall voting process, the paper contains presentation of the results of the initial tests conducted on the prototype of the system.

Keywords: E-voting · Blockchain · E-voting system
Audit · Verification

1   Introduction

An individual (or a group) under a pseudonym Nakamoto introduced a new digital currency in 2008 [1]. It was called Bitcoin and was based on blockchain technology. Since then both became considered by many to be revolutionary not only in the financial field [2]. In simple terms, blockchain technology is a distributed system of ledgers stored in a chain-like structure of connected blocks, which content is collectively negotiated and validated in a peer-to-peer network via dedicated algorithm [3,4]. Blockchain technology gained a lot of attention and its various possible applications are researched [2,5]. One such application lies in a field of electronic voting (e-voting).

The ability to vote is a foundation of a democracy. However, despite its importance and complex security measures, it is not free from frauds and manipulations [6,7]. In general, most modern voting systems are slow and prone to manipulations. This is the result of their dependence on ballots collected and counted by a single central institution. Furthermore, results obtained this way are not verifiable because voters do not have the ability to ensure that their votes were correctly and fairly handled.

E-voting systems were created to solve all of these problems [8]. Unfortunately, the systems used today are still not ideal and have many different

A. Castiglione et al. (Eds.): CSS 2018, LNCS 11161, pp. 209–223, 2018.
https://doi.org/10.1007/978-3-030-01689-0_17

issues with authentication, privacy, data integrity and transparency [6]. However, blockchain technology may be a solution to e-voting problems. Blockchain can be used for a creation of platforms allowing for public verification of the data stored inside, which in turn would allow the voters to audit and verify the results without dedicated institutions and officials. Some countries already started researching and implementing e-voting systems based on blockchain technology [9,10]. In 2017 South Korea conducted a successful community voting and in 2018 Sierra Leone conducted a nationwide election using Agora blockchain system [11].

The existing electronic voting systems based on blockchain technology have many advantages. The most important one is the ability to securely and anonymously cast vote via the Internet, which can be verified. However, these systems still have issues with identification and authentication. In fact, most of them leave this process to the election officials or depend only on cryptography, which removes the benefits of remote voting and creates a possibility of voter impersonation.

The goal of this paper is to describe an end-to-end verifiable blockchain-based electronic voting system, which is intended as an enhancement of the existing voting process in Poland. The system is intended to provide the voters with the ability to follow and verify votes and election results.

The paper is organised in the following way: Sect. 2 describes the theoretical and technical aspects of blockchain technology and e-voting, Sect. 3 presents an overview of works related to this field. Section 4 deals with the original e-voting systems and results of its testing, while Sect. 5 contains the conclusion drawn from this stage of the research.

2 Background

In this section theoretical background of blockchain technology and electronic voting is described in detail. Each of these topics is presented in a dedicated subsection.

2.1 E-voting

Electronic voting, also known as e-voting, is defined as any type of election or referendum that utilizes electronic means facilitating voting procedures (at minimum for casting votes) [21]. E-voting systems provide many benefits, for example, due to reduction of human factor in tallying process they can increase results accuracy and minimize potential of frauds. Furthermore, they can improve voting accessibility with multilingual interfaces or with dedicated interfaces for disabled people. Finally, e-voting can reduce time and costs of the voting procedure due to reduction of spoiled ballots and removal of distribution and shipment of ballots [18].

On the other hand, electronic voting is connected with many significant challenges. One of the most important ones is lack of trust in such systems. This is the result of inadequate transparency and poor understanding of e-voting solutions by non-experts. Despite reduction of human factor, electronic voting is not free from frauds as privileged insiders or hackers may be able to manipulate votes. This is a severe flaw as e-voting systems are centralized, which means a single entity controls a code base, databases and voting equipment. Furthermore, devices used for the voting process mostly come from third parties and full verification of them all is impossible. Another important problem of e-voting is lack of widely accepted standards and certifications, which can further decrease trust which is crucial for democratic voting [18, 33].

Similarly to traditional voting systems, electronic voting consists of six phases: (i) voter registration, done personally or by an authority; (ii) authentication, that is confirming voter identity; (iii) authorization, that is allowing identified voters to vote; (iv) vote casting; (v) vote counting; (vi) vote verification, which is checking if the vote was conducted correctly and without frauds. In addition, all electronic voting solutions must have the following properties [6, 19, 22, 23]:

- voter authentication and authorization,
- voter privacy,
- correctness,
- transparency,
- verifiability,
- integrity,
- availability,
- fairness.

Voter authentication and authorization property means that only eligible people are allowed to cast votes. *Voter privacy* property ensures that only voters themselves know the value of their votes. *Correctness* means that all valid votes are included in the final tally. *Transparency* property means that the procedures of the voting system are open to scrutiny and are understandable for non-experts. *Verifiability* property ensures that the system can be inspected by an independent entity to check whether the voting was conducted correctly. *Integrity* property refers to immutability of any cast votes. *Availability* property means that all eligible voters can cast their votes in the election time-frame. Finally, *fairness* property ensures that participants have equal chances and have no advantage from the system itself.

Electronic voting systems can be classified in many different ways. In the most general way they can be differentiated by two key characteristics [24]:

- remoteness,
- supervision.

Remoteness refers to whether the ballots are transmitted through some communication channel to some central location (remote voting) or are just recorded locally on some medium (non-remote voting). *Supervision* describes if the voting process is conducted from a location controlled by some authority (e.g. polling station) or is conducted remotely from a location outside any control.

Furthermore, electronic voting solution can be divided into four types depending on the usage of information and communication technologies (ICT). The first type is *voting by dedicated voting machines*, which uses electronic devices for recording, storing or transmitting user votes. Sometimes, they are accompanied by voter-verified audit paper trail, which are printed copies of the recorded votes. They provide fast data collection, fast vote counting and prevent ballot spoiling. However, they are expensive to deploy and maintain. Furthermore, they are vulnerable to manipulation as it is impossible to inspect every single device [18, 24, 25].

The second type is *voting with optical scanning machines*, which record votes by scanning machine-readable paper ballots. They are easy to implement because they do not change the voting process from the point of view of the voters. Like most electronic voting solutions they provide fast and accurate results. On the other hand, they depend on paper ballots and suffer from the same lack of auditability as the previously described dedicated voting machines [18, 24, 25].

The third type consists of *voting with electronic ballot printers*, which are similar to dedicated voting machine but they produce machine-readable ballot or token which is used in another device to record votes instead of recording them on the machine itself. They leave a physical trail in a form of a printed ballot which can be verified before being cast. However, this solution is expensive due to a need of maintaining separate devices for printing and counting [18, 24, 25].

The fourth type is *voting by the Internet*, in which votes are cast on devices connected to the Internet and then transmitted to the central counting server. This type of voting provides fast and accurate results. It allows remote and non-supervised voting which seems to be currently the most desirable method of voting. Unfortunately, it also has the most security concerns, for example, hacker attacks, potential lack of anonymity and privacy, "creation" of votes, third parties influencing voters [18, 24, 25].

Finally, electronic voting systems can be classified depending on cryptographic primitives and schemes they are utilizing. The most common cryptographic primitives used in electronic voting are: (i) *zero knowledge proofs*, which allow one party to prove to the other that it knows some value without revealing any additional information; (ii) *secret sharing*, in which a secret information is shared among a group in such a way that each participant obtains only a part of the whole information; (iii) *homorfic encryption*, which allows to perform operations on encrypted data and obtain valid results; (iv) *blind signatures* that allow authorities to sign an encrypted data without decrypting it; (v) *mixnet* which create difficult to trace communications by sending messages through a network of authorities which shuffle received messages before sending them forward [19, 23].

As can be seen, there are many different ways to analyse electronic voting systems. Each type has its own advantages and disadvantages, which cannot be overlooked. Some are connected to the whole concept of e-voting, while others come directly from the specific implementation.

2.2 Blockchain Technology

Blockchain technology is composed of two elements [3, 34]:

- blockchain data structure,
- blockchain system or network.

Blockchain data structure is an ordered list of connected data units called blocks. Each block is composed of block header and transaction data. The block header contains block metadata, which contains information about block itself, for example, index and creation timestamp. Most important field in the header is hash representation of the previous block. This value is generated from the contents of the previous block and is used to connect block to each other. The transaction data contains a list of transaction and their respective data. Figure 1 presents a model of the blockchain data structure. The two main components of each block are represented by rectangle with thicker lines, standard rectangles represent component subelements and arrows illustrate connections between blocks.

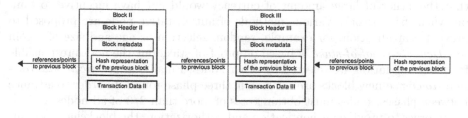

Fig. 1. Model of a blockchain, adapted from [3]

The hash representations are result of application of one of cryptographic one-way hash functions to the contents of each block. It maps data of arbitrary size to a unique bit string of a fixed size called hash value (or reference). Due to the properties of these functions, the value is easy to calculate but difficult to invert from the point of view of computational theory. Another important property of the cryptographic hash functions is sensitivity to change of input data. Even a small modification of the input will result in a different hash value [12]. This ensures immutability of the ordered list of blocks because a change of a single block would force modification of all subsequent blocks. Furthermore, due to hash value uniqueness, each block can be identified and tracked allowing verification of their correctness. There exist many cryptographic hash functions used in various blockchain implementations, the most popular include SHA256, RIPEMD160, Merkle trees and the Elliptic Curve Digital Signature Algorithm [13, 15].

On the other hand, *blockchain system* is a distributed peer-to-peer network of connected nodes which store and negotiate the information content of the blockchain. Each node validates incoming transactions and, if they are valid, propagates them to other nodes which continue this process until all nodes of the system are aware of the new transactions. Nodes maintain their own copies of the blockchain and add new blocks to it in a process called *mining*, in which transactions are validated and aggregated into blocks and appended to the chain. Each new block is broadcasted to the other nodes so they can modify their copies of the blockchain. In order to maintain consistency the system attempts to reach a consensus about which blocks must be added. This is done via *consensus algorithms*, which there are many types. The most common are [14,15,34]:

- proof-of-work,
- proof-of-stake,
- delegated-proof-of-stake,
- practical-byzantine-fault-tolerance.

In *proof-of-work* nodes compete in solving mathematical problem, which is computationally expensive. The node which first solves the puzzle is allowed to append a new block to the blockchain and gets a reward. The new block is validated by the other nodes and appended to their chains. The algorithm assumes that the longest chain is the most authoritative due to the amount of total work. *Proof-of-stake* is based on ownership of a digital currency. It assumes that the owner of large amount of currency would not have incentive to tamper with the network. Various methods of authoritative node are proposed to prevent centralisation, for example, random selection or age and size of a coin set. *Delegate-proof-of-stake* is based on proof-of-stake but the nodes responsible for block validation are selected by other nodes. Finally, in *practical-byzantine-fault-tolerance* new blocks are selected in three phase round. In order to advance between phases, nodes must obtain votes of more than 2/3 of all nodes.

In order to provide authentication and authorization, the blockchain systems use asymmetric cryptography. This approach utilizes public and private keys, which can be used to encrypt and decrypt messages. It is important to note that a messages encrypted with one key can only be decrypted with the other (Fig. 2).

Public-to-private is a method of encryption, in which messages are encrypted with the available to everyone public key and then decrypted with the private key. This is similar to a mailbox which can receive mail from anyone but only the owner can open it. In blockchain systems accounts are identified by addresses, which are also cryptographic public keys. This allows the transactions to be encrypted, so only the receiver can decrypt them. Private-to-public is a method, in which messages are encrypted with the private key and are decrypted with the public key. This is a method of proving ownership as only the owner of the private key could create a message, which can be decrypted with the corresponding public key. Blockchain systems use this method for transaction authorization [3,4].

Blockchain technology is constantly developed and there exist many different implementations and applications. In general, blockchain-based systems can be divided by two characteristics [3]:

1. read rights,
2. write rights.

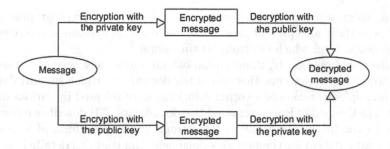

Fig. 2. Illustration of asymmetric cryptography, adapted from [3]

Read rights divide the blockchain-based systems into two classes: (i) *public* where users and nodes all have access to the contents of the blockchain and transactions; (ii) *private* where rights to access the blockchain is restricted to only a selected group. On the other hand, write rights groups blockchain-base systems into: (i) *permissionless* which allow every user and node to participate in the consensus algorithm; (ii) *permissioned* in which only a selected group of users and nodes can verify transactions and add new blocks to the chain.

As mentioned previously, many implementations of the technology exist. The best-known is Bitcoin virtual currency, from which the technology originates. It is fully distributed, public and permissionless system using proof-of-work algorithm. Second popular system is Ethereum Platform created by Ethereum Foundation [16]. It is blockchain platform which uses both proof-of-work and smart contracts. It provides a platform for creation of blockchain-based applications. Lastly, Multichain platform allows creation of private blockchain systems utilizing consensus protocol similar to practical-byzantine-fault-tolerance algorithm [17].

From the point of view of electronic voting, blockchain technology provides many potential benefits. It is censorship-proof because it is distributed among a peer-to-peer network of nodes without central authority. It is very secure on transaction and system level. Finally, because each node not only stores the blockchain but supervises transactions anyone with access to node can view the blockchain data. This can potentially provide a solution to problems with transparency from which most of the e-voting systems suffer.

3 Related Works

There are numerous publications concerning electronic voting. The authors of [23] provide a thorough overview of electronic voting schemas. The paper starts with a review of security properties of e-voting systems and the most used cryptographic primitives used in a construction of the schemes. Finally, the paper describes sixteen electronic voting schemes and their comparison.

Similarly, in [22] the authors describe the current state of electronic voting. The work presents various methods of attacking e-voting systems and different design schemas divided with respect to utilized cryptographic primitives. The authors also present chosen existing e-voting systems and discuss still open problems form which electronic voting suffer.

As discussed previously, there are no official and widely accepted standards for electronic voting systems. However, a few documents, which support development and implementation of e-voting solutions, were released by various organisations. The Council of Europe created two documents. [31] describes recommendations for conducting elections with electronic means in a form of a checklist. [32] is an explanation for the previous document and contains detailed technical recommendations. Finally, [21] was developed as a mean of providing assistance and guidelines for introducing e-voting.

Another standard was developed by The International Institute for Democracy and Electoral Assistance (International IDEA). This intergovernmental organisation created [18], which contains guidelines, recommendations and considerations for implementing electronic voting systems.

Despite being relatively new technology, there is ongoing research of blockchain application in various fields. In [9] the authors present research on possible applications of the technology in e-governance conducted by the Digital5 (D5) countries. This includes research of its usage in electronic voting. The two most active countries in this field are Estonia and South Korea. The latter was able to conduct a successful community vote using blockchain technology in 2017.

In [20] the authors present system SAVE, which is a supervised e-voting system for medium and large scale voting, for instance, elections on university. The paper describes all components and processes of the system. SAVE utilizes commonly available personal computers and smartphones as voting machines for supervised voting. Furthermore, the system uses symmetric encryption for signing its software components, asymmetric encryption (RSA with 2048 bit key length) for data encryption and HMAC-SHA256 for message authentication. Finally, it is worth noting that SAVE utilizes VVPATs generated by printers for vote verification.

It is important to mention the most successful electronic voting system. Estonian i-voting was introduced in 2005 and it is being in constant use since [29]. It provides a remote unsupervised internet voting based on "envelope scheme" [30]. Before casting votes, the voters are required to authenticate with ID-cards or mobile phones with special SIM cards containing an encrypted ID of the owner. Multiple votes can be cast but only the most recent one is considered. The votes can be verified by the common voters using a dedicated application. Furthermore, the system is being constantly upgraded and improved.

There exist some working blockchain-based e-voting solutions. The main example is Agora [26], which is customizable multi-layer system. It allows supervised and unsupervised internet voting with a hybrid of permissionless and permissioned public blockchain. The system was successfully implemented in elections in Sierra Leone in 2018 [11]. It is worth noting that Agora leaves authentication and authorization to the election officials. However, it also offers a system based on digital signatures for facilitating this process.

Another solution is Ethereum-based FollowMyVote [28] voting platform. It is designed for remote and unsupervised internet voting. The system uses elliptic curve cryptography for security and webcams for identification and authorization by ID scanning. FollowMyVote provides the users with an ability to supervise the election process in real time and to switch their votes during the election.

In [27] an end-to-end verifiable, Bitcoin-based system is presented. The solution conducts authentication and transactions using a protocol called Anonymus Kerberos. The system represents votes as "tokens", which are the smallest transferable amount of bitcoins (including fees). The system assumes that the voters must register with election officials before they can participate in the voting process. The authors note that the system fulfils most of the e-voting requirements with the exception of voter's privacy, which can be violated dude to possibility of linking the voters to their transactions.

4 Auditable Blockchain Voting System

In this section Auditable Blockchain Voting System (ABVS) is presented. It is designed as a non-remote and supervised voting system that uses blockchain system to store and verify the voting procedure. ABVS is intended to enhance the existing critical voting processes in Poland. The system is in a development stage, in which prototypes are developed and tested. In the following subsections ABVS components, process overview and result of initial testing are presented.

4.1 Auditable Blockchain Voting System Components

Auditable Blockchain Voting System is a public and permissioned blockchain-based electronic voting system. It is made of six components:

1. client applications (polling stations),
2. system of trusted nodes,
3. Vote Identification Tokens,
4. voter-verified paper audit trail (VVPAT),
5. vote error notification module,
6. counting application.

Figure 3 illustrates relations between the components of ABVS. Ovals represent components and relations are shown as labelled arrows.

Client applications are lightweight programs installed on computers located at polling stations used for casting votes in a form of blockchain transactions. Each transaction contains information about transaction creation, voter's choice (vote value), vote identification token and polling station identifier. The transactions are broadcasted to the nodes in accordance with the blockchain technology

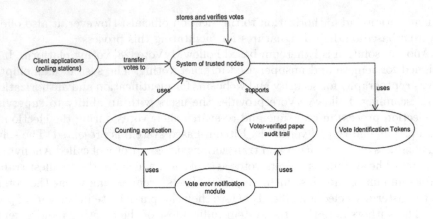

Fig. 3. Model of relations between Auditable Blockchain Voting System components

paradigm. For security purposes, each application should be signed during election preparation in order to prevent unauthorized participation.

System of trusted nodes is a set of blockchain nodes which store the chain containing blocks with votes and mine new ones. One node, called super-node, represents central national electoral authorities (National Electoral Commission in case of Poland). It is responsible for creation of the initial block (*genesis block*) aggregating all information about the voting in its transaction. The block is then broadcasted to other trusted blockchain nodes, which are pre-selected and verified public institutions (e.g. universities). Figure 4 illustrates interactions between the nodes and the client applications.

Vote Identification Tokens (VITs) are alphanumerical codes used for authentication and authorization of the voters. Furthermore, they allow vote following and vote identification during and after the election. They may be contained on paper sheets hidden in envelopes or any other medium which can be randomly selected by voters without showing their contents in advance. VITs must be generated and distributed during the election preparation stage. Each node stores a list of VIT-polling station pairs for vote verification.

Voter-verified paper audit trails (VVPATs) are paper representations of votes. Each VVPAT contains the same vote information as ABVS transaction. They are printed by standard printers after voters cast their votes and are disposed into traditional ballot boxes. This is implemented to provide additional audit and verification capabilities.

Vote error notification module is a service for reporting inconsistencies in the recorded votes. In order to send notification to the service, the voters have to provide a valid VIT and error explanation. The inconsistencies are resolved by comparison of the given block with the corresponding VVPAT.

Counting application is a certified and signed program for iterating over blockchains and producing results of the voting. Each node is equipped with its own instance of the application in order to created multiple comparable results for verification purposes.

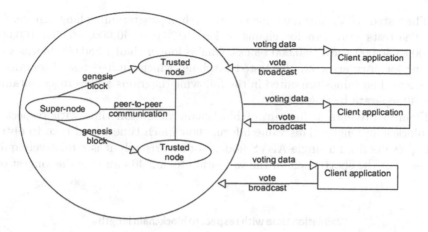

Fig. 4. Schema of the Auditable Blockchain Voting System network

4.2 Auditable Blockchain Voting System Process Overview

The voting in ABVS is organized in a three phases: (i) election preparation or setup; (ii) voting; (iii) counting and verification. In the setup stage software and hardware components are signed and certified. The election officials select institutions which will function as nodes of the blockchain system. Finally, vote identification tokens are generated and distributed.

In the voting phase, the voters identify themselves at their polling stations and randomly select voter identification tokens. They cast their votes using VITs and the client applications. Moreover, they receive VVPATs which are disposed into ballot boxes for verification in the final stage. The trusted-nodes mine blocks containing votes and reach consensus. It is important to note that at this stage, the blockchain remains private.

In the final stage, the system is deactivated and the counting applications determine the result of the voting. Lists of remaining VITs are made public in order to allow verification of the number of votes in the chain. Furthermore, when the nodes reach the final consensus the blockchain is made public, so each voter can check his vote and report inconsistencies through the dedicated application.

4.3 Auditable Blockchain Voting System Initial Testing

The initial tests of ABVS were focused on two main elements:

- the blockchain validation time,
- RAM space required by the blockchain.

The main goal of these tests was to determine a reference point for the equipment needed for a real voting. The tests were conducted one a machine with the following specification:

1. Processor: Intel(R) Core(TM) i5-7300 CPU @ 2.60 GHz 2.70 GHz.
2. RAM: 32.0 GB (31.8 GB usable).
3. System type: 64-bit operating system, x64-based processor.

The tested ABVS was implemented in Python programming language version 3.6. The tests were run for chains of length 20,000, 40,000, 80,000, 160,000, 320,000, 640,000 and 1,280,000 blocks. Chains longer than 1,280,000 blocks were causing memory error on the tested machine, which limited tested lengths at this stage. The values presented in the following diagrams are averages obtained form 40 separate testing cycles.

Figure 5 presents a diagram of blockchain validation time with respect to the blockchain length. This value informs how much time would take to obtain voting results from a single ABVS node. Not surprisingly it is a relatively quick process. For the shortest chain the validation took 2.46 s and for the longest one 158.51 s.

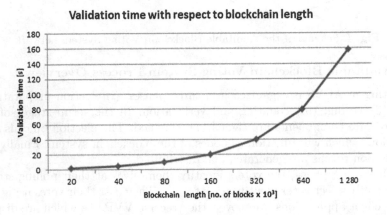

Fig. 5. Validation times with respect to blockchain length

Figure 6 presents a diagram of blockchain size in RAM with respect to blockchain length. The shortest chain takes 6.5 MB of RAM memory and the longest takes 415.1 MB of RAM memory. As mentioned above longer chains

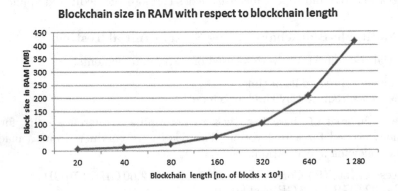

Fig. 6. RAM size of the blockchain with respect to its length

caused memory errors, which prevented testing of longer chains at this stage. This may be a result of limits forced by operating system on operational memory for a single process or optimisation problem. These issues must be solved before the next stage of the testing.

5   Conclusions

There are many existing voting solutions, which have different benefits and issues. However, they share a few common problems, for example, lack of transparency and verifiability, or lack of commonly accepted standards. Recently developed blockchain technology may be a solution to the problems of auditability of e-voting systems. Integration of blockchain and electronic voting may provide the voters with a system, in which they can follow their vote and supervise the calculation of the results. Due to this, election frauds would become much more difficult.

Auditable Blockchain Voting System is a non-remote supervised internet voting system, which utilizes blockchain technology. It is intended as an end-to-end verifiable electronic voting system, allowing the common voters to follow their votes and verify the final results. To achieve this, ABVS utilizes voter-verified paper audit trails to provide point of reference for blockchain verification and Vote Identification Tokens allowing the voters to identify their votes without providing any personal information. It is important to note that the goal of the system is to improve and enhance the existing voting process in Poland.

In this paper, ABVS components and its overall voting process are described. Furthermore, the results of the initial testing are presented. The conducted tests showcased that the equipment used for testing is inadequate for the task of handling long blockchains or there exists some optimization issues of the ABVS prototype.

References

1. Satoshi, N.: Bitcoin: a peer-to-peer electronic cash system (2008). https://bitcoin.org/bitcoin.pdf. Accessed 2018
2. Zhao, J.L., Fan, S., Yan, J.: Overview Of Business Innovations and Research Opportunities in Blockchain and Introduction to the Special Issue Financial Innovation, pp. 2–28. Springer, Heidelberg (2016). https://doi.org/10.1186/s40854-016-0049-2
3. Drescher, D.: Blockchain Basics: A Non-technical Introduction in 25 Steps, 1st edn. Apress, Frankfurt am Main (2017). https://doi.org/10.1007/s11408-018-0315-6
4. Karame, G., Audroulaki, E.: Bitcoin and Blockchain Security. Artech House Inc., Norwood (2016). https://doi.org/10.1007/s11408-018-0315-6
5. Risius, M., Spohrer, K.: A blockchain research framework - what we (don't) know, where we go from here, and how we will get there. Bus. Inf. Syst. Eng. 59(6), 385–409 (2017)
6. De Faveri, C., Moreira, A., Arajo, J.: Towards security modeling of e-voting systems, In: Proceedings of IEEE 24th International Requirements Engineering Conference Workshops (REW), Beijing (2016)

7. Lehoucq, F.: Electoral fraud: causes, types, and consequences. Ann. Rev. Polit. Sci. **6**(1), 233–256 (2003)
8. Willemson, J.: Bits or paper: which should get to carry your vote? J. Inf. Secur. Appl. **38**, 124–131 (2018)
9. Ojo, A., Adebayo, S.: Blockchain as a next generation Government 3.0 - information infrastructure: a review of initiatives in D5 countries. In: Ojo, A., Millard, J. (eds.) Government Next Generation Government Technology Infrastructure and Services Public Administration and Information Technology, vol. 32, pp. 283–298. Springer, Cham (2017)
10. Enterprise Estonia, Factsheet on Estonian blockchain technology (in English) (2012). https://e-estonia.com/wp-content/uploads/facts-a4-v03-blockchain.pdf. Accessed 8 Feb 2018
11. Akwei, I.: Sierra Leone is first country in the world to use blockchain technology to vote, March 2018. https://face2faceafrica.com/article/sierra-leone-first-country-world-use-blockchain-technology-vote. Accessed 22 Apr 2018
12. Stallings, W.: Cryptographic Hash Functions. In: Cryptography and Network Security: Principles and Practice, (6th edn.), pp. 313–354. Pearson Education Inc. (2013)
13. Morabito, V.: The Security of Blockchain Systems, pp. 61–78. Business Innovation Through Blockchain, Springer, Cham (2017)
14. Zheng, Z., Xie, S., Dai, H., Chen, X., Wang, H.: An overview of blockchain technology: architecture, consensus, and future trends. In: Proceedings of IEEE International Congress on Big Data (BigData Congress), Honolulu (2017)
15. Mingxiao, D., Xiaofeng, M., Zhe, Z., Qijun, C.: A review on consensus algorithm of Blockchain. In: Proceedings of IEEE International Conference on Systems, Man, and Cybernetics (SMC), Banff (2017)
16. Ethereum Foundation: "Ethereum Project", Ethereum Foundation, August 2014. https://www.ethereum.org/. Accessed 20 Apr 2018
17. Coin Sciences: MultiChain, Coin Sciences (2015). https://www.multichain.com/. Accessed 20 Apr 2018
18. Wolf, P., Nackerdien, R., Tuccinardi, D.: Introducing electronic voting: essential considerations. International Institute for Democracy and Electoral Assistance, 1 December 2011. https://www.idea.int/publications/catalogue/introducing-electronic-voting-essential-considerations. Accessed 22 Jan 2018
19. Zhou, Y., Zhou, Y., Chen, S., Wu, S.S.: MVP: an efficient anonymous E-voting protocol. In: Proceedings of Global Communications Conference (GLOBECOM), Washington (2016)
20. Ochoa, X., Pelez, E.: Affordable and secure electronic voting for university elections: the SAVE case study. In: Proceedings of 4th International Conference on eDemocracy & eGovernment (ICEDEG), Quito, Ecuador (2017)
21. Caarls, S.: E-voting handbook: key steps in the implementation of e-enabled elections. Council of Europe, November 2010. https://www.coe.int/t/dgap/goodgovernance/Activities/E-voting. Accessed Jan 2018
22. Schneider, A., Meter, C., Hagemeister, P.: Survey on remote electronic voting. arXiv preprint arXiv:1702.02798 (2017)
23. Fouard, L., Duclos, M., Lafourcade, P.: Survey on Electronic Voting Schemes. project AVOT, University of Grenoble (2017)
24. National Democratic Institute: Common Electronic Voting and Counting Technologies. https://www.ndi.org/e-voting-guide/common-electronic-voting-and-counting-technologies. Accessed 22 Jan 2018

25. United Nations Development Programm: Feasibility study on Internet Voting for the Central Electoral Commission of the Republic of Moldova: Report and preliminary roadmap. Central Electoral Commission of the Republic of Moldova, Chisinau (2016)
26. Agora Technologies: Agora_Whitepaper_v0.2.pd (2015). https://agora.vote/Agora_Whitepaper_v0.2.pdf. Accessed 20 Apr 2018
27. Bistarelli, S., Mantilacci, M., Santancini, P., Santini, F.: An end-to-end voting-system based on BITCOIN. In: Proceedings of Symposium on Applied Computing, SAC2017, New York (2017)
28. Follow My Vote: The online voting platform of the future. https://followmyvote.com. Accessed 26 Jan 2018
29. State Electoral Office of Estonia: General framework of electronic voting and implementation thereof at national elections in Estonia, 20 June 2017. https://www.valimised.ee/sites/default/files/uploads/eng/IVXV-UK-1.0-eng.pdf
30. Heiberg, S., Willemson, J.: Verifiable internet voting in Estonia. In: Proceedings of 6th International Conference on Electronic Voting: Verifying the Vote (EVOTE), Lochau (2014)
31. Council of Europe – Committee of Ministers: Recommendation CM/Rec(2017) 51 of the committee of ministers to member states on standards for E-voting, 14 June 2017. https://search.coe.int/cm/Pages/result_details.aspx?ObjectID=0900001680726f6f. Accessed 26 Jan 2018
32. Ad hoc Committee of Experts on Legal, Operational and Technical Standards for e-voting (CAHVE): Explanatory memorandum to recommendation CM/Rec(2017) 5 of the committee of ministers to member states on standards for E-voting, 14 June 2017. https://search.coe.int/cm/Pages/result_details.aspx?ObjectID=090000168071bc84
33. Noizat, P.: Blockchain Electronic Vote. In: Handbook of Digital Currency, Elsevier Inc., pp. 453–460 (2015)
34. Xu, X., et al.: A taxonomy of blockchain-based systems for architecture design. In: Proceedings of IEEE International Conference on Software Architecture (ICSA), Gothenburg (2017)

Privacy-Preserving SAT Solving Based on Projection-Equivalence CNF Obfuscation

Ying Qin[1]([⊠]), Xiao Yang Shen[2], and Zhen Yue Du[3]

[1] College of Computer, National University of Defense Technology,
Changsha 410073, China
yingqin@nudt.edu.cn
[2] Attached School of National University of Defense Technology, Changsha, China
[3] Fuzhou University, Fuzhou, China

Abstract. In this paper, we study the problem of privacy-preserving SAT solving in the cloud computing paradigm. we present a CNF obfuscation algorithm and its corresponding solution recovery algorithm, to prevent unauthorized third party obtaining sensitive information. By obfuscation, the CNF formula is transformed into another formula with different circuit structure and projection-equivalence over-approximated solution space. Solution of the original CNF can be extracted from the solution of obfuscated CNF by projection based solution recovery algorithm. Theoretical analysis demonstrates that, obfuscation algorithm can change the structure of CNF formula with polynomial time complexity, while solution recovery algorithm can filter out solution with linear time complexity.

Keywords: SAT · Obfuscation · Privacy preserving

1 Introduction

In the cloud computing paradigm, high-performance-computing centers play a fundamental role as the major computing infrastructure providers. Computing-centers provide the Virtual Machines (VM) service to end users through Internet [26,27]. Propositional satisfiability (SAT) [1] has been widely used in hardware and software verification [2,3,23], cryptography [4] etc. With the rapid increase of the hardware and software system size, the size of SAT problem generated from verification also increases rapidly. which make outsourcing hard SAT problem to public Cloud [19,20] very attractive.

To take advantage of computing and storage resources provided by Cloud infrastructure providers, end users are required to deploy computing and data into the VMs on computing-centers through cloud service providers. While the Cloud vendors can be trusted, the VMs cannot. Literature [12] points out security

---

Supported by NSF China.

A. Castiglione et al. (Eds.): CSS 2018, LNCS 11161, pp. 224–239, 2018.
https://doi.org/10.1007/978-3-030-01689-0_18

vulnerability that Amazon EC2 suffered from: Since Amazon Machine Image (AMI) are widely shared among the EC2 community, a malicious AMI could flood the community with hundreds of infected virtual instances. Literature [13] also points out the possibility of attacking VM through another VM in the same physical machine.

These facts show that input and output data of SAT problem may be exposed to untrusted third party, who may inspect valuable information from these data. For example, SAT program originated from verification may suffer from leakage of privacy, such as circuit structure information. Roy [9] and Fu [10] suggest the possibility of extracting circuit information from CNF formula. Furthermore, Du [18] called solution of hard SAT problem generating from cryptograph etc. as high-value rare events, and point out that the solution of SAT problem should also be treated as privacy, because it may be leaked to third party by hoarding participants [18]. Moreover, the SAT solver deployed in Cloud may also be compromised by adversary, who may compel SAT solver to return incorrect result to mislead verification.

These threats put customers who plan to outsource SAT solving in a dilemma: using public Cloud in open environment is cost-efficiently, but may suffer from leakage of privacy or incorrect result. Such security issues make many end users hesitate to move their critical computation tasks, e.g., SAT-solving, to Cloud.

In order to meet this challenge, we develop novel techniques for privacy-preserving SAT solving in Cloud, which can preserve privacy of input and output of SAT problem, while ensure the correctness of solution. These novel techniques consist of four parts: **First**, A Cubic Husk formula generation algorithm, which can generate Cubic Husk formula to act as noise. **Second**, A structure aware obfuscation algorithm, which blend original CNF formula with Cubic Husk formula seamlessly. By obfuscation, confidential information in the original CNF formula, such as circuit structure,will be destroyed in the obfuscated CNF formula. **Third**, The state-of-the-art SAT solver deployed in Cloud, which will solve obfuscated CNF formula. With the aid of Cubic Husk formula, solution space of obfuscated CNF is over-approximated and projection-equivalent to that of original CNF. **Fourth**, A projection based solution recovery algorithm, with which solution of the original CNF can be recovered from over-approximated solutions of the obfuscated CNF, which keep the solution a privacy even for the SAT solver.

Furthermore, obfuscation algorithm is polynomial complexity and solution recovery algorithm is linear complexity, which reduce the impact on the overall performance of SAT solving.

This paper is organized as follows. Preliminaries are presented in Sect. 2. Section 3 describes the threat model, while our algorithms are presented in Sect. 4. Section 5 analyzes correctness and effectiveness of our algorithms. Section 6 give the performance analysis; while Sect. 7 concludes this paper.

2   Preliminaries

The Boolean value set is $B = \{T, F\}$. For a Boolean formula F_C over a variable set V, the propositional satisfiability problem (abbreviated as SAT) is to find a satisfying assignment $A : V \rightarrow B$, so that F_C evaluates to T. If such a satisfying assignment exists, then F_C is satisfiable, and the satisfying assignment is called solution of F_C; otherwise, it is unsatisfiable. An unsatisfiable subset of formula is an unsatisfiable core. A computer program that decides the existence of a satisfying assignment is SAT solver [11].

Normally, a SAT solver requires the formula to be in conjunctive normal form (CNF), in which a formula is a conjunction of its clause set, and a clause is a disjunction of its literal set, while a literal is a variable or its negation. The number of literals in clause C is denoted as $|C|$. The number of clauses in a CNF formula F is denoted as $|F|$. Variable set of CNF formula F_C is denoted as V_{F_C}. When variables in CNF formula F_C are assigned with solution S_C, we denote it as $F_C(S_C/V_{F_C})$.

In hardware verification, circuits and properties are converted into CNF formula by Tseitin encoding [6], and then CNF formula is solved by SAT solver. Circuits can all be expressed by a combination of gate AND2 and INV, so we only list Tseitin encoding of gate AND2 and INV here. For gate INV $z = \neg x$, its Tseitin encoding is $(x \vee z) \wedge (\neg x \vee \neg z)$. For gate AND2 $z = x_1 \wedge x_2$, its CNF formula is $(\neg x_1 \vee \neg x_2 \vee z) \wedge (x_1 \vee \neg z) \wedge (x_2 \vee \neg z)$. For a complex circuit C expressed by a combination of AND2 and INV, its Tseitin encoding $Tseitin(C)$ is a conjunctive of all these gates' Tseitin encoding.

3   Motivation

In our research, there are two types of Cloud, private and public Cloud. Private Cloud is trusted but has only limited computation power and memory to handle simple computation. Public Cloud can provide elastic computation and memory resource to deal with complex computation. CNF formula will be generated from netlist or program in private Cloud, SAT solver is deployed in public Cloud to handle the CNF formula and return solution to the private Cloud.

Algorithms [7–10] have been proposed to extract and utilize circuit structure in CNF formula. Circuit structure extraction algorithms [9,10], are based on subgraph isomorphism and pattern matching technique, and can recover lots of circuits from CNF formula. These pattern matching or subgraph isomorphism techniques are available freely. In public Cloud computing environment, adversary who has controled VM [12,13] may use these algorithms to recover the circuit structure from the CNF formula. According to [18], since solutions to difficult instances of NP-complete problems are rare events, with the practical importance of many of these problems, hoarding participants may keep these solutions for economic value.

Therefore both CNF formula and its solutions should be treated as privacy. So in our research, we assume there are curious and hoarding participants [18] in public Cloud. That means, the participants conduct all the required computations to get solutions of SAT problem; But they may try to get information from CNF formula as much as possible, such as circuit structure information; And if the solution are valuable, they may keep the computation results and leak it to third party.

4 System Design

4.1 Privacy-Preserving SAT Solving Framework

When we design the Cloud oriented SAT solving framework, the following four goals are taken into consideration:

1. As for the portability, current SAT solvers with conflict analysis [11] are very efficient. So we would like to use them directly instead of developing new algorithms like [17].
2. As for the stealth [21], the framework should be able to prevent circuit structure from being recovered from CNF formula.
3. As for the resilence [21], the framework should prevent accurate solution from being known even by the SAT solver, which is deployed in public Cloud.
4. As for the cost, the framework should not incur too much overhead.

Thus, we present a privacy-preserving SAT solving framework based on CNF formula obfuscation. To obfuscate the CNF formula, according to SSH rules and CSA strategies described below, we embed extra literals into CNF clauses and insert extra clauses into CNF formula. The extra literals and part of new clauses are from another CNF formula, which we called Cubic Husk formula. SSH rules and CSA strategies ensure the original CNF formula to be blended with Cubic Husk formula seamless, to attain goals (2) and (3). Cubic Husk formula ensures that solution space of obfuscated CNF is Projection-Equivalent to that of original CNF. SSH rules and CSA strategies are described in Sect. 4.3).

Definition 1 (Cubic Husk formula). *Cubic Husk formula is a satisfiable CNF formula with more than one solution, and assignments of variables in every solution are non-uniform. Assignments of some variables are same in every solution, and these same assignments is called* **Cubic Solution**.

The SAT problem is solved in 4 steps. **Step 1**, GENERATOR algorithm generates a Cubic Husk formula F_H and one of its solution R_H. **Step 2**, OBFUSCATOR algorithm obfuscates the Original CNF F_C to obtain a new CNF formula F_O. **Step 3**, F_O is solved by SAT Solver deployed in public Cloud, which returns solution S_O. **Step 4**, MAPPER and VERIFIER algorithm maps S_O to S_C, and check if F_C is satisfied under S_C. The **Step 3** run in public Cloud, while other steps run in trusted private Cloud. These algorithms will be described in Subsects. 4.2, 4.3 and 4.4 respectively.

4.2 Cubic Husk Formula Generation

In this paper, Cubic Husk formula is constructed based on prime factorization method [15, 16].

First, given two primes $p_A \neq p_B$, we assign $p_A \cdot p_B$ to the output of a multiplier M with constraint $I_1 \neq 1$ and $I_2 \neq 1$. I_1 and I_2 are inputs of M. **Second**, we convert the multiplier M into CNF formula $Tseitin(M)$. To satisfy $Tseitin(M)$, the two inputs of M must be $\{I_1 = p_A, I_2 = p_B\}$ or $\{I_1 = p_B, I_2 = p_A\}$, which makes the $p_A|p_B$ or $p_B|p_A$ and corresponding assignments is CNF formula $Tseitin(M)$ the two solutions of $Tseitin(M)$. We filter out common assignments from two solutions of $Tseitin(M)$, and take them as R_H.

4.3 Circuit Structure Aware and Projection-Equivalenct Obfuscation

Input and Output Privacy-Preserving Scheme. To prevent information carried by CNF formula and its solution from leakage, a privacy-preserving scheme is proposed, the scheme is based on the following facts and anticipations:

Fact 1: Changing CNF signature and key clause in CNF formula will make circuit recovering based on pattern matching or subgraph isomorphism impossible.

Fact 2: Solution space should not be under-approximated after obfuscation, otherwise the result will be incorrect.

Anticipation 1: According to Fact 2, solution space have to be over-approximated after obfuscation, so as to mislead hoarding participants in public Cloud.

Anticipation 2: The solution of obfuscated CNF formula should be easily mapped back to the original formula.

The proposed scheme, denoted as OBFUSCATOR, generates a new CNF formula F_O, by embedding Cubic Husk formula F_H into the original formula F_C, with Circuit Structure Aware (CSA) strategy and Solution Space Hold (SSH) rules. By CSA strategy, the scheme changes the clause set and literal set of F_C, to prevent its structure from being recovered. By SSH rules and Cubic Husk formula, the solution space is over-approximated and projection-equivalent after obfuscation, so as to prevent its accurate solutions from being known even by SAT solver in public Cloud. We will describe them in Subsect. 4.3).

Solution Space Hold Rules. Let us consider an interesting problem: We outsource CNF formula generated from SAT problem, and wish SAT solver deployed in Cloud to give solutions to the SAT problem, without knowing exactly what the SAT problem is and what the exactly solution is.

A simple approach is to blend CNF formula of real SAT problem with that of another satisfiable SAT problem. But partition based technique [22] can easily separate the two independent formulas. Let us consider an incremental approach: An arbitrary formula F_C, and a Cubic Husk formula F_H with $\mathbf{R_H}$ as Cubic solution, and there is no common variable between F_C and F_H, viz. $V_{F_C} \cap V_{F_H} = \phi$. We blend F_C with F_H seamlessly, so as to hide F_C. At the same time, we keep all solutions of F_C still in the new formula.

To blend F_C and F_H seamlessly, an intuitive approach is to insert variables of F_H into clauses of F_C, and generate new clauses with variables in F_C and F_H. According to property of CNF, for any CNF formula F_C, inserting new variables into its clauses may expand its solution space; On the contrary, adding new clauses which consist variables in F_C, may narrow down its solution space. How can we ensure all the solutions of F_C still in new formula? Before answering this question, we need some new concepts.

Definition 2 (*Solution $S_C \subseteq$ Solution S_O*). *CNF formula F_C and F_O have n_{F_C} common variables $x_1, \ldots, x_{n_{F_C}}$ and $|V_{F_C}| \equiv n_{F_C}$, $|V_{F_O}| \equiv n_{F_O}$, $n_{F_O} \geqslant n_{F_C} > 0$. S_C and S_O are solutions of F_C and F_O respectively, and assignments to n_{F_C} common variables are same in S_C and S_O, viz. $S_C = \{x_1 = B_1, \ldots, x_{n_{F_C}} = B_{n_{F_C}} | B_i \in \{T, F\}, 1 \leqslant i \leqslant n_{F_C}\}$, $S_O = \{x_1 = B_1, \ldots, x_{n_{F_C}} = B_{n_{F_C}}, \ldots, x_{n_{F_O}} = B_{n_{F_O}} | B_i \in \{T, F\}, 1 \leqslant i \leqslant n_{F_O}\}$. Then Solution S_C is subset of Solution S_O, denoted as $S_C \subseteq S_O$.*

Definition 3 (**Solution Space Projection-Equivalence(SSP)**). *CNF formula F_C has n_C solutions $\{S_{C_1}, \ldots, S_{C_n}\}$; By obfuscation, F_C has been transformed into F_O, which has $m \times n_C$ solution, $\{S_{O_1}, \ldots, S_{O_n}, \ldots, S_{O_{mn}}\}$, $m > 1$, while for $i \in [1, n]$ and $j \in [1, m]$, $S_{C_i} \subseteq S_{O_{ij}}$. Then, we say F_O is Solution Space Projection-Equivalent to F_C, denoted as $F_C =_{SSP} F_O$, also denoted as $F_C \vdash_{SSP} F_O$.*

In order to keep all solutions of F_C in new formula, we use Solution Space Hold (SSH) rules to obfuscate F_C with F_H and its Cubic solution R_H, so as to make the solution space Projection-Equivalent after obfuscation.

Solution Space Hold Rules (SSH Rules)

> **Rule 1:** For any clause $c \in F_C$, take one variable from R_H. If this variable is T in R_H, insert its negative literal into c; Otherwise, insert its positive literal. Then clause c is replaced with the resulted clause.
>
> **Rule 2:** Generating new clauses with literals from R_H and variables in F_C according to the following rule: If this variable is T in R_H, insert its positive literal into clause; Otherwise, insert its negative literal.

Definition 4 (**Obf(F_C, F_H, R_H)**). *For formula F_C, and satisfiable formula F_H with R_H as one of its assignments, $Obf(F_C, F_H, R_H)$ is the result of applying SSH Rules when blending F_C with F_H.*

Definition 5 (**SSP obfuscation**). *For formula F_C, and satisfiable formula F_H with R_H as one of its assignments, $Obf(F_C, F_H, R_H)$ is the result of applying SSH Rules when blending F_C with F_H. If F_H is Cubic Husk formula and R_H is its Cubic solution, $Obf(F_C, F_H, R_H)$ is called **SSP obfuscation**.*

For SSH based obfuscation, we have theorem, Proof in Subsect. 5.1.

Theorem 1 (SSP Obfuscation). *For arbitrary CNF formula F_C, Cubic Husk formula F_H, if $V_{F_C} \cap V_{F_H} \equiv \phi$, and R_H is Cubic solution of F_H. then $F_C \vdash_{ssp}$ $Obf(F_C, F_H, R_H)$.*

Obviously, an obfuscated CNF formula $F_O = Obf(F_C, F_H, R_H)$ generated by SSP obfuscation consists of all the variables of F_C and F_H. As for the assignment of variables, variables from F_H are assigned with R_H, then we have: $F_O(R_H/V_{F_O}) = Obf(F_C, F_H(R_H/V_{F_H}), R_H)$. According to Lemma 1 in Subsect. 5.1, $F_H(R_H/V_{F_H})$ can be expressed as a Singular Husk formula with unique solution R_H. For CNF formulas F_C and its obfuscated formula F_O, we have:

1. F_C is unsatisfiable iff F_O is unsatisfiable. And the unsatisfiable core of F_C can be obtained from unsatisfiable core of F_O by deleting literals in F_H.
2. F_C is satisfiable iff F_O is satisfiable. And the solution of F_C can be obtained by projecting solution of F_O into variables set of F_C.

Algorithm 1. OBFUSCATOR

Data: The original CNF F_C, Cubic Husk CNF F_H, Cubic Husk result R_H
Result: The obfuscated CNF F_O, variable mapping M

1 **begin**
2     $mark(F_C)$;
3   **foreach** $c \in F_C$ **do**
4   **if** $c \in$ *Key Clause Set* **then**
5           $lit =$ get literal $\in R_H$;
6           $c = c \cup \neg lit$;
7           $nc = generate\_new\_clause(c, lit)$;
8           $F_C = F_C \cup nc$;

9   **foreach** $c \in F_C$ **do**
10       $averagelen = \frac{\sigma_{c' \in F_C} |c'|}{|F_C|}$;
11   **while** $|c| < averagelen$ **do**
12          $lit =$ get literal $\in R_H$;
13   **while** $\neg lit \in c$ **do**
14             $lit =$ get literal $\in R_H$;
15          $c = c \cup \neg lit$;
16       $M =$ remap all variable in $F_C \cup F_H$;
17       $F_O =$ reorder all clause in $F_C \cup F_H$;

Thus, each solution of F_O can be partitioned into solutions of F_C and F_H. So the solution of F_C can be extracted from that of F_O by projection on variables set of F_C. If solution number of F_C and F_H is m and n, The solution number of F_O will be mn. **In conclusion**, the solution space of F_O is over-approximation and projection-equivalence of F_C. As a result, F_O can be solved with the same SAT solver as F_C, but solution of F_C can not be recovered from that of F_O without knowing R_H.

Circuit Structure Aware Strategy. Since we want to protect circuit structure in CNF formula, let us first study how the circuit can be recovered from CNF formula. Literatures [9,10] have proposed algorithms to recover circuit structure from CNF formula in details. Before discussing them, some concepts should be introduced first.

Definition 6 (CNF signature). *CNF signature of gate g is its Tseitin encoding Tseitin(g). Each clause in CNF signature is called characteristic clause. A characteristic clause containing all variables in CNF signature is a* **key clause**. *Variable of a gate's output is* **output variable**.

Algorithm 2. mark and **generate_new_clause**

---

1 **mark**;
   Data: CNF formula S
   Result: marked S
2 **begin**
3   **foreach** $(C \in S)$ & $(|C| \equiv 3)$ **do**
4   **foreach** $l \in C$ **do**
5   **foreach** $(C_1 \in S)$ & $(\neg l \in C_1)$ & $(|C_1| \equiv 2)$ **do**
6   **foreach** $l_1 \in C_1$ **do**
7   **if** $(\neg l_1 \in C)$ & $(l_1 \neq l)$ **then**
8                   $match + +$;

9   **if** $match \equiv 2$ **then**
10   mark l as output literal ;
11   mark C as Key Clause;

12 **generate_new_clause**;
   Data: key clause C in AND2, Husk literal *lit*
   Result: new clause C_1
13 **begin**
14   *olit*=Getting output literal from C ;
15    $C_1 = lit \cup \neg olit$;

As mentioned in [9], gates with the same characteristic functions will be encoded into the same CNF signature. Roy [9] first converts the CNF to an Hypergraph G, and then matches the CNF signatures of all types of gates in G to recover gates by subgraph isomorphism, finally creates a maximal independent set instance to represent the recovered circuit. Fu [10] presents another algorithm that first detects all possible gates with key clause and CNF signature based pattern matching, and then constructs a maximum acyclic combinational circuit by selecting a maximum subset of matched gate. Potential attackers can exploit these knowledge to recover the circuit structure. Thus, CNF signature and key clause are important information that should be protected.

Since gates are basic blocks to construct circuit, and CNF signature and key clause are clues to detect circuit structure, We try to change the CNF signature and key clause of gate by adding literals and clauses. Furthermore, in order to mislead adversary, literals and clauses added may construct new legal CNF signature with clauses in original CNF signature, so as to hide original circuit structure seamlessly.

For example, Fig. 1(a) is CNF signature of AND2 gate a. By inserting A into key clause c_1 and generating clause c_4 with A and a, we transform gate a from AND2 into AND3, with a new input variable A, which is distinguishable with b and c, the input variables of AND2. The clauses for OR, NAND, and NOR gates, which are quite similar to that of AND gates, can also be transformed in this way.

$$a = \wedge(b,c) \rightarrow \begin{cases} c_1 : (a \vee \neg b \vee \neg c) \\ c_2 : (\neg a \vee b) \\ c_3 : (\neg a \vee c) \end{cases} \qquad a = \wedge(b, \ c, \ A) \rightarrow \begin{cases} c_1 : (a \vee \neg b \vee \neg c \vee \neg A) \\ c_2 : (\neg a \vee b) \\ c_3 : (\neg a \vee c) \\ c_4 : (\neg a \vee A) \end{cases}$$

a)AND2 gate a b)AND2 gate a after obfuscation

Fig. 1. Obfuscating AND2 into AND3.

All in One: *OBFUSCATOR algorithm* The proposed OBUFSCATOR algorithm obfuscates CNF formula F_C with SSH rules and CSA strategies, so as to prevent structure of F_C and its accurate solution from being known by adversary. SSH and CSA based obfuscation procedure implemented in Algorithms 1 and 2 is described below.

Procedure 1 *(Obf$_{SSH\_CSA}$)*

1. Input: Formula F_C, Cubic Husk formula F_H, Cubic solution R_H of F_H.
2. Output: Formula F_O.

    *According to Algorithm 1, F_C consists of **key clause**(line 4) and **non-key** **clause**, corresponding clause sets denoted as F_{Ck} and F_{Cn}.*
    STEP 1:
    action 1: For key clause $c \in F_{Ck}$, take one literal $lit \in R_H$, and insert $\neg lit$ into c (at line 6, 15 in Algorithm 1) according to SSH rule 1. The resulting clause set is denoted as S_3.
    action 2: Generating new clauses (line 7 in Algorithm 1) with literal lit from R_H and output variable of c in F_C according to SSH rule 2 (line 15 in Algorithm 2). New clauses set generated in this way is denoted as S_4.
    STEP 2: *Combining and randomly reordering S_3, S_4, F_H, and F_{Cn}, to produce F_O (line 6, 15, 8, 17 in Algorithm 1).*
    *end **Procedure**.*

To achieve these goals, OBFUSCATOR detect gates in CNF formula, then transform them into gates with different CNF signature. Detailed implementation of OBFUSCATOR is in Algorithm 1, which use $mark$ (line 2) to detect key clauses and output variables in CNF formula, and use $generate\_new\_clause$ (line 7) to generate new clause. As all circuits can be represented by a combination of AND2 and INV, and the $mark$ algorithm for INV is trivial, so we only present the implementation of $mark$ for AND2 in Algorithm 2. Similarly, we also present only the implementation of **generate_new_clause** for AND2 in Algorithm 2. These two algorithms can transform a CNF signature of AND2 to that of AND3.

4.4   Solution Recovery

After SAT Solving finished in public Cloud, S_O, the solution of F_O, will be returned to the private Cloud. In accordance with OBFUSCATOR, MAPPER and VERIFIER are used to filter solution of F_C out from S_O. According to Theorem 1, If result is UNSAT, then the original CNF formula is UNSAT. If result is SAT, MAPPER projects solution into variables of F_C and F_H, to get S_C and S_H, which are the candidate solution of F_C and F_H respectively. VERIFIER checks if S_H is equal to R_H, if yes, S_C is real solution of F_C. Otherwise, S_C may be false solution, hence, it is necessary to ask for a new solution from SAT Solver.

5   Security Analysis

5.1   Correctness

According to Theorem 1, under SSH rules, original CNF formula can be blended with Cubic Husk formula seamless, without narrowing down the solution space. In this section, we prove these theorems. First let us introduce some lemmas.

Most of lemmas list below has been proved in [25], We only give proof to Lemma 2, which is introduced for the first time in this paper.

Lemma 1 (Singular Husk Equation (SHE))
For singular Husk formula F_H with $|V_{F_H}| = n$, and unique solutions $S_H = \{(y_i = B_i, y_j = B_j)|B_i \equiv T, B_j \equiv F, 1 \leqslant i, j \leqslant n\}$. Let $F_{sH} = F_H \wedge (\bigwedge_{1\leqslant i\leqslant n}^{B_i \equiv T} y_i) \wedge (\bigwedge_{1\leqslant j\leqslant n}^{B_j \equiv F} \neg y_j)$, then $F_H \equiv F_{sH}$.

Lemma 2 (Cubic Husk Equation (CHE))
For Cubic Husk formula F_H and $|V_{F_H}| = n$, its cubic solution $R_H = \{c_i|1 \leqslant i \leqslant n_c\}$, n_c is number of variables in R_H. F_H has m solutions and $\{S_{H_l}|1 \leqslant l \leqslant m$ and $m \geqslant 2\}$, Solution $S_{H_l} = \{c_i = B_i, y_{l_i} = B_{l_i}|B_i, B_{l_i} \in \{T, F\}, 1 \leqslant i \leqslant n_c < l_i \leqslant n\}$. According to R_H, let $F_{RH} = (\bigwedge_{1\leqslant i\leqslant n_c}^{B_i \equiv T} c_i) \wedge (\bigwedge_{1\leqslant j\leqslant n_c}^{B_j \equiv F} \neg c_j)$. For any solution S_{H_l} of Cubic Husk formula F_H, let $F_{slH} = F_{RH} \wedge (\bigwedge_{n_c<l_i\leqslant n}^{B_{l_i} \equiv T} y_{l_i}) \wedge (\bigwedge_{n_c<l_j\leqslant n}^{B_{l_j} \equiv F} \neg y_{l_j})$ and let $F_{sH} = \bigvee_{1\leqslant l\leqslant m} F_{slH}$, we have $F_{sH} \equiv F_H$.

Proof. (1) Since $F_{sH} \equiv T$ we have:

$$F_{slH} = F_{RH} \wedge (\overset{B_{l_i} \equiv T}{\underset{n_c < l_i \leqslant n}{\bigwedge}} y_{l_i}) \wedge (\overset{B_{l_j} \equiv F}{\underset{n_c < l_j \leqslant n}{\bigwedge}} \neg y_{l_j}) \equiv T \qquad (1)$$

we have:

$$S_{H_l} = \{c_i = T, c_j = F, y_{l_i} = T, y_{l_j} = F|$$
$$B_i \equiv T, B_j \equiv F, B_{l_i} \equiv T, B_{l_j} \equiv F, 1 \leqslant i, j \leqslant n_c, n_c < l_i, l_j \leqslant n,\} \quad (2)$$

Let B_i, B_{l_i} and B_j, B_{l_j} replace T in $c_i = T$, $y_{l_i} = T$ and F in $c_j = F$ $y_{l_j} = F$, we have

$$S_{H_l} = \{(c_i = B_i, c_j = B_j, y_{l_i} = B_{l_i}, y_{l_j} = B_{l_j})|$$
$$B_i \equiv T, B_j \equiv F, 1 \leqslant i, j \leqslant n_c, B_{l_i} \equiv T, B_{l_j} \equiv F, n_c \leqslant l_i, l_j \leqslant n\} \quad (3)$$

Since index i and j have same range, we call them a joint name i. Since index l_i and l_j have same range, we call them a joint name l_i. Then Eq. (3) can be simplified as:

$$S_{H_l} = \{c_i = B_i, y_{l_i} = B_{l_i}|B_i, B_{l_j} \in \{T, F\}, 1 \leqslant i \leqslant n_c < l_i \leqslant n\} \qquad (4)$$

Since S_{H_l} is one solution of F_H we have $F_H(S_H/V_{F_H}) \equiv T$. we have:

$$F_{sH} \vdash F_H \qquad (5)$$

(2) Since $F_H \equiv T$, there must be existed one solution of F_H which can be expressed as Eq. (6), and let $F_H(S_{H_1}/V_{F_H})$ True.

$$S_{H_l} = \{c_i = B_i, y_{l_i} = B_{l_i}|B_i, B_{l_i} \in \{T, F\}, 1 \leqslant i \leqslant n_c < l_j \leqslant n\} \qquad (6)$$

According to Eq. (6) construct F_{s1H} we have:

$$F_{slH} = (\overset{B_i \equiv T}{\underset{1 \leqslant i \leqslant n_c}{\bigwedge}} c_i) \wedge (\overset{B_j \equiv F}{\underset{1 \leqslant j \leqslant n_c}{\bigwedge}} \neg c_j) \wedge (\overset{B_{l_i} \equiv T}{\underset{n_c < l_i \leqslant n}{\bigwedge}} y_i) \wedge (\overset{B_{l_j} \equiv F}{\underset{n_c < l_j \leqslant n}{\bigwedge}} \neg y_j) \equiv T \quad (7)$$

$$F_{sH} = F_{s1H} \vee (\underset{2 \leqslant l \leqslant m}{\bigvee} F_{slH}). \qquad (8)$$

Since $F_{s1H} \equiv T$, According to Eqs. (7) and (8), we have:

$$F_{sH} \equiv T \qquad (9)$$

$$F_H \vdash F_{sH} \qquad (10)$$

According to Eqs. (5) and (10), we have:

$$F_{sH} \equiv F_H \qquad (11)$$

Lemma 3 (OR Hold Obfuscation). *For formula F_C and $F_{RH} \vee F_{sH}$, with R_H is an assignment of $F_{RH} \vee F_{sH}$, then $Obf(F_C, F_{RH} \vee F_{sH}, R_H) \equiv Obf(F_C, F_{RH}, R_H) \vee Obf(F_C, F_{sH}, R_H)$.*

Lemma 4 (AND Hold Obfuscation). *For formula F_C and $F_{RH} \wedge F_{sH}$, with R_H is an assignment of $F_{RH} \wedge F_{sH}$, then $Obf(F_C, F_{RH} \wedge F_{sH}, R_H) \equiv Obf(F_C, F_{RH}, R_H) \wedge Obf(F_C, F_{sH}, R_H)$.*

Lemma 5 (Unique Positive literal SSE Obfuscation). *For any CNF formula F_C, we have $Obf(F_C, B = b, b \equiv T) \equiv F_C \wedge b$.*

Lemma 6 (Unique Negative literal SSE Obfuscation). *For any CNF formula F_C, we have $Obf(F_C, B \equiv \neg b, b \equiv F) \equiv F_C \wedge \neg b$.*

According to Lemmas 1 and 2, a singular Husk formula is equivalent to conjunction of all its solution literals. and a cubic Husk formula is equivalent to disjunction of its solutions clauses, while each solution clause is conjunction of literals in the solution. According to Lemma 3 and 4, for Husk formula F_H, AND and OR relation are true after obfuscation. According to Lemmas 5 and 6, after unique literal obfuscation, solution space is unchanged. With Lemmas listed above, let's discuss SSP Obfuscation based on Cubic Husk formula.

Theorem 1 Solution Space Projection-Equivalence (SSP) Obfuscation. For formula F_C and Cubic Husk formula F_H with n variables and m solutions ($n > 1$ and $m > 1$), if

1. $V_{F_C} \cap V_{F_H} = \phi$.
2. $R_H = \{c_i = B_i | B_i \in \{T, F\}, 1 \leqslant i \leqslant n_c \leqslant n - 1\}$ is Cubic solution of F_H.
3. $F_O = Obf(F_C, F_H, R_H)$.

then $F_C \wedge F_H \equiv F_O$. And we have $F_C \equiv_{ssp} F_O$.

Proof. According to **Procedure** 1, construct formula F_O in steps list below:

(1) let $F_{Op} = F_C$. for $y_i \in \{y_i | (y_i = B_i) \in R_H \| B_i \equiv T)\}$, let $F_{Op} = Obf(F_{Op}, B = y_i, y_i \equiv B_i)$.
(2) let $F_{On} = F_{Op}$. for $y_j \in \{y_j | (y_j = B_j) \in R_H \| B_j \equiv F)\}$, let $F_{On} = Obf(F_{On}, B = \neg y_j, y_j \equiv B_j)$.
(3) $F_O = F_{On} \wedge F_H$.

According to Lemmas 4, 5 and step (1), we have:

$$F_{Op} \equiv F_C \wedge (\bigwedge_{1 \leqslant i \leqslant n_c}^{B_i \equiv T} y_i) \tag{12}$$

According to Lemmas 4, 6 and step (2), we have:

$$F_{On} \equiv F_{Op} \wedge (\bigwedge_{1 \leqslant j \leqslant n_c}^{B_j \equiv F} \neg y_j). \tag{13}$$

According to step (3) and Eqs. (12) and (13), we have:

$$F_O \equiv F_C \wedge (\overset{B_i \equiv T}{\underset{1 \leqslant i \leqslant n_c}{\bigwedge}} c_i) \wedge (\overset{B_j \equiv F}{\underset{1 \leqslant j \leqslant n_c}{\bigwedge}} \neg c_j) \wedge F_H \tag{14}$$

R_H is Cubic Solution of F_H, let

$$F_{RH} = (\overset{B_i \equiv T}{\underset{1 \leqslant i \leqslant n_c}{\bigwedge}} c_i) \wedge (\overset{B_j \equiv F}{\underset{1 \leqslant j \leqslant n_c}{\bigwedge}} \neg c_j) \tag{15}$$

For any solution of Cubic Husk formula S_{H_l}, construct formula

$$F_{slH} = F_{RH} \wedge (\overset{B_{l_i} \equiv T}{\underset{n_c < l_i \leqslant n}{\bigwedge}} y_i) \wedge (\overset{B_{l_j} \equiv F}{\underset{n_c < l_j \leqslant n}{\bigwedge}} \neg y_j) \tag{16}$$

Construct formula $F_{sH} = \bigvee_{1 \leqslant l \leqslant m} F_{slH}$, we have:

$$F_{sH} = \underset{1 \leqslant l \leqslant m}{\bigvee} (F_{RH} \wedge (\overset{B_{l_i} \equiv T}{\underset{n_c < l_i \leqslant n}{\bigwedge}} y_i) \wedge (\overset{B_{l_j} \equiv F}{\underset{n_c < l_j \leqslant n}{\bigwedge}} \neg y_j)) \tag{17}$$

According to Lemma 2, we have:

$$F_H = F_{sH} = \underset{1 \leqslant l \leqslant m}{\bigvee} (F_{RH} \wedge (\overset{B_{l_i} \equiv T}{\underset{n_c < l_i \leqslant n}{\bigwedge}} y_i) \wedge (\overset{B_{l_j} \equiv F}{\underset{n_c < l_j \leqslant n}{\bigwedge}} \neg y_j)) \tag{18}$$

According to Eq. 18 and distributive law, we have

$$F_H = F_{RH} \wedge (\underset{1 \leqslant l \leqslant m}{\bigvee} ((\overset{B_{l_i} \equiv T}{\underset{n_c < l_i \leqslant n}{\bigwedge}} y_i) \wedge (\overset{B_{l_j} \equiv F}{\underset{n_c < l_j \leqslant n}{\bigwedge}} \neg y_j)) \tag{19}$$

According to Eqs. (14) and (15), we have:

$$F_O \equiv F_C \wedge F_{RH} \wedge F_H \tag{20}$$

According to (20), (19), and Absorption law, we have:

$$F_O \equiv F_C \wedge F_H \tag{21}$$

Since F_H is satisfiable, $V_{FC} \cap V_{FH} = \phi$, and Solution number of F_H is m $(m > 1)$. According to definition 3, we have:

$$F_O \equiv_{ssp} F_C \tag{22}$$

5.2   Effectiveness

Input Obfuscation through Transforming circuit structure. By appending redundant literals and clauses, OBFUSCATOR can change signatures in CNF formula into other legal signatures. After SSO obfuscation, the original CNF formula is transformed into another formula, mixed with noisy circuit structure. Since obfuscated CNF formula is outsourced as input of SAT solver, circuit structure in original CNF formula will not be exposed to adversary. **Output Camouflage by over-approximating solution space.** According to Theorem 1, the solution space after SSP obfuscation is an overapproximation of the original one. So even SAT solver can't tell which is the real solution. First, they can not tell real valuable variables from variables of Husks formula, which are meaningless to verification. Second, they cannot tell if a satisfied solution means whether the original SAT problem is also satisfiable, because some false solutions are produced by obfuscation. Through overapproximation, We just turn an obvious Rare Events into a Camouflaged Rare Events, as anticipation in [18].

6   Performance Analysis

According to our Cloud oriented SAT solving framework, in Private Cloud, computation overhead consists of Husk formula generation, CNF formula Obfuscation, and result recovery and verification, while in public Cloud, computation overhead consists of SAT Solving, which corresponds to state-of-the-art SAT Solver, in the paper we use MiniSat. **Husks generation algorithm complexity.** Husks generation algorithm is implemented based on genfacbm [16]. Its main procedure will take industrial design multiplier circuit, and sets the given number as the output, its complexity is $O(n)$. **Obfuscation algorithm complexity.** Obfuscation is implemented in Algorithm 1. Its main procedure consists only one layer of loop, but one of it sub-procedure **mark** (Algorithm 2) consists 4 layers of loop, and the runtimes of the 2 inner loops are bounded by length of clauses. So the complexity of the obfuscation algorithm is $O(n^2)$. **Solution recovery algorithm complexity.** Solution recovery algorithms is to get solution by projection which only consists one layer of loop, its complexity is $O(n)$. According to Theorem 1, result from honest SAT solver will not consist of false solution, so the algorithm should be runned only once to get correct solution. Since the algorithm is of linear complexity, it incurs minor impact on performance of SAT Solving. Since SAT problem is NP-complete, the customer will not spend more time to obfuscate SAT problem and solve the problem in the cloud than to solve the problem on his own. Therefore, in theory, the proposed mechanism would allow the customer to outsource their SAT problems to the cloud and gain great computation savings.

7   Concluding Remarks

In this paper, we formalize the problem of securely outsourcing SAT Solving. We proposes a practical mechanism which fulfill input/output privacy and efficiency. We define Cubic husk formula and design circuit structure aware CNF obfuscation algorithm, which can prevent the confidential information, such as circuit structure, from being recovered by adversary. we protect output information by over-approximate the solution space to projection-equivalent. Theoretical analysis demonstrate the immediate practicality of the proposed mechanism.

Acknowledgment. This work was supported by the National Key Research and Development Program of China under grant No. 2018YFB1003602.

References

1. Davis, M., Putnam, H.: A computing procedure for quantification theory. J. ACM **7**(3), 201–215 (1960)
2. Hachtel, G., Somenzi, F.: Logic Synthesis and Verification Algorithms, vol. I-XXIII, pp. 1–564. Springer, Heidelberg (2006)
3. Clarke, E., Grumberg, O., Jha, S., Lu, Y., Veith, H.: Counterexample-guided abstraction refinement. In: Emerson, E.A., Sistla, A.P. (eds.) CAV 2000. LNCS, vol. 1855, pp. 154–169. Springer, Heidelberg (2000). https://doi.org/10.1007/10722167_15
4. Soos, M., Nohl, K., Castelluccia, C.: Extending SAT solvers to cryptographic problems. In: Kullmann, O. (ed.) SAT 2009. LNCS, vol. 5584, pp. 244–257. Springer, Heidelberg (2009). https://doi.org/10.1007/978-3-642-02777-2_24
5. Hyvärinen, A.E.J., Junttila, T., Niemelä, I.: Grid-based SAT solving with iterative partitioning and clause learning. In: Lee, J. (ed.) CP 2011. LNCS, vol. 6876, pp. 385–399. Springer, Heidelberg (2011). https://doi.org/10.1007/978-3-642-23786-7_30
6. Tseitin, G.: On the complexity of derivation in propositional calculus. Stud. Constr. Math. Math. Logic (1968)
7. Li, C.: Integrating equivalency reasoning into Davis-Putnam procedure. In: AAAI/IAAI 2000, pp. 291–296 (2000)
8. Ostrowski, R., Grégoire, É., Mazure, B., Saïs, L.: Recovering and exploiting structural knowledge from CNF formulas. In: Van Hentenryck, P. (ed.) CP 2002. LNCS, vol. 2470, pp. 185–199. Springer, Heidelberg (2002). https://doi.org/10.1007/3-540-46135-3_13
9. Roy, J., Markov, I., Bertacco, V.: Restoring circuit structure from SAT instances. In: IWLS 2004, pp. 361–368 (2004)
10. Fu, Z., Malik, S.: Extracting logic circuit structure from conjunctive normal form descriptions. In: VLSI Design, pp. 37–42 (2007)
11. MiniSat-SAT Algorithms and Applications Invited talk given by Niklas Sorensson at the CADE-20 workshop ESCAR. http://minisat.se/Papers.html
12. Balduzzi, M., Zaddach, J., Balzarotti, D., Kirda, E., Loureiro, S.: A security analysis of Amazon's elastic compute cloud service. In: SAC 2012, pp. 1427–1434 (2012)
13. Ristenpart, T., Tromer, E., Shacham, H., Savage, S.: Hey, you, get off of my cloud: exploring information leakage in third-party compute clouds. In: CCS 2009, pp. 199–212 (2009)
14. Achlioptas, D., Gomes, C., Kautz, H., Selman, B.: Generating satisfiable problem instances. In: AAAI/IAAI 2000, pp. 256–261 (2000)
15. Jarvisalo, M.: Equivalence checking hardware multiplier designs. SAT Competition 2007 Benchmark Description

16. Pyhala, T.: Factoring Benchmark for SAT-solvers. http://www.tcs.hut.fi/Software/genfacbm/
17. Brakerski, Z., Rothblum, G.: Black-box obfuscation for d-CNFs. In: ITCS 2014, pp. 235–250 (2014)
18. Du, W., Goodrich, M.T.: Searching for high-value rare events with uncheatable grid computing. In: Ioannidis, J., Keromytis, A., Yung, M. (eds.) ACNS 2005. LNCS, vol. 3531, pp. 122–137. Springer, Heidelberg (2005). https://doi.org/10.1007/11496137_9
19. Paralleling OpenSMT Towards Cloud Computing. http://www.inf.usi.ch/urop-Tsitovich-2-127208.pdf
20. Formal in the Cloud OneSpin: New Spin on Cloud Computing. http://www.eejournal.com/archives/articles/20130627-onespin/?printView=true
21. Zhang, X., He, F., Zuo, W.: Theory and practice of program obfuscation. In: Crisan, M. (ed.) Convergence and Hybrid Information Technologies, p. 426. INTECH, Croatia, March 2010. ISBN 978-953-307-068-1
22. Karypis, G., Aggarwal, R., Kumar, V., Shekhar, S.: Multilevel hypergraph partitioning: application in VLSI domain. In: DAC 1997, pp. 526–529 (1997)
23. Shen, S.Y., Qin, Y., Li, S.K.: Minimizing counterexample with unit core extraction and incremental SAT. In: Cousot, R. (ed.) VMCAI 2005. LNCS, vol. 3385, pp. 298–312. Springer, Heidelberg (2005). https://doi.org/10.1007/978-3-540-30579-8_20
24. Qin, Y., Shen, S., Kong, J., Dai, H.: Cloud-oriented SAT solver based on obfuscating CNF formula. In: Han, W., Huang, Z., Hu, C., Zhang, H., Guo, L. (eds.) APWeb 2014. LNCS, vol. 8710, pp. 188–199. Springer, Cham (2014). https://doi.org/10.1007/978-3-319-11119-3_18
25. Qin, Y., Shen, S.Y., Jia, Y.: Structure-aware CNF obfuscation for privacy-preserving SAT solving. In: MEMOCODE 2014, pp. 84–93 (2014)
26. Li, X., Wang, H., Ding, B., Li, X., Feng, D.: Resource allocation with multi-factor node ranking in data center networks. Futur. Gener. Comput. Syst. **32**, 1–12 (2014). https://doi.org/10.1016/j.future.2013.09.028
27. Ren, Y., Liu, L., Zhang, Q., Wu, Q., Guan, J., Kong, J., Dai, H., Shao, L.: Shared-memory optimizations for inter-virtual-machine communication. ACM Comput. Surv. **48**(4), 49:1–49:42 (2016). https://doi.org/10.1145/2847562

A Fragile Watermarking and Bilinear Fuzzy Equations

Ferdinando Di Martino[✉] and Salvatore Sessa[✉]

Dipartimento di Architettura, Università degli Studi di Napoli Federico II,
Via Toledo 402, 80134 Naples, Italy
{fdimarti, sessa}@unina.it

Abstract. We present a fragile colour image watermarking based on the greatest solution of a bilinear fuzzy relation equation. The original image is coded with fuzzy transforms and divided in sub-images of sizes 2×2 called blocks. The watermark is applied on these blocks. A pre-processing phase is used to determine the best compression rate for the coding process. We test this scheme in tamper detection analysis on a sample of colour images of different sizes. Comparisons with various block-based fragile watermarking methods are presented as well.

Keywords: Fragile watermarking · Bilinear fuzzy relation equation
Fuzzy transform · Tamper detection · Tamper localization

1 Introduction

Today's availability of image processing software allows to manipulate and to alter an image maliciously. Some known image analysis techniques can detect these manipulations, but an expert attacker can make unrecognizable his manipulations.

Digital watermarking techniques can be applied to prevent unauthorized alteration and to detect tampers on the published image. Generally they are classified in three categories [6, 17]:

- *robust watermarking*, applied to preserve the image copyright. The information encapsulated in the image information cannot be destroyed by any attack;
- *fragile watermarking*, applied to detect and localize alterations in the image; the information encapsulated in the image can be easily destroyed and is used to detect and localize tampered zones;
- *semi-fragile watermarking*, applied to detect only malicious manipulations of the image, ignoring manipulations due to "routine processes" such as, for example, lossy compressions, brightness adjustments or filtering operations.

Fragile watermarking scheme is further classified into the following:

- *block-wise scheme*, in which the image is partitioned into blocks; in each block a secret random signature is inserted into the pixels;
- *pixel-wise scheme* in which a binary authentication watermark was produced by difference between pixels.

© Springer Nature Switzerland AG 2018
A. Castiglione et al. (Eds.): CSS 2018, LNCS 11161, pp. 240–253, 2018.
https://doi.org/10.1007/978-3-030-01689-0_19

Pixel-wise algorithms [2, 3, 13, 16] can localize precisely the tampered pixels, but they can be too expensive in terms of CPU time and memory storage.

Recently some block-wise scheme variations were proposed to improve the tamper detection and localization precision. In [19] a new block-based scheme is proposed where the 2×2 blocks are scrambled via a chaotic map and has high tamper localization accuracy. In [1] the image is partitioned in 4×4 blocks and the singular value decomposition technique is applied to each block.

Due to the large size that today reaches the dataset of images published on WEB sites, it is necessary to preserve the watermark from the compression of the image to be published. In [7, 8] a new block-wised scheme is presented in which the watermark is applied to images compressed by using fuzzy relation equations (see also, e.g., [11, 14]).

In [9] a new block-wise scheme is proposed in which the watermark is applied directly on the image compressed via fuzzy transforms (F-transforms) [15]. The watermark insertion is performed by applying the block-based watermarking scheme described in [5], where a fuzzy partition of the 2×2 blocks of the compressed image is performed by using FCM to realize the block-wise independency and a relationship between blocks. An authentication data is generated for each block by using a pseudo-random sequence seeded with a secret key. Here we describe in Sect. 2 the watermark insertion process and the tamper analysis, given in [9], and an example of watermark applied to a 2×2 block is also presented. We think the reader which is familiar with F-transforms theory [15], here not recalled for making brief the paper. In Sect. 3 the algorithm for finding the greatest solution of a bilinear fuzzy relation equation is described as well. In Sect. 4 the BFRE image watermarking method is presented. In Sect. 5 we point out many tests comparing the detection performances of the BFRE, moreover we show comparisons with other block-wise fragile watermarking algorithms. Final considerations are reported in Sect. 6.

2 Watermark in 2×2 Blocks

In Fig. 1 we show the process used in [9] to mark a new image and storing the compressed marked image in a dataset. The process is partitioned as follows:

- *Image coding:* the new image is compressed by using the direct F-transform method;
- *Watermark insertion*: the watermark insertion marks the coded image that is stored in the new compressed image dataset;
- *Image decoding*: the marked image is decompressed by using the inverse F-transform, and is ready to be distributed.

In Fig. 2 we show the tamper analysis process given in [9]. The tampered image is compressed and compared with the compressed original marked image. The tamper localization function localizes the tampered regions, producing the two levels of the tamper localization image.

In this paper we present a new color image watermarking algorithm in which we apply a Bilinear Fuzzy Relation Equation (BFRE) [12] on the 2×2 blocks of the compressed image to be marked. The BFRE algorithm was used in [10] for image

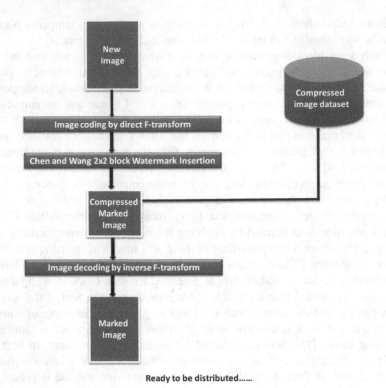

New
Image

Compressed
image dataset

Image coding by direct F-transform

Chen and Wang 2x2 block Watermark Insertion

Compressed
Marked
Image

Image decoding by inverse F-transform

Marked
Image

Ready to be distributed......

Fig. 1. Watermark insertion process given in [9]

comparison, but here our objective is to improve the tamper detection process. Formally, the BFRE algorithm finds the greatest solution of a system of n bilinear fuzzy relation equations with n unknowns. We consider two fuzzy matrices A and B of dimensions n × n, where A = [a_{ij}] and B = [b_{ij}], a_{ij}, b_{ij} in [0, 1] and i, j = 1, 2,..., n.

We calculate the greatest solution of a system of fuzzy bilinear equations given by A·x = B·x, where "·" is the known max-min composition in [0, 1], with the vector solution x = (x_1, x_2,..., x_n)^T and $0 \leq x_j \leq 1$, j = 1, 2,..., n. The general form of an above mentioned system is the following:

$$\vee_{i=1}^{n}\left(a_{ij} \wedge x_j\right) = \vee_{i=1}^{n}\left(b_{ij} \wedge x_j\right) \tag{1}$$

where $\vee$ and $\wedge$ are the max and min operators, respectively.

The previous equations form a so-called *system of fuzzy bilinear equations*. Obviously the least solution is $x_0 = (0, 0,..., 0)^T$. If A = B, we obtain the trivial greatest solution $x_1 = (1, 1,..., 1)^T$. Hence from now on we suppose A ≠ B and an algorithm to find the greatest solution is given in [12].

Here the original image is compressed by the direct F-transform and the compressed image is stored in the dataset. Then the watermark is applied on the compressed image by using the BFRE algorithm and the marked decompressed image is published as well.

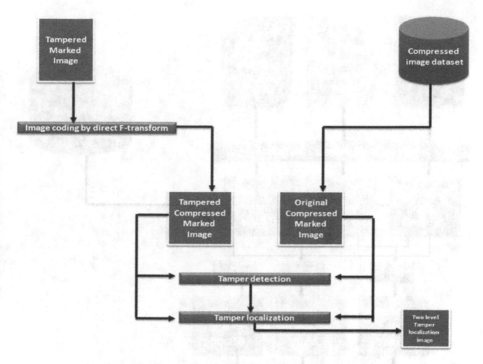

Fig. 2. Tamper analysis process in [9]

Consider a $N \times M$ color image compressed with the F-transform algorithm as described in [10]. Each band of the compressed image is partitioned in K blocks of dimensions 2×2. Let $\hat{x}_h = (\hat{x}_{1h}, \hat{x}_{2h})$, $h = 1,\ldots, K$, the greatest solution obtained for the hth block. We calculate the mean value of the two components given a $\bar{x}_h = (\hat{x}_{1h} + \hat{x}_{2h})/2$, then we obtain an integer $s_h = 255 \cdot \bar{x}_h$, where $s_h \in [0, 255]$.

For each block we apply the Chen and Wang scheme [5], in which the authentication data is embedded in the 8 LSB's for each image block. For achieving this aim, a random sequence, $(r_1, r_2,\ldots, r_K)$, $r_h \in \{0, 1,\ldots, 255\}$, is considered creating a pseudo random number generator seeded with a secret key (SK). For the hth block the corresponding authentication data is constructed as

$$d_h = s_h \oplus r_h \tag{2}$$

where the operator $\oplus$ is the XOR operator. Each two bit couple in the 8 bit authentication data d_h is embedded in the two LSB's of the corresponding pixel of the block.

This process is repeated in the compressed images of the two bands G, B, applying the BFRE algorithm over each 2×2 block. The compressed original unmarked image is stored in the image dataset with all information necessary to obtain the marked compressed image. The BFRE watermark insertion process is schematized in Fig. 3.

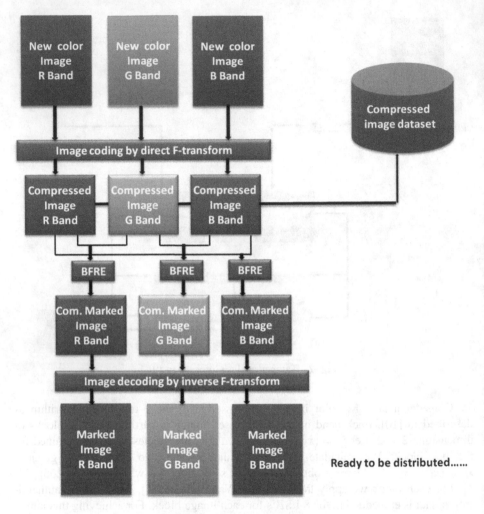

Fig. 3. BFRE watermark insertion process

In order to find the best compression rate ρ to be applied for coding the original image, a pre-processing phase is performed in where the trend of the mean Peak Signal to Noise Ratio (PSNR) is obtained for the marked image in any band. The PSNR index of a marked image is defined as

$$PSNR = 20 \log_{10} \frac{255}{RMSE} \tag{3}$$

where RMSE is the Root Mean Square Error calculated by comparing the decompressed marked image and the original image in any band. In [10] the optimal compression rate is given by the least ρ for which the RMSE is not greater than the value $2.5 \cdot (RMSE)_0$, where $(RMSE)_0$ is the RMSE obtained without compression of the image ($\rho = 1$). For a value of RMSE equals to $2.5 \cdot (RMSE)_0$, we obtain a threshold given as

$$(PSNR)_{TH} = 20 \log_{10} \frac{255}{2.5 \cdot (RMSE)_0} \qquad (4)$$

For compression rates such that the PSNR is less than the threshold (4), the loss of information is considered enough to invalidate both tamper detection and localization analysis. For color images the threshold $(PSNR)_{TH}$ is given by the arithmetic average of the thresholds obtained in any band. In order to ensure high tamper detection performance, we set the maximum compression rate for which the PSNR index results greater or equal the threshold (4), then we set as compression rate the minimum of the compression rates found in the three bands. So we ensure that in no band the loss of information due to compression can affect the results of the tamper analysis.

A tampered image is compressed via direct F-transform and the corresponding compressed image in the three bands is extracted from the image dataset. Afterwards the BFRE watermark insertion is applied and finally the tamper localization function localizes the tampered zones, producing the two level tamper localization binary images for each band. In Fig. 4 this process is schematized in detail.

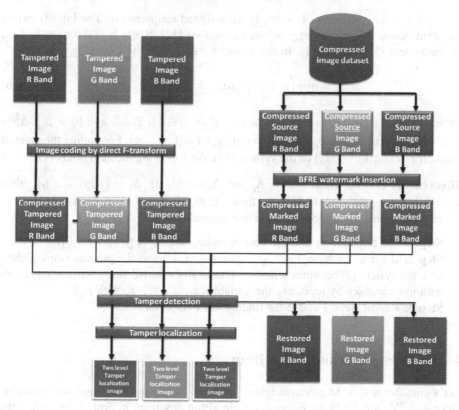

Fig. 4. BFRE tamper analysis process

We have that

- the advantage of the F-transform tamper detection is preserved in terms of storage of the published image dataset. F-transform based algorithm is used for coding the source image, moreover the compressed image is tampered and stored in the dataset;
- the CPU time performance of the F-transform tamper analysis is preserved and the tamper detection and localization processes are made on the compressed images;
- the block-wise independency watermarking scheme is applied to the compressed source image. Then the tampered image is compressed and compared with the coded source marked image.

3 The BFRE Algorithm

Let $A = [a_{ij}]$ and $B = [b_{ij}]$ two fuzzy relations of dimensions m × n, (i = 1,..., m and j = 1,..., n) and a vector $\mathbf{x} = (x_1, x_2,..., x_n)$. We consider the following system of fuzzy relation equations:

$$a_i \vee (\vee_{j=1}^n (a_{ij} \wedge x_j)) = b_i \vee (\vee_{j=1}^n (b_{ij} \wedge x_j)) \tag{5}$$

for any i = 1, 2,..., m and a_i, $b_i \in [0, 1]$ are assigned real numbers. The Eq. (5) form a so-called *system of external fuzzy bilinear equations* [12]. If $a_i = b_i = 0$ for i = 1, 2,..., m, the system (5) becomes (1). In the sequel we deal with the following quantities:

$$\rho_i = \min\left(a_i \vee (\vee_{j=1}^n (a_{ij}), \; b_i \vee (\vee_{j=1}^n (b_{ij}) \right) \tag{6}$$

for any i = 1, 2,..., m. Let us consider the sets $\Delta_i^1 = \{j \in \{1, 2, \ldots, n\} : b_{ij} > \rho_i\}, \Delta_i^2 = \{j \in \{1, 2, \ldots, n\} : a_{ij} > \rho_i\}$. Let $\rho_k = \min\{\rho_i : i = 1, \ldots, m\}$. For finding the greatest solution $\hat{x} = (\hat{x}_1, \hat{x}_2, \ldots, \hat{x}_n)$ of the system (13), the following theorem holds [12]:

Theorem 1. Let be either $\Delta_k := \Delta_k^1$ or $\Delta_k := \Delta_k^2$. If $\Delta_k = \{j_1, j_2, \ldots, j_t\}$, then $\hat{x}_{j_1} = \hat{x}_{j_2} = \ldots = \hat{x}_{j_t} = \rho_k$. If $\Delta_k = I_n$, then $\hat{x} \in [0, 1]^n$ with $\hat{x}_i = \rho_k$ for i = 1,..., n.
   In other words, the following recursive algorithm holds:

Step 1: We calculate ρ_k and the corresponding set $\Delta_k = \{j_1, j_2, \ldots, j_t\}$.
Step 2: If t = n, we have $\hat{x} = (\rho_k, \ldots, \rho_k) \in [0, 1]^n$ and the process stops. Otherwise the system (5) becomes a new system of m-t external fuzzy bilinear equations with m-t variables by replacing the variables $x_{j_1}, x_{j_2}, \ldots, x_{j_t}$ with ρ_k.
Step 3: Repeat steps 1 and 2 for finding each component $\hat{x}_j$.

4 The Watermarking Algorithm

Let's consider a N × M colour original image for applying the image watermarking algorithm. We use the block F-transform algorithm described in Sect. 2 for coding the image. Then the compressed image is partitioned in blocks 2 × 2. The greatest solution of a BFRE system is found for each block of a band. For marking the R band (resp., G-band) compressed image, each 2×2 block is normalized to form the bilinear fuzzy relation Eq. (5). The greatest solution is de-normalized and the Chen and Wang scheme [5] is applied embedding an authentication data in the LSB's for each block. The same process is applied to the corresponding 2×2 blocks of the G and B bands (resp., B and R bands) of the compressed image to mark the G (resp., B) block. The marked compressed image is then stored in the image dataset and the images are decompressed by using the inverse F-transform and ready to be published. Strictly speaking, the BFRE watermarking insertion consists of the following steps:

BFRE Watermarking insertion	
Step 1	The original image is compressed in any band with a compression rate ρ by using the block F-transform compression method. The image is partitioned in K blocks of sizes $N(D) \times M(D)$, compressed in blocks of size $n(D) \times m(D)$, being the compression rate equal to $(N(D) \times M(D))/(n(D) \times m(D))$. The direct F-transform is calculated by using uniform fuzzy partitions
Step 2	The compressed images in the R and G bands are partitioned in 2×2 blocks and the pixels are normalized in $[0, 1]$ in every block
Step 3	For each 2×2 block in the R and G bands of the compressed image, a BFRE system composed by two equations is constructed. The BFRE algorithm is applied for finding the greatest solution $\hat{x} = (\hat{x}_1, \hat{x}_2)$
Step 4	Let $\hat{x}_h = (\hat{x}_{1h}, \hat{x}_{2h})$, $h = 1,\ldots,$ K, the greatest solution (vector) obtained for the hth window. We calculate the mean value $\bar{x}_h = \frac{\hat{x}_{1h} + \hat{x}_{2h}}{2}$, and the integer $s_h = 255 \cdot \bar{x}_h$, where $s_h \in \{0, 1, \ldots, 255\}$. Then the Chen and Wang scheme is applied, generating a random sequence $(r_1, r_2, \ldots, r_K)$, $r_h \in \{0, 1, \ldots, 255\}$ by creating a PRNG seeded with a SK. For the hth block the corresponding authentication data is constructed as in (6); the authentication data is embedded in each LSB's of the four pixels in the 2×2 block of the compressed image in the R and G bands. This step is repeated for all 2×2 blocks
Step 5	Step 3 and 4 are repeated by considering the compressed images in the G, R (resp., B, R) bands for marking the compressed image in the G (resp., in B) band
Step 6	A copy of the unmarked compressed original image is stored in the image dataset in which are preserved the information necessary to mark it (number of blocks, dimension of the original image, compression rate, random sequence $(r_1, r_2, \ldots, r_K)$
Step 7	The marked compressed image is decompressed in every band by calculating the inverse F-transform. Then the marked decompressed image is ready to be published

Like in [9], we apply a pre-processing phase to finding the optimal compression rate ρ here not described for brevity. In each band we calculate a threshold for the PSNR index for the decompressed marked image, given by (4); this threshold is given by the PSNR for which the RMSE is given by $2.5 \cdot (RMSE)_0$, where $(RMSE)_0$ is the RMSE obtained marking the image without compression (i.e., $\rho = 1$).

In the tamper analysis process the compressed original image is extracted from the image dataset along with the information necessary to obtain the marked compressed image. The tampered image is compressed with the same compression rate of the corresponding compressed marked image in the image dataset. Then the tamper detection function applies the BFRE algorithm on the original compressed image: the pixels (which are not corresponding in the tampered images) are marked as invalid pixels. Thus the published marked image is reconstructed. Finally, the tamper localization identifies the invalid pixels, detecting the tampered zones.

The BFRE tamper analysis process is composed by the following steps:

BFRE Tamper analysis	
Step 1	From the image dataset the compressed original image is extracted the corresponding one to the published image tampered. The BFRE watermarking insertion function is applied to it for obtaining the compressed marked image
Step 2	The tampered image is compressed by using the F-transform compression method to the blocks. The image is partitioned in K blocks of size $N(D) \times M(D)$ and compressed with rate $\rho = (N(D) \times M(D))/(n(D) \times m(D))$
Step 3	The tampered image can be reconstructed and republished decompressing the compressed marked image
Step 4	The two compressed images are compared and the tampered pixels are detected
Step 5	In every band the tampered zones are detected

Fig. 5. Original image "Baboon"

Fig. 5a. R band

Fig. 5b. G band

Fig. 5c. B band

Fig. 5. Original image "Baboon". (a) R band, (b) G band, (c) B band

5 Tests

For brevity of exposition, we present the detailed results for the image "Baboon" downloaded from dataset available at https://www5.cs.fau.de/research/data/image-manipulation). The original image of sizes 256×256 is shown in Fig. 5. Figure 5a (resp., Fig. 5b and c) contains the same image in the R (resp., G, B) band.

Table 1. $(PSNR)_0$ and $(PSNR)_{TH}$ obtained in each band for the image "Baboon" $(\rho = 1)$

Band	$(PSNR)_0$	$(PSNR)^i_{TH}$, i = R, G, B
R	31.72	23.76
G	31.67	23.71
B	31.65	23.69

Table 2. PSNR in each band obtained for the marked image "Baboon" $(\rho = 0.25)$

Band	$PSNR$	$(PSNR) - (PSNR)^i_{TH}$
R	23.90	0.14
G	23.90	0.19
B	23.84	0.15

Fig. 6. Marked "Baboon" $(\rho=0.25)$

Fig. 6a. R band

Fig. 6b. G band

Fig. 6c. B band

Fig. 6. Marked "Baboon" $(\rho = 0.25)$. (a) R band, (b) G band, (c) B band

In the pre-processing phase we use the BFRE algorithm marking the original image (i.e., without compression). We obtain the values of $(PSNR)_0$ and $(PSNR)_{TH}$ shown in Table 1 for each band.

Then we have $\rho = (2 \times 2)/(4 \times 4) = 0.25$. By applying the BFRE watermarking algorithm, we obtain the following values of the PSNR in each band (Table 2):

In Fig. 6 we show the image of Fig. 5 marked by using the BFRE watermarking insertion process. Figure 6a (resp., Fig. 6b and c) shows the marked image in the R (resp., G, B) band.

The marked image of Fig. 6 has been tampered as shown in Fig. 7. Figure 7a (resp., Fig. 7b and c) shows the tampered image in the R (resp., G, B) band.

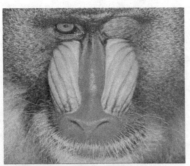 

Fig.7. The tampered image "Baboon"   **Fig. 7a.** R band

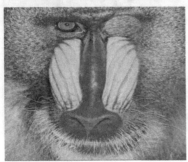 

Fig. 7b. G band   **Fig. 7c.** B band

Fig. 7. The tampered image "Baboon". (a) R band, (b) G band, (c) B band

We apply the BFRE detection algorithm to the tampered image of Fig. 8. The marked image is extracted, decompressed and compared with the tampered image. Figure 8a (resp., Fig. 8b and c) shows the tamper localization zone detected in the R (resp., G, B) band.

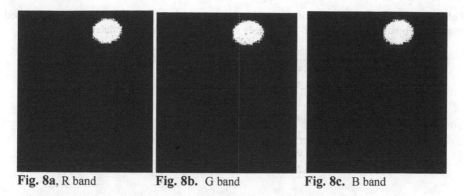

Fig. 8a, R band   **Fig. 8b.** G band   **Fig. 8c.** B band

Fig. 8. (a) R band, (b) G band, (c) B band

In Table 3 we show the Sensitivity, Specificity and Accuracy values obtained in the R, G, B bands for the tampered image of Fig. 7 under several compression rates.

Table 3. Sensitivity, specificity and accuracy for several ρ in each band (Baboon)

ρ	Band	Sensitivity	Specificity	Accuracy
1 (No compression)	R	99.47%	99.96%	99.72%
	G	99.41%	99.97%	99.69%
	B	99.38%	99.97%	99.68%
0.25	R	95.93%	99.94%	97.94%
	G	94.66%	99.95%	97.30%
	B	95.97%	99.95%	97.96%
0.0625	R	94.97%	99.92%	97.10%
	G	94.73%	99.93%	97.22%
	B	95.39%	99.93%	97.60%
0.015625	R	92.65%	99.63%	96.14%
	G	92.89%	99.58%	96.24%
	B	93.14%	99.73%	96.44%

In Table 4 we show the mean values of the three indices obtained for the 200 images (extracted from the above dataset) by applying the BFRE algorithm and other block-wise fragile watermarking algorithms like FCM, Hierarchical, DCT, Chaos, SVD dealt in [1, 4, 5, 18, 20], respectively.

Table 4. Mean sensitivity, specificity and accuracy obtained by using various block-based fragile watermarking methods for 200 images extracted from the above dataset

Method	Mean sensitivity	Mean specificity	Mean accuracy
BFRE	95.45%	99.93%	97.69%
F-transform [9]	94.31%	99.91%	97.11%
FCM [5]	96.12%	99.96%	98.04%
Hierarchical [4]	95.99%	99.95%	97.97%
DCT [18]	96.23%	99.97%	98.10%
Chaos [20]	96.04%	99.96%	98.01%
SVD [1]	96.28%	99.97%	98.13%

6   Conclusions

Comparison results show that the proposed method is better than our previous method [9] in terms of sensitivity, specificity and accuracy and comparable with other block-wise fragile watermarking methods in which no compression of images is considered.

Funding. This research did not receive any specific grant from funding agencies in the public, commercial, or not-for-profit sectors.

References

1. Ansari, I.A., Pant, M., Ahn, C.W.: SVD based fragile watermarking scheme for tamper localization and self-recovery. J. Mach. Learn. Cybern. **7**, 1225–1239 (2016). https://doi.org/10.1007/s1304201504551
2. Al-Otum, H.A., Al-Taba'a, A.O.: Adaptive color image watermarking based on a modified improved pixel-wise masking technique. Comput. Electr. Eng. **5**, 673–695 (2009)
3. Barni, M.: Improved wavelet-based watermarking through pixel-wise making. IEEE Trans. Image Process. **10**(5), 783–791 (2002). https://doi.org/10.1109/83.918570
4. Chang, Y.F., Tai, W.L.: A block-based watermarking scheme for image tamper detection and self-recovery. OPTO−Electron. Rev. **21**(2), 182–190 (2013). https://doi.org/10.2478/s1177201300884
5. Chen, W.C., Wang, M.S.: A fuzzy C-means clustering-based fragile watermarking scheme for image authentication. Expert Syst. Appl. **36**, 1300–1307 (2009). https://doi.org/10.1016/j.eswa.2007.11.018
6. Cox, I.J., Miller, M., Bloom, J., Fridrich, J., Kalker, T.: Digital Watermarking and Stenography, 2nd edn. Morgan Kaufmann, New York (2007). ISBN 0123725852
7. Di Martino, F., Sessa, S.: Digital watermarking in coding/decoding processes with fuzzy relation equations. Soft. Comput. **10**, 238–243 (2006). https://doi.org/10.1007/s0050000504779
8. Di Martino, F., Sessa, S.: Digital Watermarking Strings with Images Compressed by Fuzzy Relation Equations. In: Chatterjee, A., Siarry, P. (eds.) Computational Intelligence in Image Processing. Springer, Heidelberg (2013). https://doi.org/10.1007/978-3-642-30621-1_9
9. Di Martino, F., Sessa, S.: Fragile watermarking tamper detection with images compressed by fuzzy transform. Inf. Sci. **195**, 62–90 (2012). https://doi.org/10.1016/j.ins.2012.01.014

10. Di Martino, F., Sessa, S.: Comparison between images via bilinear fuzzy relation equations. J. Ambient Intell. Humaniz. Comput. (2017). https://doi.org/10.1007/s1265201705763
11. Hirota, K., Pedrycz, W.: Data compression with fuzzy relational equations. Fuzzy Sets Syst. 126(3), 325–335 (2002). https://doi.org/10.1016/S01650114(01)000094
12. Li, J.X.: A new algorithm for the greatest solution of fuzzy bilinear equations. Fuzzy Sets Syst. 46, 193–210 (1992). https://doi.org/10.1016/0165-0114(92)90132N
13. MeenakshiDevi, P., Venkatesan, M., Duraiswamy, K.: Fragile watermarking scheme for image authentication with tamper localization using integer wavelet transform. J. Comput. Sci. 5(11), 831–837 (2009). https://doi.org/10.3844/jcssp.2009.831.837
14. Nobuhara, H., Pedrycz, W., Hirota, K.: A digital watermarking algorithm using image compression method based on fuzzy relational equations. In: Proceedings of FUZZ-IEEE 2002, vol. 2, pp. 1568–1573. IEEE Press, New York (2002). https://doi.org/10.1109/fuzz.2002.1006740
15. Perfilieva, I.: Fuzzy transforms. Fuzzy Sets Syst. 157(8), 993–1023 (2006). https://doi.org/10.1016/j.fss.2005.11.012
16. Qin, C., Ji, P., Zhang, X., Dong, J., Wang, J.: Fragile image watermarking with pixel-wise recovery based on overlapping embedding strategy. Signal Process. 138, 280–293 (2017). https://doi.org/10.1016/j.sigpro.2017.03.033
17. Shih, F.Y.: Digital Watermarking and Steganography: Fundamentals and Techniques. CRC Press, Boca Raton (2007). ISBN 9781420047578
18. Singh, D., Singh, S.K.: DCT based efficient fragile watermarking scheme for image authentication and restoration. Multimed. Tools Appl. 76, 953–977 (2017). https://doi.org/10.1007/s110420153010x
19. Tong, X., Liu, Y., Zhang, M., Chen, Y.: A novel chaos-based fragile watermarking for image tampering detection and self-recovery. Signal Process.: Image Commun. 28, 301–308 (2013). https://doi.org/10.1016/j.image.2012.12.003
20. Walton, S.: Information authentication for a slippery new age. Dr. Dobbs J. 20(4), 18–26 (1995)

Privacy Preserving Biometric Identification on the Bitcoin Blockchain

Neyire Deniz Sarier[✉]

TUBITAK BILGEM, Gebze, Turkey
denizsarier@yahoo.com

Abstract. In this paper, we describe the first Privacy Preserving Biometric Identification (PPBI) protocol built into the Bitcoin blockchain using the cryptographic construction of Zerocoin. Biometric templates are stored as encrypted in the Bitcoin blockchain and matching is performed by the Bitcoin network in the encrypted domain. This way, the centralized server in biometric systems that presents a single point of compromise will be replaced by the blockchain. Since the matching is performed in parallel to the processing of the spend transaction, much of the infrastructure required for the identification is outsourced to the Bitcoin network which maintains strong integrity of its data. Due to the anonymity in Zerocoin system, minting a Zerocoin breaks the link between the pseudo-identity of an authenticating Bitcoin user and its encrypted fresh biometrics attached to the spend transaction. Finally, we also discuss how biometric identification via Bitcoin transactions and resulting transaction fees can be a natural prevention against hill climbing attacks that are applicable even if the templates are stored as encrypted.

Keywords: Privacy Preserving Biometric Identification (PPBI) Blockchain · Zerocoin · Bitcoin · Hill climbing attacks

1 Introduction

Traditionally, biometrics have been used for secure identification and authentication, where only one centralized database is in charge of storing the biometric data either in cleartext or as encrypted. In the identification mode, the biometric system identifies a person from the entire enrolled users in the system by searching a database for a match. This is sometimes called 'one-to-many' matching. The system can also be used in authentication (i.e. verification) mode, where the biometric system authenticates a person's claimed identity from their previously enrolled pattern. This is also called 'one-to-one' matching. In either case, the privacy of biometrics stored on a central database should be guaranteed. This is especially vital if the database that stores the biometric data of each

---

N. D. Sarier—The work was done when the author was an external researcher at Cosec, b-it, Bonn, Germany.

A. Castiglione et al. (Eds.): CSS 2018, LNCS 11161, pp. 254–269, 2018.
https://doi.org/10.1007/978-3-030-01689-0_20

user is outsourced to a cloud to reduce the storage costs. However, cloud storage requires trust to a third party and threats to data integrity as tampering with data should be prevented. The process of replicating and distributing data over a set of nodes prevents the violation of data integrity: an attacker should compromise, without being detected, all the replicated data. This replication approach is widely adopted in practice, for instance, in the context of cloud computing environments, where there is abundance of distributed storage resources [7].

Although replication surely increases the burden for a successful attack in a cloud setting, cloud providers themselves can collude with attackers for easily violating data integrity. Besides, data owners cannot control fundamental data aspects, like the physical storage of data and the control of its accesses [7]. In this context, Blockchain has recently emerged as a new technology for data integrity. To inhibit these collusion attacks and to avoid blind trust on the integrity guarantees claimed by cloud providers, blockchain technology enables a distributed, secure blockchain-based database for cloud computing environments [7].

Blockchain can be seen as a replicated database distributed among thousands of nodes belonging to diverse parties. In its first conception it has been used as public ledger for Bitcoin transactions [12]. Other areas that blockchain has emerged as a new technology are identity management, access control, secure multiparty computation, blockchain storage for cloud, health data and IoT.

1.1 Related Work

Traditionally, biometrics is used for identification/authentication purposes, although recently, biometric cryptosystems such as fuzzy commitment, fuzzy extractors and fuzzy vault have emerged that aim to guarantee biometric template protection. Fuzzy commitment scheme [10] is suitable for hamming distance and specific for biometrics that can be represented as an ordered set of features, i.e. a feature vector. However, biometrics can be affected from two types of noise, i.e. *white noise* that represents the slight perturbation of each feature and the *replacement noise* caused by the replacement of some features. Thus, *fuzzy vault* [9] assumes that biometrics consists of an unordered set of features and is designed for the set difference metric.

In addition to biometric cryptosystems, several privacy preserving biometric authentication/identification (PPBA/PPBI) schemes are designed based on various architectures (distributed with additional non-colluding parties/client-server) or security models (semi-honest/malicious). An overview of research on PPBA is given in [4,15,17], where current research focuses on PPBA schemes that can be outsourcable both in terms of storage and/or computation [4,17], resisting hill climbing attacks [8,17] with a distributed architecture as in [3] or providing private matching [16,19] within a simple client/server model.

For outsourced biometric authentication, encrypted storage with processing in the encrypted domain is a must. In this context, [14] encrypts biometric vectors using homomorphic Public Key Encryption (PKE) and compares them using bilinear pairings similar to the concept of 'PKE with equality testing' [21].

For unordered feature sets, [14] proposes biometric matching by combining RSA encryption and Zero Knowledge Proof of Knowledge (ZKP).

Recently, decentralized identity management systems [1,2] are proposed which are built into the Bitcoin blockchain to guarantee a reliable, public identity proving system. [13] is based particularly on biometric-based identities. The different entities in [1] communicate via Bitcoin transactions, allowing identity issuers to outsource much of the infrastructure required for this system to the Bitcoin network maintaining strong integrity of data through the miner's work.

The identity management system of [1] requires the users to have different Bitcoin addresses in order to obfuscate the link between their identity transactions. While users may employ many identities (or pseudonyms) to enhance their privacy, anyone can de-anonymize Bitcoin by using information in the blockchain such as the structure of the transaction graph as well as the value and dates of transactions. Zerocoin [11] solves this issue by extending Bitcoin to allow for fully anonymous currency transactions. An alternative construction is called as Pinocchio Coin that builds Zerocoin from a Succinct Pairing-based Proof System improving the size of the zero knowledge proof [6].

The startup CryptID [5] stores encrypted records of fingerprints (along with a password) in the Factom blockchain, which is itself periodically committed to the Bitcoin blockchain, replacing the traditional centralized server in fingerprint identification [1]. Similarly, [13] describes a new decentralized authentication protocol that relies on decentralized identifiers (DIDs) and the concept of self sovereign identity, where the latter utilizes blockchain technology to establish a web-of-trust. The multiple shares of biometric templates are spread across alternate off-chain storage (like Dropbox, Google drive, etc.) and securely referenced to them by blockchains technology. Contrary to [13], the systems of [1,2] publish the commitments to identities of each user as a transaction and in [1] a special transaction called as *authentication token* will be spent by the user upon using her identity leaving a transaction output for future authentications. The necessary proofs for the commitments can be stored either off-chain or a link to a site storing the proofs is added to this special transaction.

1.2   Motivation and Contributions

Most user authentication methods and identity proving systems rely on a centralized database. Such information storage presents a single point of compromise, hence system failure causes enough information to be extracted to compromise the user's digital identity. Apart from the storage risks, biometric authentication systems are vulnerable to various attacks with respect to user and data privacy [8,15,17,20]. Since biometrics and personal identity are linked together, users should authenticate anonymously and biometric data should stay private. For the latter, encrypted storage with processing in the encrypted domain is the standard solution although hill-climbing attacks can still be performed even in encrypted domain. In particular, hill-climbing attacks generate data resembling the originally acquired biometrics by updating the data generated at a given step iteratively to improve the resulting matching output, till a successful recognition is achieved. Hence, this leakage of information enables a hill-climbing attack against any biometric scheme designed according to semi-honest security model such that, given a sample that matches the template, could lead to the full recovery of the reference biometric template even if it is stored as encrypted. In this context, biometric identification on the Bitcoin network offers a possible solution, at least by increasing the cost of an attacker for impersonation or hill climbing attacks using the Bitcoin network. These costs are further affected by the choice of the transaction fees, entropy of the biometric template and quantization of the matching scores. Besides, Bitcoin transactions are by their nature public, posing risks to user anonymity. The typical suggestion to ensure (pseudo-)anonymity in Bitcoin is to use each Bitcoin address exactly one time as proposed in current identity management schemes of [1,2,13] on the Bitcoin network. However, for biometric matching, we need stronger anonymity guarantees since biometrics is sensitive data and the link between the identity and biometrics should be protected with provable security. In summary, we should have the following goals for a Privacy Preserving Biometric Identification (PPBI) on the blockchain.

- Biometric identification should be performed anonymously on the blockchain using the infrastructure of the Bitcoin network.
- Matching should be performed in the encrypted domain without any decryption operation.
- Identity privacy should be guaranteed that breaks the link between the pseudonym identity, i.e. Bitcoin address of the user and his encrypted biometrics that is stored on the blockchain.
- The cost of a hill climbing attack using the Bitcoin network should be made expensive and the identity of the user can be revoked using a transaction performed by the identity provider.

In this paper, we describe the first PPBI protocol on the Bitcoin network that is resistant to hill climbing attacks. Due to the encrypted storage and matching in the encrypted domain, biometric templates are protected and user privacy is guaranteed as a result of the anonymity of Zerocoin. As opposed to the current identity management systems on the blockchain, we build our system on Zerocoin [6,11], which is an anonymous decentralized e-cash system that uses Bitcoin both as an append-only bulletin board and a backing currency. We define the security notions of the new system that provide the privacy of the link between the pseudo-identity (i.e. Bitcoin address) and biometrics of the user, where user privacy should be guaranteed against any attacker whereas identity privacy is restricted to the malicious insider attacker, namely the service provider.

Intuition Behind Our Construction: The different entities of PPBI, namely the service provider ($\mathcal{SP}$), the identity provider ($\mathcal{IP}$) and the user ($\mathcal{USR}$) communicate via Bitcoin and Zerocoin transactions. Specifically, enrollment and revocation of a user is performed by the offline $\mathcal{IP}$, who publishes only the encrypted biometric template of the user via a standard Bitcoin transaction sent to $\mathcal{IP}$. As different from [1], the user's Bitcoin address is not tied to his encrypted biometrics. Before authenticating to the system, the user should already have minted a Zerocoin so that during authentication, the user spends it with a Zerocoin spend transaction, where a fresh encrypted biometrics is inserted into the OP_RETURN output of this transaction that is normally used to store arbitrary information. The Bitcoin network verifies that the transaction is valid, i.e. not double spending a previously spent output/having valid proofs. Next, the network compares the encrypted fresh biometrics to each enrolled biometric data that are published by $\mathcal{IP}$ as part of Bitcoin transactions.

The comparison is performed in the encrypted domain without a decryption operation using the modified versions of protocols in [14] for ordered and unordered biometric features, respectively. If there exists a match, the transaction is authorized in parallel to the processing of a spend transaction. The coin serial number S together with the match/non match decision of the network is added to the list of spent serial numbers held by the user and $\mathcal{IP}$. This way, $\mathcal{IP}$ keeps track of the non-valid authentication attempts of dishonest users or a malicious $\mathcal{SP}$ masquerading as a user, which perform hill climbing attack using the Bitcoin infrastructure. The total difference between the authorized spent serial numbers and non-authorized ones reveals the matching failures. Hence, anonymity of a coin is upper bounded by the total number of minted coins. Identity privacy is upper bounded by the total number of authorized spent coins.

In particular, we adapt the RSA based protocol in [14] for unordered biometrics such as fingerprint minutia and elliptic curve signed ElGamal scheme for ordered biometric features such as face, fingercode, etc. so that matching is performed only remotely. These systems could be integrated into the Bitcoin network, where miners check for the validity of each transaction in parallel to the authorization of the transactions through biometric identification. Besides, the parameters of the protocols in [14] are common with Zerocoin, which uses RSA based accumulators together with Schnorr signatures and is built on top of Bitcoin that uses elliptic curve cryptography.

2   Background on Biometrics and Zerocoin

2.1   Biometric Representation

Early biometric cryptosystems such as fuzzy vault were implemented on fingerprints, where we need query fingers to be pre-aligned so that stored minutiae matching with query minutiae are of sufficient similarity, namely stored minutiae significantly overlap fresh minutiae. Next, prealigned minutia data are quantized and mapped to a fixed finite field. In this case, the similarity measure has to consider set difference metric since the biometric features are represented as an unordered set of features. Fingerprint matching can also be performed using a different type of information extracted from fingerprint image, i.e. FingerCode, that uses texture information from a fingerprint scan to form fingerprint representation. Similar to fingercode representation, other biometrics modalities such as face, online handwritten signatures, iris, voice, etc. can be represented as an ordered set of features (i.e. a sequence of k points) [15,17]. Due to page limitations, details of feature set/vector extraction can be found in [15,18].

2.2 Secure Biometric Matching

Firstly, we employ the modified version of the first protocol in [14] that is based on the elliptic curve ElGamal encryption scheme, bilinear pairings for equality testing and a non-malleable ZKP based on the Schnorr signature. We assume that biometrics is represented as an ordered set of features such as face. For simplicity, we omit the stable/nonstable separation of features as in [14], where the stable parts are matched remotely and non-stable parts on card for a multi-factor biometric authentication. Instead, we employ secure sketches for error correction and alignment as described in [15].

Setup Phase: The parameters of the elliptic curve ElGamal encryption scheme are initialized with a pairing friendly elliptic curve group $\mathbb{G}$ and bilinear pairing $\hat{e} : \mathbb{G} \times \mathbb{G} \to \mathbb{F}$ and a map to map each biometric feature (integer value) to a group element before encryption. Each user generates an ElGamal key pair (pk_U, sk_U) that is used to encrypt the biometric features.

Enrollment Phase: $\mathcal{IP}$ extracts the user's biometrics B and each feature μ_j is encrypted using the public key pk_U of the user to obtain $w_j = \mathsf{Encrypt}(\mu_j, pk_U) = (w_j^1, w_j^2) = (g^{r_j}, y^{r_j}\mu_j)$. The user registers his ID at the $\mathcal{SP}$. User does not store the secret key x of his public key $pk_U = y = g^x$ as it will not be used further.

Verification Phase: The user authenticates to $\mathcal{SP}$ as follows:

1. The user extracts his fresh biometrics B' and encrypts the fresh features (μ_j's) using his ElGamal public key pk_U. Alignment and error-correction through a secure sketch scheme can be performed before encryption.
2. The encrypted features $w_j' = (w_j'^1, w_j'^2) = (u_j', v_j')$ are sent to the system together with the associated ZKPs: namely $w_j' = (g^{r_j'}, y^{r_j'}\mu_j')$ and the Schnorr ZKP (z_j, c_j), where $z_j = g^{k_j}, c_j = r_j' \cdot H(g, u_j', v_j', z_j) + k_j$ as described in [14].
3. The system first checks the ZKP as $g^{c_j} = (u_j')^{H(g,u_j',v_j',z_j)} \cdot z_j$. However, this non-malleable scheme is still vulnerable to replay attacks as an attacker can obtain the encrypted biometrics and the corresponding ZKP of a user and later impersonates this user. This can only be prevented by adding a time stamp t to the ZKP as $H(g, u_j', v_j', z_j, t)$, thus the attacker cannot use the same ciphertext for a replay attack at a later time t' [14].
4. The system verifies the ZKPs and compares the fresh encrypted features w_j's to the enrolled w_js by using the homomorphic property of ElGamal encryption scheme. For $1 \leq j \leq k$, $s_j \xleftarrow{R} \mathbb{Z}_p^*$ is selected to compute $R_j = (R_j^1, R_j^2) = \left(\left(\frac{w_j^1}{w_j'^1}\right)^{s_j}, \left(\frac{w_j^2}{w_j'^2}\right)^{s_j}\right)$. The system checks for $1 \leq j \leq k$ whether $\hat{e}(g^x, R_j^1) = \hat{e}(g, R_j^2)$ by computing $2k$ pairings. Finally, the system counts the number of the equations satisfying the above condition and computes the matching score ms to check that it is less than the predefined threshold of the system. If so, the user is authenticated.

Although some biometric modalities can be represented as an ordered set of features such as face biometric, for fingerprints this is not a trivial task [15]. Fuzzy vault based systems try to find a solution for biometrics that consists of an unordered set of features using error correcting codes and alignment. Since ordering or grouping of features is not possible for some biometric modalities, we cannot use a probabilistic encryption scheme such as ElGamal encryption system as the comparison cannot be made in the encrypted domain without decryption. However, if we use a deterministic scheme like RSA as in [14], the system does not need to compute in worst case $O(k^2)$ bilinear pairings and modular divisions when elliptic curve ElGamal is used, where the computation of one bilinear pairing is approximately 9 modular exponentiations. (k is the size of the feature set). Thus, our previous system is impractical compared to a deterministic encryption scheme for unordered biometric features. Finally, dictionary and replay attacks should be considered when a deterministic scheme is used as encryption of the same message results in the same ciphertext, whereas the encryption of the same message results in a different ciphertext due to the random coins used in the probabilistic encryption scheme. Thus, ZKPs designed for RSA should be attached to the ciphertext with a time stamp as before. For dictionary attacks, we have to apply a blinding of each ciphertext, i.e. by multiplying the ciphertext w_j by a randomly picked p_j raised to the public key e as applied in anonymous e-cash. The random value p_j has to be stored secretly by the user, who applies it during each verification. Since the structure of enrollment and verification is almost identical except for the bilinear pairing computations for equality testing and the replacement of ElGamal encryption with RSA (and the corresponding ZKPs), we omit the details and refer the reader to [14].

2.3   Bitcoin and Zerocoin Relevant Definitions

All Bitcoins exist in the form of Unspent Transaction Outputs (UTXOs). Each transaction may have several inputs, each of which was an output UTXO for some previous Bitcoin transaction, and it may have several outputs. The given inputs and outputs of a given transaction are provably linked together. Most transaction outputs correspond to a Bitcoin address, the hash of the public key that can spend it. The scripts for each input that satisfy the requirements set up when the corresponding input UTXO was created, generally include a signature from a corresponding private key. Also relevant to our work will be OP_RETURN outputs; each such output contains up to 80 bytes of space in which the sender of a transaction can store arbitrary information. Note, OP_RETURN outputs must have zero Bitcoins associated to them; as such, they are provably not usable as inputs to later transactions [1]. Miners are compensated by fees. The amount paid in fees for a given transaction is the difference between the combined values of the inputs and the combined values of the outputs. We denote the fees for a given transaction by $F_{\text{NameOfTransaction}}$ in our protocol.

Zerocoin [11] extends Bitcoin to allow for fully anonymous currency transactions. To prevent de-anonymization and transaction graph analyses, Zerocoin allows the Bitcoin users to generate their own coins provided that they have sufficient classical Bitcoins. In particular, the user first generates a random coin serial number S, then commits to S using a secure digital commitment scheme. The resulting commitment is a coin, denoted c, which can only be opened by a random number r to reveal the serial number S. Instead of a public key, coins are identified by a commitment c to a pair of fresh, random secrets: S and r. The user pins c to the public bulletin board, namely blockchain.

To redeem his coin c, the user first scans the bulletin board to obtain the set of valid commitments C that have thus far been posted by all users in the system. Zerocoin authenticates coins by proving, in zero knowledge, that they belong to a public list C of valid coins on the blockchain. The opening r to the commitment of the coin being spent is never revealed but is used to compute a proof π for a signature of knowledge that replaces the conventional signature of a Bitcoin spend transaction. It provides anonymity by unlinking a payment transaction from its origin address. To guarantee anonymity, a Zerocoin spend transaction involves revealing S and proving knowledge of r for any c in a large, public collection C of previously-logged commitments. The signature of knowledge proves that the spending party can open one of the commitments to the serial number, -by hiding which commitment can be opened in this way, Zerocoin provides anonymity-. At the same time, if the commitment and zero-knowledge proof are secure, then the user cannot double-spend any coin without re-using the serial number S and thus being detected by the network participants [11]. Hence, the uniqueness of the serial number prevents double spending [6]. Due to the storage costs, the required proofs are stored in a separate, well-known location (a simple server). Alternatively, a Distributed Hash Table or non blockchain backed storage in Bitcoin could be used.

3   Our Proposal

3.1   Architecture of the System

Our system will have three types of actors: Identity Providers ($\mathcal{IP}$), Service Providers ($\mathcal{SP}$), and Users ($\mathcal{USR}$). We consider that both the Bitcoin addresses of $\mathcal{IP}$ and $\mathcal{SP}$ are well-established and public, $a_{\mathcal{IP}}$ and $a_{\mathcal{SP}}$ respectively. In contrast, $\mathcal{USR}$ may have different Bitcoin addresses, but this is not required as in [1] to obfuscate the link between her identity transactions due to the use of Zerocoin. Zerocoin uses a fixed Bitcoin amount, i.e. all Zerocoins have the same denomination, which is not a drawback for PPBI, as each of these transactions is thought of as having symbolic meaning, their Bitcoin values are secondary; indeed, they are assigned values slightly larger than the minimum amount $\mathcal{D}$ of standard Bitcoin transaction around .01 USD as in [1]. We assume that $\mathcal{IP}$ validates a user's real world identity and then publishes documents that are correct. Furthermore, $\mathcal{IP}$ should handle user personal data in a way that respects user-privacy. Note that $\mathcal{IP}$ does not need to stay online for the identities it issues to be used, and only participates for issuing and revocation of identities.

We will use the public ledger functionality of Bitcoin as in [1,2] and provide anonymity using Zerocoin since Bitcoin has significant limitations regarding privacy. Specifically, the Bitcoin transaction log is completely public and users' privacy is protected only through the use of pseudonyms [11]. While users may employ many identities (or pseudonyms) to enhance their privacy -as in the ID management system of [1]-, anyone can de-anonymize Bitcoin by using data in blockchain such as the structure of the transaction graph as well as the value and dates of transactions. For instance, [1] records the committed identity of each user in the blockchain, a transaction is sent from $\mathcal{IP}$ to the $\mathcal{USR}$ that ties the user's address to his identity. Hence, [1] requires the users to have different Bitcoin addresses to obfuscate the link between their identity transactions.

3.2 Identification Workflow

There are three steps for our protocol: a Setup phase, an Enrollment phase, and an Identification phase.

Setup Phase: $\mathcal{IP}$ will choose the public parameters *params* that will serve as the base for the Zerocoin and biometric identification depending on the type of the biometrics, i.e. ordered/grouped or unordered features, where the latter shares the parameters of Zerocoin since both are based on RSA. $\mathcal{IP}$ could create a series of Bitcoin transactions with inputs from his address in which pairing friendly elliptic curve group parameters for ordered biometrics and RSA parameters for unordered biometrics are stored in OP_RETURN outputs.

Enrollment Phase: $\mathcal{USR}$ brings to $\mathcal{IP}$ the (physical, biometric, etc) elements required to prove his identity. Also, $\mathcal{USR}$ should provide $\mathcal{IP}$ with a Bitcoin address $a_{\mathcal{USR}}$ that he controls and his public key to encrypt the biometrics B. Then, $\mathcal{IP}$ can form a single Bitcoin transaction, $TX_{PUBLISH}$ as shown in Fig. 1, that stores the encrypted template $b_{\mathcal{USR}}$ of the user in OP_RETURN outputs.

Input Addresses	Amounts	Output Addresses	Amounts
$TX_{PUBLISH}$			
$a_{\mathcal{IP}}$	$\mathcal{D} + F_{PUBLISH}$	$a_{\mathcal{IP}}$	$\mathcal{D}$
		OP_RETURN $\left(b_{\mathcal{USR}} \right)$	
		Fees:	$F_{PUBLISH}$

Fig. 1. Structure of $TX_{PUBLISH}$

The primary purpose of this transaction is to record the encrypted biometric template $b_{\mathcal{USR}}$ of the user in the blockchain as described in Sect. 2.2. Moreover, $\mathcal{IP}$ can revoke the identity of the user by sending a transaction to $\mathcal{IP}$. Finally, an OP_RETURN contains $b_{\mathcal{USR}}$, which denotes the encrypted feature set (or vector).

Identification Phase: is made up of four further Bitcoin transactions: TX_{Mint}, TX_{Spend}, $TX_{Service}$ and the decision of the $\mathcal{SP}$, namely either TX_{Accept} or TX_{Reject}.

1. *Minting a Zerocoin* (TX_{Mint}): Firstly, USR creates a transaction, in particular mints a Zerocoin, where the input is the Bitcoin address of the USR as a_{USR}. The output's scriptPubKey contains ZEROCOIN_MINT instruction and a coin c_1 as shown in Fig. 2. Nodes receiving this transaction should validate that c_1 is a well-formed coin.

2. *Spending a Zerocoin* (TX_{Spend}): The user first constructs a partial transaction ptx that references an unclaimed mint transaction $\overline{TX}_{Mint}$ as input and includes SP's public key as output as shown in Fig. 2. She then traverses all valid mint transactions in the blockchain, assembles the set of minted coins C, and runs $Spend(params, \overline{b}_{USR}, c_1, skc_1, hash(ptx), C) \rightarrow (\pi_1, S_1)$. Finally, she completes the transaction by embedding (π_1, S_1) and a reference to the block containing the accumulator used in π_1 in the scriptSig of the input of ptx, and $\overline{b}_{USR}, c_2$ into the OP_RETURN of the TX_{Spend}. Hence, the primary purpose of this transaction is to record the fresh encrypted biometric feature set (or vector) $\overline{b}_{USR}$ and a commitment c_2 to another S_2 similar to a TX_{Mint} transaction. The proof for the commitment c_2 will be used later in a $TX_{Service}$ for anonymous biometric identification.

TX $_{Mint}$ Input Addresses	Amounts	Output Addresses	Amounts
a_{USR}	$D + F_{Mint}$	scriptPubKey(ZEROCOIN_MINT, c_1)	D
		Fees:	F_{Mint}

TX$_{Spend}$ Input Addresses	Amounts	Output Addresses	Amounts
$\overline{TX}_{Mint}$	$D + F_{Spend}$	a_{SP}	D
scriptSig(π_1, S_1, refBlockAcc$_1$)		OP_RETURN $\left(\overline{b}_{USR}, c_2 \right)$	
		Fees:	F_{Spend}

Fig. 2. Structure of TX_{Mint} and TX_{Spend}

When this transaction appears on the network, the nodes extract the accumulator from the referenced block and, using it, validate the spend via $Verify(params, \pi_1, S_1, hash(ptx), C) = 1$ and check that S_1 does not appear in any previous transaction. If these condition hold and the referenced mint transaction is not claimed as an input into a different transaction, the network accepts the spend as valid and allows the user to redeem the Bitcoin.

In parallel to this verification, the nodes perform the comparison of $\overline{b}_{USR}$ against all published templates in the encrypted domain without a decryption operation using the modified versions of protocols in [14] described in Sect. 2.2. If there exists a single match, the transaction is authorized in parallel to the processing of a spend transaction. The coin serial number S_1 together with the match/non match decision of the network is added to the list of spent serial numbers held by the user and $\mathcal{IP}$. If there exists two matches, the nodes check whether there exists a TX_{REVOKE} as shown in Fig. 3 and store the index of this transaction together with the index of the associated $TX_{PUBLISH}$ in the list of revoked identities for future comparisons. This way, revoked users are not processed further after the validation of the spend transaction for matching.

Hence, if there exists a single match meaning the match does not involve a revoked transaction, the transaction is authorized in parallel to the processing of a spend transaction. If a match decision is listed, the associated coin c_2 embedded to the OP_RETURN of this transaction is accumulated by the nodes to the second accumulator that contains the list of coins associated to a match decision. We note that the coin c_2 associated to a non-match decision of the nodes is not accumulated to the second accumulator employed for a service request of the user from the $\mathcal{SP}$. This way, if the spend transaction is authorized with a match decision, $\mathcal{USR}$ is able to prove to $\mathcal{SP}$ the knowledge of a coin c_2 committed to a second serial number S_2 without revealing it as described in Sect. 2.3 allowing for an anonymous identification among the coins attached to the spend transactions with a match decision.

	Input Addresses	Amounts	Output Addresses	Amounts
TX_{REVOKE}				
	$a_{\mathcal{IP}}$	$\mathcal{D} + F_{REVOKE}$	$a_{\mathcal{IP}}$	$\mathcal{D}$
			OP_RETURN $\left(b_{\mathcal{USR}} \right)$	
			Fees:	F_{REVOKE}

Fig. 3. Structure of TX_{REVOKE}

3. *Request for Service* ($TX_{Service}$): The user creates a transaction where the input is his Bitcoin address. Here, the user should choose a Bitcoin address that is different than the one used during minting a Zerocoin. The output is sent to $a_{\mathcal{SP}}$ together with the OP_RETURN that contains (π_2, S_2) and a reference to the block containing the accumulator used in π_2 as shown in Fig. 4.

A verifier, namely $\mathcal{SP}$ will extract the accumulator from the referenced block and, using it, validates the proof in the decision phase. A user can store in the OP_RETURN of $TX_{Service}$ a link to a site where the proofs are stored externally as well as a hash of the relevant contents of this site as done in [1]. The hash will be included in mined blocks, so the information on the site has the same protections against mutability as other information on the blockchain. We note that, if the spend transaction of the previous stage is authorized with a match decision, $\mathcal{USR}$ is able to prove to $\mathcal{SP}$ the knowledge of a coin committed to a second serial number S_2 without revealing it as described in Sect. 2.3. We note that an unauthorized user or a revoked user cannot do this since, only authorized spend transactions are accumulated in C_2 by the nodes.

4. *Decision of $\mathcal{SP}$* (TX_{Accept} or TX_{Reject}): Upon validating the proof of the user, namely extracting the accumulator from the referenced block, validating the proof by $\mathsf{Verify}(params, \pi_2, S_2, hash(ptx_2), C_2) = 1$ and checking that S_2 does not appear in any previous authentication request, $\mathcal{SP}$ gives his decision about the user's authentication request as shown in Fig. 4. If these condition hold in the decision phase, $\mathcal{SP}$ accepts the user's authentication and uses its output from $TX_{Service}$ to send Bitcoins to $a_{\mathcal{IP}}$. Otherwise, he rejects and sends a TX_{Reject} transaction to $\mathcal{IP}$. This way, $\mathcal{IP}$ can verify that $\mathcal{SP}$ behaves correctly by comparing the number of authorized spent serial numbers and the number of TX_{Accept}s, and vice versa.

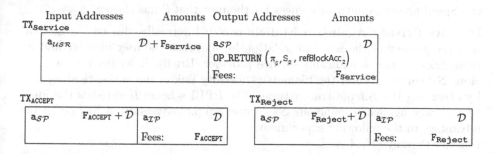

Fig. 4. Structure of $TX_{Service}$, TX_{Accept} and TX_{Reject}

3.3   Security Analysis

Here, we describe the security notions of PPBI on the blockchain, namely user privacy and identity privacy. First, we analyze the user privacy experiment, which ensures that the adversary cannot link a given biometric data within the Zerocoin spend transaction (π_1, S_1) to the Bitcoin address within the Zerocoin associated to it (i.e. TX_{Mint}), even when the attacker provides many of the coins used in generating the spend transaction. Given an adversary $\mathcal{A}$ running against the PPBI scheme Π and a challenger $\mathcal{C}$ that simulates the setup, enrollment and identification phases of Π, consider the following game between $\mathcal{A}$ and $\mathcal{C}$.

User Privacy: The PPBI scheme $\Pi = $ (Setup; Enrollment; Identification) satisfies the user privacy requirement if every probabilistic polynomial time (p.p.t.) adversary $\mathcal{A}$ has negligible advantage in the following experiment. Here, R denotes a transaction information string as in [11].

User privacy$(\Pi, \mathcal{A}, \lambda)$

$\quad$ $params \leftarrow \mathsf{Setup}(1^\lambda)$

$\quad$ For $j \in [1, n] : \mathsf{TX}_{\mathrm{PUBLISH}}(B_j) \leftarrow \mathsf{Enrollment}(ID_j, B_j)$

$\quad$ For $i \in \{0, 1\} : \mathsf{TX}_{\mathrm{Mint}}, \mathsf{TX}_{\mathrm{Spend}} \leftarrow \mathsf{Identification}(ID_i, B_i')$

$\quad\quad$ $(c_{1i}, skc_{1i}) \leftarrow \mathsf{Mint}(params, \mathsf{a}_{\mathcal{USR}_i})$

$\quad\quad$ $(C, R, z) \leftarrow \mathcal{A}(params, c_{10}, c_{11}); d \leftarrow \{0, 1\}$

$\quad\quad$ $(\pi_1, \mathsf{S}_1, c_2, skc_2) \leftarrow \mathsf{Spend}(params, \overline{b}_d, c_{1d}, skc_{1d}, R, C \cup \{c_{10}, c_{11}\})$

$\quad$ Output: $d' \leftarrow \mathcal{A}(z, \pi_1, \mathsf{S}_1)$

We define $\mathcal{A}$'s advantage in the above game as $\Pr[|d = d'] - 1/2|$.

Here, $\mathcal{C}$ generates the identification data for n users in the system by simulating the enrollment phase. $\mathcal{C}$ picks at random two users with identity ID_i and biometrics B_i' of $i \in [0, 1]$ and simulates the identification phase by minting two Zerocoins c_{10}, c_{11} one for each user. The rest of the game is identical to the anonymity game of [11] except for the Spend phase, where OP_RETURN output contains the fresh encrypted biometrics $\overline{b}_d$ and the commitment c_2 for a second serial number S_2 for the randomly chosen user with ID_d. Here, embedding of c_2 imitate the minting of a Zerocoin, although no coin is generated. After running the Spend phase, $\mathcal{A}$ outputs a guess for the user that $\mathcal{C}$ has chosen.

Identity Privacy Against a Malicious $\mathcal{SP}$: Informally, this notion guarantees the privacy of the sensitive relationship between the user identity and its biometrics against a malicious service provider. Briefly, it means that a malicious $\mathcal{SP}$ cannot recover the biometrics/identity link of the authenticating user by observing the Bitcoin transactions. The PPBI scheme Π satisfies the identity privacy against a malicious $\mathcal{SP}$ if every p.p.t. adversary $\mathcal{A}$ has negligible advantage in the following experiment.

Identity Privacy $(\Pi, \mathcal{A}, \lambda)$

$\quad$ $params \leftarrow \mathsf{Setup}(1^\lambda)$

$\quad$ For $j \in [1, n] : \mathsf{TX}_{\mathrm{PUBLISH}}(B_j) \leftarrow \mathsf{Enrollment}(ID_j, B_j)$

$\quad$ For $i \in \{0, 1\} : \mathsf{TX}_{\mathrm{Mint}}, \mathsf{TX}_{\mathrm{Spend}} \leftarrow \mathsf{Identification}(ID_i, B_i')$

$\quad\quad$ $(\pi_{1i}, \mathsf{S}_{1i}, c_{2i}, skc_{2i}) \leftarrow \mathsf{Spend}(params, \overline{b}_i, c_{1i}, skc_{1i}, R, C \cup \{c_{10}, c_{11}\})$

$\quad\quad$ $(C_2, R, z) \leftarrow \mathcal{A}(params, c_{20}, c_{21}); d \leftarrow \{0, 1\}$

$\quad\quad$ $(\pi_2, \mathsf{S}_2) \leftarrow \mathsf{Service}(params, \mathsf{a}_{\mathcal{USR}}, c_{2d}, skc_{2d}, R, C_2 \cup \{c_{20}, c_{21}\})$

$\quad$ Output: $d' \leftarrow \mathcal{A}(z, \pi_2, \mathsf{S}_2)$

We define $\mathcal{A}$'s advantage in the above game as $\Pr[|d = d'] - 1/2|$.

Theorem 1. *PPBI protocol Π achieves user privacy against any attacker based on the security of the Zerocoin.*

Theorem 2. *PPBI protocol Π achieves identity privacy against a malicious $\mathcal{SP}$ based on the security of the Zerocoin and the security of the encrypted biometrics.*

The proofs will be presented in the full version of the paper.

3.4   Discussion

For ordered features, since no blinding is applied, we require higher entropy for biometric features. As analyzed in [15], the scheme with signed ElGamal can achieve only OW-CCA security, thus, if an attacker (trying to learn the biometric template of a particular user with a published encrypted biometric feature b) picks a candidate biometric feature, computes its encryption b' using the public key of that user and runs the (public) test on input b and b', then the attacker can learn much information about the ciphertexts from the test results as in the scheme of [21]. Since one factor limiting the security of biometric cryptosystems is the entropy of the biometric features, to prevent the attacker from breaking the identity privacy, it is necessary to impose higher entropy for the features as suggested in [16]. To further increase the input-entropy, multimodal biometrics can be employed and a user password can be concatenated to the biometric inputs, where a random 8-character password can have 52-bit entropy [16]. Blinding in RSA encryption for unordered sets prevents this attack due to the randomly picked blinding factor for each feature.

We know that $s \leq m$, namely the total number of spend coins s is less than the total number of generated (minted) coins m due to the Balance property as proved in [11]. Hence, the probability of identity privacy against a malicious service provider is $1/s$, whereas the probability of user privacy against any attacker is $1/m$ similar to the probability of anonymity of Zerocoin. Hence, an internal attacker as the $\mathcal{SP}$ has a higher success on guessing which biometric encrypted template is associated to the user, nevertheless the security of the encryption scheme prevents $\mathcal{SP}$ from inverting the encrypted template to obtain the fresh biometric template of the user. However, our main goal is to break the link between the pseudo-identity of the user and its biometrics as achieved in the user privacy notion since the pseudo-identity of the user is not published together with its (encrypted) biometric data as opposed to the TX$_{\text{PUBLISH}}$ of [1]. (Remember that the Bitcoin address of the user is bound to its ID in the TX$_{\text{PUBLISH}}$ of [1]). Even if any attacker has complete knowledge of all the biometric templates registered in the PPBI, if the attacker has no *a priori* knowledge of which biometrics belongs to which user identity, the attacker cannot extract this information from PPBI. Here, $\mathcal{IP}$ is assumed to be honest and trusted by anyone in the system.

Finally, our system has one drawback. As authentications are encoded in Bitcoin transactions, this requires paying transaction fees to miners. This will not cause any problem for honest users who present valid encrypted templates to the Bitcoin network for comparison, but for insider attackers who use the Bitcoin network infrastructure for many authentication attempts during a hill climbing attack, the cost will be high. Hence, this drawback turns out to be a natural prevention against this attack performed on the Bitcoin network.

4   Conclusion

In this paper, we describe the first anonymous PPBI protocol built into the Bitcoin blockchain using the cryptographic construction of Zerocoin. We define the security notions for the new system, i.e. user and identity privacy that provide the privacy of the sensitive relationship between the identity of the user and his biometrics. Future work could be analysis of the transaction fees to avoid hill climbing attacks, improving the efficieny of the system by employing other credential systems to decrease computational and storage costs, and integration of multimodal/multi-factor PPBI schemes to increase the entropy of biometrics.

References

1. Augot, D., Chabanne, H., Chenevier, T., George, W., Lambert, L.: A user-centric system for verified identities on the bitcoin blockchain. In: Garcia-Alfaro, J., Navarro-Arribas, G., Hartenstein, H., Herrera-Joancomartí, J. (eds.) ESORICS/DPM/CBT -2017. LNCS, vol. 10436, pp. 390–407. Springer, Cham (2017). https://doi.org/10.1007/978-3-319-67816-0_22
2. Augot, D., Chabanne, H., Clémot, O., George, W.: Transforming face-to-face identity proofing into anonymous digital identity using the bitcoin blockchain. CoRR abs/1710.02951 (2017)
3. Bringer, J., Chabanne, H., Izabachène, M., Pointcheval, D., Tang, Q., Zimmer, S.: An application of the Goldwasser-Micali cryptosystem to biometric authentication. In: Pieprzyk, J., Ghodosi, H., Dawson, E. (eds.) ACISP 2007. LNCS, vol. 4586, pp. 96–106. Springer, Heidelberg (2007). https://doi.org/10.1007/978-3-540-73458-1_8
4. Chun, H., Elmehdwi, Y., Li, F., Bhattacharya, P., Jiang, W.: Outsourcable two-party privacy preserving biometric authentication. In: ACM ASIACCS 2014, pp. 401–412 (2014)
5. CryptID. https://github.com/cryptidid/cryptid, http://cryptid.xyz/. Consulted May 2018
6. Danezis, G., Fournet, C., Kohlweiss, M., Parno, B.: Pinocchio coin: building zerocoin from a succinct pairing-based proof system. In: PETShop 2013, pp. 27–30. ACM (2013)
7. Gaetani, E., Aniello, L., Baldoni, R., Lombardi, F., Margheri, A., Sassone, V.: Blockchain-based database to ensure data integrity in cloud computing environments. In: ITASEC 2017, vol. 1816, pp. 146–155. CEUR-WS.org (2017)
8. Higo, H., Isshiki, T., Mori, K., Obana, S.: Privacy-preserving fingerprint authentication resistant to hill-climbing attacks. In: Dunkelman, O., Keliher, L. (eds.) SAC 2015. LNCS, vol. 9566, pp. 44–64. Springer, Cham (2016). https://doi.org/10.1007/978-3-319-31301-6_3
9. Juels, A., Sudan, M.: A fuzzy vault scheme. Des. Codes Cryptogr. 38(2), 237–257 (2006)
10. Juels, A., Wattenberg, M.: A fuzzy commitment scheme. In: ACM CCS, pp. 28–36 (1999)
11. Miers, I., Garman, C., Green, M., Rubin, A.D.: Zerocoin: anonymous distributed e-cash from bitcoin. In: SP 2013, pp. 397–411. IEEE (2013)
12. Nakamoto, S.: Bitcoin: a peer-to-peer electronic cash system (2008)
13. Othman, A., Callahan, J.: The Horcrux protocol: a method for decentralized biometric-based self-sovereign identity. CoRR abs/1711.07127 (2017)
14. Sarier, N.D.: Practical multi-factor biometric remote authentication. In: BTAS 2010, pp. 1–6. IEEE (2010)
15. Sarier, N.D.: Biometric cryptosystems: authentication, encryption and signature for biometric identities. Ph.D. thesis, Bonn University, Germany (2013)
16. Sarier, N.D.: Private minutia-based fingerprint matching. In: Akram, R.N., Jajodia, S. (eds.) WISTP 2015. LNCS, vol. 9311, pp. 52–67. Springer, Cham (2015). https://doi.org/10.1007/978-3-319-24018-3_4

17. Sarier, N.D.: Privacy preserving multimodal biometric authentication in the cloud. In: Au, M.H.A., Castiglione, A., Choo, K.-K.R., Palmieri, F., Li, K.-C. (eds.) GPC 2017. LNCS, vol. 10232, pp. 90–104. Springer, Cham (2017). https://doi.org/10.1007/978-3-319-57186-7_8

18. Sarier, N.D.: Multimodal biometric identity based encryption. Future Gener. Comp. Syst. **80**, 112–125 (2018)

19. Shahandashti, S.F., Safavi-Naini, R., Ogunbona, P.: Private fingerprint matching. In: Susilo, W., Mu, Y., Seberry, J. (eds.) ACISP 2012. LNCS, vol. 7372, pp. 426–433. Springer, Heidelberg (2012). https://doi.org/10.1007/978-3-642-31448-3_32

20. Simoens, K., Bringer, J., Chabanne, H., Seys, S.: A framework for analyzing template security and privacy in biometric authentication systems. IEEE TIFS **7**(2), 833–841 (2012)

21. Yang, G., Tan, C.H., Huang, Q., Wong, D.S.: Probabilistic public key encryption with equality test. In: Pieprzyk, J. (ed.) CT-RSA 2010. LNCS, vol. 5985, pp. 119–131. Springer, Heidelberg (2010). https://doi.org/10.1007/978-3-642-11925-5_9

Iris Quality Assessment: A Statistical Approach for Biometric Security Applications

Andrea F. Abate[2], Silvio Barra[1]([⊠]) [iD], Andrea Casanova[1], Gianni Fenu[1], and Mirko Marras[1]

[1] Department of Mathematics and Computer Science, University of Cagliari, Cagliari, Italy
{silvio.barra,casanova,fenu,mirko.marras}@unica.it
[2] Department of Computer Science, University of Salerno, Salerno, Italy
abate@unisa.it

Abstract. Biometric recognition is often affected by low quality images. This is especially true in iris recognition fields, due to the fact that the area of the iris is quite small and wrong detection are very common when standard iris detection methods are used, like the Hough transform. In this paper, the iris quality assessment of over 1200 images is achieved, from three different datasets. The evaluation of the iris is done by using shallow learning techniques. Two different experiments have been carried out and the results obtained show good accuracy performance on the test sets.

Keywords: Iris quality assessment · Statistical approach
Machine learning · SVM

1 Introduction

The iris is considered as one of the most safe biometric traits, mainly due to the random way the features are generated. In [5] Daugman introduces the iris as a biometric traits; this work is a must-to-read for the reader to be properly introduced in the topic. The two biggest areas of research involving iris biometric are related with the segmentation and recognition of the iris features. The segmentation is related to the cropping of the iris from an image, cutting out all the noises present in the area, like eyelids, eyelashes, reflections and so on. In this area, [6] is one of the most used technique, for the segmentation of the iris. Also, in the last years fuzzy methods revealed to be very effective in denoising images of irises. In [3] the authors developed a Mamdani fuzzy controller in order to quickly segment an iris, by keeping out all the noise factors which affected the iris. As regards the recognition field, most of the methods proposed in literature are oriented to perform always better in terms of recognition rate, without focusing a lot on the quality of the irises involved in the processing phases. In this

© Springer Nature Switzerland AG 2018
A. Castiglione et al. (Eds.): CSS 2018, LNCS 11161, pp. 270–278, 2018.
https://doi.org/10.1007/978-3-030-01689-0_21

field of research, for example, in [2] and in [1] the authors proposed a method for recognizing subjects by using kurtosis and skewness measurements, and hence differentiating the irises depending on their statistical inner patterns. In [4] the recognition has been achieved over mobile phones by using spatial histograms as matching features. The iris quality assessment techniques can positively affect these steps, since evaluating an iris before its processing may lighten the process of segmentation of the iris, and also the feature extraction phase would be more safe. Also, it could be possible to automate some processes in video surveillance purposes like shown in [14] and [8]. In literature most of the methods involving iris quality assessment are oriented to the liveness, spoofing and fake iris detection as in [9] and [10]. In [17] the authors tried to improve the quality of an iris affected by motion blur, occlusion or defocus, while in [15] the author evaluated the quality by analyzing its spectral information. The main differences between the cited papers and the proposed method rely on the fact that in this work the nature of the iris is not known a priori; therefore, the method tries to understand if the image actually contains an iris and, if so, it tries to assess its quality. Also, the method has been tested over three different datasets, acquired in different periods and with different cameras; this broaden the use of the method to any environment or device. The source code, along with the experimental data, is provided.

2   The Approach

In this section, the whole approach is presented, starting from the detection of the circles into the image and arriving to the evaluation of the irises extracted.

2.1   The Problem

Usually, an iris recognition process starts with the acquisition of an image which is supposed to contain an iris. The fastest and most efficient method for detecting irises is the Hough Transform approach [11]; this method does not take into account about the semantic structure of the iris, but it is only based on the localization in the image of a circle, which is the usual shape of an iris. Therefore, even if quite fast, it does not ensure reliability about the quality of the iris which is extracted from the image. As a consequence, it becomes quite complicated to automate an iris recognition process, if, as it often happens, the extracted area is not an iris. The proposed iris quality assessment approach is based on the measurements of several statistical measures about the circle extracted, which aim at evaluating if that circle is actually an iris or just noise. In order to approximate a circle, the Hough method starts by standing out the edges of an image; for this operation, usually, a common edge detector is used. In the example in Fig. 1, the rightmost image shows the output of a canny edge detector, applied of the image on its left.

As for the example above, the circles detected are the following in Fig. 2: only the image with the green frame regards a good iris detection. Those in red frame

Fig. 1. On the left the original image, while on the right the canny edge detector output.

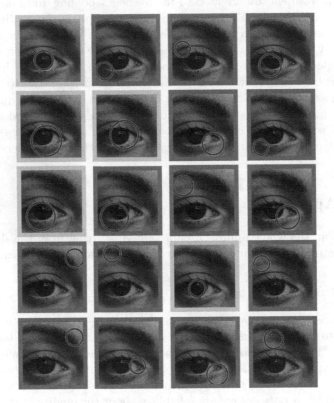

Fig. 2. The circles detected from the Hough Transform method. In green the correct detection of the iris; those in red are wrong detection, whereas those in yellow contain iris, but are needed of further processing. (Color figure online)

are not useful at all, since regard areas which are not iris but eyelids, eyebrows or skin, whereas those in yellow contain iris, but they need further processing operation before stating that the circle detected is actually an iris.

2.2   The Aim

Obtaining many circles related to potential irises is not an advantage, since it becomes difficult to automatize a process if we are not sure that the image is actually what we need. The aim of the proposed method is to considerably reduce the number of the outliers yield by the Hough transform. In the best case, we only want one circle left, which is exactly the one describing the iris position in the image. Many algorithms pose the attention on the fact that the iris, usually contains another circle, which is the one describing the pupil. Unfortunately, with high resolution images, this process does not lead to any optimal solution due to big amount of edges obtained by the Hough; therefore, in many cases, many circles have other circles inscribed. The reckoning to pay for this solution is even higher with respect to not apply any iris quality assessment approach, since we decided to apply twice the Hough transform, without obtaining fair benefits.

2.3   The Solution

The solution proposed aims at analyzing the circles that usually are yield by the Hough transform; each iris has been transformed from cartesian to polar coordinates, in order to have a rectangle-shaped iris. This technique is common when dealing with irises, since it allows to obtain an easily processable image. Each polarized iris is then divided in 32 section, 4 rows and 8 columns. In Fig. 3 this step is shown.

For each section, 6 metrics have been measured: (1) Average Gray Level, (2) Average Contrast, (3) Smoothness, (4) 3rd order moment, (4) Uniformity and the (5) Entropy. Hence, we created 3 different sets of irises:

- a set containing excellent irises, in terms of shape and quality (SET1)
- a set containing good irises, but still deserving processing (SET2)
- a set containing other but no irises. This images can be discarded (SET3).

The sets cited are the classes we aimed at classifying. In the Fig. 4 some examples of the images belonging to the three classes and the related measures are shown.

From the Fig. 4, it is possible to notice that the last four sections of each image does not give any insight about iris quality. This mainly happens because this part is related to the outer circumference of the iris, which is more prone to noise, due to the distortion cause by the polarization step. That's the reason why these sections have been discarded from the analysis. For all the other sections, the measures defined above have been computed and classified with an ensemble of machine learning classifiers.

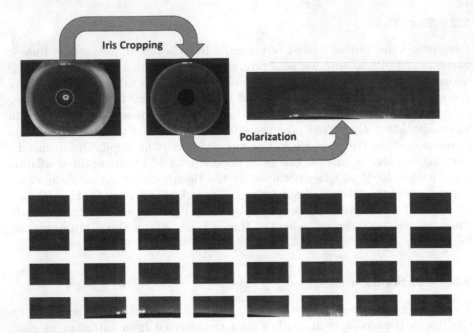

Fig. 3. The iris is first cropped and polarized; then the obtained rectangle-shaped image is divided in 32 sections.

3 The Evaluation

For evaluating the proposed approach, three well known iris datasets have been used. The UPOL dataset (University of Palackeho and Olomouc, available at http://phoenix.inf.upol.cz/iris/) consists of 384 images collected by 64 subjects. The images were captured at a close distance (optometric device) with subject cooperation; therefore these images turned to be perfect, since the entire iris is visible and easily processable. The UBIRIS dataset [16], consists of about 1900 images acquired from 241 subjects. In contrast to the UPOL dataset, UBIRIS introduces many noise factors caused by motion blur, poor focus images, eyelids, eyelashes and even closed eyes images. The MICHE dataset [7] consists of images from 90 subjects, collected from three mobile devices: Apple iPhone5, Galaxy Samsung IV and Galaxy Tab II. The images are acquired in both indoor and outdoor environments, so providing images with different light sources and, in most cases, with totally unconstrained conditions.

The images of the datasets have been processed with the Hough transform and all the circles area produced have been saved in a folder. Then, with respect to the quality of the images obtained, these have been moved in three further folders, related to the three sets, SET1, SET2 and SET3, how described in Sect. 2.3. The sets consist of 383, 920 and 1942 images respectively. The 70% of the images has been used for training and the remaining for testing.

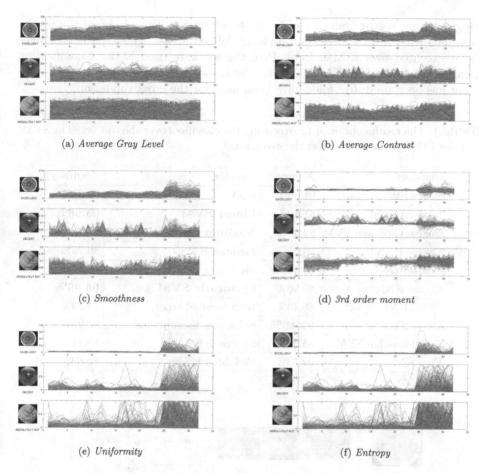

(a) *Average Gray Level*

(b) *Average Contrast*

(c) *Smoothness*

(d) *3rd order moment*

(e) *Uniformity*

(f) *Entropy*

Fig. 4. In the figure, the images analyzed and the related plot for each metric are shown. On the x-axis, the section number is defined. On the left of each plot, the three images shown belong respectively to SET1, SET2 and SET3

Currently the state-of-the-art works related with the iris quality assessment are oriented at evaluating the factors that actually reduce the quality of the image, without giving a final response in order to automate the biometric process. In [13], the author estimated some factors that could reduce the quality of an iris image, like motion, blur, defocus, off-angle and so on. Based on this analysis, they evaluated the CASIA and WVU databases. The work in [12], presented at CVPR Workshops 2018, also evaluates the quality difference between an enrolled iris image and a new acquired image, but still does not provide an index or a response giving information above the overall quality of the image.

Two different experiments have been carried out: the first aimed at analyzing the quality of the iris, by concatenating the measures of the single sections. Since for each image 24 sections are available and 6 metrics have been computed, the single feature vector trained consisted of 144 entries. Table 1 shows the results obtained with train and test subdivision defined above. The experiments have been executed over a Mac Book Pro; the software used is the Classification Learner Toolbox of MATLAB 2018a. The standard configuration for each classifier has been used; five folds have been used for the cross validation.

Table 1. The results obtained by executing the classifiers over the test set. The SVMs obtained the best accuracy over the given sets.

Classifier	Accuracy	Classifier	Accuracy
Bagged trees	91.65%	LDA	90.92%
Boosted trees	81.80%	**Linear SVM**	**95.66%**
Coarse Gaussian SVM	82.50%	**Medium Gaussian SVM**	**95.90%**
Coarse KNN	79.35%	Medium KNN	88.75%
Coarse tree	80.16%	Medium tree	85.46%
Cosine KNN	89.96%	**Quadratic SVM**	**96.86%**
Cubic KNN	88.43%	RUS boosted trees	91.24%
Cubic SVM	**97.19%**	Subspace discriminant	91.25%
Fine Gaussian SVM	85.38%	Subspace KNN	88.11%
Fine KNN	92.53%	Weighted KNN	89.63%
Fine tree	87.80%		

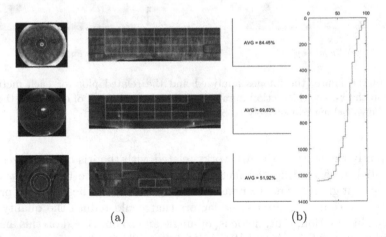

(a)   (b)

Fig. 5. The (a) image shows the example of the execution of the Cubic SVM over the single section of an image. In green the sectors that have been classified as iris; in red are those classified as non-iris. In the (b) image, instead, the overall accuracy over all the images of the set. In the best case we have an average accuracy of almost 85% over the entire image. (Color figure online)

More deeply, the second experiment aimed at classifying the single section. The entry for each section consists of 6 values, one per metric computed. The training set and the test set have been the same as for the previous experiment. The classifier used has been the Cubic SVM, which obtained the best accuracy result in the previous experiment. In Fig. 5 the results for this experiment are shown. On the left part of the image, 3 irises have been chosen, in order to show how the Cubic SVM classifier performs over the single sections of the image. The section contoured in green are properly recognized as iris., whereas those in red are recognized as non-iris sections. In the bottommost image in the (a) image, in fact, only 5 sections out of 24 have been classified as iris, therefore, the entire image is stated not to be an iris. On the right, the (b) image shows the accuracy over the test set. The accuracy is related to the entire iris and not to the single sections.

Acknowledgments. Mirko Marras gratefully acknowledges Sardinia Regional Government for the financial support of his PhD scholarship (P.O.R. Sardegna F.S.E. Operational Programme of the Autonomous Region of Sardinia, European Social Fund 2014-2020, Axis III "Education and Training", Thematic Goal 10, Priority of Investment 10ii, Specific Goal 10.5). The Italian Ministry of University, Education and Research (MIUR), partially supported this work, under the project ILEARNTV (announcement 391/2012, SMART CITIES AND COMMUNITIES AND SOCIAL INNOVATION).

Source Code. In order to have the source code of the method, along with the experimental data.

References

1. Abate, A., Barra, S., Gallo, L., Narducci, F.: SKIPSOM: Skewness Kurtosis of iris pixels in self organizing maps for iris recognition on mobile devices. In: 23rd International Conference on Pattern Recognition (ICPR) 2016, pp. 155–159 (Dec 2016). https://doi.org/10.1109/ICPR.2016.7899625
2. Abate, A.F., Barra, S., Gallo, L., Narducci, F.: Kurtosis and skewness at pixel level as input for SOM networks to iris recognition on mobile devices. Pattern Recogn. Lett. **91**, 37–43 (2017). https://doi.org/10.1016/j.patrec.2017.02.002, http://www.sciencedirect.com/science/article/pii/S0167865517300338. mobile Iris CHallenge Evaluation (MICHE-II)
3. Abate, A.F., Barra, S., Fenu, G., Nappi, M., Narducci, F.: A lightweight mamdani fuzzy controller for noise removal on iris images. In: Battiato, S., Gallo, G., Schettini, R., Stanco, F. (eds.) ICIAP 2017. LNCS, vol. 10485, pp. 93–103. Springer, Cham (2017). https://doi.org/10.1007/978-3-319-68548-9_9
4. Barra, S., Casanova, A., Narducci, F., Ricciardi, S.: Ubiquitous iris recognition by means of mobile devices. Pattern Recogn. Lett. **57**, 66–73 (2015). https://doi.org/10.1016/j.patrec.2014.10.011, http://www.sciencedirect.com/science/article/pii/S0167865514003286, mobile Iris CHallenge Evaluation part I (MICHE I)
5. Daugman, J.: How iris recognition works. In: The essential guide to image processing, pp. 715–739. Elsevier (2009)
6. De Marsico, M., Nappi, M., Daniel, R.: IS_IS: Iris segmentation for identification systems. In: Pattern Recognition (ICPR), 20th International Conference on 2010, pp. 2857–2860. IEEE (2010)

7. De Marsico, M., Nappi, M., Riccio, D., Wechsler, H.: Mobile iris challenge evaluation (MICHE)-I, biometric iris dataset and protocols. Pattern Recogn. Lett. **57**, 17–23 (2015)

8. Fenu, G., Marras, M., Boratto, L.: A multi-biometric system for continuous student authentication in e-learning platforms. Pattern Recogn. Lett. (2017). https://doi. org/10.1016/j.patrec.2017.03.027, http://www.sciencedirect.com/science/article/ pii/S0167865517300909

9. Galbally, J., Marcel, S., Fierrez, J.: Image quality assessment or fake biometric detection: application to iris, fingerprint, and face recognition. IEEE Trans. Image Process. **23**(2), 710–724 (2014)

10. He, X., Lu, Y., Shi, P.: A fake iris detection method based on FFT and quality assessment. In: Pattern Recognition, CCPR 2008 Chinese Conference on 2008, pp. 1–4. IEEE (2008)

11. Illingworth, J., Kittler, J.: A survey of the hough transform. Comput. Vis. Graph. Image Process. **44**(1), 87–116 (1988)

12. Jenadeleh, M., Pedersen, M., Saupe, D.: Realtime quality assessment of iris biometrics under visible light. In: CVPR 2018: IEEE/CVF Conference on Computer Vision and Pattern Recognition, pp. 556–565 (2018)

13. Kalka, N.D., Zuo, J., Schmid, N.A., Cukic, B.: Estimating and fusing quality factors for iris biometric images. IEEE Trans. Syst. Man Cybern. Part A Syst. Hum **40**(3), 509–524 (2010). https://doi.org/10.1109/tsmca.2010.2041658. http://gen.lib.rus.ec/scimag/index.php?s=10.1109/tsmca.2010.2041658

14. Neves, J.C., Moreno, J.C., Barra, S., Proena, H.: Acquiring high-resolution face images in outdoor environments: a master-slave calibration algorithm. In: 2015 IEEE 7th International Conference on Biometrics Theory, Applications and Systems (BTAS), pp. 1–8 (Sept 2015). https://doi.org/10.1109/BTAS.2015.7358744

15. Proença, H.: Quality assessment of degraded iris images acquired in the visible wavelength. IEEE Trans. Inf. Forensics Secur. **6**(1), 82–95 (2011)

16. Proença, H., Alexandre, L.A.: UBIRIS: a Noisy Iris Image Database. In: Roli, F., Vitulano, S. (eds.) ICIAP 2005. LNCS, vol. 3617, pp. 970–977. Springer, Heidelberg (2005). https://doi.org/10.1007/11553595_119

17. Wei, Z., Tan, T., Sun, Z., Cui, J.: Robust and fast assessment of iris image quality. In: Zhang, D., Jain, A.K. (eds.) Advances in Biometrics, pp. 464–471. Springer, Berlin (2005). https://doi.org/10.1007/11608288_62

Social Security, Ontologies and Smart Applications

Enhancing Information Security Culture to Reduce Information Security Cost: A Proposed Framework

S. G. Govender, M. Loock[✉], and E. Kritzinger

University of South Africa (UNISA), Pretoria, Gauteng 0001, South Africa
32393113@mylife.unisa.ac.za,
{loockm, kritze}@unisa.ac.za

Abstract. As data breaches in mid to large organizations become more frequent and more public, there is a need to focus less on technological solutions to information security management but rather, sociological solutions. This paper identifies cost saving information security initiatives and proposes a framework for organizational and behavioral change in technical human resources, to better address information security concerns.

Keywords: Information security · Security culture · Security cost

1 Introduction

Information security breaches have gained significant publicity and become more frequent. Studies conducted by IBM and Kaspersky indicates that even though the cost per breach has been reduced incrementally with the adoption of better technology, organizational structures and awareness, the number of breaches have gone up [15, 21, 29]. This implies that the overall cost to protect an organization has and will continue to increase. The factors that are considered as remediation to the major data breach vectors are a combination of social (structural and awareness) and technical (product and service acquisition). With the likelihood of breaches increasing, technical solutions are progressively more employed to reduce risk. This article proposes a social alternative to reduce risk and thereby reduce the cost of information security management in organizations.

2 Information Security Culture

As organizations need information systems to survive and prosper and thus need to be serious about protecting their information assets, many of the processes needed are, to a large extent, dependent on human cooperative behavior [11]. The definitions of information security focuses on the technology that supports the cause as opposed to the people [8]. Employees, whether intentionally or through negligence, often due to a lack of knowledge, are the greatest threat to information security [19].

A. Castiglione et al. (Eds.): CSS 2018, LNCS 11161, pp. 281–290, 2018.
https://doi.org/10.1007/978-3-030-01689-0_22

The vast majority of security breaches originate from human actions and the number of potential reasons for this are [11]:

- People are poorly trained and have poor security awareness
- People are not motivated to perform at the required level
- People are malicious and deliberately expose the organization to risk
- People are aware of the problem of security, but as managers and employees make poor decisions.

As a result, people, their behavior, attitude and hence culture must become an integral defense in information security [22].

Establishing an organizational sub-culture of information security, which is a fragmentation of overall organizational culture, is key to managing (mitigating) the human factors involved in information security breaches [28]. As the scope of connected devices becomes greater and more information is shared between future internet (FI) technology, the context of how organization secure these devices becomes more important [5]. Organizations will be unable to do business without access to their information resources. However, protecting any information resources often has no direct return on investment. Securing information resources does not, as a rule, generate income for an organization [30]. Business people are therefore rarely interested in how their information resources are protected [28].

Organizations are cognizant of the importance of information security and information assurance to the value of their business. As a result, organizations are moving to respond to the threat in a more context aware manner. Context awareness allows information security managers to address information security risk from a contextualized and focused perspective [3]. One of the key methods is by organizations creating or elevating Chief Information Officer positions to senior planning roles, removing the position from the Information Technology (IT) department, and integrating security planning and policy development into the strategic management process [1]. However, the problems related to creating a security culture are not always solved by a top-down management approach. The way in which employees interact with technology and the controls that need to be in place for information security is a complex issue. The influence of individual differences in personalities and cognitive abilities impacts the effectiveness of any security programme [20]. Furthermore, personal bias and personal experience will have an effect on people's perception of risk, thus affecting the security decisions they make [20]. Knowledge and the involvement of employees are key to securing an organization. If the security culture of an organization is not strong, then even adequate (minimal) technology security measures will become inadequate [25].

2.1 The Human Factor of Information Security Culture

Studies have shown that the establishment of an information security culture in the organization is necessary for effective information security [9]. However, security culture cannot be assessed in isolation from the overall corporate culture [23]. Culture may not be uniform throughout an organization but may be split into sub-cultures. Sub-cultures can be observed in different job levels, functions and roles within an organization resulting in differences in attitudes, beliefs and values among the members of an organization [13]. Differing sub-cultures may fully align with corporate culture or somewhat align with corporate culture or be completely incongruent to corporate culture [17]. Sub-cultures within an organization can be problematic and can negatively affect performance when the sub-cultures have different priorities and agendas [10].

In organizations, the information security culture is usually managed through basic awareness and training programmes. These programmes deal with simple issues and are generally not assessed to provide an honest view of the actual learning taking place. Furthermore, these awareness programmes are usually focused on general staff, without a focus on management and more importantly the technical IT staff. Security culture amongst IT staff is far more important in an organization in relation to general staff, as these IT staff members manage and implement security controls. Sub-cultures are formed within the IT department, reducing the concentration of security efforts but focusing on the technical specifics of each environment. In addition, technical staff do not consider security as a primary concern even though technical actions that support information security management, such as patching, updates, application enhancement and upgrade equipment lifecycle management, is implemented by them. It has been established that technical security measures are key to information security management success [6, 14].

Considering that technical staff have a greater influence on factors that support information security management, it would be reasonable to contend that enhancing the information security behavior and values of these technical staff members would improve information security [7, 14, 27] and in turn reduce information security cost.

3 Information Security Breach Vectors

Information security breach vectors are defined as the methods or means by which attackers may gain access, deliver malicious software or exploit system vulnerabilities. In the Ponemon study of 419 large companies in 13 countries [21], the average cost of a data breach was found to be $3.62 million (US), where the cost was determined by:

- the unexpected or unplanned loss of customers due to the data breach
- the size of the breach in terms of number of records lost
- the time taken to identify a data breach
- the detection and escalation costs of the breach
- and post data breach costs.

The Kaspersky study [15] of 5500 organizations of varied size in 26 countries showed that the average cost was greater than $600 000 (US). Ultimately, this implies that the larger the organization the greater potential cost of limited information security management controls.

These studies broadly categorized the types of breaches as malicious or criminal attacks, cyber espionage, system glitches, third party failures, human error or employee fraud. In most organizations the attacks or breaches are focused on applications, while the greatest security spend is on networks [12].

Irrespective of the type of breaches, 50% were attributed to malware, 20% were related to phishing attacks and 20% were attributed to data leakage by employees.

The per breach type cost was also equivalent to similar ratios. It can therefore be inferred by reducing malware, phishing and data leakage that an organization may significantly increase its information security posture and significantly reduce its cost of security events.

In organizations the approach to remediating these types of breaches are a combination of technical and social solutions. The technical solutions include operational products such as Intrusion Detection or Prevention (IDS/IPS) devices, anti-virus and malware products, web and email traffic analysis products, and Data Loss Prevention (DLP) tools. The social solutions are generally awareness and training programmes.

Literature on information security budgeting, indicates that the cost-benefit analysis for information security is difficult and applying traditional IT budgeting techniques is counter-productive [1, 18, 24]. Furthermore, investment is focused on reducing security breaches through technical means [4]. The caveat to these types of technical solutions is that the products are relatively expensive, the expertise to implement and maintain these is scarce and therefore expensive, and most importantly the processes and periodic analysis of information and remediating activities as a result of information generated by these products is dependent on the human intervention, skill and motivation.

Positive motivation theory for workers has a direct impact on information security systems and controls [16], and a positive improvement on overall information security posture of an organization. It therefore follows that having an approach to enhancing information security core values and behaviours, focusing on specific cost saving remediation factors will improve information security postures and will significantly reduce information security management cost.

4   Information Security Remediation Factors

In the study conducted by Ponemon [21], 20 factors were considered as remediation for security breaches. Of these factors, 12 were considered to have an effect of decreasing the cost of a breach while 8 were considered to increase the cost. These cost reducing factors were as follows:

- Having an Incident Response Team
- Extensive use of Encryption
- Employee Training
- Business Continuity Management Processes
- Participation in Threat Analysis and Sharing
- Use of Security Analytics Services
- Extensive use of Data Loss Prevention (DLP) products, policies and processes
- Data Classification
- Cyber Security Insurance
- Having a Chief Information Security Officer appointed
- Board level involvement in Information Security spend
- Having a Chief Privacy Officer appointed.

The cost increasing factors were as follows:

- Provision of ID protection
- Consultant Engaged after the breach
- Rush to notify after the breach
- Lost or stolen devices
- Extensive use of mobile platforms
- Compliance failures
- Extensive Cloud Migration
- Third party/Outsourced Management.

Figure 1 shows the cost reducing factors, of which six are socially influenced (human, managerial or structural) and six factors are technically influenced. Therefore, concentrating the information security management effort on these twelve factors will provide the best information protection at a lowest cost.

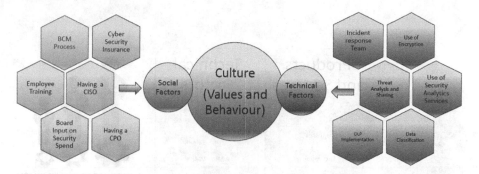

Fig. 1. Social and technical security cost reduction factors

For each of the six technical factors, there is a requirement for some human intervention and response, for these factors to be successful. The technical factors may include management, participation, configuration, administration, continuous monitoring and evaluation and periodic, ad-hoc processes to remediate [2, 26]. Since this human interaction is social in nature, people's behavior and values within an organization has a direct influence on whether these actions supporting information security management are successful. Improving the values and behavior of technical resources (e.g. server and network administrators, application developers, desktop support specialists and email and file-server administrators), that support information security remediation requirements, will also assist in reducing the risk of information security breach incidents. In effect, developing and enhancing the socially relevant factors creates a stronger foundation for success of the technical factors.

5 Proposed Framework

Organizations determine the information security landscape using several methods such as ISO 27001 assessments, through risk assessments, or through longer term strategy defined by a security architecture programme. The outcomes of these assessments or programmes are supported by the selection of products and/or solutions that fit the information security and business needs. Information security products and solutions are complex in nature and require many technical inputs to function appropriately or effectively within the organization. Products and solutions purport to being autonomous and self-running but in reality require significant human input and intervention in order to function in a valuable way for the business (Fig. 2). Security tools are not always managed by the security function within the organization and staff that do manage these solutions, are from alternative functional areas, i.e. application development, infrastructure or networks. The motivation and behavior for these staff members to consider security first is generally incongruent to their motivation for their primary job responsibilities. The effect of what staff considers additional work to their primary job responsibility, is a lower motivation to consider their information security responsibilities as important.

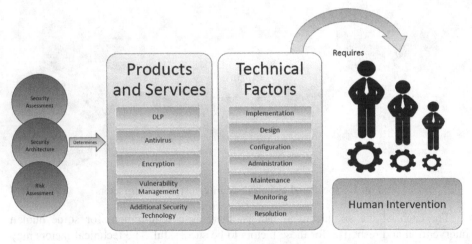

Fig. 2. Human intervention in information security capability

The model in Fig. 3 proposes five pillars of cultural change that are applicable in re-defining the values and behaviors of IT staff members which will develop and enhancing the socially relevant factors that lead to information security cost reduction. The effects of improving employees information security culture is twofold: firstly that staff will be motivated within their job functions to consider information security a priority and secondly the enhancement of information security cultural aspects will allow for long term value for the organization and create the foundation for information security practices to become a prioritized norm.

Pillar 1 - Common Security Values and Principles
Information Security Management is the responsibility of different functional areas within an IT department. The areas are generally managed with a focus on the functional discipline and consider cross-functional responsibility a secondary matter. This pillar informs the creation of common security values and principles that need to be shared amongst each IT discipline. The value of security must be embodied and communicated

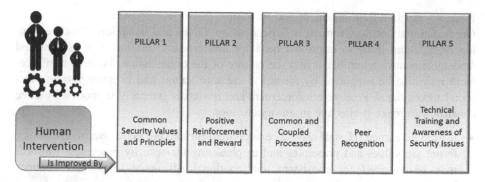

Fig. 3. 5 Pillars of Information Security Culture Enhancement Model. The five pillars for the enhancement of information security culture in IT staff is discussed as follows:

with the common view to responsibility of information security amongst all role-players. The principles of information security must become part of the IT principles of the organization and not considered a stand-alone discipline. IT Security as a concept must be supported and championed by executive and senior management and structures and roles must be developed to support these common values and principles.

Pillar 2 - Common and Coupled Security Processes
When considering technical implementation, IT staff are generally internally focused on their area of expertise. The impact of layering security onto 'their' technology is rarely considered in the context of the IT disciplines that they support or are supported by. IT staff should understand the effects of security monitoring, blocking, patching and processes as it affects each IT discipline in the IT value chain. Information security managers should develop and socialise 'common-thread' information security processes where the impact of each IT discipline is transparent.

Pillar 3 - Technical Training and Awareness of Security Issues
Security awareness and training programmes in organizations focus predominantly on the general user. While this is useful, it was established in Sect. 3 that the key factors to the success of information security management and the reduction of information security costs lies in the technical factors of security products and solutions. IT staff should receive significant technical training in the security solutions that are implemented and be made aware of technical security issues that are prevalent. IT staff should understand the scope of products selected and how these can be leveraged to support the information security values and principles. IT staff should also understand their value in threat remediation through patching and vulnerability management. Threat analysis and aggregated information from security analysis resources and information security staff, should be shared with general IT staff. Lastly, information security awareness and training is rarely targeted at senior and executive management. As most governance best practices place data breach responsibility with the accounting officer of an organization, a greater focus on information security awareness and training for senior and executive management should be part of the cultural enhancement programme.

Pillar 4 - Positive Reinforcement and Reward

Organizational accomplishment is dependent on values and behaviors. Positive reinforcement often leads to improved behavior and creating this into a consistent and repeatable behavior imbibes it into the culture of the organization. Positive reinforcement may also be supported by reward to enhance values and behavior through less social mechanisms. Positive reinforcement and reward is generally supported by three constructs to make it effective in an organization:

- It must be earned. IT staff should be supported for making good security decisions, living the values and principles and emphasizing the security processes. Rewards may be awarded for consistent and continual adherence to positive security behavior.
- It must be quick. IT staff should get immediate feedback and recognition for their adherence to the positive values of information security in the organization.
- It must be frequent. The organization should consider smaller more frequent rewards. When values and behavior are supportive of the information security programme short term communication to those staff members involved should be commonplace.

Pillar 5 - Peer Recognition

Several studies show that peer recognition is one of the greatest motivators in the workplace. In the context of information security management, organizations should consider implementing a peer recognition programme that is managed and controlled by the IT staff themselves. Peer programmes that are managed by the staff and supported by senior management, fosters an environment of recognition and reward that is perceived to be less biased than that which is driven by management. Through this process, staff will be informed of the positive value that their peers, in all IT disciplines, are inputting into information security management and may be motivated to follow suit. Staff will also be able to see the impact of their contribution to information security and this in turn will create a more consistent information security behavior profile, thereby supporting the overall information security culture.

6   Conclusion

Information security data breaches are becoming larger and more frequent. The reporting on such events is a part of mainstream media reports making people and organizations much more aware of such threats. Organizations have focused their security management efforts in technology at significant cost and complexity. Organizations have however neglected incorporating information security into the culture of the IT staff members that support these technologies. The framework proposed in this research, looks at focusing on building the correct behaviors and values in IT staff members, to better support information security management.

References

1. Bodin, L.D., Gordon, L.A., Loeb, M.P.: Evaluating information security investments using the analytic hierarchy process. Commun. ACM **48**(2), 78–83 (2005)
2. Bojanc, R., Jerman-Blazic, B., Tekavcic, M.: Managing the investment in information security technology by the use of a quantitative model. Inf. Process. Manag. **48**, 1031–1052 (2012)
3. Casillo, M., Colace, F., Pascale, F., Lemma, S. and Lombardi, M.: A tailor made system for providing personalized services. In: Proceedings of the International Conference on Software Engineering and Knowledge Engineering, SEKE 2017, pp. 495–500 (2017)
4. Cavasoglu, H., Cavasoglu, H., Son, J., Benbasat, I.: Institutional pressures in security management: direct and indirect influences on organizational investment in information security control resources. Inf. Manag. **52**(4), 385–400 (2015)
5. Colace, F., et al.: A context-aware framework for cultural heritage applications. In: Proceedings 10th International Conference on Signal-Image Technology and Internet-Based Systems, SITIS 2014, p. 469 (2014)
6. Crossler, R.E., Johnston, A.C., Lowry, P.B., Hu, Q., Warkentin, M., Baskerville, R.: Future directions for behavioral information security research. Comput. Secur. **32**(February), 90–101 (2013)
7. D'Arcy, J., Hovav, A.: Deterring internal information systems misuse. Commun. ACM **50**(10), 113–117 (2007)
8. Drake, P. Clarke, S.: Social aspects of information security. IGI Global (2009)
9. Eloff, M.M., Von Solms, S.H.: Information security management: an approach to combine process certification and product evaluation. Comput. Secur. **19**(8), 698–709 (2000)
10. Furnham, A., Gunter, B.: Corporate culture: diagnosis and change. In: Cooper, C.L., Robertson, I.T., International Review of Industrial and Organizational Psychology, Wiley, Chichester (2003)
11. Garret, C.: Developing a security awareness culture -improving security decision making. In: SANS Institute InfoSec Reading Room (2004)
12. Gunter, S.: Digitally secure transformation. IT Now, June 2017, pp 12–13 (2017)
13. Hampden-Turner, C., Trompenaars, F.: The seven cultures of capitalism, Piatkus (1994)
14. Hsu, J., Shih, S.-P., Hung, Y.W., Lowry, P.B.: How extra-role behaviors can improve information security policy effectiveness. Inf. Syst. Res. **26**(2), 282–300 (2015)
15. Kaspersky lab: damage control: the cost of security breaches, IT security risks special report series (2016)
16. Lowry, P.B., Moody, G.D.: Proposing the control? Reactance Compliance Model (CRCM) to explain opposing motivations to comply with organizational information security policies (2015)
17. Martin, J., Siehl, C.: Organizational culture and counterculture: an uneasy symbioses. Am. Manag. Assoc. **12**(3), 52–64 (1983)
18. Mecuri, R.T.: Analyzing Security Costs. Commun. ACM **46**(6), 15–18 (2003)
19. Mitnick, K.D., Simon, W.L.: The Art of Deception: Controlling the Human Element of Security. Wiley Publishing, Hoboke (2002)
20. Parsons, K., Mccormac, A., Butavicius, M., Ferguson, L.: Human Factors and Information Security: Individual. Culture and Security Environment. Government Research Paper edn. Australian Government, Department of defence, defence science and technology organization (2010)
21. Ponemon : Cost of data breach study. Ponemon Institute Research Study (2017)

22. Rotvold, G.: How To Create Security Culture in Your Organization [Homepage of Information Management]. http://content.arma.org/IMM/NovDec2008/How_to_Create_a_Security_Culture.aspx [June, 2018]. (2008)
23. Ruighaver, A.B., Maynard, S.B., Chang, S.: Organizational security culture: extending the end user perspective. Comput. Soc. **26**, 56–62 (2007)
24. Schatz, D., Bashroush, R.: Economic valuation for information security investment: a systematic literature review. Inf. Syst. Front. **19**(5), 1205–1228 (2017)
25. Siponen, M.T.: Five dimensions of information security awareness. Comput. Soc. **31**(2), 24–29 (2001)
26. Takemura, T., Komatsu, A.: An empirical study on information security behaviors and awareness. In: Böhme, R. (ed.) The Economics of Information Security and Privacy. Springer, Heidelberg (2013). https://doi.org/10.1007/978-3-642-39498-0
27. Vance, A., Lowry, P.B., Eggett, D.: A new approach to the problem of access policy violations: increasing perceptions of accountability through the user interface. MIS Quart. **39**(2), 345–366 (2015)
28. Van Niekerk, J.F., Von Solms, R.: Information security culture: a management perspective. Comput. Secur. **29**, 476–486 (2010)
29. Verizon: 2017 Data Breach Investigation Report, 10th Edition, accessed from http://www.verizonenterprise.com/verizon-insights-lab/data-breach-digest/2017/ (2017)
30. Wylder, J.: Strategic Information Security. CRC Press, Boca Raton Florida (2004)

Chatbot: An Education Support System for Student

Fabio Clarizia[1](✉), Francesco Colace[1](✉), Marco Lombardi[1](✉),
Francesco Pascale[1](✉), and Domenico Santaniello[2](✉)

[1] DIIn, University of Salerno, 84084 Fisciano, SA, Italy
{fclarizia, fcolace, malombardi, fpascale}@unisa.it
[2] DICIV, University of Salerno, 84084 Fisciano, SA, Italy
dsantaniello@unisa.it

Abstract. In the last few years there has been a fast growing up of the use of Chatbots in various fields, such as Health Care, Marketing, Educational, Supporting Systems, Cultural Heritage, Entertainment and many others. This paper presents the realization of a prototype of a Chatbot in educational domain: the purpose has focused on the design of the specific architecture, model to manage communication and furnish the right answers to the student. For this aim, it has been realized a system that can detect the questions and thanks to the use of natural language processing techniques and the ontologies of domain, gives the answers to student. Finally, after the implementation of the designed model, experimental campaign was conducted in order to demonstrate its utility.

Keywords: Chatbot · E-learning · Educational support systems

1 Introduction

A Chatbot (or Chatterbot) is a software (machine) that talks with a user (human): it is a virtual assistant able to answer a number of user questions, providing the correct responses. Major companies have developed several Chatbots both for industrial solutions and for research: some of the most famous are Apple Siri, Microsoft Cortana, Facebook M and IBM Watson. These are just some of the most popular systems. There is a wide range of a less famous Chatbots that have a greater relevance for research and for their applications, some of which will be discussed in the next chapter [15].

One of the most challenging research tasks is the development of effective Chatbots: the emulation of human dialogues, in fact, is a really difficult task and involves problems related to the NLP (Natural Language Processing) research field [1]. Thanks to the use of NLP algorithms and techniques it is possible to understand what the user is writing, and which are his requests. Generally, this task represents the core of system but there are some problems: it is not possible to map all user requests, and the current Chatbots do not show remarkable performances because of the unpredictability of user thought during a conversation [2]. The correct design of conversational flow plays an important role in the development of a Chatbot. In fact, for a successful conversation, it is important to handle with all user requests and provide the right answers. In the literature we find several examples and researches works on the management of

A. Castiglione et al. (Eds.): CSS 2018, LNCS 11161, pp. 291–302, 2018.
https://doi.org/10.1007/978-3-030-01689-0_23

conversational workflow. Most of this works use ontologies, based on the knowledge base of the domain, that can be used to interpret the intentions of the user and solve the problem of interpretation of sentences written by the user [3].

As previously said, one Chabot field of application is Educational. Recently there has been an increase of Chatbots for e-learning platforms to support student learning [14]. Chatbot technology can be considered an important innovation for e-learning: in fat they are turned out to be the most innovative solution in filling the gap between technology and education. The implication of Chatbots creates an interactive learning experience for the students, like the one-to-one interaction with the teacher. From testing the student's behavior and in order to keep track of their improvements, bots play an essential role in enhancing the skills of an individual student. Moreover, they can also serve a major role in encouraging a student to work by sending regular reminders and notifications. There are several other cases of use of Chatbots for e-learning, for example is possible to provide a system for a personalized learning experience: each student earns and absorbs things at a different pace. Using Chatbots is possible to adapt the speed at which a student can learn without being too pushy [19]. Chatbot can also be used as a source of social learning, in fact students from different backgrounds can share their views and perspectives on a specific matter while the bot can still adapt to each one of them individually [16]. This technology can improve engagement among students and encourage interaction with the rest of the class by assigning group works and projects like teachers usually do. Chatbots can help teachers in their work routine, answering to student's questions or even checking their homework [18]. Often, they are used as online assessments: if in a class there are many students, give attention to each one of them becomes very demanding for teachers, while Chatbots can work with multiple students and groups at the same time [22]. They can also work as a support for teachers by identifying spelling and grammatical mistakes, checking homework, assigning projects and especially keeping track of progress and achievements of each student.

This paper presents the realization of a Chatbot prototype for supporting students during their learning activities. Chatbot aims to be an e-Tutor for students. The aim of this paper is the introduction of a framework for:

- The automatic identification of the students' needs thanks to the adoption of Natural Language Processing Techniques
- The selection of the best answer thanks to the use of the ontological representation of knowledge domain.

An experimental campaign has been developed for the evaluation of the performance of the system. In the next section, the related works are presented [17].

2 Related Works

In literature, there are many approaches related to Chatbots, in particular on e-learning systems [24–26]. From the beginning of the last decade the use of artificial intelligence as e-learning support has captured the interest of many researchers for its many applications. One of these research works is [4], in which Farhan M. et al. using a web bot in an e-learning platform, to address the lack of real-time responses for the students. In fact, when a student asks a question on e-learning platform the teacher could answer at a later stage. If there are more students and more questions, this delay increases. Web bot is a web-based Chatbot that predicts future events based on keywords entered on the Internet. In this work Pandora is used, a bot that stores the questions and answers it on XML style language i.e. Artificial Intelligence Markup Language (AIML). This bot is trained with a series of questions and answers: when it cannot provide a response to a question, a human user is responsible for responding. In the last recent years some interesting research works can be found. In [5] Niranjan et al. discussed about an interesting approach using Bayesian theory to match the request of student and furnish the right response. In particular, Chatbot agent accepts to student's answers and extracts the keywords from the question using a lexical parser, then the keywords are compared with the category list database. The Bayesian probabilities are obtained for all categories in the list. Once the category is selected keywords are compared with the questions under the category using Bayesian probability theory. The answer to the question, which has the highest posterior probability, is then fed into the text to speech conversion module and thus the student receives the answer to his question as a voice response. In [6] Satu et al. many Chatbot applications based on AIML are analyzed: in particular an integrated platform which consists of a basic AIML knowledge is presented. In this project, Chatbot is called Tutorbot because it is functionality backing of didactics done in e-learning environments. It contains some features as natural language management, presentation of contents, and interaction with search engine. Besides, e-learning platforms work is linked to indispensable services to web service. A continuous monitoring service has been created on e-learning platform servers which is another controlling machine: Daemon. In [7] Nordhaug et al. proposed a game-based e-Learning tool called The Forensic Challenger (TFC), used to teach digital forensic investigation. A Chatbot inside the learning platform helps students. A multiple-choice question-based quiz is implemented for kinesthetic learners, and there is a pedagogical Chatbot agent that assists users. It provides easy navigation and interaction within the content. The Chatbot is implemented to be a pedagogical agent for the users, which is meant for discussions and help with the topics. It also acts as a navigation tool and can play video or use the advanced wiki if there are somethings to ask. In [8] Nenkov et al. have investigated about the realization of intelligent agents on platform IBM Bluemix with IBM Watson technology. These agents in the form of Chatbots have to automate the interaction between the student and the teacher within the frames of Moodle learning management system. Watson is a cognitive system that combines capabilities in Natural Language Processing, analytics, and machine learning techniques. In this case, a Chatbot through the Facebook Messenger is realized to simplify communication between a teacher and a student: it could be arranged by acquiring Moodle test basis by Facebook Messenger Bot GUI Builder. A motivating example will be illustrated in the next session.

3 Motivating Example

A bot (short for "robot") is an automated program that runs over the Internet. Some bots run automatically, while others only execute commands when they receive specific input [21]. There are many different types of bots, but some common examples include web crawlers, chat room bots, and malicious bots. Chatbots were one of the first types of automated programs to be called "bots" and became popular in the 1990s, with the rise of online chatrooms [20]. These bots look for certain text patterns submitted by chat room participants and respond with automated actions. For example, a chat bot might warn a user if his or language is inappropriate. If the user does not heed the warning, the bot might kick the user from the channel and may even block the user from returning. A more advanced type of chat bot, called a "chatterbot" can respond to messages in plain English (or other languages), appearing to be an actual person. Both types of chat bots are used for chatroom moderation, which eliminates the need for an individual to monitor individual chatrooms.

The introduction of bots in schools as a tool to support traditional didactic activities can renew the way school works from the point of view of learning; it can help to modernize a blocked school in fixed schemes to keep up the pace of a third millennium society [23].

The main feature of this work is the use of bots in teaching field, particularly in e-learning: this expression means a form of independent training from space and time of distribution and characterized by the physical separation between teacher and student. This is very important if we consider the difficulties that can be encountered by working students and by those ones who live far from centers that provide training or who can't access them (disabled, hospitalized ...). It is equally relevant with a view to continuing education, that is, a training that accompanies the individual throughout life and is not limited to the first years of existence.

A teaching-oriented platform, however, is really useful when it allows the student to take an active role in building his/her knowledge through dialogue, exchange and deepening tools (forums, chat, site links etc.).

Three privileged didactic uses for the e-learning bot can be highlighted:

- Lectures
- Recovery actions.
- Ways of deepening.

Differing significantly from textbooks, dealing with a subject that is not contemplated or treated differently from what is desired, the bot for e-learning can be a useful broadcast tool because, compared to the simple oral lesson, allows to offer students a text that can be consulted.

This type of work implies a considerable commitment on the part of the teacher, who evidently has to prepare the text of the lesson in writing, or at least a map or summary of the irreplaceable content that will then expand in a voice but has the great benefit of saving the contents and make them usable (and editable or implementable) every time that he/she later wants to develop the same topic.

Organizing the material on the platform implies, therefore, by the teacher or in general by a system administrator, significant preliminary work. However, the platform can be considered as a permanent work in progress because it is continuously implemented over time.

By dividing the tasks among teachers, in relation to the activities to be set up, it is possible to have, in a short time, standardized and reusable packages from year to year.

When discussing a topic, it may be necessary to evaluate, in terms of formative verification, the level of understanding or assimilation of a content.

For the provision of verifications, the platform can offer different modes, including multiple response, true/false and short response. Finally, when the score for each item is set, the system automatically corrects and calculates the score.

4 System Architecture

As previously said, an e-learning Chatbot has been made: its architecture is shown in Fig. 1.

The architecture of our model is composed of:

- Front-End
- Back-Office
- Knowledge Base Module
- E-learning BOT Module.

The first module represents the presentation layer (front end) through providing a user-friendly interface: it consists of different kinds of device like tablets, smartphones, PCs and so on.

The Back-Office is used to manage operations that are not seen by end user. This module works in the background to better satisfy user demand: it handles business logic and data storage, working in collaboration with the knowledge base.

The Knowledge Base Module is a special type of database, where data is processed by a server, for the management of knowledge and information: in particular, "Users", representing all users of the application (Students, Professors, etc.); "Learning object" is a collection of content items, practice items, and assessment items that are combined based on a single learning objective.

The E-learning BOT Module is the main engine of the proposed system. It's composed of:

- **Interaction Quality Tracker**: this module monitors interactions between users and Chatbot, evaluating conversation logs based on quality indicators and highlighting critical aspects of Human-machine interactions.
- **Human-Computer Interaction Supervisor**: it supervises dialogue, tracks interaction times, identifies ambiguous questions, recognizes non-convergent interaction sessions, and indicates the need for community support if it is not possible to give a correct answer.
- **Context-Aware Information Manager**: this module allows to drive the dialogue based on contextual parameters (for example, user profile, user position, etc.). The goal is to provide a mechanism of dynamic and automatic invocation of information considering the context through the Context Dimension Tree [9, 10, 27, 28].
- **Inference Engine**: it is designed to provide right answer to the user through Latent Dirichlet Allocation Algorithm and Workflow Manager. In particular, the design of a Workflow Manager is divided into two main phases. The first phase is the definition of an ontology for the description of a certain knowledge domain: in this

case, E-learning domain. It's obtained thanks to the support of domain experts and the adoption of pre-existing ontologies. The second phase is related to the definition of a workflow navigation module. In this way, according to the conversation (through word analysis), this module can surf the ontology and select the more appropriate sentences. So, a way for the description of the workflow is needed: an effective way is the Petri Net [11].

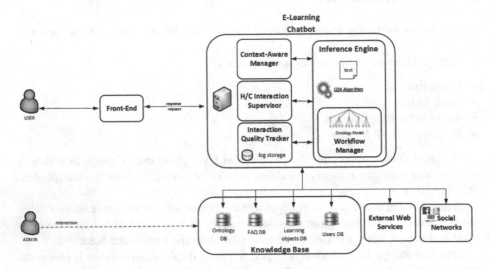

Fig. 1. System architecture

As previously said, a surfer to navigate the ontology is needed. Therefore, an approach based on the Petri Nets could be effective. In particular, the aim is to describe a typical workflow by the adoption of a Petri Net. Each phase of the conversation is modelled as a node of a Petri Net while the transaction is obtained thanks to some structures that are identified in the sentences. The aim is the identification of the right intent/request of the end user.

Therefore, in this scenario, the first aim has been to build an ontology, shown in Fig. 2, to describe the reference taxonomy.

The ontology model is composed of:

- Topic of Study: it represents a field of study for a set of subjects (for example Computer Science);
- User is a Student or a Professor;
- Course is an instance of specific Topic of Study (for example, Fundamentals of Computer Science or Computer Networks);
- Lesson is a didactic module of Course;
- Learning Object is a modular resource, usually digital and web-based, that can be used and re-used to support learning activities.

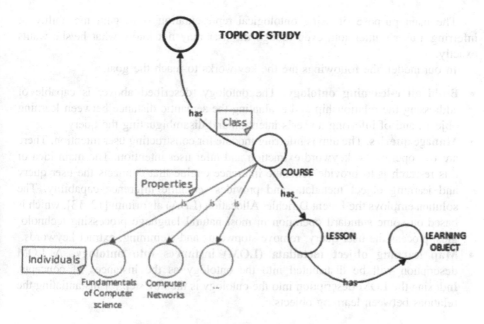

Fig. 2. Ontology

We propose a framework by applying the ontology technology to the e-learning environment, e-learning systems can be more intelligent, powerful, and adaptive; it is shown as in Fig. 3.

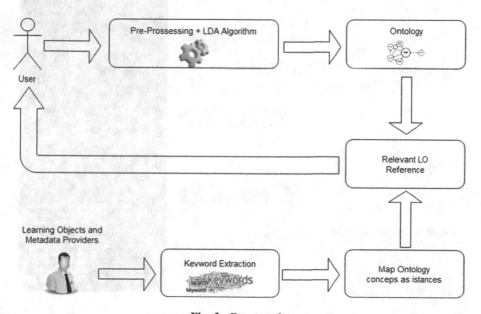

Fig. 3. Framework

The main purpose of using ontological representation is to gain the ability of inferring a user's intention, even though the user may not know what he/she wants exactly.

In our model, the followings are the key works to reach the goal:

- **Build an e-learning ontology**. The ontology, described above, is capable of addressing the relationship and evaluating the semantic distance between learning objects, and of inferring a user's intention and disambiguating the query.
- **Manage queries**. The aim is inferring module for constructing user intention. There are two operations: keyword extraction and infer user intention. The main idea of this research is to provide semantic inference engine that connects the user query and learning object metadata, and provides semantic inference capability. The solution employs the Latent Dirichlet Allocation (LDA) algorithm [12, 13], which is based on some standard operation in most natural language processing technologies: process the user query, remove stopwords and stemming, extract keywords.
- **Map learning object metadata (LOM) instances into ontology**. A LOM description will be distributed into the ontology as the instances of concepts. Indexing the LOM description into the ontology is the key step for instantiating the relations between learning objects.

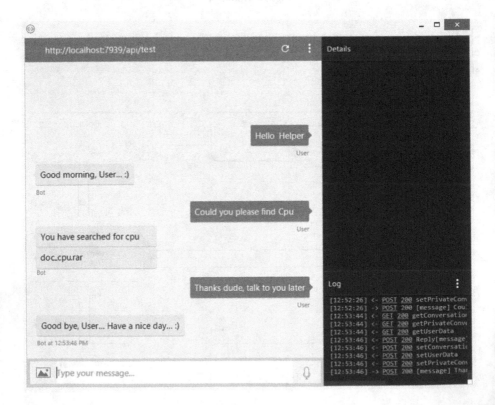

Fig. 4. Screenshot of proposed system

Moreover, as can be seen from the Fig. 3, in our framework there are a back-end and a front-end. The back-end is learning objects provider. Each learning object metadata will be pointed to one or some ontology concepts. The front-end receives queries from user and then enters the inference procedure to infer users' intention. In Fig. 4 there is an example of this system.

We can consider the example of the proposed solution in the field of e-learning: a student of the University courses of Fundamental of Computer Science accesses our system in order to ask for an in-depth study on a specific topic such as CPU. The bot receives the request, elaborates it and answers to the student by sending he/she the attached material or through textual insights on the subject. The example just described can be seen in Fig. 4.

5 Experimental Results

To evaluate the performances of the proposed system an experimental campaign has been developed. In particular, the aim of the experimentation has been the evaluation of the system effectiveness in the recognition of students' requests. Moreover, the usability of the system has been evaluated. An implementation of the Chatbot has been developed and inserted in e-learning platform at University of Salerno. Two study courses were considered: Fundamentals of Computer Science and Computer Networks. The first class was composed by 167 students and the second one by 124 students. During the semester, all students used the platform and the Chatbot: the experimental analysis has been conducted about only the students who passed the exams at the first call, which were 121 for Fundamentals of Computer Science and 87 for Computer Networks. At the end of the session, an email with a questioner has been sent to the students who passed the exam, and in three months about 187 of them responded: the experimental analysis has been conducted on these ones. First of all, the performance of the Chatbot in providing the correct suggestions to the user has been evaluated. In particular, three different situations have been considered:

- Chatbot furnishes a correct suggestion
- Chatbot furnishes a correct suggestion, but it does not fit with the real needs of the student
- Chatbot furnishes a wrong suggestion.

The obtained results are the following:

1. Correct Suggestion: 133–71,13%
2. Correct Suggestion, but not suitable for the needs of the student: 30–16,04%
3. Wrong Suggestion: 24–12,83%

Analyzing the Wrong Suggestion case, it's possible to see that the system fails when students talk about an argument that have various meanings because the bot proposes a response that was not what the student was looking for. Another critical aspect occurs when the system does not understand what kind of language the student is considering: it happens, for example, when it's not clear if the student is considering a C or a C++ language programming. In case of Correct Suggestion, but not suitable for the needs of the student, the main problem is the identification of the real user needs, for example when the student ask a question about an argument on a specific book, but the system fails to identify the correct one. From the point of view of the usability a questionnaire about his/her interaction with the Chatbot has been submitted to each student: generally, they find the Chatbot easy to use and user friendly. Comparing it with other Chatbots (for example Messenger Chatbot or similar) students says that it is more simple and effective.

6 Conclusions

In this paper, an original approach to a Chatbot has been introduced. In particular, the proposed system is based e-learning platform for students. A real case has been investigated developing a Chatbot for the students of Fundamentals of Computer Science and Computer Networks courses. The results obtained by the experimental campaign are satisfying and show the good perspective of this kind of approach [29]. Further developments involve the application of the proposed approach in various contexts and an improvement of e-learning platform.

References

1. Yan, M., Castro, P., Cheng, P., Ishakian, V.: Building a Chatbot with serverless computing. In: Proceedings of the 1st International Workshop on Mashups of Things and APIs (2016). Article no. 5
2. Bi, Y., Deng, K., Cheng, J.: A keyword-based method for measuring sentence similarity. In: Proceedings of the 2017 ACM on Web Science Conference, pp. 379–380 (2017)
3. Lin, L., D'Haro, L.F., Banchs, R.: A Web-based platform for collection of human-chatbot interactions. In: Proceedings of the Fourth International Conference on Human Agent Interaction, pp. 363–366 (2016)
4. Farhan, M., et al.: Automated reply to students' queries in e-learning environment using Web-BOT. In: Eleventh Mexican International Conference on Artificial Intelligence: Advances in Artifical Intelligence and Applications, Special Session - Revised Paper (2012)
5. Niranjan, M., Saipreethy, M.S., Kumar, G.T.: An intelligent question answering conversational agent using naïve bayesian classifier. In: International Conference on Technology Enhanced Education (ICTEE) (2012)
6. Satu, S., Parvez, H., AI-Mamun, S: Review of integrated applications with AIML based chatbot. In: First International Conference on Computer and Information Engineering (ICCIE) (2015)
7. Nordhaug, Ø., Imran, A.S., Alawawdeh, A., Kowalski, S.J.: The forensic challenger. In: International Conference on Web and Open Access to Learning (ICWOAL) (2015)
8. Nenkov, N., Dimitrov, G., Dyachenko, Y., Koeva, K.: Artificial intelligence technologies for personnel learning management systems. In: Eighth International Conference on Intelligent Systems (2015)
9. Clarizia, F., Lemma, S., Lombardi, M., Pascale, F.: A mobile context-aware information system to support tourism events. In: Au, M.H.A., Castiglione, A., Choo, K.-K.R., Palmieri, F., Li, K.-C. (eds.) GPC 2017. LNCS, vol. 10232, pp. 553–566. Springer, Cham (2017). https://doi.org/10.1007/978-3-319-57186-7_40

10. Clarizia, F., Lemma, S., Lombardi, M., Pascale, F.: An ontological digital storytelling to enrich tourist destinations and attractions with a mobile tailored story. In: Au, M.H.A., Castiglione, A., Choo, K.-K.R., Palmieri, F., Li, K.-C. (eds.) GPC 2017. LNCS, vol. 10232, pp. 567–581. Springer, Cham (2017). https://doi.org/10.1007/978-3-319-57186-7_41

11. Colace, F., De Santo, M., Lemma, S., Lombardi, M., Pascale, F.: BotWheels: a petri net based chatbot for recommending tires. In: The 3rd Edition of Special Session on Knowledge Discovery Meets Information Systems: Applications of Big Data Analytics and BI - Methodologies, Techniques and Tools (KomIS), within the 6th International Conference on Data Science, Technology and Applications (DATA) (2017)

12. Colace, F., De Santo, M., Greco, L., Napoletano, P.: Improving relevance feedback-based query expansion by the use of a weighted word pairs approach. J. Assoc. Inf. Sci. Technol. **66**(11), 2223–2234 (2015)

13. Colace, F., De Santo, M., Greco, L., Napoletano, P.: Weighted word pairs for query expansion. Inf. Process. Manage. **51**(1), 179–193 (2015)

14. D'Aniello, G., Gaeta, A., Gaeta, M., Tomasiello, S.: Self-regulated learning with approximate reasoning and situation awareness. J. Ambient Intell. Hum. Comput. **9**, 1–14 (2016)

15. D'Aniello, G., Gaeta, M., Orciuoli, F., Tomasiello, S., Loia, V.: A dialogue-based approach enhanced with situation awareness and reinforcement learning for ubiquitous access to linked data. In: Proceedings - 2014 International Conference on Intelligent Networking and Collaborative Systems, IEEE INCoS 2014, pp. 249–256 (2014). https://doi.org/10.1109/incos.2014.73. Article no. 7057098

16. Hussain, S., Athula, G.: Extending a conventional chatbot knowledge base to external knowledge source and introducing user based sessions for diabetes education. In: 32nd International Conference on Advanced Information Networking and Applications Workshops (WAINA) (2018)

17. D'Angelo, G., Rampone, S.: Cognitive distributed application area networks. In: Security and Resilience in Intelligent Data-Centric Systems and Communication Networks, Intelligent Data-Centric Systems, pp. 193–214 (2018)

18. Albayrak, N., Özdemir, A., Zeydan, E.: An overview of artificial intelligence based Chatbots and an example chatbot application view document. In: 26th Signal Processing and Communications Applications Conference (SIU) (2018)

19. Su, M.H., Wu, C.H., Huang, K.Y., Hong, Q.B., Wang, H.M.: A chatbot using LSTM-based multi-layer embedding for elderly care. In: International Conference on Orange Technologies (ICOT) (2017)

20. Abdul-Kader, S.A., Woods, J.: Question answer system for online feedable new born Chatbot. In: Intelligent Systems Conference (IntelliSys) (2017)

21. Scheuer, M.S., Sandbank, T., Konopnicki, D., Nakash, O.P.: Exploring the universe of egregious conversations in Chatbots. In: Proceedings of the 23rd International Conference on Intelligent User Interfaces Companion (2018). Article no. 16

22. Athreya, R.G., Ngomo, A.C.N., Usbeck, R.: Enhancing community interactions with data-driven Chatbots–the DBpedia Chatbot. In: Companion Proceedings of the Web Conference, pp. 143–146 (2018)

23. Mihnev, P., Stefanov, K., Stefanova, E.: Integrated education in e-learning design and development through synchronised assignments and assessments of courses. In: Proceedings of the 17th International Conference on Computer Systems and Technologies, pp. 383–390 (2016)

24. Wong, J.S., Pursel, B., Divinsky, A., Jansen, B.J.: An analysis of cognitive learning context in MOOC forum messages. In: Proceedings of the 2016 CHI Conference Extended Abstracts on Human Factors in Computing Systems, pp. 1315–1321 (2016)

25. Basogain, X., Olabe, M.A., Olabe, J.C.: Transition to a modern education system through e-learning. In: Proceedings of the 2017 International Conference on Education and E-Learning, pp. 41–46 (2017)
26. Clarizia, F., Colace, F., De Santo, M., Lombardi, M., Pascale, F., Pietrosanto, A.: E-learning and sentiment analysis: a case study. Paper presented at the ACM International Conference Proceeding Series, pp. 111–118 (2018). https://doi.org/10.1145/3178158.3178181
27. Casillo, M., Colace, F., Pascale, F., Lemma, S., Lombardi, M.: Context-aware computing for improving the touristic experience: a pervasive app for the Amalfi coast. Paper presented at the 2017 IEEE International Workshop on Measurement and Networking, M and N 2017 - Proceedings (2017). https://doi.org/10.1109/iwmn.2017.8078373
28. Colace, F., Lemma, S., Lombardi, M., Pascale, F.: A context aware approach for promoting tourism events: the case of artist's lights in salerno. Paper presented at the ICEIS 2017 - Proceedings of the 19th International Conference on Enterprise Information Systems, vol. 2, pp. 752–759 (2017)
29. Casillo, M., Colace, F., Pascale, F., Lemma, S., Lombardi, M.: A tailor made system for providing personalized services. Paper presented at the Proceedings of the International Conference on Software Engineering and Knowledge Engineering, SEKE, pp. 495–500 (2017). https://doi.org/10.18293/seke2017-151

A Multilevel Graph Approach
for Road Accidents Data Interpretation

Fabio Clarizia[1(✉)], Francesco Colace[1(✉)], Marco Lombardi[1(✉)],
Francesco Pascale[1(✉)], and Domenico Santaniello[2(✉)]

[1] DIIn, University of Salerno, 84084 Fisciano, SA, Italy
{fclarizia,fcolace,malombardi,fpascale}@unisa.it
[2] DICIV, University of Salerno, 84084 Fisciano, SA, Italy
dsantaniello@unisa.it

Abstract. Nowadays, due to the massive low-cost technology and mobile
devices spread, our society is increasingly projected towards data production.
Often, we find ourselves surrounded by data that, however, does not always lead
to the knowledge, or toward information that we need. This is liable to eclipse
the desire to use this data trying to predict the future. So much has been done in
literature in regard to the extraction of information and interpretation of these
data. However, in this field does not seem to be present a universal methodology
for solving the problem, leading us to research new approaches more cus-
tomized on the available dataset. The aim of this paper is to introduce an
approach for the interpretation of data from sensors located within a city using
three graphical views: Context Dimension Tree, Ontologies and Bayesian
Networks. Through the Ontologies and the Context Dimension Tree it is possible to analyze the scenario from a syntactic and semantic point of view,
assisting the construction of the he Bayes network structure that allow to estimate the probability that some events happen. A first preliminary analysis
conducted on a London borough seems to confirm the effectiveness of the
proposed method.

Keywords: Big Data · Context Awareness · Smart City
Knowledge management

1 Introduction

An ever-increasing digitization of our lives involves the production of such a large and
rich amount of data which can not be processed by conventional methods. Being able
to develop solutions and algorithms capable to interpret and interact with this huge
amount of information is a key challenge which Big Data poses in today's world [1].
However, many questions remain: How to conduct this transformation? How to
properly use these data to increase the competitiveness and efficiency of services? And,
how could they contribute to social development? [2].

Data management has grown along three dimensions: volume, velocity and variety
[3]. According to Tole [4] the so-called "3Vs" represents key elements regarding the
characteristics of Big Data systems. Volume refers to the amount of structured or

A. Castiglione et al. (Eds.): CSS 2018, LNCS 11161, pp. 303–316, 2018.
https://doi.org/10.1007/978-3-030-01689-0_24

unstructured data generated, which is being manipulated and analysed in order to obtain the desired results. Commonly, these data are generated by heterogeneous sources such as traditional databases, social media, sensors, logs, events, etc. Velocity refers not only to the speed of data generation, but also to the need, of this information, to be processed in real time. Variety deals with the different types of data that are generated, collected and used. These data, which belong to the most disparate codification, suggests the use of different storage and retrieval approaches.

These pervasive data are mainly the result of two independent phenomena that reached critical mass simultaneously: the advent of the Internet of Things and the increase in volume of user-generated content produced by social networks and smart mobile terminals [5].

The internet has allowed us to create a powerful information network, through which more and more services are spread: from information to communication, from banking services to the purchasing. In addition, it has given us the opportunity to connect human beings to each other, to communicate and share anything anywhere instantly. In this sense, in 1999 Kevin Ashton defined the term Internet of Things (IoT) [6] which refers to the concept of a network in which human beings and machines are connected, using common public services. According to Atzori [7] the main strength of the IoT idea is the high impact it will have on several aspects of everyday-life and behaviour of potential users. The spread of low-cost sensors makes a significant contribution to create an impressive amount of data. Moreover, thanks to their pervasiveness they appear able to influence our daily actions more and more. This leads us to pose further questions: How can we properly process this data? Is it necessary to understand the underlying processes generating the data precisely? How are the data sources linked with each other? Is it sufficient to have high level general views in order to mine useful results? How to turn these data into knowledge? Are there specific techniques and methodologies able to analyse this important amount of data? Much has been done regarding to manage these huge volumes of data (Hadoop, Spark, Storm, Google BigQuery, etc.), but what has been done for the interpretation of these data?

It's been a while since the literature no longer refers to the 3Vs but to the 5Vs [8], Value and Veracity are introduced as fundamental characteristics to analyse the problems related to the Big Data. Value is a key aspect of the data, which is defined by the added-value that the collected data can bring to the intended process, activity or predictive analysis/hypothesis; obviously this aspect is related to the capability to transform data into Knowledge Database. The veracity dimension of Big Data includes data consistency and data trustworthiness, related to a number of factors including statistical reliability, data origin, processing methods etc. It is important to ensure the reliability of the data considering that results may be generated on which important decisions are made. Assigning a veracity index to data on which the analyses are based is essential in order to have a measure of the general reliability of the system. These aforementioned issues are all key when dealing with data generated in a smart cities context.

Increasing populations and rapid large-scale urbanization creates a demand to increase the quality of life through economic development, environmental efficiency and stability. This could be performed by designing urban areas which take advantage of integrated technologies and the optimization of resources in order to improve some key objectives such as mobility, communication, economy, work, environment, administration and construction. It was 2008 when IBM, during the years of the global financial crisis, suggested a smart approach to deal with problems afflicting economic growth launching the concept of a smarter planet. Smart cities are able to use data such as traffic congestion, power consumption statistics, and public safety events, in order to upgrade the city services, through three foundational concepts: instrumented, interconnected, and intelligent supplies [9]. Instrumented is referring to sources of data from physical or virtual sensors, interconnected refers to the capacity of the integration and management of those data into an enterprise computing platform and their communication, Intelligent refers to the capacity of complex analytics, modelling, optimization, and visualization in order to make better operational decisions.

Many applications, on smart cities concept, have been proposed in literature; in particular, Zanella et al. present and discuss the technical solutions and best-practice guidelines adopted in the Padova Smart City project. Added-value services for citizens and the administration of the city have been highlighted in many areas of interest such as: Structural Health of Buildings, Waste Management, Air Quality, Noise Monitoring, Traffic Congestion, City Energy Consumption, Smart Parking, Smart Lighting [10].

Information management environments, or more generally pervasive data contexts, may be supported by context representation approaches and enhanced through adopting probabilistic approaches such as Bayesian Network (BN) [5]. BNs can offer a framework for risk and maintenance analysis through their ability to model data transparently. Some of the advantages of probabilistic approaches are the capability to model complex systems, to make predictions as well as diagnostics, to compute the probability of an event, to update the probabilities according to evidence, to represent multimodal variables and offer a user-friendly graphical and compact approach [11].

As previously mentioned, a further element of added value could be given by the introduction of methodologies capable to represent the context, in particular, the Context Dimension Tree (CDT). The CDT represents a valid tool used for applications which include the choices of places of interest [12]. In addition, CDT, or more generally context-aware approaches, leads to the rationalization of information delivered to the users and to the personalized distribution of information [13]. An undisputed and widely used method for representation of reality are ontologies. An ontology can adequately support pervasive context-aware systems [14], in addition, there is a strong connection with Bayesian Networks [22]. In particular, according to Helsper et al. is possible to build BNs through Ontologies [15], and vice versa Colace et al. propose a novel algorithm for Ontology building through the use of BNs [16].

Thinking about the mentioned context representation methodologies and the ability of the BNs, which from experimental evidences and through probabilistic approach are able to identify probable events, it is necessary to introduce techniques and methodologies able to manage the context in real time, in order to improve the quality of life in smart cities. The aim of this paper is to introduce a methodology for merging context representation techniques, which are CDT and Ontology, and probabilistic approach based on BN in order to help expert user to handle emergency conditions or provide suggestions for the liveability of the citizens. Sample Heading (Third Level). Only two levels of headings should be numbered. Lower level headings remain unnumbered; they are formatted as run-in headings.

2 The Proposed Approach

In a great number of cases, the problem we have to sort out is the following one: given a series of data, facts or observations, we are interested in identifying their most likely source and the reason that they have been generated, with a view to optimizing our own decisions. Although this seems quite a simple operation, making a decision in uncertain conditions is a process, which is far from being trivial. In this respect, the goal here is to identify an architecture to be used as an extremely flexible inferential/decision-making tool. Such architecture will not only enable the managing of complex problems, featuring a great variety of variables inter-linked through both logical-deterministic and probabilistic relationships, but also provide an effective graphic representation of the phenomenon at stake, formulating a problem description that will enhance the degree of comprehension and allow the identification of key variables. The innovative characteristics of the proposed architecture concern mainly the informational content that is intended to be made available to the end users with three point of view: Data management and organization, Representation of the context and Inferential engines.

2.1 Data Management and Representation

Data represents the key to build up and enable services and actions to be made: the goal is then to implement a Knowledge Base (KB) with a view to collecting, elaborating and managing information in real time. In this respect, we use a Knowledge Organization System (KOS), by which we mean well known schemes such as Taxonomies, Thesaurus and further types of vocabulary that, together with Ontologies, constitute valid tools to shape the reality of interest into concepts and relations between concepts [17]. Many benefits stem from this: using ontologies, for instance, allows to fix a series of key concepts and definitions relating to a given domain that can be shared, thus making the appropriate terminologies available (collaborative knowledge sharing); furthermore, an ontology allows a full re-usage of the knowledge that it codifies, even within other ontologies or rather for their completion (non-redundancy of information) and, being susceptible to interpretation by electronic calculators, enables the automatic treatment of knowledge with relevant significant advantages (Semantic Web).

2.2 Representation of the Context

The goal is primarily to deliver to different categories of users, in a given moment, information which is useful in a given context. In practice, the objective would be to set up an architecture characterized by a high degree of Context Awareness. Real time understanding of the context where users are, via a representation by means of graphs, enables the provision of a wide array of personalized, "tailored" services and suggestions regarding the decisions to make, that can help them in professional and private daily life, managing in the best possible way both the time and resources they have, hence meeting their needs [18]. Context Awareness should be understood as a set of technical features capable of providing added value to services in different operational segments. Context Aware Computing applications can exploit, in this specific case, such features in order to provide context-related information to users, or suggest them an appropriate selection of actions. In order to achieve a better representation of the various features, formal tools of context representation have been adopted, capable to define in details the user's needs in the context where he is acting, through an approach « where, why, when, how » . In detail, the representation of the context has been implemented by means of formal models of representation, such as the Context Dimension Tree (CDT). The CDT is a tree composed of a triple <r; N; A> where r indicates its root, N is the set of nodes of which it is made of and A is the set of arcs joining these nodes. CDT is used to be able to represent, in a graphic form, all possible contexts that you may have within an application. Nodes present within CDT are divided into two categories, namely dimension nodes and concept nodes. A dimension node, which is graphically represented by the colour black, is a node that describes a possible dimension of the application domain; a concept node, on the other hand, is depicted by the colour white and represents one of the possible values that a dimension may assume. Each node is identified through its type and a label. The children of the root node r are all dimension nodes, they are called top dimension and for each of them there may be a sub-tree. Leaf nodes, instead, must be concept nodes. A dimension node can have, as children, only concept nodes and, similarly, a concept node can have, as children, only dimension nodes. A Context Element is defined as an assignment dimension_namei = value, while a Context is specified as an "and" among different context elements: several context elements, combined with each other, give rise to a context.

2.3   Inferential Engines

The system collects data from various sources without interruption and immediately processes them, with a view to activating precise actions, depending on the users and on the events. These events, detected and analysed, will have to be translated into facts associated to specific semantic values: it is therefore necessary to use an inferential engine capable to draw conclusions by applying certain rules to reported facts, which could be imagined as a sequence of if-else statements. The approach selected to implement this inferential engine stems from Bayesian Networks: powerful conceptual, mathematic and application tools allowing the management of complex problems with a great number of variables interlinked by means of both probabilistic and deterministic relations.

3   The System Architecture

The system architecture, sketched out in Fig. 1, envisages functional blocks with three main phases. In the first phase, defined as the Collection Phase, data (referred to as "rough data"), are provided by different types of sensors. The set of data that are most significant with a view to the analysis that is meant to be carried out, is saved within a database. Then, in the Pre-Processing Phase, data are transformed in order to adapt them to the system that will have to use them. In general, data arrives from different sources and therefore show inconsistencies such as, for instance, the usage of different denominations to identify the same value of a feature. In addition, this phase envisions the cleaning of the collected data, in order to eliminate any error, and the treatment of missing data. The phase ends up with sampling and discretization of data. Finally, the Elaboration Phase aims at providing a representation and interpretation of the acquired knowledge, starting from information correctly memorized. To this end, an approach is followed which is based on the three views previously described, leading to implementing and using "decisional models". Such models are constantly improved based on newly collected data and experiences, or previously treated cases.

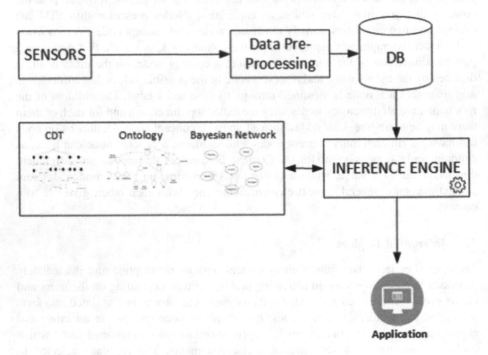

Fig. 1. The system architecture

Summing up, the need to make a decision, in a given context, can be met through the fruition of the right information delivered by the architecture. This information is featured by innovative elements based on: knowledge management and organisation, formal context representation, inferential engines.

4   Experimental Results

This section presents the experimental results of the proposed approach: the architecture is designed to collect and analyse a vast amount of data, making it available to different categories of users. The results shown are aimed at highlighting the strength of the system, which would be the ability to adapt quickly and the exploitation of human-machine interaction in order to provide automatic and reliable answers. The study area is the city of London where, for data availability reasons, it was possible to collect a sufficient number of data to provide a preliminary example that allow us to show the capability of the system to provide a reliable Bayesian Network capable to predict accident risk. In particular, the selected borough is Westminster, which is an inner London borough that occupies much of the central area of Greater London including most of the West End, and the observation period of data set is throughout the 2016 year. The data, obtained from sensors spread throughout the borough, were aggregated at 3-h intervals, resulting in the observation period of one year being made of 2920 instances. The data are organized as shown in the table below (Table 1).

Table 1. Dataset

DayDate	This data refers to the date of the day with the following format: yyyy-mm-dd, HH:MM:SS
Interval	This information refers to the time interval in which a day is divided
WeekDay	This data refers to the day of the week; therefore, the days of the week are specified for each instance
Month	Like been done for the day of the week, even the month are specified for each instance
Rainfall	This data refers to the instantaneous measure of precipitation, expressed in mm
Temperature	This data refers to the outside temperature, expressed in Celsius degree.
WindSpeed	This data refers to the instantaneous speed of the wind, expressed in m/s.
Accidents	This data refers to the modest and hight severity accidents that occurred in the borough.

To explain the capability of the presented system, the experimental phase is shown by comparing three different cases. The data set, in order to perform the analysis, is divided in a Training data Set (TrDS), which represents 75% of the data (2190 instances), and in a Test Data Set (TeDS), which represents 25% of the data (730 instances). The analysis is performed through R-Studio IDE [19]. The results of the analysis are provided in the form of Confusion Matrix, also known as error matrix, which is a specific matrix containing observed data and predicted results that allows valuation of the performance of an algorithm. Through Confusion Matrix is possible to give results in terms of Accuracy, which is a description of systematic errors, a measure of statistical bias. In this way three Bayesian Networks, obtained according to three different approaches, will be compared. The cases are the follows: Defined Bayesian Network, Learned Bayesian Network, MuG Bayesian Network.

4.1   Case #1

An expert defined BN structure, shown in Fig. 2, is taken into account, it is combined with the TrDS in order to obtain the conditional probabilities. At this point we can test the obtained BN comparing the predicted results and the observed data.

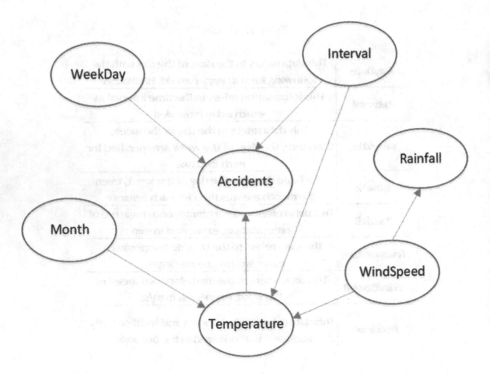

Fig. 2. Defined Bayesian network

4.2   Case #2

The BN is defined and learned with a chosen structural learning algorithm through the TrDS. The so learned network is tested with the TeDS in order to obtain the confusion matrix. The Score-based Learning Algorithm chosen is K2 Hill Climbing [20]. It has been possible to use this algorithm through the bnlearn package [21] available for the programming language R. The Bayesian Network structure is shown in Fig. 3.

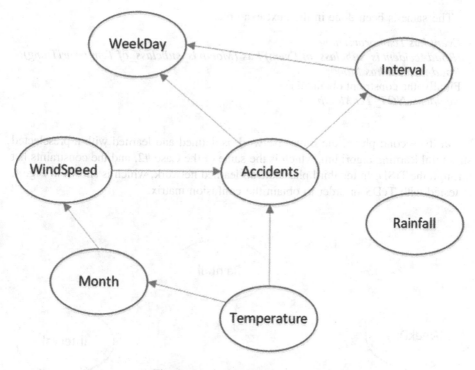

Fig. 3. Learned Bayesian network

4.3   Case#3

In this case, our approach has been applied combining CDT and Ontology in order to obtain a reliable BN. In the first phase the CDT (Fig. 5) and the Ontological view (Fig. 6) are taken into consideration. The system automatically makes a selection of all the nodes in all possible combinations according to the target. Starting by selecting some nodes of the CDT, the same nodes will be selected on the Ontological view by extracting their relationships. These relationships are turned into a constraints list, which is an essential tool in the BN building process. For example, a relation found combining CDT and Ontology is the follow:

WeatherConditions **has_influence_on** *Randomness*
This is automatically manipulated, obtaining:
(Rain   is_subclass_of   WeatherCondition)   has_influence_on   (Randomness is_subclass_of RoadAccident)
Rain **has_influence_on** *RoadAccident*
Finally, it is turned into a constraint:
Rainfall TO Accidents

The same is been done in the next example:

*Event **has** TemporarlThing*
*(RoadAccident **is_subclass_of** Event) **has** (Month **is_subclass_of** TemporarlThing)*
*RoadAccident **has** Month*
Finally, the constraint obtained is
*Accidents **NOT_TO** Month*

In the second phase, the Bayes Network is defined and learned with a preselected structural learning algorithm, which is the same of the Case #2, and the constraints list through the TrSD. In the third phase the so-learned network, which is shown in Fig. 4, is tested with TeDS in order to obtain the confusion matrix.

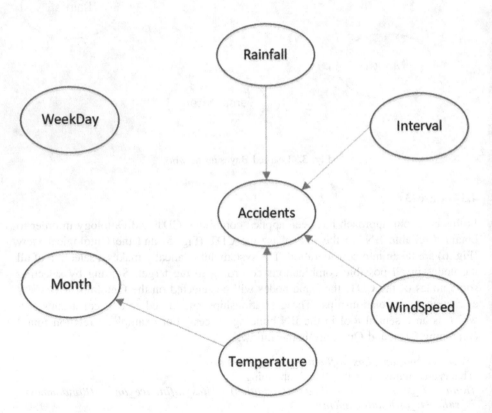

Fig. 4. The Bayesian network obtained by the use of the MuG approach

The results in terms of Confusion Matrix are shown in the following Tables 2, 3 and 4.

Table 2. Confusion matrix defined Bayesian network

Reference

Prediction		Low	Medium	High
	Low	80	40	1
	Medium	41	102	70
	High	5	76	237

Accuracy : 64%

Table 3. Confusion matrix learned Bayesian network

Reference

Prediction		Low	Medium	High
	Low	0	40	149
	Medium	0	37	215
	High	0	47	363

Accuracy : 47%

Table 4. Confusion matrix using the MuG approach

Reference

Prediction		Low	Medium	High
	Low	112	12	12
	Medium	48	73	88
	High	3	45	321

Accuracy : 71%

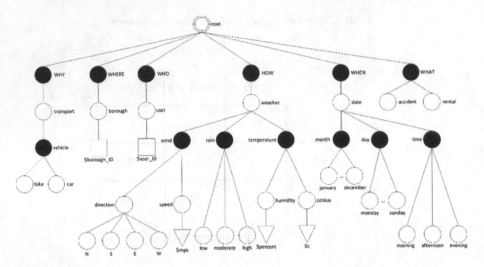

Fig. 5. CDT view

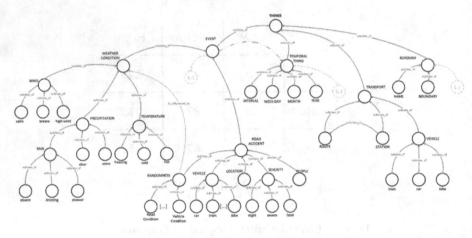

Fig. 6. Ontology view

5   Conclusion

Although the learned Bayesian Network structure by our system is not complete, its reliability in terms of Accuracy increase between Case #1 and Case #3, as shown in the tables. Therefore, we could argue that our system, which is ready to provide reliable answers, can raise its performance over time with increasing volumes of data. Moreover, the potential of such built systems lies in the fact that it is able to automatically update and adapt itself. In addition, it is capable, through Ontologies and CDT, to interface with other similar systems based on different contexts sharing and exchanging knowledge in order to improve its performance more and more.

References

1. deRoos, D., Eaton, C., Lapis, G., Zikopoulos, P., Deutsch, T.: Understanding Big Data: Analytics for Enterprise Class Hadoop and Streaming Data. McGraw-Hill, New York City (2011)
2. Boyd, D., Crawford, K.: Critical questions for BIG DATA. Inf. Commun. Soc. **15**(5), 1–18 (2012)
3. Laney, D.: 3D Data management: controlling data volume, velocity, and variety. META Group (2001)
4. Tole, A.A.: Big data challenges. Database Syst. J. **4**(3), 31–40 (2013)
5. Colace, F., De Santo, M., Moscato, V., Picariello, A., Schreiber, F.A., Tanca, L.: Data Management in Pervasive Systems. Springer, Cham (2015). https://doi.org/10.1007/978-3-319-20062-0
6. Ashton, K.: That "Internet of Things" thing. RFiD J. **22**, 97–114 (2009)
7. Atzori, L., Iera, A., Morabito, G.: The Internet of Things: a survey. Comput. Netw. **54**(15), 2787–2805 (2010)
8. Demchenko, Y., Grosso, P., De Laat, C., Membrey, P.: Addressing big data issues in scientific data infrastructure. In: 2013 International Conference on Collaboration Technologies and Systems (CTS), pp. 48–55 (2013)
9. Harrison, C., Eckman, B., Hamilton, R., Hartswick, P.: Foundations for smarter cities. IBM J. Res. Dev. **54**(4), 350–365 (2010)
10. Zanella, A., Bui, N., Castellani, A.P., Vangelista, L., Zorz, M.: Internet of Things for smart cities. IEEE IoT J. **1**(1), 22–32 (2014)
11. Weber, P., Medina-Oliva, G., Simon, C., Iung, B.: Overview on Bayesian networks applications for dependability, risk analysis and maintenance areas. Eng. Appl. Artif. Intell. **25**(4), 671–682 (2012)
12. Colace, F., Lemma, S., Lombardi, M., Pascale, F.: A context aware approach for promoting tourism events: the case of artist's lights in Salerno. Paper presented at the ICEIS 2017 - Proceedings of the 19th International Conference on Enterprise Information Systems, vol. 2, pp. 752–759 (2017)
13. Panigati, E., Rauseo, A., Schreiber, F.A., Tanca, L.: Aspects of pervasive information management: an account of the green move system In: 2012 IEEE 15th International Conference on Computational Science and Engineering (CSE), pp. 648–655 (2012)
14. Chen, H., Finin, T., Joshi, A.: An ontology for context-aware pervasive computing environments. Knowl. Eng. Rev. **18**(3), 197–207 (2003)
15. Helsper, E.M., Van Der Gaag, L.C.: Building Bayesian networks through ontologies. In: Proceedings of the 15th Eureopean Conference on Artificial Intelligence, ECAI 2002, Lyon, France, July 2002
16. Colace, F., De Santo, M.: Ontology for E-learning: a Bayesian approach. IEEE Trans. Educ. **53**(2), 223–233 (2010)
17. Clarizia, F., Lemma, S., Lombardi, M., Pascale, F.: An ontological digital storytelling to enrich tourist destinations and attractions with a mobile tailored story. In: Au, M.H.A., Castiglione, A., Choo, K.-K.R., Palmieri, F., Li, K.-C. (eds.) GPC 2017. LNCS, vol. 10232, pp. 567–581. Springer, Cham (2017). https://doi.org/10.1007/978-3-319-57186-7_41
18. Clarizia, F., Lemma, S., Lombardi, M., Pascale, F.: A mobile context-aware information system to support tourism events. In: Au, M.H.A., Castiglione, A., Choo, K.-K.R., Palmieri, F., Li, K.-C. (eds.) GPC 2017. LNCS, vol. 10232, pp. 553–566. Springer, Cham (2017). https://doi.org/10.1007/978-3-319-57186-7_40

19. R.C. Team: R: a language and environment for statistical computing. R Foundation for Statistical Computing, Vienna, Austria, 2013 (2014). ISBN 3-900051-07-0
20. Cooper, G.F., Herskovits, E.: A Bayesian method for the induction of probabilistic networks from data. Mach. Learn. **9**(4), 309–347 (1992)
21. Scutari, M.: Learning Bayesian networks with the bnlearn R package. J. Stat. Softw. **35**(3), 1–22 (2010)
22. Tucker, A., Trifonova, N., Maxwell, D., Pinnegar, J., Kenny, A.: Predicting ecosystem responses to changes in fisheries catch, temperature, and primary productivity with a dynamic Bayesian network model. ICES J. Mar. Sci. **73**(10), 1334–1343 (2017)

Cyber Safety Awareness and Culture Planning in South Africa

E. Kritzinger[(⊠)], M. Loock, and E. N. Mwim

School of Computing, University of South Africa, Pretoria, South Africa
{kritze,loockm,mwimen}@unisa.ac.za

Abstract. Cyber-safety awareness projects are active in rural and township schools and communities, but people (adults and children) are still not cyber safe. Information technology (IT) practitioners in academia and industry are active in creating cyber safety awareness programmes among children in schools and among eager and available adults. The interesting questions currently being asked are, what trends are these programmes following and should new trends be added to existing programmes to make awareness more effective. The purpose of this research is to explore possible new trends in creating awareness among cyber users. A group of conference attendees from different research fields was asked to share their current cyber-safety awareness programme trends and any possible new trends that may better the general results of cyber-safety awareness programmes. The conclusion is made that the responsibility of educating cyber-security awareness rests on the shoulders of a wide group of people, including government. This education effort should be done in a collaborative and holistic manner.

Keywords: Cyber-safety awareness · Secure · Data management

1 Introduction and Background

1.1 Introduction

Information and communication technology (ICT) has become part our daily life and the advances in ICT have changed the manner in which ordinary citizens conduct their daily activities relating to information finding, social networking, electronic transactions and entertainment (Dlamini and Modise 2012; de Lange and von Solms 2012). These activities take place in cyberspace where the use of the internet has become second nature to millions of people (Kritzinger and von Solms 2010) due to the proliferation of smart mobile phones and increased bandwidth. Dodge and Kitchin (2001) define cyberspace as the digital arena where computer systems are connected. The involvement in cyberspace provides numerous benefits for business and non-business users alike (Dlamini and Modise 2012). However, the benefits of and dependence on cyberspace carries its own risks as it increases vulnerability to cybercrime and attack, in the process threatening national security (Dlamini and Modise 2012). For these reasons, it is important for cyberspace users to be schooled in safe and secure ways to operate in the cyberspace environment (von Solms and von Solms 2014).

South Africa is considered one of the top three countries in the world to have been targeted by phishing attacks over the years (RSA 2011). Cyber safety is considered vitally

A. Castiglione et al. (Eds.): CSS 2018, LNCS 11161, pp. 317–326, 2018.
https://doi.org/10.1007/978-3-030-01689-0_25

important to all South Africans who participate in cyberspace (von Solms and von Solms 2014). Initiatives and efforts have been made by various entities to create cyber-safety awareness among different internet users in South Africa. Since there is no national cyber-security and cyber-safety policy, all awareness efforts, initiatives and programmes are delivered through a variety of independent, uncoordinated mechanisms, each with its own specific focus areas and objectives (Dlamini and Modise 2012). The next section discusses the trends in the different cyber-safety awareness programmes in South Africa.

1.2 Cyber-Safety Awareness Trends

Cyber-safety awareness in South Africa has been approached from different perspective and the focus has been on different members of society. This section presents the different angles from which cyber-safety awareness has been approached in South Africa. In their cyber-safety awareness work, von Solms and von Solms (2014) prepared three different syllabus tables for teachers to use in a classroom to educate and train school learners between the age of 7 and 13 years. The syllabus was prepared by identifying publicly available online resources. The authors aimed the work at empowering teachers to play a crucial role in preparing and equipping primary school learners for their activities in cyberspace.

Since there is no formal long-term national approach towards enhancing cyber safety within South African schools, Kritzinger has done research and proposed the implementation of a short-term national approach and short-term initiatives (Kritzinger 2016). This research argues that despite intense research on the proposed approaches of incorporating cyber-safety awareness into the school curriculum, the national school curriculum in South African does not make provision for cyber-safety awareness education, and the availability of supporting materials and training for ICT teachers in South Africa is limited. This results in a lack of knowledge and skills about cyber security (Kritzinger 2016). Before proposing the short-term approach, Kritzinger and Padayachee (2013) conducted cyber-safety awareness research focusing on using educators as the key role players in disseminating e-safety information, particularly in school curricula (Kritzinger and Padayachee 2013). A cyber-safety curriculum was also developed by using open educational resources (von Solms and von Solms 2015).

In an attempt to bridge the gap in cyber-safety education, Kritzinger (2015) proposed the concept of gaming as a way to approach and create awareness of cyber-safety issues in South Africa (Kritzinger 2015). Research by Labuschagne et al. (2011) used an interactive game hosted by a social networking site to create awareness of information security threats and vulnerabilities (Labuschagne et al. 2011).

Work has also been done in proposing a framework to contribute to the development of an e-safety culture in South Africa (de Lange and von Solms 2012). In 2015 a practical framework, called the ICT Security Awareness Framework for Education (ISAFE) was proposed for the integration of ICT security awareness into the South African education system (Walaza et al. 2015). In the ongoing effort to create cyber-security awareness, a study by researchers at the Nelson Mandela Metropolitan University proposed a cyber-security awareness education framework for South Africa aimed to assist in creating a cyber-secure culture in South Africa among all internet users (Kortjan and Von Solms 2014).

Research at the University of Venda in 2011 also focused on an intensive awareness campaign with the purpose of educating novice internet and technology users about basic security. The second stage of the awareness evaluation project was aimed at developing cyber-security awareness training modules for local communities in their native tongue, in order to improve the current level of awareness (Grobler et al. 2011a).

It is evident from research that the work done towards cyber-safety awareness in South Africa has targeted different parts of society, such as school children, university students, teachers, organisations for the elderly, home users and non-home users. The majority of the work has focused on the area of framework, gaming, training modules, school syllabi and curricula, presentations or formal lectures, movie clips, and online and offline discussions (Dlamini and Modise 2012).

1.3 Objectives of Cyber-Safety Awareness

Table 1, adapted from Dlamini and Modise (2012), summarises some of the objectives of cyber-safety awareness in South Africa.

Table 1. Objectives of cyber-safety awareness. Adapted from Dlamini and Modise (2012)

Objectives of cyber-safety awareness in South Africa
To equip individuals with the necessary knowledge to make the right decision in cyber-related situations
To increase awareness and an understanding of cyberspace
To educate users about information security and the role each individual should play in the effectiveness of one type of control
To contribute towards the creation of an awareness culture

1.4 Role Players in Cyber-Safety Awareness

Various people and groups play a role in ensuring cyber-safety awareness in South Africa. Some of the role players include universities, researchers, schools, teachers, parents, communities and organisations such as non-profit organisations. However, government has played no role or only a limited role in the various cyber-security safety initiatives in South Africa and this is a serious concern (Dlamini and Modise 2012). Of all the role players, universities are the most active. The findings of this study suggest other role players who could still play a role in cyber-safety awareness in South Africa.

The major problem with cyber-safety trends and initiatives in South Africa over the years is that the different efforts operate in cycles. There is no coordination, resulting in duplications (Dlamini and Modise 2012) – there is a need for a change of trends. This supports Dlamini and Modise's (2012) recommendation that a single body is needed to integrate all activities of cyber-security awareness initiatives. The single body should be established with the support of all organisations, institutions, businesses and, most importantly, the government.

2 Methodology

The research followed a questionnaire approach. The questionnaire was distributed under university lecturers, government workers and industry workers in a conference setting. The following questions were asked:

1. Are you currently involved in a cyber-safety awareness project?
   If YES, please continue with question 2.
   If NO, please continue with question 3.

2. Please explain your own involvement in questions 2A to 2H.
   (A) Name of project:
   (B) Involvement in project:
   (C) Collaboration with other projects/industry/academic institution:
   (D) Short description of your project:
   (E) What is the aim of your project?
   (F) Who is the targeted community for your cyber-security awareness project?
   (G) Funding:
      (G.1) Do you have funding for this project?
      (G.2) If YES, what type of funding?
   (H) Is electronic access to this project available? (e.g. website, e-mail).
      If YES, please give the electronic address.

3. Do you know of other cyber-safety awareness projects worth noting?
   If yes, please complete questions 3A to 3C.
   (A) Who is the project leader of this project?
   (B) Give a short description of the project.
   (C) At which institution is this project hosted?

4. What is your vision for cyber-safety awareness in South Africa?
5. What initiatives are still needed to improve cyber-safety awareness in South Africa?
6. What are the possible methods to implement these initiatives?
7. Who are the role players that must be involved in future cyber-safety awareness initiatives?
8. What other factors can or should contribute to the maturity of a cyber-safety awareness culture in South Africa?
9. What are your ideas on how cyber-safety awareness can be improved for the future?

The data was collected on the second day of the African Cyber Citizenship Conference in Port Elizabeth, South Africa in November 2016. A slot was allocated for the researchers of this paper in the conference programme to distribute the questionnaires, answer any relevant questions and gather all the completed questionnaires again. The conference audience was made up of researchers, academics, students, industry people, government workers and individuals from non-profit organisations. The researchers introduced themselves and then distributed the questionnaires. The conference audience was divided into four groups for discussion purposes. The groups were small enough for active participation and also big enough to allow diversity of opinions from those present. The survey questions were open-ended questions designed to focus on qualitative questions. Twenty-five questionnaires were distributed manually and 92% of conference participants responded. Since the data were collected in a conference setting, the choice of respondents was restricted to the conference participants. The research findings are presented in the next sections. The study adopted a qualitative research analysis of the questionnaires' content using an inductive approach.

3   Analysis of Data

3.1   Code Families and Their Members

All completed questionnaires were analysed with AltlasTi. The different inputs and comments received from the questionnaires were coded. All the codes were then grouped under code families. A list of code families and their code members are depicted in Table 2.

Table 2. List of code families and their code members

Code family	Codes
Cyber-security awareness (CSA) improvement	• CSA improvement: Co-ordinated efforts • CSA improvement: Educational interventions • CSA improvement: Legislative enforcement • CSA improvement: Psychological interventions • CSA improvement: Resources
CSA mature culture creation	• CSA culture creation • CSA through digital literacy
CSA methods	• CSA methods: Information dissemination • CSA methods: Needs-based initiatives
CSA needs	• CSA needs: Broader all-inclusive approaches • CSA needs: Empower parents • CSA needs: National approach
CSA role players	• CSA role players • CSA through digital literacy
Vision for CSA	• Vision for CSA: Broad and diverse involvement • Vision for CSA: Focus on educating youth • Vision for CSA: Societal awareness and empowerment

3.2   Relationships of Quotations by Code

The relationships between the different codes are depicted in Fig. 1. These relationships were gathered from the different questionnaires. One of the many examples that can be read in this figure is that the target of the CSA improvement family's educational intervention member should not only be on educating the youth, but should also be on empowering the parents.

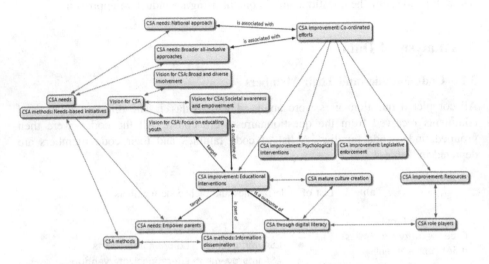

Fig. 1. Relationships of concepts gathered from questionnaires

3.3   Cyber Needs

The data analysis provided the weighting of the different cyber needs that was identified in the qualitative analysis of the feedback of the participants. These cyber needs (as depicted in Sect. 3) can be seen as critical aspects that must be addressed to grow a cyber culture within an organisation, community or a country (Clarizia et al. 2017a; Clarizia et al. 2017b). The weighting of the cyber needs (Annunziata et al. 2016) are relevant to identify the current lack of a cyber-safety process in South Africa. Figure 2 depicts an analysis via a word-o-gram that indicates the weighting of the cyber needs.

Possible interventions and cyber activities to improve cyber safety and address cyber needs can be derived from these cyber needs. It is important to note that these cyber needs must be visualised and addressed by a wide range of cyber-safety collaborators. These different collaborators (role players) should engage with the current cyber needs and assist where possible. The next section will investigate the different collaborators that can contribute to the elimination of cyber needs with the main goal of growing a cyber-safety culture in South Africa.

Fig. 2. Word-o-gram of the cyber needs

3.4 Cyber-Safety Collaborators and Cyber Activities

According to one participant: "Cyber safety needs to be targeted because the South African paradigm is very diverse and has broad users. It is everybody's responsibility". This responsibility should be shared among all cyber collaborators from a wide range of sectors in South Africa. However, from the findings of the survey it is clear that participants strongly feel that collaborators should not function in a silo or vacuum, but rather that a "multidisciplinary" and a "holistic collaboration" approach must be established. Different sectors in South Africa were identified from the data analysis as well as the collaborators within each sector.

Government
The first sector identified is government. Participants identified the following cyber activities for the government sector:

- assessing preparedness for the ongoing technological revolution and implementing measures according to the required knowledge/skills
- a focal point in the National eSkills Initiative
- CSERT
- collaboration across different platforms
- large-scale collaborative efforts on a national level
- cooperation between institutions and government participation
- legislation
- statistical analysis of the current cyber situation
- establishing a cyber-safety vision for South Africa

Schools
The second sector is the Department of Education with the focus on schools. The participants identified the following activities for this collaborator:

- mandatory introduction into the basic education curriculum
- school events
- skills training awareness for teachers

Communities
Thirdly, the participants indicated that a "community-centric approach must be adapted according to culture within community". The community approach has a strong-routed tradition within South Africa. Some cyber activities identified include:

- story-telling in communities
- peer-to-peer activities
- social community learning

Multidisciplinary Involvement
Lastly, the participants identified the following collaborators to be part of the multi-dimensional integrated approach to cyber safety:

- media
- psycho-educational workshops/follow-ups
- using social media – something people use every day
- university courses
- ISPs
- legal sector
- psychologists
- social workers
- mental health workers
- the banking environment
- law professionals
- governing bodies

Cyber-Safety Activities
The participants also identified the following cyber-safety activities to be addressed by all cyber users:

- moving from knowledge to attitude to behavioural change
- incorporating a systems approach
- incorporating behavioural theories
- focusing on motivation approaches
- attitude change

Challenges for Cyber-Security Awareness
The participants identified the following challenges of ensuring that cyber safety is proactively addressed between all collaborators:

- lack of focus among different projects
- too much involvement (too many projects)
- blame issues (different role players blame each other)
- funding and manpower

- lack of policies supporting cyber security
- insufficient media used to create publicity, for example, billboards and posters
- denial of women's rights
- lack of cyber security skills by some identified role players
- lack of collaboration among different role players

It is clear from the feedback what can be done, created or implemented in the process of building a cyber-safety culture in South Africa.

4 Conclusion

The different comments in the questionnaires were analysed and grouped into code families and code members. This was done to recognise trends and similar arguments in the different responses to the questions posed to all participants.

The participants argued that the current information dissemination does not take into account the digital literacy of the different target groups, therefore their main request was that this should be addressed by educational interventions in a coordinated effort. It was expressed that such a coordinated effort should create a culture of cyber safety among any target audience. It was also voiced that social awareness and empowerment among the different target audiences should be established by concentrating on coordinated efforts. These target audiences should be as wide as possible, but educating the youth should be the first priority.

References

Annunziata, G., Colace, F., De Santo, M., Lemma, S., Lombardi, M.: ApPoggiomarino: a context aware app for e-citizenship. In: Proceedings of the 18th International Conference on Enterprise Information Systems, ICEIS 2016, p. 273 (2016)

Clarizia, F., Lemma, S., Lombardi, M., Pascale, F.: An ontological digital storytelling to enrich tourist destinations and attractions with a mobile tailored story. In: Au, M.H.A., Castiglione, A., Choo, K.-K.R., Palmieri, F., Li, K.-C. (eds.) GPC 2017. LNCS, vol. 10232, pp. 567–581. Springer, Cham (2017a). https://doi.org/10.1007/978-3-319-57186-7_41

Clarizia, F., Lemma, S., Lombardi, M., Pascale, F.: A mobile context-aware information system to support tourism events. In: Au, M.H.A., Castiglione, A., Choo, K.-K.R., Palmieri, F., Li, K.-C. (eds.) GPC 2017. LNCS, vol. 10232, pp. 553–566. Springer, Cham (2017b). https://doi.org/10.1007/978-3-319-57186-7_40

de Lange, M., von Solms, R.: An e-safety educational framework in South Africa. In: Proceedings of the Southern Africa Telecoms and Network Applications Conference (2012)

Dlamini, Z., Modise, M.: Cyber security awareness initiatives in South Africa: a synergy approach. In: The Proceedings of ICIW (2012)

Dodge, M., Kitchin, R.: Mapping Cyberspace. Routledge, London and New York (2001). ISBN 0-415-19885-4

Grobler, M., Jansen van Vuuren, J., Zaaiman, J.: Evaluating cyber security awareness in South Africa. In: ECIW Conference, July 2011a

Kortjan, N., von Solms, R.: A conceptual framework for cyber-security awareness and education in SA. South African Comput. J. **52**, 29–41 (2014)

Kritzinger, E.: Enhancing cyber safety awareness among school children in South Africa through gaming. In: Proceeding of Science and Information Conference, London, UK (2015)

Kritzinger, E.: Short-term initiatives for enhancing cyber-safety within South African schools. South African Comput. J. 28(1), 1–7 (2016)

Kritzinger, E., Padayachee, K.: Engendering an e-safety awareness culture within the South African context. In: Proceeding of AFRICON (2013)

Kritzinger, E., von Solms, S.: Cyber security for home users: a new way of protection through awareness enforcement. Comput. Secur. 29(2010), 840–847 (2010)

Labuschagne, W., Veerasamy, N., Burke, I., Eloff, M.: Design of cyber security awareness game utilizing a social media framework. In: Information Security South Africa (ISSA), pp. 1–9 (2011)

RSA: Cyber security awareness month fails to deter phishers (2011). http://www.rsa.com/solutions/consumer_authenticcation/intelreport/11541_Online_Fraud_report_1011.pef

von Solms, S., von Solms, R.: Towards cyber safety education in primary schools in Africa. In: Proceeding of Eighth International Symposium on Human Aspects of Information Security and Assurance (HAISA), pp. 184–197 (2014)

von Solms, S., von Solms, R.: Cyber safety education developing countries. In: Proceeding of 9th International Multi-Conference on Society, Cybernetics and Informatics (IMSCI), pp. 173–178 (2015)

Walaza, M., Loock, M., Kritzinger, E.: A pragmatic approach towards the integration of ICT security awareness into the South African education system. In: 2015 Second International Conference on Information Security and Cyber Forensics (InfoSec), pp 35–40. IEEE (2015)

Author Index

Printed in the United States
By Bookmasters